Software Process
Improvement

Software Process Improvement

Practical Guidelines for business success

SAMI ZAHRAN

Software Engineering Institute
SEI Series in Software Engineering

 Addison-Wesley

An imprint of **Pearson Education**

Harlow, England · London · New York · Reading, Massachusetts · San Francisco
Toronto · Don Mills, Ontario · Sydney · Tokyo · Singapore · Hong Kong · Seoul
Taipei · Cape Town · Madrid · Mexico City · Amsterdam · Munich · Paris · Milan

PEARSON EDUCATION LIMITED

Head Office:
Edinburgh Gate
Harlow CM20 2JE
Tel: +44 (0)1279 623623
Fax: +44 (0)1279 431059

London Office:
128 Long Acre
London WC2E 9AN
Tel: +44 (0)207 447 2000
Fax: +44 (0)207 240 5771

Website: *www.awl.com/cseng*

First published in Great Britain 1998

ISBN 0-201-17782-X

British Library Cataloguing in Publication Data
A catalogue record for this book is available from the British Library.

Library of Congress Cataloging in Publication Data
Applied for.

The programs in this book have been included for their instructional value.
The publisher does not offer any warranties or representations in respect of
their fitness for a particular purpose, nor does the publisher accept any
liability for any loss or damage arising from their use.

Many of the designations used by manufacturers and sellers to distinguish
their products are claimed as trademarks. Pearson Education has made
every attempt to supply trademark information about manufacturers and
their products mentioned in this book. A list of the trademark designations
and their owners appears on p. vi.

10 9 8 7 6 5

Typeset by Dobbie Typesetting.
Printed and bound in Great Britain by Biddles Ltd, Guildford and King's Lynn.
Cover designed and illustrated by Odb Design & Communication, Reading.

The publishers' policy is to use paper manufactured from sustainable forests.

I dedicate this book to Watts Humphrey – the 'prophet' of the Software Process.

This book is a contribution towards the Software Engineering Institute's vision:
'Bringing engineering discipline to the development and maintenance of software'.

This book analyses and discusses a number of software process improvement initiatives, models and standards developed by a number of organizations. By the very nature of this analysis activity, some of the discussions quote the original material for those initiatives, models and standards. Both the author and the publisher fully acknowledge the original copyright of all organizations concerned and wish to thank the following for their permission to reproduce some of their material for the purpose of analysis and discussions in this book.

ISPI (Institute for Software Process Improvement) for the material on Guidance for Action Plan (GAP) in Chapter 9.

ami Consortium for material on the ami methodology in Chapter 12.

Software Engineering Institute (SEI), Carnegie Mellon University for the material on the Capability Maturity Model and the SEI-Assessment method in Chapters 13, 14 and 19.

The International Organization for Standardization (ISO), Mr Jacques-Olivier Chabot and Mr Jean-Normand Drouin for the material on the ISO/IEC 15504 Draft Technical Report for Software Process Assessment in Chapters 15 and 16.

The Department of Defense (DoD) for the material on the MIL-STD-498 in Chapter 18.

Bell Canada and the Trillium technical committee for the material on Trillium in Chapter 18.

European Commission for the material on the ESSI Programme and Process Improvement Experiments (PIE) in Chapter 19.

While the publisher has made every attempt to trace all copyright owners and obtain permission to reproduce material, in a few cases this has proved impossible. Copyright holders of material which has not been acknowledged are encouraged to contact the publisher.

Contents

Foreword

by Watts S. Humphrey

It is a pleasure to introduce this book by Sami Zahran. He covers an important topic in an interesting way. I enjoyed reading the book and I am sure you will as well. In addition to talking about process improvement, Sami provides useful guidance from a practitioner's perspective. He clearly explains the purposes and methods of process improvement and he compares the leading methods, their principal features and their characteristics. Most importantly, he discusses the issues that you, the user, will face as you pursue process improvement on your own.

As you read this book and think about what Sami says, I suggest you keep some special topics in mind. They should provide a useful perspective and help ensure that your process improvement efforts are most effective.

In the change business, there is something called unfreezing. People are naturally resistant to change and unfreezing breaks through their resistance. It shows the engineers and their managers what is wrong today. It makes them even more unhappy with the current situation, and convinces them that there are better and more effective ways to do their jobs. When the engineers and their managers see all the key problems in one big pile, they realize they really must do something about them.

A properly done assessment walks through the issues in great detail, breaks the ice, and starts unfreezing. Then you can begin to talk about what to improve. Until you get to that point, all improvement talk will be just that – talk. And nothing much will happen. This is why the assessment process was invented. By involving the engineers and managers, and asking them what is wrong and what can be improved, the assessment becomes a way of learning from the organization. When you get their ideas on what should be improved, the people are most likely to support and participate in the change process.

Another area of misunderstanding is the role of Capability Maturity Model (CMM)^{SM} goals. In first developing the CMM, we did not want to block good ideas. The software community is full of creative people. Once they are involved, they will see many ways to improve things. Also, software engineering is a relatively new and rapidly changing field. What seems appropriate today could be hopelessly out of date in just a few years. A CMM that is too specific could easily inhibit change instead of encouraging it.

This is why the real CMM objective is the goals; everything else is examples of how the goals could be met. I thus suggest that you keep your eye on the goals, and use all the detail for guidance on possible ways to achieve them.

Another difficult issue is maturity ratings. These can be very helpful in focusing attention on immediate priorities. While they are an important means of communication, they can also cause the wrong behaviour. People can easily lose sight of the principal objective of improving the process. They begin to see the next CMM level as the target.

When people focus on the level, they think of assessment as a way to measure the level. Then they become concerned with the accuracy of the CMM as a measurement tool. Some even seek sophisticated measures that will precisely determine the maturity level. This is nonsense. Software processes are far too complex to measure with one or even a few numbers. The critical need is for a framework engineers and managers can use to examine and talk about their processes. Then they can use their detailed knowledge of the organization to identify the key problems, and to decide what and how to improve.

The level measure provides so much value that we decided to keep it. The need, however, is to focus on those few improvements that will make a difference right now. The CMM can guide you in identifying these opportunities. Other than that, don't worry about the maturity level. If you continue working on process improvements, the level will follow. If you focus on the level, however, improvement is much less likely.

To keep this perspective, I suggest you do the following:

1 Use maturity levels to do assessments and evaluations, and to set priorities
2 Keep your objectives focused on making specific improvements
3 Make improvement the job of every manager and track his or her performance against these goals
4 Plan to get the highest-priority key process areas (KPAs) in place as soon as possible
5 When those plans are well along, plan and implement the next most important KPAs.

If you do this, when you next do an assessment, you will see significant improvements. And the levels will take care of themselves.

Watts S. Humphrey
Sarasota, Florida, USA
April 21, 1997

Foreword

by Mark C. Paulk

Anyone familiar with computers is familiar, often painfully so, with the 'software crisis'. Our ability to build software-intensive systems is orders of magnitude greater today than it was five decades ago, but our appetite for software has grown even faster, and the software industry is still evolving from a craft to an engineering discipline. Historically, the result has been the chronic software crisis: software is (almost) always later than expected, more expensive than planned, and with less functionality than hoped. There is hope, however, that we have turned the corner on the software crisis.

If we are overcoming the software crisis, one of the major reasons is the topic of Dr Sami Zahran's book: software process improvement. Peter Freeman stated in the foreword to Watts Humphrey's *Managing the Software Process* that 'The "software crisis" is dead!' and that Humphrey's book was one of the best signs of that change.

Eight years later, the increasing ability of mature software organizations to deliver high-quality software products on budget and on schedule shows that Freeman was correct – at least for that part of the software community that has adopted a systematic approach to software process improvement.

Unfortunately only a minority of software organizations have chosen to pursue systematic improvement. The reasons are manifold, but perhaps the crux of the problem is that disciplined software engineering is easy to describe but devilishly hard to do.

Much of the problem lies in the fact that 'changing the way we do things around here' requires behavioural change across the board. True software process improvement requires that management, especially senior management, take an active role in process improvement. It also requires that the workers in the trenches participate in defining and implementing usable and effective processes. This means a diversion from the 'real work' of shipping product. If software process improvement is considered a 'silver bullet' rather than an investment in the future, then it will wind up being another 'flavour of the month' fad, and its value will never be attained.

Improvement also implies facing a sometimes unpleasant reality. Some of the pain of the software crisis is caused by human nature. In response to the question 'Why does software cost so much?', Jerry Weinberg replies 'Compared to what?'. Tom DeMarco suggests that this assertion is a negotiating position; people complain because they know we work harder when they complain. In one survey, most of the responding professional software managers reported that their estimates were dismal, but they weren't on the whole dissatisfied with the estimating process! All too many software professionals would agree with DeMarco, but many software managers and customers are vitally interested in understanding how to manage software projects more effectively.

Customers and managers who use schedule pressure and overtime as motivational tools have to deal with the resulting quality trade-off. Customers and managers who are interested in truly managing software projects – and facing up to a sometimes unpleasant reality – have available a number of approaches for systematically improving the process for developing and maintaining software. The results of successfully applying these approaches give us hope that the software crisis is finally coming to an end.

Perhaps the best-known approaches to software process improvement are the International Organization for Standardization's ISO 9001 standard for quality management systems, the Software Engineering Institute's Capability Maturity Model for Software, and the ISO 15504 (frequently referred to as SPICE) standard for software process assessment. These approaches, among others, apply Total Quality Management principles to the software process and are described by Dr Zahran in this book. Hopefully the comments in this book will help the reader navigate the quagmire of alternative approaches!

As the product manager for the Software CMM, I have a biased view of the various approaches to software process improvement. We are incorporating a number of process implementation and management ideas from the various standards and models described in this book in the next version of the Software CMM. While I believe that the Software CMM is the best foundation for software process improvement, and we are actively working to maintain this position, any systematic approach to improvement can help an organization succeed. Regardless of the approach chosen, process improvement is becoming essential to survival in today's highly competitive world.

The importance of high-quality software products cannot be overemphasized. Recent UK court decisions and proposed changes to the US Uniform Commercial Code foreshadow a potential for legal action by dissatisfied customers. The concept that software should be sold free of major bugs and should work as intended, like other commercial goods, may be a major paradigm shift for many software developers!

To survive, much less thrive, modern organizations must continually improve all aspects of their business. Improvement in software-intensive products and services is crucial and difficult. The challenge is to implement good software engineering and management practices in the high-pressure environment software organizations face. A disciplined and systematic approach to software process and quality improvement, such as these models and standards support, is necessary to survive and thrive.

Process improvement is not, however, sufficient for success. Other issues are also fundamental, such as:

- building the right product – one that customers want to buy;
- hiring, selecting, and retaining competent staff;
- overcoming organizational barriers (for example, between systems engineering and software staff).

An effective software process improvement programme should be aligned with other organizational initiatives, perhaps under a Total Quality Management umbrella, to address the totality of business issues that are related to process improvement.

Regardless of the approach selected, building competitive advantage should be focused on improvement, not on achieving a score, whether the score is a maturity level, a certificate or a process profile. Dr Zahran's book should help the reader understand the trade-offs and issues associated with effective software process improvement.

Mark C. Paulk
Software Engineering Institute
Pittsburgh, Pennsylvania, USA
22 September, 1997

Preface

Software development is a challenging endeavour

Developing reliable software on time and within budget represents a difficult endeavour for many organizations. As the role of software becomes increasingly critical for business as well as for human lives, the problems caused by software products that are late or over budget, or that do not work, become magnified. Loss of life or widespread inconvenience caused by unreliable software makes big headlines in the news media. It is estimated that in the last few years around 4000 people have died as a result of software defects. In a modern aircraft, if software stops functioning for more than 200 milliseconds, the aircraft is irrecoverable. In June 1996 a European Space Agency rocket carrying a number of European satellites exploded seconds after its launch. The accident was attributed to software failure. A few years ago, unreliable software made big news in the UK, from emergency services disasters to social security payment blunders, let alone the failure of a large project for the London Stock Exchange. Improved software quality is essential to ensure reliable products and services, and to gain customer satisfaction. The US Government Accounting Office (GAO) reported recently on 'cost rising by millions of dollars, schedule delays of not months but years, and multi-billion dollar systems that do not perform as envisioned' (Paulk *et al.*, 1994).

CASE tools are not enough

Stories about failure of software projects that still excite the press are in sharp contrast to the inflated promises of CASE tools that filled the same press back in the mid and late 1980s. The industry has realized that tools are not enough.

One fact that the software industry has established is that 'a fool with a tool is still a fool!'. Usually business solutions have three main aspects: people, process, and technology. It is evident from industry experience that, when implementing a business solution or introducing a change, the least problematic aspect is usually technology, while processes and people are the critical factors that could make the difference between success and failure. People are an integral part of the process, since they are the enablers of the process activities, process monitoring and process management.

Competent individuals are not enough

The software industry's experience with CASE tools has proved that the main reason for failing software projects has little to do with technology and tools, and much to do with lack of process discipline. Software development is a team effort. In the absence of process discipline, a team may follow different processes, or more commonly use no defined process at all. In such a case it will be 'like a ball team with some team members playing soccer, some baseball, and others football. Under these conditions, even the best individual players will form a poor team' (Humphrey, 1995). In contrast, a team that follows consistent process definitions can better coordinate the work of individual members, direct the efforts of the team members towards the common goal and more precisely track the progress.

Process focus offers better chances for success

Software development as a discipline has existed for more than four decades, but we have not yet turned the software industry into an engineering discipline. The recent focus on the software development process is a step in the right direction. Only by creating a disciplined process for software development can we manage and control the quality of software products. Organizations are realizing that their fundamental problem is the immaturity of their software development process. All the evidence is that investing in software process improvement promises to offer better hope for the software industry, as it has done for other industries such as manufacturing. Also, there is a difference in motivation between a software movement based on tools and one based on process improvement. Process improvement is the responsibility of the organization developing the software and there are no tool vendors with vested interest. The use of tools to automate a chaotic process will lead to more (automated) chaos. Examples are abundant, but one striking example outside the software industry is the shipping of sophisticated armoury and destructive weapons to a chaotic war between two tribal factions in a primitive country. These 'technological tools' are not likely to result in stability, but will probably increase human suffering. Experience has shown that introducing new technology and tools in an immature or undisciplined environment is likely to increase the chaos. A software project without defined processes for control and management (for example quality assurance, configuration management and project management) will not benefit from tools. Dumping tools into such a project is likely to increase the chaos, to speed up the production of faulty software and to multiply user dissatisfaction. Such projects could ultimately end up as a disappointment to all concerned. Such disappointments take various forms, such as wasted effort, time, money and resources, and possibly unavoidable disasters.

Software process movement: the second wave in the software industry

Structured methods were developed in the 1970s to cater for the increasing demands and complexity of software, and consequently the increasing size of development teams. That was the first wave of the software industry. It came as a response to the growing need to build complex interactive commercial applications using shared systems and to make such systems maintainable. Structured methods focus on ways to formalize the definition of requirements and on the traceability of requirements through design and build into finished systems. Some of these transformations have been assisted to varying degrees by automated tools. Although this was the beginning of transforming software development from a 'cottage industry' to mass production, it was not quite enough. Real issues that make or break software projects, such as project management and requirements management, were not a mainstream focus. The software process movement came as a response to the increasing rate of failure of software projects. Focus on process started through sponsorship by the US Department of Defense (DoD) which funded the Software Engineering Institute (SEI) to come up with a method for assessing the capability of the Deparment's software subcontractors. Watts Humphrey first joined the SEI in an undefined position and in a couple of months was named Director of the Process Program. Since that time the process message coming out of the SEI has gone from strength to strength to influence the whole software industry worldwide.

One can easily trace the roots of the software process to the quality movement that started in the 1930s and prevailed throughout the 1970s, 1980s and 1990s. The concepts of quality gurus such as Edwards Deming and Philip Crosby gained popularity across manufacturing industry all over the world. Watts Humphrey applied those same quality principles to software development. The process maturity movement prepares the way for the third wave of the software industry: 'software industrialization'. In the third wave software development will become like an assembly and manufacturing process. Enabling technologies for the third wave include object-oriented technology and reusable component libraries. It will then be possible to assemble software from standard reusable components. A critical enabling factor for the third wave is a disciplined software engineering process with predictable quality, schedule and functionality.

Aims of this book

This book offers a pragmatic approach to the effective implementation of software process improvement. It provides guidelines for creating process support infrastructure, and makes the case for adopting a process view to software development. It outlines a practical approach for setting up a disciplined and continuously improving software process environment. In summary, the book presents a framework for establishing an effective environment for continuous software process improvement.

The arguments in the book put emphasis on the people aspect. Understanding and following the process is as important as the process definition. Another equally important emphasis is on the impact of process discipline on team performance and business goals and objectives.

The concepts offered in this book are the result of more than thirty years of the author's practical work in the software industry. Most of those years were spent in practical experience and research on different facets of software engineering. This included experiencing the pains and pleasures associated with developing software and managing software projects. The projects covered business and industrial applications for a variety of industry sectors ranging from oil, banking and government, to defence, manufacturing and aerospace. They also included involvement in the development of operating systems, database management systems, data dictionary systems, transaction processing systems and a large number of commercial applications. Having lived through both successes and failures of software projects, I readily identified with the process message and teachings which I first received at the Software Engineering Institute, Carnegie Mellon University, in February 1992. Since that time my dedication to the software process has been uninterrupted.

Intended audience

This book is relevant to and readable by a wide audience, including those who already have some knowledge of software process assessment and improvement and those who have little knowledge beyond knowing that the subject is significant for them. In other words it contains new ideas and approaches that will interest those who have prior knowledge, and is simple and readable enough to interest those who do not. In particular, it is aimed at the following special interest groups.

Software engineering managers and professionals
The whole book should be of interest to everyone involved in software engineering activities including management, coordination, development and control. This includes business managers with interest in software, project managers, team leaders, software engineers, and software support functions, such as configuration management, quality assurance and process improvement teams. Also the book is suitable for inclusion in graduate software engineering degrees within a unit on software process improvement.

Process improvement teams
The first part of the book discusses process thinking in generic terms. It should be beneficial to all those interested in process improvement activities including business process re-engineering, business process redesign and business process improvement.

Process research scientists
The book offers a holistic approach to a process improvement environment. The concepts and discussions in the book are intended to provide inspiration for further research effort on process modelling and quality concepts.

Structure of the book

The book is structured in five parts, followed by a glossary and list of references.

Part 1: Process thinking
This part lays the intellectual foundation for the rest of the book. It defines and explains process thinking, relates the concepts discussed to process discipline, and describes the characteristics of an effective process environment. It also relates these concepts to the software process environment. Part 1 contains four chapters:

Chapter 1. Process thinking
Chapter 2. Process discipline
Chapter 3. Effective process environment
Chapter 4. Process maturity: the second wave of the software industry

Part 2: A framework for software process improvement
This part describes the framework proposed for the software process environment. It describes the components of the framework, the process infrastructure, process improvement roadmaps, process assessment methods, and process improvement plans. This framework should lead to a continuous process improvement environment. Part 2 contains five chapters:

Chapter 5. A framework for software process improvement
Chapter 6. Software process infrastructure
Chapter 7. Process improvement roadmaps
Chapter 8. Fundamentals of software process assessment
Chapter 9. Software process improvement action plan

Part 3: Making software process improvement happen
Part 3 describes strategies and plans for planning and launching a software process improvement programme in your organization. It discusses steps for converting the assessment results into an improvement plan and highlights the need for measuring the benefits of software process improvement. It discusses

the critical success factors for software process improvement and summarizes some approaches suggested for implementing and institutionalizing the software process, and for measuring its business benefits. Part 3 contains three chapters:

Chapter 10. Launching software process improvement
Chapter 11. Implementing and institutionalizing software process improvement
Chapter 12. Measuring the benefits of software process improvement

Part 4: Current models and standards for software process improvement
Part 4 describes some of the most significant models and standards for software process assessment and improvement. These include the Software Engineering Institute's Capability Maturity Model (CMM) and CMM-based assessments, the International Standards Organization's ISO/IEC 15504 and its draft guide for assessments, and the BOOTSTRAP assessment method. It also discusses other initiatives and models including ISO 9001, MIL-STD-498, Trillium and the V-Model. Part 4 contains six chapters:

Chapter 13. The Capability Maturity Model (CMM)
Chapter 14. CMM-based software process assessment
Chapter 15. ISO/IEC 15504 Draft Standard to Software Process Assessment
Chapter 16. ISO/IEC 15504 draft guide to conducting assessment
Chapter 17. BOOTSTRAP software process assessment
Chapter 18. Other initiatives (ISO, MIL-STD-498, Trillium and the V-Model)

Part 5: Business benefits of software process improvement
Part 5 describes the business benefits of software process improvement, and summarizes some of the case studies in Europe and the USA which have tracked and measured the benefits. Finally it discusses some scenarios for the future of software process improvement. Part 5 contains two chapters:

Chapter 19: The evidence: business benefits of software process improvement
Chapter 20: Epilogue: future of software process improvement

How to use this book

Each part of the book focuses on one topic and can be read as a self-contained source of information for that subject. The following diagram illustrates the structure of the book and possible reading routes.

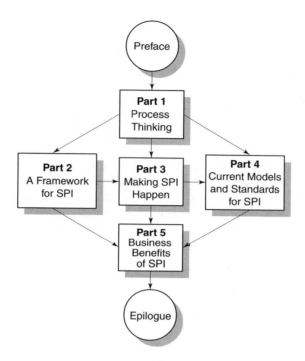

Unique features

This book takes you through a journey from 'fire fighting' behaviours in software projects to a culture of disciplined processes, defect prevention and continuous improvement. The book has some special features:

- It provides a holistic framework for a software process improvement environment supported by models and architectures that can help organizations build an effective process improvement environment.
- It proposes a framework for establishing a software process improvement infrastructure and a process discipline.
- It describes well-known software process improvement initiatives and standards, including the CMM, ISO/IEC 15504, ISO 9000, MIL-STD-498, Trillium, the V-Model, ISO 12207 and BOOTSTRAP.
- It suggests a generic model for software process assessment, and a method for organizations to design their own process assessment method based on available assessment standards and methods.
- It provides practical steps for successfully establishing and managing a software process environment.
- Every chapter contains illustrations and models that help in emphasizing the main concepts discussed. This is followed by a summary at the end of each chapter to help the reader understand the main concepts.

- The book contains five parts. Each part discusses one of the main components of the framework proposed for software process environment. Effectively, you have five books for the price of one.

Disclaimer

The methods and standards summarized in this book are undergoing continuous evolution. The author cannot guarantee that the information provided in this book represents the latest state of these methods and standards. The material presented represents the author's own interpretations and are based on the sources of information that were available at the time of developing this book. It is hoped that the explanations and summaries will provide the reader with a reasonable view of these methods and standards. Readers who are interested in the latest offerings are advised to contact the organizations concerned.

Acknowledgements

This book has evolved over the last five years. Many of the ideas in this book have come as a result of discussions and interactions with several of the world's prominent figures in the software process area. Although it is hard to list everyone that I have discussed my ideas with, I feel indebted to the following colleagues who most influenced my thinking.

From the Software Engineering Institute
My thanks are due to Watts Humphrey whom I met on paper through his work for nearly a decade, and met in person in 1996 in Barcelona. His presence, leadership and overwhelming conviction and beliefs in the process focus make him the undisputed 'prophet' of the software process movement. My thanks are also due to Tim Kasse, Jeff Purdue and Jim Hart whom I met at the Software Engineering Institute, Carnegie Mellon University, in 1992 when I went to receive the 'message' of the software process. They have been loyal evangelists of the process teachings and they converted me to the process belief. I also thank Mark Paulk of the Software Engineering Institute whom I met over the pages of his work on the CMM years before we met in person in London and Barcelona. Mark's impressive clarity of the CMM and the software process has strengthened my ideas on the critical role of process improvement in the software industry. My thanks are also due to David Kitson of the Software Engineering Institute whom I met through a video recording of his CMM training before we met in person in Cambridge, England. All of the above are pioneers of the software process movement who have succeeded in influencing the software industry worldwide. Lastly, I thank Charles Weber and Suzanne Garcia for reviewing the CMM material and providing useful comments and guidance for the latest development in the CMM.

From the European Commission
David Talbot, Brian Holmes and their colleagues at the European Commission in Brussels drive the European Commission's Software Best Practice Programme that has played a major role in sponsoring and encouraging a large number of software process improvement projects throughout Europe. As a result of their European Software and Systems Initiative (ESSI), process improvement experiments (PIEs) mushroomed in European software projects, leading to real benefits to the software industry and increasing awareness of the software process.

From the UK
My thanks are due to Harry Barker, of the UK Defence Research Agency, and his team who pioneered software process improvement programmes in the UK Ministry of Defence. Also, thanks to Colin Tully for his leadership role in promoting the software process improvement message throughout Europe; to Jennifer Stapleton, Mike George, Jane Searles, Bev Wilson and Alec Dorling for the fruitful discussions we had at various locations in England and their useful comments; to Roy Farmer and David Booth of the International Standards Organization; and to Robin Whittey for his review and comments on the *ami* material and fruitful discussions on the metrics for the software process, and Professor A. Furnham for useful discussions on the strategies for organizational change. Thanks to Peter Goodhew, Agnes Donaldson and Richard Thomas for providing information on IBM benchmark on software development practices. Finally, special thanks to the many individuals who influenced my career in the computing profession. Special thanks are due to Essam Isa, Norman Ward and Professors Sam Waters and Peter King.

From the rest of Europe
I wish to thank Dr Ch. Avratoglou of Greece for his valuable comments on sharing his experience of running three ESPRIT software process improvement experiments; Dr Roland Simon, Rolf Kaul and Hans Rene Klaey of Switzerland for their comments and for sharing their experiences of implementing software process improvement; Anne-Mett Jonassen, Jorn Johanssen and Carsten Joergensen of Denmark, who support and promote software process improvement in Denmark; Jose Oliveira and Daniel Ferreira of Portugal for sharing their experiences of software process improvement; Dr Hans Stienen and Hartmut Gierszøl for their review and comments on BOOTSTRAP material; and Pasi Kuvaja of the BOOTSTRAP Institute.

From Addison Wesley Longman
My sincere thanks are due to Dr Sally Mortimore, Commissioning Editor at Addison Wesley Longman, for her patience, encouragement, guidance and comments, and to her assistant Fiona Kinnear for her efficiency and responsiveness. Thanks also to the production team for their hard work and dedication.

My family
My thanks are due to my wife Nadia, my daughter Reem, and my son Wesam for their encouragement, patience and support.

Software process improvement champions
Finally, I am sure there are thousands of software engineers and managers who promote the software process all over the world and participate in the software process improvement networks (SPINs). My thanks go to those software process champions in all types of organizations all over the world.

Sami Zahran
Iver, Buckinghamshire, England, UK
email: sami@cloud9.win-uk.net
21 November 1997

PART I

Process thinking

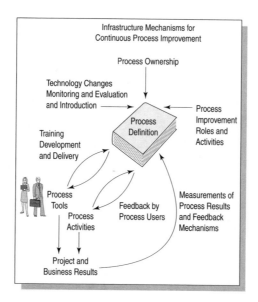

Infrastructure Mechanisms for
Continuous Process Improvement

Process Ownership

Technology Changes
Monitoring and Evaluation
and Introduction

Process
Improvement
Roles and
Activities

Process
Definition

Training
Development
and Delivery

Process
Tools

Process
Activities

Feedback by
Process Users

Measurements of
Process Results
and Feedback
Mechanisms

Project and
Business Results

This first part provides the intellectual foundations for the rest of the book. It presents the overall framework suggested in this book for software process improvement. It describes the tour that you are about to start when reading this book. The tour into the 'process universe' shows you how to move from 'a chaotic process environment' to 'a continuously improving process environment'. After reading this part, the reader should be able to identify the most suitable point to continue his or her reading.

CHAPTER I

Process thinking

1.1 WHAT IS PROCESS THINKING?

1.1.1 START THINKING PROCESS

Process thinking is here, and is already taking place at the highest level of business. Task oriented thinking has failed in modern businesses owing to changes happening around us. Michael Hammer and James Champy vehemently advocate the need for all businesses to think in terms of process. They declare that the shift to process thinking is already underway and that 'Many business people are not process oriented; they are focused on tasks, on jobs, on people, on structures, but not on processes. Task-based thinking – the fragmentation of work into its simplest components and their assignment to specialist workers – has influenced the organisational design of companies for the last two hundred years' (Hammer and Champy, 1993).

Another strong advocate for adopting process thinking in business is James Harrington. In his book *Business Process Improvement* he advocates the need to start thinking in terms of process: 'You have to stop thinking about organisational structure and start focusing on the processes that control customer interfaces. A completely different thought pattern occurs when you focus your emphasis on the process' (Harrington, 1991).

So what is process thinking and how can it affect the software process? Watts Humphrey pioneered the application of process management principles to software development for a long time. He introduced the concept of process discipline in the software industry through his classic book *Managing the*

Software Process. In that book he advocates: 'An important first step in addressing software problems is to treat the entire software task as a process that can be controlled, measured, and improved' (Humphrey, 1989).

Process thinking is like a religion. It challenges and tries to change your conventional way of thinking. Either you believe or you disbelieve. In the September 1995 issue of *IEEE Software* John Baumert likens process improvement to religion, a matter of faith: 'If you believe in the CMM and its role in process improvement, you will march forward and try to convert the unbelievers within your organisation – and perhaps become a martyr in the process. Yet if you encounter a true unbeliever, no amount of cajoling nor hours of haranguing will convert him' (Baumert, 1995). If process thinking for software is a religion, then Watts Humphrey is its main 'Prophet' without dispute. After 27 years with IBM he joined the Software Engineering Institute (SEI), Carnegie Mellon University, in 1986, where he was soon appointed as the first Director of the Process Program. He led the initial development of the Software Capability Maturity Model, and introduced the concepts of Software Process Assessment and Software Capability Evaluation.

1.1.2   PROCESS THINKING IS DIFFERENT

Process thinking is different from the conventional way of thinking. It has some apparent consequences, especially when adopted by a group of individuals who have a common goal to achieve. Common process thinking across a group of individuals aligns the behaviour and activities of those individuals towards achieving their common goal. It brings consistency and uniformity to the group's behaviour, which turn into improved capability and better quality of results. It acts like a magnetic force aligning the particles of a piece of metal in one direction. Imagine members of a special forces team on a critical mission. Each team member should act in complete harmony with the rest of the team to support the mission. Team members will focus their activities to be in perfect alignment with the goals they want to achieve. Without a focus and alignment towards common goals, the activities of the different team members could contradict each other, thus degrading the total effectiveness of the team. Similarly in a software project, a process focus brings discipline to the individuals' activities and alignment towards achieving the project goals.

1.1.3   PROCESS THINKING IS A NATURAL WAY OF THINKING

In one sense process thinking could reflect the way our brains store and use knowledge and experience. A human brain contains hundreds of millions of neurones. Knowledge is stored as connections between these neurones. These connections start as 'weak' connections, leading to what is known as the 'weak memory'. Once we acquire knowledge and go through practical experience, the relevant connections turn into strong connections, leading to what is known as the 'strong memory'. Once you have experience and knowledge of a certain situation 'wired' into your brain, this knowledge is automatically retrieved when you face a similar situation. Your actions will be nearly automatic. The process has been 'internalized' by you. You can perform the process as part of your natural behaviour. Following an 'internalized' process is 'painless'. You can think of countless situations in which knowledge acquisition and training have led to the 'internalization' of the process. For example, think of the time when you as a young person started learning how to drive a car. As a new learner the first few lessons were difficult, and you must have practised the difficult manoeuvres several times before mastering the skill of driving. Continuous practice and learning gradually shifts the knowledge from the 'weak' memory to the 'strong' memory. The process becomes 'internalized'; performing the process becomes repeatable and painless.

1.2   WHAT IS A PROCESS?

1.2.1   DEFINITION OF A PROCESS

In my process training and discussions, I ask a group of participants to define what each one understands by the word 'process'. In almost all cases they come up with different definitions. Even in the literature, process definitions vary widely. Table 1.1 illustrates a spectrum of the most common definitions. Note the variations in breadth, coverage or orientation.

Table 1.1   A spectrum of definitions of the word 'process'

Source/reference	Definition of process
Concise Oxford Dictionary	'a course of action or proceeding, esp. a series of stages in manufacture or some other operation'
Webster's Dictionary	'a system of operations in producing something . . . a series of actions, changes or functions that achieve an end result'
IEEE-STD-610	'a sequence of steps performed for a given purpose, for example the software development process'
Hammer and Champy (1993)	'a collection of activities that takes one or more kinds of input and creates an output that is of value to the customer'
Olson *et al.* (1989)	'a set of actions, tasks, and procedures that when performed or executed obtain a specific goal or objectives. More specifically, a software process is a software development process'
SEI CMM (Humphrey, 1989; Paulk *et al.*, 1993a)	'the set of activities, methods, and practices used in the production and evolution of software'

1.2.2 THREE ASPECTS OF THE PROCESS

Most of the definitions in Table 1.1 vary in their focus. They emphasize a certain aspect of the process and ignore other aspects. This book presents a holistic view of the definition of a process. A process has three aspects. To start with, the process must be defined, hence the first aspect is the process definition. It usually takes the form of a document (paper or electronic) which specifies the activities and procedures for the process. Second, the process knowledge must pass to those who will perform it, hence the second aspect is the process learning. This should lead to the process knowledge being transferred to the brains and memories of those performing the process activities. The process knowledge should drive the behaviours and activities of those performing the process. The third aspect is the process results as manifested by the products produced as a result of executing the process activities. Figure 1.1 illustrates these three essential aspects. My advice is that when someone asks you to define a process, draw the diagram in Figure 1.1 rather than quoting a long English sentence. A verbal definition may fail to convey the essential aspects of the process.

The three process aspects discussed are all important. Consider the following scenarios in which one aspect is missing. A process definition that exists only on paper, with no one knowing about it, is little more than 'shelfware'. A defined process that everyone has been trained in but no one follows, is a 'waste of time'. On the other hand, a defined process, in which

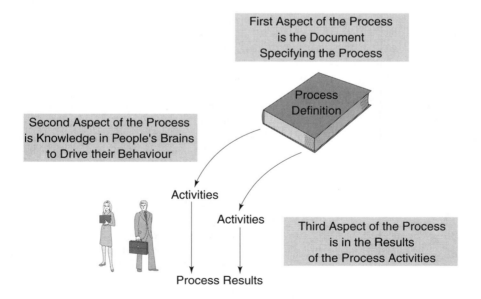

Figure 1.1   Three aspects of the process

everyone has been trained, and which everyone follows to perform their tasks, is an effective process. This model and its three aspects are a major theme in this book.

1.2.3 PROCESS INTERNALIZATION AND PROCESS INSTITUTIONALIZATION

A process shapes the way we act and react. The behaviours, activities and tasks we perform to achieve a certain goal represent the process for achieving that goal. A disciplined process will manifest itself in ordered and consistent patterns of behaviours, whether by an individual or by a group of people following a common process. The process defines the way we act or react in a certain situation, or the activities to fulfil a certain task. We have a process for 'eating', a process for 'going to work', a process for 'performing work activities', and so on. When a process is performed professionally and naturally by a person it is described as 'internalized' by that person. One can draw similarities with organizations. In organizations the processes involve groups and teams of people. To get process discipline, the process needs to be established or 'institutionalized' in the organization. Without established processes across the organization, every individual will follow his or her own way of performing the task. Adherence to a common process is likely to be *ad hoc* and sometimes chaotic. This could cause organizational stress owing to the potential conflict between those who follow the common process and those who ignore it. On the other hand, in organizations where common processes are 'institutionalized', staff will perform the process 'painlessly', smoothly and in harmony with each other. The process itself becomes 'transparent' because it becomes the natural way of performing business activities. When you see someone struggling when performing his or her duties, you deduce that he or she is a novice or amateur. On the other hand when you see that person performing his or her duties and activities naturally and painlessly, you deduce that such a person is a professional. He or she has been properly trained to follow a well-defined process that has been performed repeatedly. We can say that such a person has 'internalized' the process and is capable of performing the process activities professionally and 'painlessly'.

1.3 PROCESS FOCUS

1.3.1 PROCESS FOCUS VERSUS PRODUCT FOCUS

Many organizations are culturally product-focused organizations. In such a culture, people are naturally inclined to put more emphasis on tangible concrete things. They expect the outcome of any activity to take a tangible form. They will misinterpret a procedural document as a process. In such organizations there is likely to be resistance to activities that do not directly contribute to short-term tangible deliverables. Management often view process-related work as a low-priority activity. Such work is considered as something that could be deferred until there is a slack time for those 'non-critical' activities.

In contrast to the above, a process-focused organization would view process problems and issues within the total business context, their impact on the business results, the organization, and the workforce and their interrelationships. Such organizations consider tangibles as just one component of the total picture. The process document is considered as only a tool to facilitate process participation, and not an objective in itself. The objective is the acceptance and consistent use of the process, and the process itself is viewed as a disciplined way of conducting the business.

1.3.2 POWER OF THE PROCESS FOCUS

To appreciate the power of the process focus, think of the example we discussed earlier: a situation where a group of individuals work together towards achieving a common goal. If they do not follow a common process, each one will be left to follow his or her own way of achieving the common goal. They do not share a common process. Imagine such a team working on a software development project. Team members could be developing different programming languages, using different naming conventions and not coordinating changes with their peers – 'the results would be chaos' (Humphrey, 1989). This is what is likely to happen in the absence of a process focus. On the other hand, if the team follows a common process that everyone adheres to, the following benefits would accrue:

- Alignment between the activities of individuals and the common goal of the group
- Consistency across the various activities, thus avoiding any contradiction or conflict across the team activities
- Ability to measure objectively the achievement of individuals in terms of their contribution to the process results
- Repeatability of earlier successes and achievements of the team. This is possible because a process focus minimizes dependence on individuals. New joiners are trained in the common process to ensure that they do not degrade the overall result.

In summary, a common process focus shared by a group of people can yield the following advantages:

- Alignment of the group activities towards achieving the common goals
- Providing the basis for objective measurement of individuals' performance by measuring their contribution to the overall process results
- Enhancing consistency and repeatability of the process results and group performance.

Within a business context, an effective process provides the opportunity to improve the overall business performance through the following:

- Process focus helps identify areas for investment that are likely to provide the most effective return.
- Process focus improves the effectiveness and efficiency of the business activities, thus assisting project managers to meet their budgets and time scales.
- Process focus helps communication, productivity and team building. A common process means that the same methods and terminology are used and shared across the team.
- Process focus enhances the management visibility of the process performance and business results.

1.3.3   ABSENCE OF PROCESS FOCUS

Project managers should manage software projects and development teams through managing the process and monitoring the process performance. A process focus for managing projects will lead to better management practices that are more likely to guarantee successful project results and effective team performance. Absence of a process focus could easily result in what Edwards Deming calls the 'fire fighting' syndrome, where: 'One gets a good rating for fighting a fire. The result is visible, can be quantified. If you do it right first time, you are invisible. You satisfied the requirements. That is your job. Mess it up, and correct it later, you become a hero' (Deming, 1982).

This sums up the culture and behaviour in an immature, *ad hoc* process environment. A closer look at behaviour in an undisciplined process environment could reveal more weaknesses and confusion. Unfortunately the 'fire fighting' culture seems to prevail in many organizations. In some cases fire fighting is the routine behaviour of middle managers. It is so embedded into the organization that middle management would have virtually nothing to do if there were no crises. It is not unlikely that some people unconsciously create fires of their own making in order to appear to be doing an important job 'fighting fires'. Table 1.2 contrasts some aspects of management with and without process focus.

1.4   PROCESS MATURITY

1.4.1   PROCESS MATURITY VERSUS PROCESS IMMATURITY

Organizations at various levels of process discipline are like people at different stages of maturity. The difference between an immature process and a mature process is like the difference between a young child and a mature adult. Process

Table 1.2 Impact of process focus

Aspect of comparison	Without process focus	With process focus
Process discipline	Processes are improvised by the staff and their management in the course of performing their activities	Processes are defined and followed by staff and management; process discipline is the norm
Organization	Functions and roles do not necessarily align with the process requirements	Functions and roles are defined in support of the process
Management	• Staff performance is measured in terms of the number of work hours (irrespective of whether they were productive or not) • Managers are usually focused on solving immediate crises (fire fighting)	• Staff performance is measured in terms of process performance and results • Such measurements are defined and agreed • Managers focus on the quality of both process and product
Skills and training	Training is *ad hoc*, and oriented towards personal inclinations	Training is planned, and is defined in support of the end-to-end process
Tools and technology	Tools and technology are acquired as *ad hoc* point solutions without an overall plan and strategy	Tools and technology are selected in support of the end-to-end process and the automation of process activities

thinking impacts on our behaviours. Our behaviours reflect the processes we have stored in our brains. Newly born babies do not have any process experience. Babies and children do not have the process knowledge engraved in their brains. They move erratically as they gradually and slowly gain process knowledge and experience through trial and error. Watts Humphrey describes processes as habits: 'Processes are like habits: hard to establish and even harder to break' (Humphrey, 1995). Table 1.3 compares the behaviours and attitudes of a child with those of a mature adult. Note that the right-hand column of Table 1.3 refers to a *mature* adult; not all adults are mature! There is more to maturity than getting older – the child needs nurturing and developing, the right environment, and opportunities to learn and grow. It is the same with processes.

Table 1.3 Comparison of the behaviours and attitudes of a child with those of a mature adult

Key behaviours	Child	Mature adult
Planning	Lives from minute to minute, experimenting, repeating mistakes (always trips over the last stair, does it most of the time . . .)	Takes a longer view, plans ahead and learns from experience
Stability	Taken off guard by unexpected events, panics over setbacks	Copes calmly with unforeseen events, reviews the situation and overcomes problems
Capability	Sometimes can do things, other times can not	Knows own capabilities
Consistency	Takes an hour to get dressed one day, ten minutes the next	Results are consistent most of the time
Predictability	Behaves differently on different occasions, changes mood and preferences frequently	Predictable, has established behaviours and preferences, can perform tasks consistently

1.4.2   CENTRAL ROLE OF THE PROCESS

Process focus should have a strong impact on the organizational roles and responsibilities, management procedures, skills and training, and technology and automation. Applying process thinking in organizational design is likely to result in a streamlined organization. Process-focused organizations will have the roles and responsibilities, management procedures, staff skills, business activities and supporting technology all streamlined to support the process. A common objective across all these aspects is to increase the process productivity and effectiveness in support of the overall business goals.

To bring this point home, let us consider the following scenario. The National Lottery in the United Kingdom runs every Saturday and every Wednesday night to create a number of new millionaires. Imagine that you won the jackpot and suddenly became a millionaire overnight, and you decided to use your winnings to build a factory. There are some logical steps that you are likely to follow. First, you will need to decide what products the factory will produce. This is equivalent to defining the process goals. Second, you will need to get the advice of some industrial experts in the product you have chosen in order to specify the steps for manufacturing the chosen product. This is organization in support of the process. Third, you will need to define the roles and management procedures and practices that will ensure the smooth running of the processes – management procedures in support of the process.

Fourth, you will need to identify the skills required to perform the manufacturing tasks, and assume the roles and responsibilities effectively. The skills will be the basis for recruitment and training of people who will work in the factory in support of the processes – skills in the processes. Finally, you will identify the infrastructure, machinery and tools to automate the tasks and activities of the process – technology in support of the process.

Figure 1.2 illustrates the point that a process should be the focus for the organization, the management, the staff and the technological infrastructure. The process is the glue that ties together people, technology, organizational structures and management in a coherent whole, focusing on the business goals and objectives. The process and how to support it should be the basis for the organizational roles and responsibilities, management practices, people's skills, and technology selection and installation. The organization should specify the functions which perform and monitor the process activities. Management should provide the strategic direction and manage the process performance. Staff should aim to be skilled in performing the process activities competently and the technology should aim to automate and enable the process activities.

In summary, the process should support business goals and objectives. The organizational roles and responsibilities should be defined to enable and support the process. Management practices should be defined and enforced to monitor and support the process. Skills should be acquired to enable effective performance of the process tasks. Finally, tools and technology infrastructure should be designed and built in such a way as to automate and enable the efficient performance of the process tasks. Some aspects of this discussion are intentionally simplified or exaggerated to stress the importance of process focus. The reality is more complicated, especially in terms of the role of technology in influencing the process steps. The technology used could influence the process; for example, using robotics in the production line could have a strong influence on the process design. Thus the relationship between the technology and the process could be stronger in reality.

Figure 1.2   Central role of the process

1.4.3 CHAOTIC FORCES CAN CAUSE PROCESS DISORDER

In an organization, the process should be the basis for organization, management, skills and technology. In a process-focused environment (disciplined process environment), process activities are aligned towards fulfilling common business goals. Forces that enforce the process discipline are the forces of order. Opposing these, there are likely to be forces of disorder that could be hindering and degrading the process discipline. Such forces of disorder are activities performed that are not consistent with the defined process. They may have goals that are not consistent with the goals of the common process. These are the 'chaotic' forces that degrade and jeopardize the process performance and business results. To preserve the process discipline, management should continuously streamline the process activities and enforce the process discipline. Management could achieve this by continuous realignment and correction of potential chaotic forces, while at the same time encouraging and strengthening the 'forces of order' that strengthen the process discipline. In a software development environment, process discipline manifests itself in the form of strict adherence to common procedures and methods for development activities, whereas chaotic forces take the form of non-compliance to the project's processes and methods, which could ultimately have a negative impact on the final project results.

SUMMARY

Process thinking

- Process thinking differs from conventional thinking. Common process thinking adopted by a group of individuals is likely to streamline the group efforts and activities towards achieving the common goals.
- Process thinking is a natural way of thinking. Our knowledge and experience are probably stored as process maps in our brains.

Three aspects of the process

A process is more than just a set of documented procedures. An effective process environment has three essential aspects:

- Process definition, which describes the process procedures, rules and activities.
- Process training, which ensures that process knowledge is effectively transferred to the people who will perform the process activities.
- Process monitoring and enforcement, which ensure that process activities are performed according to the documented procedures and that the business goals are achieved.

Absence of process focus leads to fire fighting

Absence of a common process focus within a group of individuals could lead to internal conflict, and misalignment between the activities and goals of the group. This could ultimately lead to 'fire fighting', minimizing the team's capability of achieving the common goal.

Process internalization and process institutionalization

- A process can be described as 'internalized' by a person when following the process becomes a 'natural' way of performing the task 'painlessly'.
- A process can be described as 'institutionalized' by an organization when everyone follows the common processes and the process discipline is enforced.

Process focus brings discipline and leads to increased capability

- A mature process environment brings discipline to the team. We can compare this with the behaviour of a mature person, being disciplined and predictable, as opposed to the behaviour of a child, being undisciplined and unpredictable.
- Process immaturity brings unpredictability. Process maturity increases predictability of the process results.
- A common process focus across a team leads to disciplined behaviour and increased capability of achieving the process goals.

Process focus leads to stable organization

Process focus should lead to stability in organizations because of the following factors:

- Roles and responsibilities are defined in support of the process.
- Management procedures are oriented towards managing the process performance.
- Performance of teams and individuals is assessed by measuring their contribution to the process results.
- Skills and training plans are defined to increase proficiency in performing the process activities.
- Finally, supporting technology infrastructure and tools are selected to automate, monitor and support the process activities.

Incomplete processes

A process is incomplete in any one of the following scenarios:

- The process definition documents exist (usually locked up in a manager's desk) but not everyone is aware of their existence. This is no more than 'shelfware'.
- The process definition document exists, but there is no process training. Staff are left to use their own initiative to learn the process. Some people take the time to learn the process and some do not.
- The process is documented, process training takes place, but many people ignore the process. There is no accountability, no monitoring, and no enforcement. Some people follow the process and some do not.

Disciplined process

The process is disciplined only if all the following conditions are satisfied:

- the process is documented;
- process training exists and takes place;
- people follow the process as the normal way of performing their activities; and
- the process is monitored and enforced.

Lack of process discipline could lead to organizational stress

These situations could lead to internal organizational stress:

- Lack of alignment between the organizational structure and the process activities. This could lead to confusion in focus and orientation.
- Lack of management belief in the process. This could lead to misalignment between the reward system and the process goals.
- Lack of induction training for new joiners. This could lead to the new recruits using the knowledge and skills they are familiar with to perform their activities, bringing possible conflict with existing processes.
- Lack of staff proficiency and skills in the process activities. This could lead to everyone improvising and using their own initiative to do things their own way.
- Lack of alignment between the automation tools and the process activities. This could lead to the tools being an obstacle rather than an enabler of the process.

CHAPTER 2

Process discipline

2.1 PROCESS DISCIPLINE

2.1.1 WHAT IS PROCESS DISCIPLINE?

According to the *Concise Oxford Dictionary* a discipline is 'the system of rules used to maintain control or order over a group of people'. Behaviour of group members is subjected to such rules. Accordingly a process is a disciplined process when it specifies the set of rules that would result in behaviour consistent with those rules. A disciplined process is a mature process. The definition of 'mature' is sensible, wise, duly careful and adequate.

An undisciplined, immature process is one that does not specify a set of rules and does not result in behaviour consistent with such rules. People come up with many reasons to justify behaviour that is inconsistent with a specified set of rules. One such excuse could be ignorance of the rules. For a process to be effective, people must be informed about it and if necessary trained in it. Process knowledge must be disseminated to those who are supposed to perform and participate in its activities. Another possible excuse could be the absence of process enforcement. In such cases, some people may follow the rules while others may get away with flouting them. For a process to be effective it must be enforced. A mature process is a process that is defined, trained, enforced and followed. Watts Humphrey adds another attribute, that a mature process is also continuously improving (Humphrey, 1989).

2.1.2   CAN PROCESS DISCIPLINE BE PROHIBITIVE?

Enthusiasm about the process focus and process discipline usually raises some questions and issues. There is the risk that some managers could opt for restrictive processes and practices that could inhibit rather than assist the performance of individuals. A bureaucratic process is one that is fraught with unnecessary authorizations and escalation procedures. This is why the process users (those who perform the activities following the process) should drive or at least have a large say in the process design. Process users should also have mechanisms available to provide feedback on whether the process helps or hinders their performance. Such measures should minimize the possibility of the process being restrictive and should enhance the chances of a process that is supportive to its users.

There is a fine line between discipline and bureaucracy. When designing a process we should first identify the management criteria and the business goals that the process will support. On the other hand, it may be that for valid business reasons, we want to deliberately design a bureaucratic process, a secure process, a restrictive process, a flexible process, and so on. Business goals and objectives should drive the process design criteria.

2.1.3   DOES PROCESS DISCIPLINE IMPEDE CREATIVITY?

An important question that process opponents often ask when arguing against process discipline is whether a disciplined process impedes creativity. One possible answer is that we should design the process so as to encourage and channel people's creativity towards improving the process effectiveness. Every user of the process should be encouraged to think of creative ways to improve the process performance.

Let us take a closer look at the validity of the arguments for and against process discipline in a creative environment. In other words, can process discipline be counteractive to creativity? Think of the great painters and artists of the world. It is highly unlikely that they really follow a rigid step-by-step process to create their great works of art! The process discipline seems to be more relevant to scientific and engineering work and to work performed by teams and groups of people. In such cases the final result depends on the collective group activities, rather than the work of a lone individual. Also, on a personal level, an individual may find that a disciplined process is the best way to achieving his or her goals.

There is always the question of how far discipline can be enforced in a creative environment. For example, a disciplined process could very well assist a group of people doing creative work together. In such cases a disciplined process gives a structure for releasing and harnessing the creativity of the individual members of the group. This happens without necessarily prescribing the results. An example of a process for creativity is a facilitated brainstorming session. It gives a group of individuals the opportunity to focus on the creative aspects of the subject under consideration without being concerned with the management, organization and recording of the results of the discussion.

The software industry continuously attempts to transform software development activity from a black art to an engineering discipline. Process discipline, at both team level and personal level, is an important step necessary for software development to achieve engineering and manufacturing standards. Process discipline at both team level and personal level is important for achieving productivity goals and improving the product quality. Fred Brooks (1995), in a comment on the twentieth anniversary edition of his legendary book *The Mythical Man-Month*, states that creativity comes from individuals and not from structures or processes. The question facing the software manager is 'how to design structure and process so as to enhance, rather than inhibit, creativity and initiative' (Brooks, 1995). This comment stresses the need for managers to be careful when designing processes not to make them restrictive and prohibitive, but rather to make them encourage creativity.

Another relevant question is when can a chaotic process be desirable? Do creativity and free experimentation require a chaotic environment? Think of infants in a playgroup. The purpose of the playgroup is to encourage their creativity without too much restriction. Probably they require a minimum amount of discipline in creativity sessions, while in some other sessions we may want to inject strict discipline to teach them how to work in groups and teams. The question of the link between creativity and chaotic processes is more relevant to the situation of creative individuals working on their own. Even in such cases it is wide open to discussion. This book discusses the work of teams, groups and individuals in software development projects, which requires a disciplined process to enhance project performance. Some of the reasons why we need a process discipline for groups and project teams are:

- Diverse levels of knowledge among members of the group
- Wide variation of maturity across the members of the group
- Various levels of knowledge and expertise among the group members
- Common purpose could be open to 'wide' personal interpretation.

2.1.4   SIGNIFICANCE OF PROCESS DOCUMENTATION

Another interesting question is whether a process focus can exist without necessarily being documented. This is possible in a small team environment under one or more of the following conditions:

- The team is small and has a strong sense of common purpose.
- The team has strong leadership which believes in the process discipline.
- The value system and rewards are aligned to achieving the process results.
- The team is highly trained and the team members are qualified, mature and disciplined.

Such teams exist when operating in well-controlled, highly focused projects where there is a common process shared by the group, and the team members are all experienced and mature individuals. The behaviours and activities of the individual team members are consistent and aligned with the common project goals. Given that the team membership remains stable, the results are highly likely to be repeatable.

Absence of process definition that everyone follows could result in the risks associated with an *ad hoc* process environment. Some of these risks are as follows.

- *Dependence on individuals*: If the team leader or an important team member is replaced by someone else, the risk is that the new joiner may impose a different process altogether. Without careful planning this could result in deterioration of performance. The other scenario is when a new team leader is too weak to enforce the process with the same vigour as his or her predecessor.
- *'Gurus' joining the team*: New recruits may try to impose their own way of performing activities. Some of these are 'gurus' who believe that their way of performing process activities is better than anyone else's. A common excuse is that they know better, and they try to impose their way on the others.
- *Disruptive new joiners*: These are immature and highly disruptive individuals. They are likely to destabilize the process and degrade the process effectiveness.
- *Inconsistency of process knowledge*: This leads to a difference of interpretation of the process rules and details amongst the team members. Lack of a process definition could raise the possibility of misunderstandings and misinterpretations by the team members.

Lack of process focus and lack of process discipline can lead to failures. Examples are abundant of situations where a group of talented individuals fails as a team owing to the absence of a process discipline.

2.2 BENEFITS OF PROCESS DISCIPLINE

2.2.1 PROCESS DISCIPLINE RESULTS IN PATTERNS OF COLLECTIVE BEHAVIOUR

Process discipline streamlines and aligns the activities of team members towards achieving the common process goals. Every process should have a set of 'measurable' goals assigned to it. These goals are usually derived from, and in support of, the overall business or project goals. Process teams should be enabled and empowered to achieve the process goals. The team should be judged on process performance which reflects the degree to which the process goals have been achieved. Managing teams by monitoring process performance is much more effective than managing them by other conventional methods. Some conventional management practices still focus on managing throughput of work by ensuring that staff come to work at 9 o'clock in the morning and leave at 5 o'clock in the afternoon! Such a pure time measure relates neither to the productivity nor to the quality of work performed during these hours.

A common process adopted by a team of individuals should streamline their activities and align them towards achieving their common goals. It should result in ordered patterns of behaviour (Figure 2.1). Only a disciplined process can result in streamlined patterns of behaviour. Process discipline is particularly evident in the case of teams on critical missions. Think of the Space Shuttle teams (both on-board and ground crews). In such teams all the members are well trained, have common goals to achieve, have documented procedures and have their performance measured by the results achieved by the whole team. Other examples of such teams can be found in other disciplines such as symphony orchestras. Ordered patterns of behaviour are evident and in most cases reflect beauty as in nature.

2.2.2   PROCESS DISCIPLINE INCREASES TEAM CAPABILITY

Process discipline leads to ordered patterns of collective behaviour of the team members. This means that they perform their tasks in harmony with each other towards achieving the common goals of the team. This increases the overall team's capability. On the other hand, undisciplined processes diminish the team's capability. In a disciplined process environment, the activities of

Non-disciplined Process 'Chaotic'

Disciplined Process 'Mature'

- Activities are not aligned towards a common goal
- The results of individual activities could nullify each other
- The total capability of the group is minimized

- Activities are aligned towards a common goal
- The results of individual activities add and strengthen each other
- The total capability of the group is maximized

Figure 2.1   Process discipline manifests itself in ordered patterns of behaviour

individuals are all aligned towards achieving the common process goals. Those who follow and enforce the process represent the 'forces of order'. There are also likely to be 'forces of disorder' represented by those who do not follow the common process when performing their activities. They may claim to have some reasons for not following the process (for example, 'I know better'). From the group's point of view, a process is like a contract between the group and the individual. Individuals who think there is a better way of achieving the process goals should channel their views through a process improvement mechanism. The whole group will benefit from their ideas and this could lead to process innovation while preserving process discipline.

There are many examples that illustrate how some groups cannot achieve their common goals without a disciplined process. Consider an orchestra trying to play a symphony

- without a maestro (the process is not managed)
- without musical notes (the process is not documented)
- without practice (the process is not trained)
- with everyone playing his or her own notes (the process is not enforced).

More likely the resulting music will be 'noise' with no relevance to the musical notes originally intended. Process discipline increases a team's capability (Figure 2.2a), whereas lack of process discipline could diminish its capability (Figure 2.2b).

2.2.3 PROCESS DISCIPLINE IS VITAL IN 'LIFE-CRITICAL' SITUATIONS

There are situations where the process goals are life-critical. Any deviation from the prescribed process and training could lead to disasters. The following examples illustrate this point.

- *A crew flying a plane*: Imagine a pilot deciding to ignore the advice of ground staff and taking a different flight path contrary to normal operating procedures and without full knowledge of the terrain or the weather conditions. The lives of passengers could then be threatened because of lack of process discipline.
- *A surgical team*: Imagine a surgical team performing a critical operation on a patient. If one of the surgeons or nurses ignores the instructions of the head surgeon and contradicts the agreed procedures, the life of the patient could be threatened owing to lack of process discipline.
- *Teams on high-risk missions*: Such teams have strictly prescribed processes. An example is the crew managing and flying the Space Shuttle (both on-board and ground crew). If one member of the team ignores the prescribed procedures and changes the plan without informing the others, the whole mission could be threatened.

(a)

(b)

Figure 2.2 (a) Process discipline increases a group's capability. (b) A lack of process discipline leads to chaos.

Although some of the above examples may seem exaggerated, the fact is that software now plays a critical role in most aspects of life. An undisciplined software project will most likely result in software that is riddled with errors. If such software is embedded in critical products such as aircraft, cars, medical apparatus or a space shuttle, then it becomes safety critical. A disciplined process for the development of such software is essential to guarantee its quality. The press is already full of stories about how failure in software has resulted in deaths and injuries. A highly publicized story in the UK in the early 1990s was about the failure of an ambulance routing computer system that was prematurely implemented before ensuring the quality of the system. The result was ambulances following the wrong routes and going to the wrong addresses. This led to the death of at least one patient. In the late 1980s a software error involving the operation of a switch on a computer-controlled radiation machine delivered excessive amounts of radiation, killing at least four people. These are just illustrative examples, but the point that they bring home is that software process discipline is a serious business.

2.3 PROCESS DISCIPLINE AND PRODUCT QUALITY

2.3.1 A DISCIPLINED PROCESS BREEDS PRODUCT QUALITY

It is a widely accepted fact that the quality of a software product is largely determined by the quality of the process used to develop and maintain it. The principle adopted by software process advocates is that a disciplined software process should result in high quality software products.

It is also important to remember that a good process does not necessarily deliver a good product. For example, a good process could deliver unwanted products or services. The issue of choosing the right product or service is a subject for the business strategy. A disciplined process is not a replacement for a successful business strategy. But once you have chosen a business strategy and selected the right products and services, an effective process should help you produce those products and services with high quality. A good process should specify activities and tasks for identifying the quality criteria and quality characteristics of the target product, agreeing them with the users, and making them known to all the project personnel. Other activities of the development processes can then be focused towards the realization of the product's critical quality criteria. The close link between the product quality and the process quality becomes more evident when the quality of parts of a software system is poor. Without a disciplined process, the development effort could become fixated on finding and fixing defects, and in the words of Watts Humphrey, 'the entire project becomes so preoccupied with defect repair that more important user concerns are ignored' (Humphrey, 1995).

Through disciplined processes the development team should be able to ensure the quality of both process and products. Team members will perform the tasks for analysing the quality of the product and for tracing the reasons for poor product quality. On the process side they will identify weaknesses in the process and plan corrective action for rectifying those weaknesses. A continuously improving process environment will have feedback loops. The feedback comes from measuring and analysing product quality and process performance. Analysis of such feedback should help the development team and their management trace the reasons for poor quality and identify areas for improving the process and product quality.

2.3.2   IS QUALITY IN AN UNDISCIPLINED PROCESS

ENVIRONMENT POSSIBLE?

There is no clear answer to this question. It is conceivably possible to achieve quality, without necessarily having an explicitly documented or enforced process, in small development teams of highly skilled, motivated and experienced individuals. For the rest of us an undisciplined environment means that quality is unpredictable and elusive. Not only will it be impossible to plan and manage quality without a disciplined process, but also when we achieve it we will not know why, nor will we be confident that we can repeat it. Some people could still find it difficult to prove a direct relationship between process discipline and product quality.

We can use some metaphors to support the argument for the impact of process discipline on product quality. Consider the following scenario. You take your spouse or friend to a top-class restaurant in London's West End. You order an expensive meal and in return you expect healthy delicious food. While in the restaurant you want to make a telephone call and by chance you walk by the kitchen. You look through the kitchen door to see a shocking scene of confusion and chaos. The chef is indecisive and the kitchen staff are running around aimlessly. The floor is dirty and cockroaches are feeding on some food remains on the floor. Equipment is outmoded and in need of replacement. The process is chaotic. The process discipline is represented by the cleanliness of the kitchen and the proficiency of the staff, and the product is represented by healthy tasty food. To relate process discipline to product quality think of the following questions:

- Can you expect tasty healthy food out of a dirty kitchen and out-of-date equipment? (Deficient process infrastructure)
- Can you expect good delicious food from an ignorant untrained chef who does not follow a well-tried recipe? (Lack of process training and absence of process documentation)
- Can you expect a consistently good result (food) from a confused undisciplined kitchen staff who are out of control? (Lack of process enforcement)

This should illustrate the low probability of getting high product quality out of an undisciplined process.

Total quality management, TQM, is the universal domain that covers both product and process quality. To understand the difference between process and product focus, let us consider the manufacturing environment. The same manufacturing process can be used for manufacturing a variety of products. The process focuses on *how* we produce things, while the product focus concentrates on *what* we produce. The quality of the process has a direct impact on the quality of the final product. Manufacturing industry provides us with a number of lessons on why process discipline is essential for ensuring product quality. Discipline on the production line is essential for performing manufacturing and engineering tasks and activities efficiently, ensuring the safety of the workforce, and ensuring product quality and functionality. Quality control procedures are enforced throughout the manufacturing stages. The software industry should learn from the manufacturing industry.

2.3.3 IMPACT OF PROCESS DISCIPLINE ON PRODUCT QUALITY

With the software process movement several years old now, there is growing evidence of the impact of software process improvement on software quality. A paper presented at the May 1995 SEPG Conference summarized a survey of process improvement efforts (Goldenson and Herbsleb, 1995b). It presented some evidence of the impact of software process improvement on both product quality and project schedule. Some results are shown in Figures 2.3 and 2.4.

An earlier study of the benefits of software process improvement was conducted by James Herbsleb and others (Herbsleb *et al.*, 1994). They reported the following benefits:

- $490–2004 invested per software engineer per year
- 9–67% annual increase in productivity
- 15–23% annual reduction in cycle time
- 10–94% annual reduction in field error reports
- return on investment ranging from 4:1 to 8.8:1.

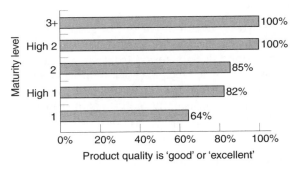

Figure 2.3 Impact of software process improvement on product quality.

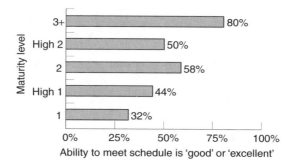

Figure 2.4 Impact of software process improvement on schedule.

2.4 PROCESS-FOCUSED ORGANIZATIONS

2.4.1 CHARACTERISTICS OF PROCESS-FOCUSED ORGANIZATIONS

Table 2.1 compares roles and responsibilities and a number of other characteristics of a mature process environment with those of an immature process environment. You could say that the mature process, like the mature adult, looks boring, and you could be right! On the other hand, a mature process, like a mature adult, has more subtle attractions. The aim of making a process mature is to make it predictable, measurable, and continuously improving. In the main, you can predict the behaviour and reactions of a mature adult in most situations based on his or her track record. On the contrary, you cannot consistently predict the behaviour of a child or an immature person. Similarly in a mature organization, you can predict the results of the organization.

The same comparison is valid for software organizations. Table 2.2 contrasts some features of immature software process environments with those of mature software process environments.

One of the most radical advocates of process focus at business level is Michael Hammer. Together with James Champy, in their pioneering book *Reengineering the Corporation*, he argues that 'it is no longer necessary for companies to organise their work in a task-oriented way. Instead they must organise work around process' (Hammer and Champy, 1993). A task-oriented or function-oriented organization is hierarchical, while a process-oriented organization is organized around horizontal process teams. Figure 2.5 illustrates some of the differences.

The following paragraphs elaborate on some of the main characteristics of horizontal process-oriented organizations and contrast them with hierarchical task-oriented organizations.

Table 2.1 A comparison between an immature and a mature process environment

Measure	Immature	Mature
Roles and responsibilities	Not well defined. Every person assumes what his or her role is. This could lead to overlapping roles and unclear ownership and responsibility	Well defined, with defined goals and measurements. Relationships are clearly defined with no overlap. Responsibilities are clearly defined
Coping with change	Different people work differently, and invent their own ways to do things	People follow a planned process, share and learn from experience and follow consistent process
Reacting to problems	Chaos reigns, fire-fighting is normal and everybody claims to be a hero	Problems are analysed and addressed from a basis of sound knowledge; professionalism rules
Reliability	Delivery sometimes late and/or over budget; estimates unreliable	Estimates are accurate and project scope is controlled and managed; targets are consistently achieved
Staff rewards	Rewards go to fire fighters. 'If you do it right the first time, you are invisible. That is your job. Mess it up, and correct it later, you become a hero' (Deming, 1986)	Rewards go to teams who produce high quality products, which satisfy the requirements with no or minimum failure. Fire prevention is rewarded rather than fire fighting
Predictability	You're never quite sure how it's going to go or what might go wrong; quality is variable and depends on individuals. Schedules and budgets are not based on historical experience	The progress of projects is predictable and so is the quality of the products. Schedules and budgets are based on historical performance and are realistic

Empowerment of process teams

In a hierarchical structure there is no single person or team who has the power to make decisions about the end-to-end process. The process spreads across organizational functions, each having responsibility and accountability only for some parts of the process. In a process-focused organization the process teams are empowered to make decisions relating to the whole process, and the team has full accountability for process performance. There are no organizational barriers. In a software engineering environment this will take the form of process teams taking responsibility for key processes such as requirements management, project planning, software quality assurance and software configuration management. A process team for a key process area will be multi-disciplined and will take total responsibility for that process. A

Table 2.2 Comparative features of immature and mature software process environments

Immature	Mature
When in doubt, code!	Formal processes are followed
No objective measures	Formal measures are taken, understood and applied
Requirements are not managed	Requirements are controlled by change control procedures
Deadlines are imposed with little regard to the requirements	Schedules are negotiated on the basis of understood and agreed requirements
Fire fighting is the accepted behaviour at time of crisis	Exceptions are considered in the process, and product and process problems analysed
No interest in the maturity of software subcontractors' processes	Subcontractors' processes are assessed and process maturity is the basis for selection
Quality focus (if it exists) is only in product quality	Quality focus always exists for both the product and the process
Performance is unpredictable	Performance is predictable
No quantitative information on product and process quality	Quantitative basis established for product and process quality

process team will be empowered to make decisions relating to their process area in order to ensure alignment between the process and the project and business goals.

Holistic end-to-end view of the process

In a hierarchical structure the process is divided between the individual functions. No one is responsible for the totality of the process performance. The total picture of the end-to-end process is rarely documented or assessed. On the other hand, in a process-focused organization the process team sees the whole picture and takes responsibility for the performance of the whole process. This improves the visibility of the total end-to-end process and its performance.

Alignment with business and project goals

In a hierarchical organization, vertical functions can 'evolve' into isolated 'silos', each with its own entrenched local goals. These local goals may or may not be aligned with business goals. In a process-focused organization, performance goals could be allocated to process teams in alignment with the overall business and project goals. Since a process team has total responsibility for process performance, it is easier to measure their effectiveness. In a

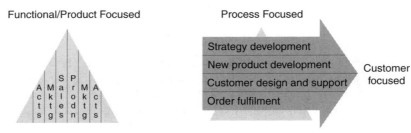

Functional/Product Focused

Process Focused

- Hierarchical structure
- Functionally focused procedures
- No department sees the big picture
- Competition between departments
- Possible conflict between department and company objectives
- No clear ownership of end-to-end process

- Empowered horizontal teams
- Devise own effective procedures
- Shared strategic and central functions
- Process teams multi-disciplinary
- End-to-end process focus
- Process teams and business objectives aligned
- Clear ownership of the end-to-end process

Figure 2.5 Function-focused versus process-focused organization

hierarchical organization, it is not always easy nor straightforward to allocate end-to-end performance goals to individual departments that handle only part of the total process.

2.4.2 LANDMARKS OF PROCESS-FOCUSED ORGANIZATIONS

There are some conditions that must be satisfied before you can say that the process is effective, or that the process contributes to the objectives and goals of the organization. These conditions represent 'landmarks' in the process environment. Some of the landmarks that distinguish a process-focused environment from a non-process-focused environment are as follows:

1   **Central role of the process**
    The process should be the basis for organization, management, skills and technology. This provides more stability to the organization and alignment of people, process and technology to support the business goals.

2   **The process has three components**
    The process is more than just a document. It has three components: the document, the training, and the mechanisms to ensure the process is followed. A document on its own is shelfware. Without effective training, people will follow their own way of performing the activities. Without monitoring the process performance, there are no guarantees that the process will achieve its goals.

3   **The process is more than a list of activities**
The process definition should include goals, activities, abilities, commitment, measurement and verification. Goals align the process to the business goals. Abilities ensure the competency of those who will perform and manage the process. Activities ensure that the process produces the correct products. Measurements ensure the quality of the process activities. Verification ensures the proper and effective implementation of the whole process and all its related activities. This model is much more comprehensive than other simple process models that focus only on the activity part of the process. This model for process design will be discussed in more detail in the following chapters.

4   **End-to-end coverage**
The process definition should cover the end-to-end horizontal flow of the process activities across all vertical functions and roles. All roles and responsibilities should be aligned with the process goals in a consistent and cooperative manner. All the activities and roles are streamlined to support the process goals.

5   **Three main types of processes: management, engineering and support**
Within a software project, key processes could be classified in three major process classes as follows:
(a) Management processes
(b) Software engineering (lifecycle) processes
(c) Support processes (lifecycle support)

2.4.3   NEED FOR PROCESS SUPPORT BY PEOPLE AND

MANAGEMENT

Under the banner of 'Personal Software Process – PSP', Watts Humphrey's recent crusade (Humphrey, 1995) is concerned with software process improvement at the personal level. PSP is now turning into a driving force that brings the process message to individual software engineers worldwide. Humphrey stresses the need for individual software engineers to have their personal software processes defined. Every software engineer should develop an improvement plan at a personal level. A process culture requires the establishment of a process focus at a number of levels: the whole business organization, projects and teams, and the software engineers' personal level. The process focus at the business level aligns and streamlines the process goals with the business goals. The process focus at the project and team management level defines the management practices to manage and evaluate the performance of teams and individuals by monitoring and evaluating the process results. The process focus at the project and team level defines the common practices in support of the project and team goals. The process focus at the personal level defines the working processes and disciplines of individuals together with actions to improve personal performance. There are risks of having a process focus at just one of these levels without the others. This could result in contradiction or conflict of the measurement goals across the levels. This in turn could lead to contradiction of goals and confusion of performance criteria used at the different levels, hence degrading the total business performance and threatening the project goals.

In this context, a word of caution is necessary. The process is just one component, albeit an important component, of the total organization. A process culture needs a sustained process focus, which in turn needs a process support infrastructure that covers organizational roles and procedures, management practices and technical infrastructures, all supporting the process in harmony. Another important point to remember is that people are the most essential part of the process. The process comes to life mainly through people. Without the people the process is likely to be a dead set of documents.

2.4.4 JUSTIFYING INVESTMENT IN PROCESS IMPROVEMENT

It is generally difficult to justify a return on investment (ROI) for software process improvement in monetary terms. There are several problems with purely monetary ROI arguments for justifying process improvement (Paulk, 1995b), for example:

- Sound management and engineering practices should not have to be return-on-investment (ROI) issues.
- Organizations with no process discipline have too few data to develop ROI arguments.
- ROI arguments ignore intangible benefits.
- Often ROI arguments are used as a stalling tactic; they are a symptom of non-commitment.

Competitive survival is hard to quantify. The quality gurus initially faced a situation of having to justify the investment in quality. The argument often used was summarized by Phil Crosby: 'The cost of quality is the expense of doing things wrong' (Crosby, 1980). We can translate this for justifying investment in software process improvement by stating that 'The cost of process improvement is the expense of tolerating the consequences of a chaotic process'.

When justifying process improvement it is important to remember that process is just one factor in the formula for business survival and growth. Other factors that can adversely affect business survival include changing customer demands, changing political and economic environments, changing technology, poor vision and strategy, and bad business decisions. Process is a key factor among these.

More arguments can be used to prove the strong link between process discipline and product quality. Product quality assurance is itself a process, and for it to be implemented effectively you need a disciplined process environment. You cannot ensure that your product quality procedures are effective unless you have in place a disciplined process to enforce them. Also you cannot monitor, measure and improve the effectiveness of the product quality controls unless you have a process improvement focus. A common reason that may hinder the acceptance of software process improvement is that many of today's software organizations cannot measure the performance of their current processes. Hence they have no baseline against which to measure the effectiveness of the process improvement efforts. They do not know what is their starting point for the process improvement journey.

SUMMARY

Process discipline

- Common process thinking should lead to disciplined behaviour across team members. Such discipline should help streamline the efforts and activities of the team members towards achieving their common goal.
- Process focus makes you look at organizations and team behaviour in a different light. One of the first questions that come to mind when seeing a group of people at work is 'Do these people follow a common process?'.

How to recognize a disciplined process

- Is the process documented, and is everyone aware of it?
- Is the process trained and practised?
- Is the process enforced? Are there mechanisms and procedures to enforce the process?
- Does the process help or hinder people's activities? Are there mechanisms to track the process performance?
- Do managers manage their teams through measuring their process conformance and process performance?

Quality of the process impacts on quality of the product

While other industries (for example, manufacturing) can provide hard evidence of the link between process discipline and product quality, the software industry needs to provide similar evidence. In software development it is logical to assume that a disciplined process is likely to lead to successful projects and higher product quality. Although this is a valid argument, we need hard evidence to prove the link between the two. Such evidence has started to filter through the literature describing the results of case studies of software process improvement.

Process discipline results in ordered patterns of behaviour

A team following a common process usually exhibits consistent ordered patterns of behaviour. The activities of individuals are aligned to the goals of the team. If everyone follows the common process consistently, consistent patterns of behaviour should be observable. Are such patterns evident in the projects and teams you know? The capability of a team following a disciplined process environment far exceeds the capability of a team that does not adhere to one.

The process maturity movement has been inspired by quality management

The software process movement has been inspired by the success of total quality management (TQM). The concepts of software process improvement have their origins in the quality concepts that started more than sixty years ago. One of the objectives of the software process movement is to apply the quality management concepts of quantitative and statistical control to managing software development. Process focus is the main enabler that can help make this achievable.

Process discipline in the context of software engineering

- A mature process results in disciplined behaviour, hence less rework, better product quality and improved project control. This is critical for software projects.
- Process discipline should not stifle creativity. Rather it channels creative ideas towards improving the process. Project managers and software engineers should be proponents of process discipline.
- A mature software process should be defined, trained, followed, enforced and continuously improving. A mature process should result in an improved software quality.

CHAPTER 3

Effective process environment

3.1   PROCESS MYTHS AND REALITIES

The process thinking and process discipline concepts described in earlier chapters should correct the view of those who believe that having procedures and standards documents is sufficient guarantee that the process is effective. An effective process environment is much more than a document. There are some myths about the nature of an effective process. A myth is 'a widely held but false notion', and the following paragraphs summarize a number of process myths and their corresponding realities. Try to relate these to your own experiences and observations.

The documentation myth

'We have a set of standards documents that specify the steps of software development and project management. We think we have a process.'
   Wrong!   A standards document on its own, without being trained and enforced, is no more than 'shelfware'. It could do harm rather than good. It gives the false impression to management that there is a process in place. A document is a dead object. It only comes to life when it turns into knowledge in people's brains and memories and only becomes effective when such knowledge drives people's behaviours.

The trust myth

'We already train our software engineers in the process. We automatically assume that they practise what they have learned. We think we do not have to monitor their activities or put enforcement procedures in place. We trust our staff.'

Wrong! This is 'wishful thinking'. An effective process environment is designed to work effectively and endure throughout generations of staff. Without follow-up, people tend to revert to their old habitual ways of performing activities. Why should they change? People can attend many training events but still act as if they had received no training. Without enforcement, you cannot guarantee that everyone in the team will follow the process.

The verification myth

'We have the software processes defined, documented and trained. We assume that things should go smoothly, the process should be self-driven. Nothing should go wrong. There is no need for external verification.'

Wrong! Without external verification, the process could be corrupted. It could be diverted from its original goals. The team performing the process could serve their own local interests rather than the overall business goals. External verification is an effective mechanism for ensuring continuing alignment between the process teams' activities and the overall business goals.

The stability myth

'We have the process defined, documented, trained and enforced. The process is stable, and it should remain effective without any changes.'

Wrong! The process will only be effective if it is aligned with the business goals. If the business goals change, the process goals must be realigned with the business goals. A stable process does not necessarily mean that the process is effective. The process should reflect the latest changes in business, technologies and methods. It should be continuously realigned to reflect any changes in the business goals.

The sponsorship myth

'We have a senior management sponsor who believes in the value of our process improvement effort. We do not have to justify our investment and effort in process improvement.'

Wrong! Unless the business benefits of the process improvement are continuously monitored, measured and made visible, management sponsorship could be lost. The process improvement effort could be stopped at the first business crisis. Business benefits attributed to process discipline should be uncovered and publicised.

The continuous enforcement myth

'We have established a disciplined software process environment. The process is defined, trained and followed. Nothing could disturb it.'

Wrong! If you do not control the process through continuous improvement, monitoring and enforcement, the forces of chaos could disrupt and degrade the process. Examples of the forces of chaos include 'gurus' who want to impose their own way, and new staff who are not properly trained in the process. Process improvement is a journey and not a destination.

3.2 WHAT IS AN EFFECTIVE PROCESS?

3.2.I SHELFWARE IS NOT A PROCESS

If you ask some managers whether they have a process in place, they point proudly to thick volumes of standards and procedures. They confuse the process specification or documentation with the process itself. Unfortunately this is an illusion. The mere existence of a document containing the definition of procedures, standards or process specifications is no evidence that the process is effective. In many cases such documents are no more than 'shelfware'. A process document does not mean that the process is understood, followed or enforced. On the other hand, an effective process, however well or poorly documented, is understood, followed, measured and enforced. 'Shelfware' is very dangerous. It could give the false impression that there is a process in place, whereas the reality could be that not everyone is even aware of the existence of the process documentation, let alone in receipt of appropriate training in the process. Another danger of 'shelfware' is that it could easily fool external observers (for example external auditors) that everything is fine – the thick standards manuals are in place!

3.2.2 SYMPTOMS OF INEFFECTIVE PROCESS ENVIRONMENT

An effective process is one that is 'producing an effect, powerful in its effect' (*Oxford English Dictionary*). For a process to be effective, three aspects must be covered: process documentation, process training, and process monitoring and enforcement. This means that for the process to be effective it needs roles and mechanisms to drive and monitor its performance. Only with the three process aspects in place can a process be effective. Any missing component could render the process ineffective, as argued in the following paragraphs.

Lack of process ownership

In situations where process ownership is neither defined nor assigned, the process could end up with no one looking after it. Without ownership the process is most likely to decay and to be ignored. The gap between the process documentation and actual practice in the real world is likely to widen over time. Also the process could turn into an obstacle that hinders rather than helps the business. Ownership implies that the process will be monitored and updated to improve its effectiveness. Figure 3.1 stresses the point that absence of explicit ownership and responsibility of a job will most likely result in it being ignored altogether.

The Story of the Four Men

This is a story about four people named **Everybody**, **Somebody**, **Anybody** and **Nobody**.

There was an important job to be done and **Everybody** was sure that **Somebody** would do it.
Anybody could have done it, but **Nobody** did it.
Somebody got angry about that, because it was **Everbody**'s job.
Everybody thought **Anybody** could do it, but **Nobody** realized that **Everybody** wouldn't do it.
It ended up that **Everybody** blamed **Somebody** when **Nobody** did what **Anybody** could have done.

(Source anonymous)

Figure 3.1 Consequences of the absence of process ownership

Lack of process monitoring

If monitoring of the process performance is absent, there will be no guarantees that the process is effective. Without monitoring, the likelihood is that the process will lose its alignment with business and management goals. Without monitoring whether activities and results conform to the process, people are likely to improvise their own processes. This will certainly lead to conflicting approaches, and will ultimately weaken the capability of the whole team.

Lack of process enforcement

If process enforcement is not evident, there would be no guarantee that the process is consistently followed. Most people will be tempted to avoid following the standard process if they feel they can get away with it (that is, if the process is not enforced). Another reason for trying to avoid the standard process could be that people may not genuinely believe that it helps them individually to achieve their objectives. Process enforcement should be linked to a scheme of rewards to encourage conformance to the process, and penalties for penalizing those who ignore the process.

Absence of process improvement

If process improvement is not actively pursued, the process could lose its effectiveness. A process without a proactive effort to improve it will decay. Without monitoring external development and progress in relevant areas, the process could lose its effectiveness. Without process improvement the process will fail to take advantage of new methods, new techniques and new tools. It will remain tied to outdated methods and techniques. It will become too inflexible to accommodate new technologies and trends.

Possible divergence of the process from its business goals

If monitoring of the external business environment is not in place, the probability of the process deteriorating (losing its effectiveness) will increase. Possible changes to the process can occur in response to political or economic changes, technological advances, or any changes to the business environment supported by the process. If the process does not keep in line with changes of business strategy and objectives, the gap between the process and its environment will widen. The process may end up as a burden rather than help business improvement.

3.2.3 CHARACTERISTICS OF EFFECTIVE PROCESS

There are a number of characteristics of an effective process environment. Table 3.1 lists some aspects and characteristics that are important for an effective process environment (assuming that the process is already defined).

Table 3.1 Characteristics of and conditions for an effective process

Key process characteristics	Conditions for an effective process
Followed	A process is effective only if it is followed consistently
Enforced	A process is followed only if it is enforced consistently
Monitored	A process is enforced only if it is consistently monitored and measured
Trained	A process is consistently performed only if those who perform it have been trained and apply their training
Measured	A process can only be improved if it is measured and the measurements are fed back into a process improvement action plan
Owned	A process will be maintained only if it has accountable ownership
Visibly supported by management	A process will be aligned to business goals only if it is visibly supported by senior management
Staff incentives are aligned with process goals	Activities of team members will only be aligned to the process goals if their productivity measurements and incentives are oriented to the process performance
New staff are properly trained in the process	The process will not be degraded by new joiners only if induction training in the process is consistently provided to new staff. If new staff do not receive such training, they will follow their own way of performing the activities which may contradict and degrade the process
Staff feedback is encouraged and analysed and leads to process improvement	The process will increase its effectiveness if the staff provide feedback on how the process helps (or hinders) them in their work and such feedback is turned into process improvement actions.
The process is adequately supported by technology	Technical infrastructure and tools are selected to support the process activities and the process monitoring and feedback

3.3 MECHANISMS FOR MAKING THE PROCESS EFFECTIVE

3.3.1 EFFECTIVE PROCESS ENVIRONMENT

An effective process should have all the key characteristics listed in Table 3.1. The process should be followed, enforced, maintained, trained, measured, owned and visibly supported by management; staff measurements and incentives should be aligned with process goals, induction of new staff mandatory, and staff feedback taking place. An environment that makes all this happen can be considered an effective process environment. It must have in place all the mechanisms shown in Figure 3.2. They should cover the roles, responsibilities and technical support required for the following:

- effectively performing the process activities;
- maintaining and updating the process definition;
- monitoring the process performance; and
- implementing corrective action as necessary.

3.3.2 MAKING THE PROCESS EFFECTIVE

An effective process environment is a dynamic environment. The process benefits are measured, process effectiveness is evaluated, and the results are fed back into

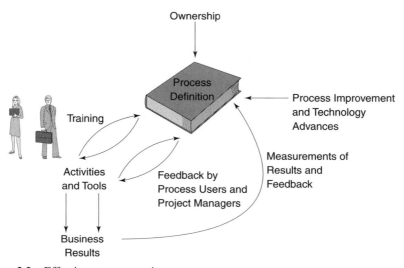

Figure 3.2 Effective process environment

process improvement actions, increasing the effectiveness of the process. In such an environment the following factors increase process effectiveness:

- The process documentation is a living document. It is owned, disseminated and maintained by a dedicated resource.
- The process users, management and staff, are keen to follow the process.
- Performance measurements provide feedback for inclusion into process improvement actions.
- The process impact on the business goals is evident, and following the process is the norm.

There are a number of organizational roles and mechanisms that should be in place for the process to be effective. These roles should cover the following areas:

- Process ownership
- Process training
- Measurement of process results
- Monitoring of process performance (as a result of monitoring of the process results)
- Feedback from process users
- Feedback from the surrounding environment (to incorporate new advanced methods, technologies, tools and concepts)
- Process inspection and enforcement (to ensure the conformance of the process and product quality with the expected standards).

3.3.3   PROCESS OWNERSHIP

A group must be assigned the responsibility for process ownership. Without ownership the process will deteriorate. It could turn into a 'disabler' rather than an 'enabler' for its users. An 'orphan' process without ownership will deteriorate. It will end up being a liability rather than a help to the business, and it is likely to be ignored by everyone. (Imagine the increase in road accidents if no one were monitoring drivers' behaviour on the road.) In most of the literature on the software process, such ownership is assumed by what is called the software engineering process group (SEPG).

3.3.4   PROCESS TRAINING

A process that is not consistently trained will be ineffective. It will be performed inconsistently, will miss its performance targets, and will deteriorate over time. An important type of training is the induction training given to new staff who join the organization or the project from outside. If these staff are not provided with process training they are likely to use old processes they were using in their previous job. This is a chaotic factor that

Table 3.2 Candidates for process training

Candidates for process training	Type of process training
Management sponsors	Awareness training of the business benefits of the process
Process groups	Detailed process, methods and techniques training
Project managers	Process management training and process improvement awareness
Functional managers	Process awareness and process management training
Project members and functional teams	Detailed process, methods and techniques training
Infrastructure specialists	Detailed process infrastructure and support training
Quality assurance teams	Detailed process inspection and monitoring training

will result in a non-uniformity of the processes used and will lead to degradation of the total process performance. Who should receive the process training? Table 3.2 illustrates potential candidates for process training, and the type of training they should receive.

The type of training for a specific group should be defined according to the role and importance of the process knowledge for the group's activities. For example, the process training scope and orientation for senior management should focus on the business benefits and the alignment between the process and the business goals.

3.3.5 MEASUREMENT AND FEEDBACK ON PROCESS RESULTS

Measurements of process results are essential to assess the contribution of the process to business and project goals. They prove the business benefits of the process discipline and highlight risks to the business in the absence of the process discipline. The results should be publicized in order to strengthen everyone's belief in the value of the process discipline to the whole business. Performance of teams as well as individuals should be measured and rewarded based on the process performance. This implies that the appropriate mechanisms to measure and assess the results are in place. Harrington (1991) suggests types of measurements for business processes. Table 3.3 provides an expanded list of potential measurements suitable for measuring the software process effectiveness.

3.3.6 FEEDBACK FROM PROCESS USERS

One of the worst scenarios for process acceptability by staff is when management impose an out-of-date or bureaucratic process on their staff, or the process is seen to add no value nor to assist anyone in performing his or her

Table 3.3 Types of process measurements

Type of measurements	Metrics
Process effectiveness	Performance Reliability Usability Cost of process activities Responsiveness Adaptability Dependability Applicability Accuracy of results Quality of output products
Process efficiency	Processing time Resources expended per unit of output Ratio of cost and benefit per unit of output Rate of improvement in the number of reported errors over a period of time
Process adaptability	Suitability for varying sizes of projects Suitability for different types of products Customizability to match different requirements Adaptability to match different users' expectations Flexibility to accommodate a variety of methods, techniques and tools

activities. Most people have had to fill in forms which no one ever referred to afterwards. Process user representatives should be involved from the start in the design and definition of the processes relevant to their work. This is an effective way to gain their buy-in and commitment to the process. Some possible mechanisms for feedback on process performance are as follows:

- Feedback forms to be completed by users when they face a problem relating to the process, its ease of use and its effectiveness
- Proactive feedback through direct elicitation from selected process users (on regular or *ad hoc* basis)
- Voluntary feedback from users who have some incentives to provide such feedback (for example, rewards for proposals that result in improving the process)
- Automatic feedback collected through monitoring and measurement mechanisms embedded into the process activities and tools, making the feedback an automatic fallout of process activities.

The following list presents the types of questions that could be used to elicit process user feedback:

- Was the process generally a help or a hindrance?
- In what way was it a help or a hindrance to you personally in performing your tasks?
- Under what conditions was the process most useful?
- What aspects of the process should be improved?
- How do you think the process could improve?
- What motivations are in place that encouraged you to follow the process?

3.3.7   FEEDBACK FROM EXTERNAL ENVIRONMENT

Change is the only constant fact in this world. A process could start as effective and completely aligned with business, project and team goals, but could end up ineffective and a hindrance to progress and competitiveness. One reason for this could be that the process remained static while the world around it has moved on. An effective process should not remain static. It should reflect the changes in its surrounding business environment. Such changes could come in the form of political, economic, legislative, social or technological changes. For example, a business process based on the assumption of separate western European countries may be completely impeding the progress of the organization to do business and compete in a unified European Community. Also a software development process based on structured methods may not be competitive for a market that requires an object-oriented or rapid application development approach. The following is a list of sources of changes that could impact the process. These should be monitored closely by the process group in order to keep the process continuously aligned with the new changes:

- Laws, regulations and product standards (for example, environmental or safety product requirements)
- Regulations for inspection and certification
- National and international trade laws and regulations
- Industry-specific and product-specific laws and regulations
- Technological and methodological advances that could impact on the process activities
- Political changes that could impact the trans-border flow of trade and labour. This could lead to changing the character and scope of target customers and their needs.

3.3.8   ENFORCEMENT AND INSPECTION MECHANISMS

Inspection is necessary to ensure conformance of the process activities and results with the process definition and standards. Enforcement mechanisms should deal with non-compliance. Inspection and enforcement of the process do not necessarily mean that you mistrust the staff. In most situations the majority of process users will conform with the process requirements.

Enforcement aims to uncover and correct the minority of non-conformers. The mere existence of enforcement mechanisms and procedures is a deterrent against the breach of the standard process. (Imagine the state of driving on motorways and roads if we abolished the traffic police and dismantled speed cameras.)

Enforcement and inspection mechanisms could take one or more of the following forms:

- Internal audits (random or regular)
- ISO 9000 certification audits
- Other standards certification audits
- Compliance audits and reviews
- Inspection for compliance (random or regular).

3.4 PROCESS CULTURE

3.4.1 PROCESS INSTITUTIONALIZATION

Process institutionalization is achieved when the process becomes embedded in the day-to-day activities of the organization. Process institutionalization is defined as broad and routine use across the whole organization (Fowler and Rifkin, 1990). This will happen when the organization has in place a process culture and a process infrastructure. Culture is a set of shared basic assumptions that a group has learned as it solved its problems or that has helped the group repeatedly in achieving its objectives (Myers, 1996). Culture is formed by what are known as cultural drivers. The process culture is driven by vision and strategic direction coming from the top of the organization. The process infrastructure provides operational support for the process activities and process management. The infrastructure covers the organization and management roles and responsibilities and the technical tools to support the process.

Figure 3.3 illustrates the two main prerequisites for process institutionalization: corporate process culture and process infrastructure.

Process Culture Driven by vision and strategic direction
Process Infrastructure Able to support the business
methods, practices and procedures, so that they
'endure after those who originally defined them have gone'

Figure 3.3 Process institutionalization requires both corporate culture and process infrastructure

3.4.2 PROCESS CULTURE AND INFRASTRUCTURE:
WHY WE NEED BOTH

What happens if one of these elements is lacking? Can a process be sustained without a supporting infrastructure *and* a process culture? Let us consider the following scenarios.

Can we have a process culture without a supporting infrastructure? In the absence of a process support infrastructure, the process culture will be little more than 'lip service'. Everyone talks about the need for the process, but management is reluctant to invest in establishing the infrastructure required to support and enforce the process discipline. They are not prepared to put their money where their words are.

Can we have an effective process infrastructure in the absence of a process culture? A process organizational infrastructure, without a process culture to encourage its use, is no more than an isolated island of roles and responsibilities. Process roles would be isolated from mainstream development and business activities, and would be confined to an 'ivory tower'. The process technical infrastructure would be little more than a collection of technical facilities with no effective use – a 'white elephant'.

3.4.3 SYMPTOMS AND BEHAVIOURS OF PROCESS CULTURE

A process-focused organization will have process behaviours ingrained into its culture. Only then can we say that the organization has a process culture. What does a process culture mean? The word culture means 'customs and civilization of a particular time or people'. In process culture people's customs and behaviours are influenced by process-oriented thinking and process management principles. Following the process is the norm and preaching the process is the exception. The process is followed naturally and everyone accepts that the process discipline helps the business achieve its objectives. This is the ultimate result of establishing all the process enforcement mechanisms described above. These mechanisms are the factors that will make the process effective.

You can recognize whether an organization has a process culture or not by comparing the behaviours of its staff and management with the process-oriented symptoms and behaviours summarized in Table 3.4.

3.4.4 EFFECTIVE PROCESS AND THE CORPORATE MEMORY

An effective process environment should have feedback mechanisms to collect feedback on the process performance. The feedback data should be collected and stored in a process database. This database in effect becomes the corporate memory in which the organization stores the experiences and results of its

Table 3.4 Process-oriented symptoms and behaviours

Key word	Description of symptom/behaviour
Process visibility	The process definition and process responsibility are visible to everybody in the organization
Process discipline	Following the process is the norm, and acting outside the process is the exception
Process institutionalization	The process is 'institutionalized' within the organization. Following the process is engraved into the organizational policies and procedures, and supported by the management
Management commitment to the process	The process is supported by top management of the enterprise as well as all other levels of management and staff
Process enforcement	Process enforcement is evident and is in force
Process ownership	The process is owned, maintained and continuously improved and supported by an organizational infrastructure
Process feedback	Feedback on the process effectiveness is practised by everyone in the organization, and is enabled by appropriate feedback mechanisms
Performance assessment	Measurement and evaluation of staff and team performance is tightly linked to the process performance (i.e. achieving the process goals)
Process training	Process awareness and training is mandatory for all staff, and process induction is mandatory for new recruits
Process improvement	Process improvement is planned and implemented through the participation of all the staff involved

process performance, successes and failures. Such information should be made available to everyone in the organization who is involved in performing the process activities. Such information represents the learning of all those who were involved in the process activities. Availability of this data could prove invaluable for the success of future projects. The organization learns from its past experiences, hence the learning organization. The capability and predictability of such an organization are much higher than those of an organization with an ineffective process environment. As will be discussed later in the book, the organization's corporate process database is a good candidate to act as the corporate memory.

3.4.5   MOVING TO AN EFFECTIVE PROCESS ENVIRONMENT

This book describes a roadmap for moving towards an effective software process environment. Such a move is likely to have an impact on all aspects of your software organization. It impacts on people, technology, management and organization. As in the case of all change programmes, process improvement should be planned properly, otherwise it could backfire. There are guidelines and principles for successful change management. In the case of changing the software process, Watts Humphrey suggests a list of six basic principles for software process change (Humphrey, 1989):

- Major changes to the software process must start at the top.
- Ultimately, everyone must be involved.
- Effective change requires a goal and knowledge of the current process.
- Change is continuous.
- Software process changes will not be retained without conscious effort and periodic reinforcement.
- Software process improvement requires investment.

Successful implementation of continuous software process improvement should apply these principles as a matter of course. The framework and the approach described in this book advocates the use of these principles by any strategy for creating a culture of software process improvement. Failure to follow these principles could have any of the following consequences:

- Process improvement initiatives that fail because of lack of top management support
- Change programmes that fail because their goals were not well defined
- Change programmes that fail because of lack of involvement by everybody.

SUMMARY

Key features of effective process

A process will be effective only if it is defined, trained, followed, owned, supported and continuously improving.

A process is more than a document

The world is full of process documentation that is no more than 'shelfware'. Shelfware is everywhere. Think of some documents or procedures in your environment that you can describe as 'shelfware'. Think of some reasons why these documents or procedures are 'shelfware'. Is it because of lack of ownership? Lack of training? Lack of monitoring and measurement of results? Lack of strong link with the reward system?

Process essentials

- The process must be supported by the appropriate organizational roles and responsibilities and management and technical infrastructure.
- A process culture will result in an effective process environment where the process will yield business benefits to the organization and the team.

- Process performance goals must be aligned with the business and project goals. This will bring conformity and increase effectiveness of the process activities.
- Inspection and monitoring of the process results should ensure that the process benefits are realized. Process enforcement is an insurance against non-conformance.
- Management commitment to the process must be visible and is mandatory for achieving process culture.

Need for process culture and infrastructure

- Process culture is driven by vision and strategic direction from the top of the organization.
- Process infrastructure provides operational support for the process activities and process management.
- In the absence of a process infrastructure, the process culture will be little more than 'lip service'.
- In the absence of a process culture, the process infrastructure will be no more than an isolated set of roles and responsibilities.

Effective Process environment

For a process environment to be effective, it should have roles and mechanisms to support the following:
- Process ownership
- Process training
- Measurement of process results
- Monitoring of process performance
- Feedback from process users
- Feedback from the external environment
- Process inspection and enforcement.

CHAPTER 4

Process maturity: the second wave of the software industry

4.1 WAVES AND MEGATRENDS OF THE SOFTWARE INDUSTRY

4.1.1 WAVES AND MEGATRENDS

The software industry has been progressing through a number of waves and megatrends. So far, three waves are evident. The first wave was characterized by the waterfall lifecycle and structured methods, the second wave is the process maturity movement, and the third wave is expected to be software industrialization (Lai, 1993). Each wave appears to emerge progressively from the preceding one. Structured methods were a step forward compared with the 'go-to' and 'spaghetti code' culture. The process maturity movement is a further step forward compared with structured methods. The scope of software process management is wider than analysis, design or coding. It covers all aspects of the software development process and its support activities. The evolution of object-oriented technology has given rise to much talk about software industrialization, where software development turns into a manufacturing and assembly of components. Having a disciplined process is a prerequisite for the realization of software industrialization.

The software industry is currently in the midst of the process maturity wave. The software process movement is gaining popularity and spreading worldwide through software process improvement networks (SPINs), and through the leadership of the Software Engineering Institute (SEI) and the International Standards Organization (ISO).

4.1.2 THREE WAVES OF THE SOFTWARE INDUSTRY

Robert Lai (1993) refers to the process maturity movement as the second wave of the software industry. He uses the model proposed by Alvin Toffler that describes an industry's maturity in terms of waves. Lai proposes that process improvement is the second maturity wave of the software industry. He states that in the first wave we developed software using the waterfall model. Today we are in the midst of the second wave – a maturity movement 'as we attempt to formally define the development process and the best ways to improve it. The third wave will involve the machination of the software industry, characterized by the mass production of uniformly high quality products' (Lai, 1993).

The first wave, started by the lifecycle models and structured methods, brought us one step nearer to understanding software development activities. One of the most powerful features the first wave gave us was the ability to represent software activities diagrammatically (Royce, 1970; Boehm, 1981). This step brought software development nearer to becoming an engineering discipline. The second wave, process maturity wave is likely to push the software industry even further towards becoming an engineering discipline. It will make the software industry a process-focused industry just like manufacturing industries have been for a long time. Although software may have special features that make it different from hardware, from a process-discipline point of view there are many aspects common to both. Process discipline can be seen in other areas of human activity and business domains. Look at the need for discipline in military operations, in large manufacturing plants or aerospace projects.

4.1.3 WATTS HUMPHREY AND THE SOFTWARE PROCESS MOVEMENT

Taking the lead in this area has been Watts Humphrey (Humphrey, 1989, 1995, 1996; Humphrey *et al.*, 1991) and the Software Engineering Institute (SEI) of Carnegie Mellon University. Watts Humphrey is the pioneer and leader of the software process movement. He laid down its founding principles. A basic principle set out early by Humphrey is the need 'to treat the entire software task as a process that can be controlled, measured, and improved' (Humphrey, 1989). Software process pioneering work was started by Watts Humphrey and his team at the Software Engineering Institute in the late 1980s. Since then, the software process movement has been gaining momentum and increasing popularity worldwide.

Lai (1993) quotes Humphrey's 'second wave' process improvement cycle as the route from the first wave to the third wave (Humphrey, 1989). The cycle has the following six steps:

- Understand the current status of your development process (perform process assessment).
- Develop a vision of the desired process (in support of the business vision).
- Establish a list of required process improvement actions, in order of priority (based on the result of process assessment).
- Produce a plan to accomplish the required actions (prepare the process improvement plan).
- Commit the resources to execute the plan (implement the plan).
- Restart the cycle (continuously improve).

The framework proposed in this book covers the whole cycle of software process improvement. It encompasses the essential components of the software process improvement environment: software process infrastructure, process improvement roadmap, process assessment method and process improvement plan.

4.2   THE SOFTWARE PROCESS MATURITY MOVEMENT

4.2.1   ROOTS OF THE MOVEMENT

The push for software process improvement came as a response to the failures of software projects. The success of total quality management (TQM) has inspired the software process movement. The origins of software process maturity can be traced back to the principles of product quality management that have existed for nearly 70 years. Well-known 'gurus' of the quality movement include such names as Shewhart, Deming, Juran and Crosby. Figure 4.1 summarizes the milestones and tracks the origins of the software process movement.

Walter Shewhart promulgated the principles of statistical quality control. These principles were further developed and successfully demonstrated in the works of Edwards Deming (1982), Joseph Juran (1988) and Phil Crosby (1980). The premise of those early pioneers of quality is that real process improvement must follow a sequence of steps. Make the process visible, then repeatable and then measurable. What you cannot measure you cannot manage and you cannot improve.

Principles of statistical process control

In its evolution the quality movement progressed from product inspection to statistical methods of process control. The roots of the software process maturity movement are easily traceable in the total quality concepts. The principle of statistical control is a theme common to both the quality

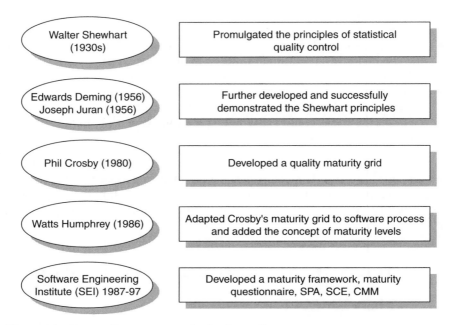

Figure 4.1   Roots of process maturity in the quality movement

movement and the software process movement. Watts Humphrey put the case for the need for statistical control of the development process: 'if the development process is under statistical control, a consistently better result can be achieved only by improving the process. If the process is not under statistical control, sustained progress is not possible until it is' (Humphrey, 1988).

In his work with Japanese industry after World War II, Edwards Deming applied the concepts of statistical process control to industry. Watts Humphrey highlighted the fact that, while there are important differences, these concepts are just as applicable to software as they are to manufacturing artefacts, such as automobiles, cameras, wristwatches and steel. In developing a framework for software process maturity, Humphrey combined Deming's principles, Juran's improvement approach and Crosby's maturity grid, and applied their underlying principles to the software development process. Further discussions of these approaches are provided in later chapters.

4.2.2 POPULARIZATION OF THE MOVEMENT

The impact of Watts Humphrey's early work that was later expanded in his book *Managing the Software Process* (Humphrey, 1989) has been enormous. It has triggered worldwide interest from managers and software engineers working for software suppliers and acquirers alike. The second wave has begun. This is evident from the increasing number of organizations investing seriously in software process improvement and from the attention that software process improvement is getting from sponsoring organizations.

The following is a selection of public initiatives which illustrate the worldwide attention given to the software process and its improvement as organizations and consortiums develop software process improvement models and standards.

- The US Department of Defense (DoD) sponsored pioneering process work by the Software Engineering Institute (SEI). At that time Watts Humphrey was appointed Director of the Software Process Program that led to the development of the CMM. Sponsorship of the SEI continued through the US Air Force. Also the new military standard for software development and documentation (MIL-STD-498) accommodates the software process concepts.
- The European Commission has set up a special investment programme, the European Systems and Software Initiative (ESSI), to encourage and sponsor organizations throughout Europe in experimenting and disseminating software process improvement experiments (PIE). The results of some of these experiments are documented. They are published and presented at European conferences where experiences with PIEs are exchanged (Holmes, 1995).
- The UK Ministry of Defence (MoD) has sponsored work on software quality standards and software process improvement through its Defence Research Agency (DRA). The resulting quality standards and initiatives were an essential contribution to the SPICE proposal to the International Standards Organization. This highlighted the need to develop an international standard for determining the software process capability of software suppliers. This has ultimately led to the development of ISO/IEC 15504 process assessment standards.
- The German Federal Armed Forces sponsored the development of the V-Model (IABG, 1992). The V-Model is a software development standard that addresses the software engineering lifecycle and its supporting activities.
- A consortium of international telecommunications corporations was formed, championed by Bell Canada and with the active participation of Bell Northern Research and Northern Telecom in Canada. The consortium has developed and published Trillium, a model for initiating continuous software process improvement (Trillium, 1994).
- The European Space Agency (ESA) has developed and published a software engineering standard, PSS-05-0, for use by ESA suppliers and affiliates for developing software (ESA, 1991).
- The International Standards Organization (ISO) has developed the ISO 9000 series of standards. A number of related documents have focused on applying ISO 9000 to software development. The most relevant of these are ISO 9000-3 (ISO, 1991, 1994), ISO/IEC 12207, and most recently the development of an international standard for software process assessment ISO/IEC 15504.

In addition to these public models and standards, there are many private initiatives. These are mostly developed by large organizations for use in software development and acquisition, and for evaluating and selecting their software suppliers. An example is British Telecom's 'Healthcheck' methodology for assessing and selecting software suppliers (Mackie and Rigby, 1993).

4.3   LEVELS OF SOFTWARE PROCESS INSTITUTIONALIZATION

4.3.1   THREE LEVELS OF PROCESS INSTITUTIONALIZATION

While process internalization is at the level of an individual, process institutionalization is at the level of teams and organizations. A process is described as 'institutionalized' when it is followed consistently and performed naturally by everyone involved in performing the process activities. Consistency in this context means that different groups and teams follow a consistent set of activities for achieving the process goals. A level of consistency of results should be expected irrespective of who are the individuals performing the process activities. This is why the predictability of an organization with an institutionalized, disciplined process is higher than that of one without disciplined processes. In a software engineering context, this implies that different software projects within the organization follow a common core of practices that should help them achieve their goals. Process institutionalization is defined as 'the building of infrastructure and corporate culture that support the methods, practices, and procedures so that they are the ongoing way of doing business, even after those who originally defined them are gone' (Paulk *et al.*, 1994).

As depicted in Figure 4.2, process institutionalization is achieved if the process focus is established at all levels of the organization – corporate,

'All three levels need to be process-focused before an
organization can be described as a process-focused organization'

Figure 4.2   Levels of process institutionalization

management and personal. The management level covers functional, project, and team management. An effective process support infrastructure should cover all of these levels. A process focus at these levels would manifest itself as discussed below.

4.3.2 PROCESS INSTITUTIONALIZATION AT THE ORGANIZATIONAL OR CORPORATE LEVEL

The organizational structure, roles and responsibilities should explicitly relate to the business goals. The business goals should be reflected and supported explicitly in the process goals. Usually 'horizontal' cross-functional process teams should be formed from different organizational functions with the purpose of analysing process performance and devising ways to improve the process. Examples of process enablers at the corporate level are corporate process groups, corporate process database, and corporate culture and infrastructure.

4.3.3 PROCESS INSTITUTIONALIZATION AT THE PROJECT AND TEAM MANAGEMENT LEVEL

The project and team managers in a process-focused organization will manage their staff through monitoring the process performance rather than monitoring individuals. Performance evaluations and rewards will be for process teams. This is quantitative process management. Managers should follow the process explicitly so the staff can see that managers are the first to respect and follow the process: 'walk the talk'. They can also encourage the creation of a continuous process improvement culture through measuring the process performance and taking corrective action to improve it.

4.3.4 PROCESS INSTITUTIONALIZATION AT THE PERSONAL LEVEL

This is reflected in the attitude of all process users, managers and staff in the organization. Adherence to the process while performing activities is the natural way followed by individuals. Circumventing the process is an exception, and often requires authorization from higher management levels. Improving the personal software process (PSP) is the subject of Watts Humphrey's recent crusade within the software process movement (Humphrey, 1995).

Table 4.1 illustrates examples of important factors that could help process institutionalization and the creation of a process focus in an organization at these three levels.

Table 4.1 Factors that could help process institutionalization

Level	Process focus	Process infrastructure	Process measurement
Organizational (Corporate)	Alignment of process with business goals	Corporate-wide process infrastructure	Process metrics linked to business results
	No organizational barriers	Corporate-level organizational ownership of the process	Corporate-wide mechanisms for process measurement and feedback
Management (Project and team)	Management sponsorship and leadership by example	Project/departmental level process infrastructure	Process performance used as basis for rewards
	Managers champion process facilitation and support	Process group to develop, nurture and monitor the process	Process metrics known and accepted by staff
Personal	Personal belief that process discipline is beneficial to the individual and the team	Availability of personal process support tools and facilities	Ability and willingness to keep records of personal process performance
	Circumventing the process requires authorization	Awareness of and competency in using process support tools	Process measurements are basis for personal process improvement

4.4   SOFTWARE PROCESS MATURITY STANDARDS AND INITIATIVES

This section briefly describes a number of process standards and initiatives. These include the Capability Maturity Model, ISO/IEC 15504, DoD Standard 498, BOOTSTRAP and other initiatives. More details of these initiatives are discussed in later chapters.

4.4.1   THE CAPABILITY MATURITY MODEL

The Capability Maturity Model (CMM) developed by the Software Engineering Institute (SEI) of Carnegie Mellon University is one of the most, if not the most, popular process improvement models in the software industry thus far. The SEI developed the CMM through sponsorship by the US Department of Defense. A detailed account of the evolution of the CMM is given in Paulk *et al.* (1994). The process programme was led by Watts Humphrey and the results started appearing in 1987. An early report entitled 'Characterizing the software process: a maturity framework' set the foundations for the software process movement (Humphrey, 1987).

Another significant milestone was the publication of Watts Humphrey's book *Managing the Software Process* (Humphrey, 1989) which popularized the message of software process maturity. A draft of the Capability Maturity Model (CMM v0.2) was distributed in June 1990 for review. It described the maturity levels in terms of key process areas. CMM version 0.6 was released in June 1991 for review. This was followed by the release in August 1991 of the CMM v1.0 (Paulk *et al.*, 1991). CMM version 1.1 was published in February 1993 as two reports, *Capability Maturity Model for Software, version 1.1* (Paulk *et al.*, 1993a) and *Key Practices of the Capability Maturity Model for Software, version 1.1* (Paulk *et al.*, 1993b). Plans for CMM version 2.0 are already in place. The CMM undergoes continuous improvement and its development has progressed consistently. Figure 4.3 illustrates milestones in CMM development. Figure 4.4 illustrates the five process maturity levels of the CMM: Initial, Repeatable, Defined, Managed and Optimizing. The Capability Maturity Model is further discussed in later chapters. The first CMM developed by the SEI focused on software engineering process. Inspired by the success of the CMM for the software process, the CMM is coordinating an international support effort to develop and maintain a number of the CMMs to address other disciplines related to software engineering. This resulted in a number of CMMs: SE-CMM for systems engineering, P-CMM for people, IPD-CMM for Integrated Systems Product Development, SA-CMM for Software Acquisition as well as the SW-CMM for Software. In this book we shall use CMM to refer to SW-CMM.

4.4.2 ISO 9000

ISO 9000 is a general standard. It is applicable to producers of virtually any commodity, from cars to software. The parts of the standard that are applicable to software developers are:

1 ISO 9001 Quality Systems – Model for Quality Assurance in Design, Development, Production, Installation and Servicing. This standard describes the quality system used to produce a product.
2 ISO 9000-3 Guidelines for the Application of ISO 9000 to the Development, Supply and Maintenance of Software. This document interprets ISO 9000 for the software developer.
3 ISO 9004-2 Quality Management and Quality System Elements – Part 2. This standard provides guidelines for the servicing of software facilities.

The quality system requirements covered by this standard include production of quality policy, documenting the system, reviewing contracts, design and document control, testing, handling and storage, quality auditing,

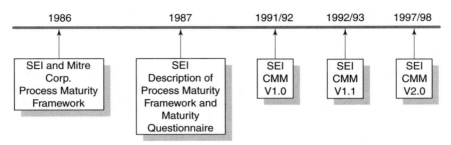

Figure 4.3 Milestones in the history of the Capability Maturity Model (CMM)

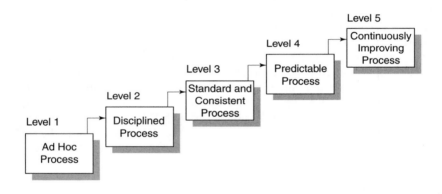

Figure 4.4 The five process maturity levels of the CMM

training, servicing and metrics. The UK Department of Trade and Industry (DTI), the British Standards Institution (BSI) and software industry representatives have developed and issued a guide for software purchasers, software suppliers and quality auditors entitled *TickIT Guide to Software Quality Management System Construction and Certification Using ISO 9001/EN29001* (BSI, 1992).

A more detailed discussion of ISO 9000-3 is provided in later chapters. The quality system defined in ISO 9000-3 is divided into lifecycle activities and supporting activities:

- Quality system – lifecycle activities:
  - Contract review
  - Purchaser's requirements specification
  - Development planning
  - Quality planning

- – Design and implementation
- – Testing and validation
- – Acceptance
- – Replication, delivery and installation
- – Maintenance
- Quality system – supporting activities (not phase dependent):
  - – Configuration management
  - – Document control
  - – Quality records
  - – Measurement
  - – Rules, practices and conventions
  - – Tools and techniques
  - – Purchasing
  - – Included software product
  - – Training.

4.4.3   ISO/IEC 15504

ISO/IEC 15504 resulted from the SPICE project. SPICE stands for 'Software Process Improvement and Capability dEtermination', El Emam *et al.* (1997). The SPICE Project, sponsored by the International Standards Organization, is an international collaborative programme developing a new international standard for Software Process Assessment ISO/IEC 15504. A series of project documents control the development work, and a quality assurance coordinator is dedicated to the project. A formal requirements specification has been produced and all of the component parts of the standard have been developed and extensively reviewed. The approval stage followed the completion of formal trials in spring 1996. The standard has now been published.

During an ISO/IEC 15504 process assessment, individual process attributes are rated by qualified and trained assessors. They are evaluated against an appropriate achievement scale using an appropriate set of indicators of process performance and an appropriate set of indicators of process capability. A process profile for an assessed process instance is made up of its attribute ratings. Ratings for several instances of a process may be aggregated into a process capability profile that indicates, for each process assessed, the frequency with which the process attributes are being achieved.

Armed with this capability profile, the supplier defines a *desired* capability profile and analyses any gaps, going on to initiate process improvement actions if necessary. This gap analysis technique can also be used to compare competing software suppliers' profiles against a *procurer*'s desired capability profile.

The ISO/IEC 15504 draft technical report includes guidance on how to develop and use assessment instruments, how to conduct assessments and how to use the results, as well as providing a reference model and rating scheme. ISO/IEC 15504 is published by the International Standards Organization (ISO). ISO/IEC 15504 is discussed in more detail later in this book.

4.4.4   BOOTSTRAP

The BOOTSTRAP methodology was described in detail in Kuvaja *et al.* (1994). It was originally developed as ESPRIT project 5441. The project ran from September 1991 to February 1994. The project consisted of the development of the BOOTSTRAP model and method. The BOOTSTRAP methodology is based on the Capability Maturity Model (CMM). The model has been extended and adapted to include guidelines in the ISO 9000 family of standards and the European Space Agency's PSS-05 software development standard. More detailed discussion of BOOTSTRAP is provided in later chapters of this book.

4.4.5   OTHER PROCESS-RELATED INITIATIVES

There is a host of other related efforts for software process improvement. Some are variants of the CMM, such as Trillium for the telecommunications industry (Trillium, 1994). The following is a non-exhaustive list of related initiatives and techniques: Engineering Maturity Model (EMM); Software Acquisition Maturity Model (SAMM); *ami* (application of measurements in industry); Goal–Question–Metric (GQM); Software Development Capability/Capacity Review (SDC/CR); Systems Security Engineering (SSE); Software Technology Diagnostic (STD); Healthcheck; Self-Assessment Method (SAM); Quantum; Software Quality Improvement Method; ImproveIT and TickIT. The focus of this book is on the most popular and established approaches, especially the CMM, BOOTSTRAP, ISO 9000 and ISO/IEC 15504.

SUMMARY

Since its start, the software industry has been and still is undergoing waves and megatrends. The first wave has been the structured methods and development lifecycles, and we are now in the midst of the second wave, the process maturity movement.

Software process maturity and total quality management

The roots of the software process maturity movement come from total quality management. Watts Humphrey has pioneered and championed the application of the concepts of statistical control to the software development process. The Capability Maturity Model is a framework for software process maturity that incorporates the major approaches to quality improvement.

Levels of software process institutionalization

For the process to be sustained, process behaviour needs to be ingrained into the organization's culture. In order to succeed in embedding the process into the organization's culture, there is a need to address all organizational levels, including corporate, management, project, team and personal. Models and techniques to embed the process into these organizational levels should be adopted as appropriate for each level to ensure that the process is institutionalized. Process thinking should endure across generations of workers and managers.

Software process maturity standards and initiatives

There are a number of international standards and initiatives for the software process. Some of these are well known in the public domain such as the CMM, ISO/IEC 15504, ISO 9000 and BOOTSTRAP. Some of the other initiatives are local either to a specific organization or to a specific industry, such as Healthcheck and Trillium.

PART 2

A framework for software process improvement

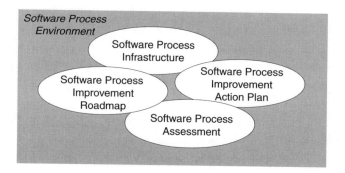

Part 2 introduces the overall framework proposed in this book for the software process improvement environment. The framework describes the main components that need to be in place in order to build a continuous software process improvement environment. The four components are software process infrastructure, software process improvement roadmap, software process assessment method, and software process improvement plan. Each of these components is described in detail in one chapter.

CHAPTER 5

A framework for software process improvement

5.1 SOFTWARE PROCESS IMPROVEMENT ENVIRONMENT

5.1.1 EFFECTIVE SOFTWARE PROCESS

A general model for an effective process environment has been described in Chapter 3. Applying this model to software development should lead to an effective software process environment as illustrated in Figure 5.1. The process definition is the software process definition, that is specification of the software lifecycle management and engineering processes, the software lifecycle management and support processes. The process users are the software engineers and project managers. The process results are the software programs, systems and documentation.

An environment for continuous software process improvement is established when all the components and mechanisms shown in Figure 5.1 are installed and working. Such mechanisms should facilitate the establishment of a process culture and infrastructure to support software development projects within the organization.

The model shown in Figure 5.1 is applicable to all types of processes. The focus here is on applying it to the software process. Applying it in the context of the framework described in this chapter should help towards achieving the creation of an effective software process culture and a software process infrastructure. According to this model, an environment for software process improvement should support not only the process definition and documentation,

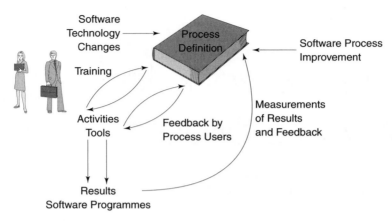

Figure 5.1 Effective software process environment

but also process monitoring, feedback and improvement roles and activities. This should lead to a continuously improving software process.

Table 5.1 applies the characteristics and measures proposed for effective processes to a software development environment. These are key indicators for symptoms and behaviour in a process-focused software development environment. An environment with these characteristics can be described as a mature software process environment. In such an environment the process discipline is the norm for software engineering and management activities.

5.1.2   A FRAMEWORK FOR SOFTWARE PROCESS

IMPROVEMENT

The framework proposed for software process improvement comprises four components:

- *Software process infrastructure:* There are two types of infrastructure necessary for supporting the process. The first is the organization and management infrastructure, and the second is the technical infrastructure. The first covers the roles and responsibilities, while the second covers the technical tools and facilities. All these need to be in place for supporting the process-related activities and for sustaining the process improvement actions.
- *Software process improvement roadmap:* This should specify a model for characterizing the software process and a logical step-by-step approach towards the realization of effective software processes. The improvement roadmap specifies stages and levels to be achieved by the software process and criteria for achieving those levels. It could be one of the standard public process roadmaps, for example the capability maturity model (CMM) or maturity levels of ISO/IEC 15504, or a tailored version to match the organization's own needs.

- *Software process assessment method:* This should specify methods and techniques for assessing the organization's current software process, practices and infrastructure. The assessment is usually performed against a process improvement roadmap. The result of the assessment should identify the strengths and weaknesses with recommendations for improving the process effectiveness. The improvement actions should lead to process maturity progressing along the improvement roadmap. The process assessment method could be one of the standard methods publicly available, for example the SEI assessment method or the BOOTSTRAP method, or a self-assessment along the guidelines specified in ISO/IEC 15504.

- *Software process improvement plan:* This involves transforming the assessment findings into specific actions for software process improvements. These are the actions that have to be undertaken to improve the process infrastructure and its effectiveness. Process improvement should lead to improved process discipline and process effectiveness.

Table 5.1 Symptoms and behaviour of an effective software process environment

Symptom/behaviour	Manifestation in software development environment
Visibility	Executive sponsorship of the software process is visible. The software process documentation and ownership are visible to everyone in the development projects
Discipline	All software developers follow the process as the norm; acting outside the process is the exception
Institutionalization	Following the software process is mandated by organizational policies and project procedures
Management support	The software process is visibly supported by both the organization management and the development project management
Enforcement	Software process enforcement is evident and is in force; conformance is checked and violations are reported
Ownership	The software process is owned, maintained and continuously improved by a dedicated software engineering process group (SEPG) or equivalent group
Feedback	Feedback on the software process is provided by developers, and feedback mechanisms are available to all project staff
Engineers' performance assessment	Measurement and evaluation of development staff and team performance are tightly linked to the process performance (i.e. achieving the process goals)
Training	Software process awareness and training is mandatory for all development staff, and process induction is mandatory for new recruits to the project
Improvement	Software process improvement is planned and implemented through the participation of all the staff involved

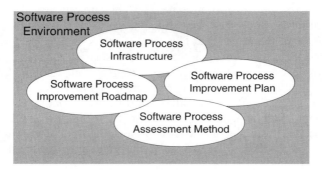

Figure 5.2 Framework for a software process improvement environment

Figure 5.2 illustrates the four-component framework for a software process improvement environment.

The four components of the framework are interrelated. They should all be covered by any strategy for software process improvement. The absence of any one of these components could lead to deficiency in the software process programme. The relationship between the components is cyclic. A full cycle for software process improvement starts with an assessment of the process infrastructure. The assessment is a catalyst for change. It is usually associated with a software process improvement roadmap. It results in an improvement plan to move the software process maturity up the levels of the improvement roadmap. A full process improvement cycle could take between 18 and 24 months depending on the size of the organization and the scope of improvement.

The rest of this chapter provides a brief definition of these components, and the remainder of the book provides a detailed description of each of them.

5.2 SOFTWARE PROCESS INFRASTRUCTURE

5.2.I WHAT IS INFRASTRUCTURE?

Infrastructure is an important concept. It is defined in the *Concise Oxford Dictionary* as 'the basic structural foundations of a society or enterprise; a substructure or foundation'. In the context of an organization, the term is defined as 'the underlying framework of an organization or system, including organizational structures, policies, standards, training facilities, and tools, that support its ongoing performance' (Paulk *et al.*, 1994). Applying these concepts and definitions to the software process environment, we could define the software process infrastructure as follows:

> The software process infrastructure is the underlying framework and structural foundations that support the software process. It covers both the organizational and management roles and responsibilities as well as the

technical tools and platforms necessary to support defining the process, performing the process activities, capturing and analysing feedback on process performance, and ongoing process improvement activities.

To establish an effective infrastructure, a software process environment must have in place two types of infrastructure, an organizational and management infrastructure, and a technical infrastructure.

5.2.2 ORGANIZATIONAL AND MANAGEMENT INFRASTRUCTURE

An organizational and management infrastructure covers the roles and responsibilities for establishing, monitoring and enforcing the process activities. Process-support roles and responsibilities are at two levels: global and local. Global support functions, such as the software engineering process group (SEPG), usually operate at a corporate level. The local support functions can be either at a project level or for a specific key process area. Process support roles and responsibilities are usually a mix of full-time functions (such as the SEPG) and part-time functions such as software process improvement teams (software PITs). These functions are referred to by different names; for example, PITs are sometimes referred to as task teams (TTs), competency circles (CCs), technical task groups (TTGs), and so on.

Figure 5.3 illustrates an organizational infrastructure for software process improvement. The roles and responsibilities shown cover two organizational levels: the corporate level and the project level. The organizational infrastructure should reflect and support the various organizational layers that may exist in the corporate hierarchy. For example in a multinational corporation, one would expect 'process-related' roles and responsibilities at both corporate and country (or division) levels as well as at project and team level.

The following roles are covered in the organizational and management infrastructure:

- *Sponsorship role:* A corporate executive sponsor for supporting the software process improvement activities. This role covers authorization of budgets and resources and monitoring the business benefits.
- *Management role:* A steering committee for providing management guidance and strategies for software process improvement activities. This role covers scoping, monitoring progress and resolving organizational issues.
- *Coordination role:* Corporate SEPG (software engineering process group) for providing coordination and technical guidance to the software process improvement teams. This group is the owner of the software process improvement plan.

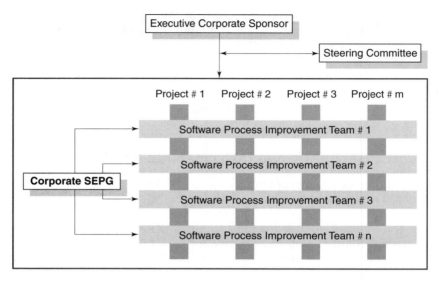

Figure 5.3   An organizational infrastructure for software process improvement

- *Improvement teams role:* The software process improvement teams (software PITs) for performing the software process improvement activities. This role covers managing and implementing a subset of the total software process improvement action plan.

The process organizational and management infrastructure will be discussed further in more detail in the following chapter.

5.2.3   TECHNICAL INFRASTRUCTURE

A software process technical infrastructure incorporates the technical platforms, computing facilities and tools that support the software engineering process group and process improvement teams.

The process technical infrastructure should cover corporate, project and team level process-related functions, as well as personal level process activities. Project level facilities should accommodate a level of flexibility that enables individual projects to choose their own technical process support environment to match their project's specific requirements. Having an effective and flexible technical process infrastructure is essential for improving and sustaining the effectiveness of the process.

Let us take an example of motorists. The support technical infrastructure covers the roads, traffic signs, road markings, speed cameras, etc. The process management primary goals cover ensuring safety on the roads and facilitating the journeys of the road users. If the roads are in a dismal state and the traffic

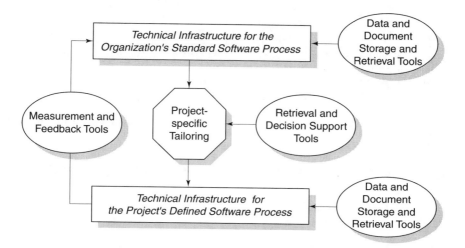

Figure 5.4 An architecture for software process technical infrastructure

lights are never in working order, would you expect the process goals to be achievable even if the cars were in good condition? A poor technical infrastructure will obstruct the process even if the process is well defined and well trained.

For a software process environment, the process-support component of the infrastructure covers the tools required to support process-related activities. Figure 5.4 illustrates an example of the architecture for the software process technical infrastructure.

The types of tools required to support the process-related activities include:

1   *Data and document storage and retrieval tools:* for the organization's standard process (corporate level). The main roles of such tools are:
   (a) to enable the software engineering process groups (SEPG) to store and modify the organization's standard process models, definitions and measurement data;
   (b) to enable project managers and software engineers to retrieve the organization's standard process models, definitions and data.

2   *Retrieval and decision support tools:* these tools assist project managers and team leaders in tailoring the organization's standard process to create the project's defined process. The main use of such tools are:
   (a) to assist project managers, team leaders and software engineers to access the organization's standard process definitions, models, data and tailoring guidelines;
   (b) to enable project managers, team leaders and software engineers to simulate various tailoring scenarios for tailoring the organization's standard process to match the specific requirements and characteristics of the project.

3   *Data and document storage and retrieval tools:*   these tools enable process users to access the project's defined process. The main use of such tools are:

(a) to assist project managers, team leaders and project process support personnel to store and modify the project's defined process models, definitions and data;

(b) to enable software engineers to retrieve the project's defined process models, definitions and data.

The software process infrastructure is covered in more detail in the next chapter.

5.3   SOFTWARE PROCESS IMPROVEMENT ROADMAP

5.3.1   NEED FOR A PROCESS IMPROVEMENT ROADMAP

To illustrate the need for a software process improvement roadmap (Figure 5.5), Watts Humphrey quotes a Chinese proverb: 'If you do not know where you are going, any road will do'. A process improvement roadmap will specify the stages for improving the process, and the characteristics and attributes that the process should satisfy in order to reach these stages.

Without adopting a process improvement roadmap, an organization could be facing some of the following risks:

• Lack of consistent basis for software process assessment and improvement
• Difficulty in ensuring that the improvement action plans focus on the most important areas; this could in turn jeopardize the business benefits of software process improvement
• Potential inconsistency of recommendations across different assessments and across successive improvement plans

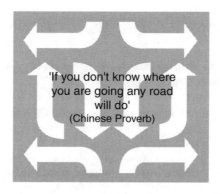

'If you don't know where you are going any road will do' (Chinese Proverb)

Figure 5.5   Why we need a software process improvement roadmap

- Inability to benchmark process effectiveness across organizations due to the variations and inconsistency of the approaches followed by different organizations.

5.3.2 REQUIREMENTS OF A PROCESS IMPROVEMENT ROADMAP

A process improvement roadmap would be expected to define successive 'levels' of process maturity. A process improvement effort will aim to move the process effectiveness up those maturity levels. The best known process improvement roadmap so far is the Software Engineering Institute's Capability Maturity Model (CMM). Figure 5.6 illustrates the process improvement levels of the CMM. Full discussion of the CMM and other roadmaps is provided in later chapters of this book.

A software process improvement roadmap is important for focusing the process improvement efforts. It should offer the following features:

- It should express a step-by-step improvement of the process effectiveness. Such steps are usually referred to as process maturity levels.
- It should identify and list process attributes at each level. For example, the Capability Maturity Model (CMM) characterizes the software process at the following levels: Level 1: ad-hoc process; Level 2: disciplined process; Level 3: standard and consistent process; Level 4: predictable process; Level 5: continuously improving process (see Figure 5.6).
- It should identify the symptoms, characteristics and attributes of software development environments at each level. These are guidelines on what is required, and the key areas that need to be addressed in order to satisfy each level.
- It should identify the challenges faced at each level. These challenges should present guidelines when drawing up an improvement plan.

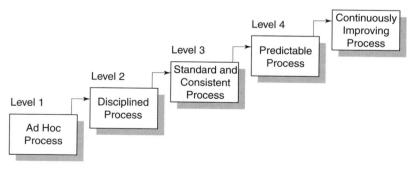

Figure 5.6   The CMM, an example of a software process improvement roadmap

The approach and granularity of improvement roadmaps vary from one approach to another. There are staged roadmaps (e.g. the CMM) which group process areas together in maturity levels, and there are flat, two-dimensional roadmaps (for example, ISO/IEC 15504) which define improvement levels for individual processes. Further details of some of the most popular software process improvement models and standards are provided in later chapters of the book.

5.4 SOFTWARE PROCESS ASSESSMENT

5.4.1 NEED FOR SOFTWARE PROCESS ASSESSMENT

Assessment helps an organization to find out the true state of the effectiveness of the software process infrastructure and environment. Watts Humphrey's famous quote stresses the need for assessment (Figure 5.7): 'If you do not know where you are, a map will not help' (Humphrey (1990)).

Process assessment provides a baseline of the current status of the prevailing software practices in the organization. This is used as the basis for improvement. The assessment usually acts as a catalyst for an improvement action plan.

An assessment method will normally be based on a process model and an improvement roadmap. The assessment takes place by comparing the state of the organization's software process against the model and the improvement scale. Without following a defined process assessment method, an organization could be facing the following risks:

'If you don't know where you are, a map won't help'

(Watts Humphrey)

Figure 5.7 The need for process assessment

- The assessment results could miss some important aspects of the software process. For example, some assessments focus on the process documentation at the expense of other important aspects. Important aspects that impact the process performance and should be covered by the assessment include the availability and effectiveness of the process training, the roles and responsibilities for process ownership, process enforcement and monitoring mechanisms.
- Different assessment teams could be adopting different approaches based on their own individual experiences, rather than following a common approach to the assessment. This could vary across individuals and across teams. This could lead to inconsistency of assessment results and discontinuity of the process improvement effort.

The generic model for software process environment described earlier in this book could effectively be used to ensure that the assessment method adopted covers all the essential components and mechanisms necessary for software process improvement. Examples of areas that should be covered by the assessment include the process documentation, process training, inspection of process results, feedback and improvement mechanisms, and associated roles and responsibilities.

5.4.2   REQUIREMENTS OF A SOFTWARE PROCESS

ASSESSMENT METHOD

A method for software process assessment should uncover the real state of the software process in the target organization. The assessment should establish the presence (or absence) and degree of utilization of all the mechanisms required to make the process effective. The following is a list of some of the general requirements of a software process assessment method:

- It should not restrict its focus to the process documentation.
- It should uncover whether software managers and practitioners have been trained in the process.
- It should establish whether the process is effective by uncovering the following:
  - whether there is management and organizational commitment
  - whether the process results are monitored and measured
  - whether feedback mechanisms are in place
  - whether the process is owned and whether the process is improving.
- It should not rely on questionnaires only. It should involve software practitioners and project managers in interviews and group discussions.
- It should be conducted by a trained team of software practitioners. The team should be trained in the assessment methods and techniques.

- It should follow a defined software process improvement roadmap. The roadmap will drive the analysis and evaluation stages of the assessment and provide the direction and basis for the process improvement plan.

5.5 SOFTWARE PROCESS IMPROVEMENT PLAN

5.5.1 NEED FOR A SOFTWARE PROCESS IMPROVEMENT PLAN

If no one is working towards improving the process, the process will not improve itself. Rather, the process most likely will deteriorate over time. Software process assessments are means to an end. The required end is a plan for improving the software process. Such a plan for process improvement should be based on the assessment results, and should be treated as a full project with a project manager, a budget, resources and milestones and deadlines. The software process improvement plan aims to overcome the weaknesses in the software process infrastructure uncovered by the process assessment. The resulting improvements should upgrade the state of the process infrastructure along the maturity scale of the improvement roadmap. Once an organization has completed an assessment and implemented the resulting improvement plan, it can be said to have undergone a full cycle of software process improvement. As Figure 5.8 illustrates, each process improvement cycle should be followed by another cycle to create a continuous improvement culture.

5.5.2 REQUIREMENTS OF A SOFTWARE PROCESS IMPROVEMENT PLAN

The implementation of a software process improvement action plan is essentially about introducing change. The changes could cover the existing organization, procedures, activities and culture. It costs money, time and effort. For an improvement plan to be effective it should satisfy the following conditions:

- It must be a proper plan with activities, schedule, allocated resources, milestones, project manager, budget, quality plan, configuration management plan, and schedule of activities.
- It must be sponsored by management. It must have a dedicated project manager and the commitment of software engineers and project managers.

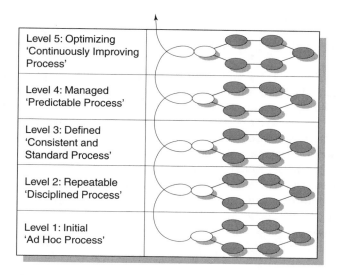

Level 5: Optimizing 'Continuously Improving Process'	
Level 4: Managed 'Predictable Process'	
Level 3: Defined 'Consistent and Standard Process'	
Level 2: Repeatable 'Disciplined Process'	
Level 1: Initial 'Ad Hoc Process'	

Figure 5.8 The software process improvement cycle moves the process effectiveness up the levels of maturity

- It must be based on the result of an assessment (which in turn must be based on an improvement roadmap).
- It must be planned, implemented and managed as a change programme, and it must take into consideration the pace of change that the organization can withstand.
- It must have well-defined scope and boundaries, with clear and explicit goals and milestones.
- It must involve everyone in the software organization. Everyone should participate somehow in the process improvement activities.

5.5.3 CRITICAL SUCCESS FACTORS FOR SOFTWARE PROCESS IMPROVEMENT

For software process improvement to succeed it must be properly managed and introduced at such a pace as not to be rejected by organizational inertia and resistance to change. The following is a selection of important factors that should be taken into consideration to ensure the success of software process improvement effort:

1 Set realistic expectations for senior management. An organization can only move forward at the pace that corresponds to its maturity and discipline.

2   Secure management support. Some middle management could feel threatened by introducing process changes, so try to educate management and highlight the potential benefits to them resulting from a disciplined process.

3   Get the buy-in from and involvement of project managers and software engineers. They are the ones who will implement the process changes and apply the new processes. Any change to the current processes must carry with it benefits to project managers and software engineers.

4   Treat process improvement as proper projects with budget, timescales, allocated resources, defined deliverables and milestones, committed resources and dedicated project management. Process improvement needs resources and dedicated skills.

5   Process improvement plans should follow a process improvement roadmap, so everyone will be aware of the target end state.

6   Continuous process improvement should be considered a journey and not a destination. Keep the momentum in order to ensure that process thinking and process focus prevails across the whole organization.

7   Measurement of staff performance and reward schemes should be linked to process performance. Reward schemes play an important role in driving staff behaviour.

8   Process performance should be evaluated in terms of the degree to which the process goals have been achieved. Every process must have associated with it a set of goals in support of the overall business and project goals. Key goals must be expressed in measurable terms, against which process performance could be evaluated.

9   Ensure continuous alignment between process goals, project goals and business goals. This should increase the visibility of the business benefits of process improvement and make it possible to relate process improvement to business improvement.

10 Involve everyone in the organization in process improvement activities. Continuous process improvement should be the objective of everyone in the organization. Sometimes the best ideas for improvement come from the most unexpected source.

SUMMARY

Need for a framework

- Your strategy for software process improvement should be based on an overall framework for a software process improvement environment.
- An overall framework should identify all important areas that need to be covered by the strategy for software process improvement.

- The four interrelated components of the framework suggested in this book are all necessary for the creation of a continuous improvement environment for the software process.

Components of the framework

- *Software process infrastructure:* organizational and managerial roles and responsibilities as well as technical facilities to support process activities. Without an effective support infrastructure, the process could be a stumbling block rather than an enabler.
- *Software process improvement roadmap:* defined steps for improvement of the process infrastructure. It defines what needs to be in place in order to move up the process improvement scale. Without such a roadmap, the improvement efforts could be diverted in the wrong direction.
- *Software process assessment method:* the assessment method should be used to assess and establish the current state of the process infrastructure. An assessment compares and evaluates the state infrastructure against the improvement roadmap. The result should lead to identifying strengths and weaknesses and point to areas that need to be addressed to move up the scale of the improvement roadmap.
- *Software process improvement plan:* this identifies the ownership of the improvement actions, and builds on the impact created by the process assessment.

Effective software process environment

An effective software process environment should reflect the following symptoms and behaviours: visibility of the process, process discipline, process institutionalization, management support of the process activities, enforcement procedures, process ownership, process feedback, process training, and continuous process improvement.

Critical success factors for software process improvement

There are some conditions and factors that, if observed and taken into consideration, should contribute to the success of the software process improvement plan. A critical factor is the need to treat the software process improvement plan in the same way as a full-scale software project is treated. It should have committed resources, project management, stage plans with milestones, a quality and configuration management plan, and so on.

CHAPTER 6

Software process infrastructure

6.1 JUSTIFICATION AND DEFINITION

6.1.1 WHY AN INFRASTRUCTURE IS NEEDED

Process institutionalization requires a process culture and a process infrastructure. The infrastructure is necessary to enable and facilitate the software process activities and to support the process-related roles and responsibilities. Generic definitions of the infrastructure and of the software process infrastructure were discussed in the previous chapter. This chapter describes the software process infrastructure components that need to be in place in order to support the process and sustain continuous process improvement.

A software process infrastructure covers two aspects:

- *Organizational and management infrastructure:* this includes roles and responsibilities that have to be in place to sponsor, manage, perform and monitor software process improvement activities.
- *Technology and tools infrastructure:* this incorporates the necessary facilities and tools for automating process activities and supporting the various process improvement roles and responsibilities.

Both of these aspects have to be covered in order to sustain an environment for software process improvement. The role of the infrastructure is to institutionalize the software process improvement behaviours into the organization's culture. This is necessary for these behaviours to survive in the organization after those who championed the original efforts have gone.

An expressive quotation from Phil Crosby (Crosby, 1980) emphasizes the need for quality to be 'engrained' in the organization: 'If quality isn't "engrained" in the organization, it will never happen'.

This is equally true for process improvement. We can convert this quote into an equally true statement for continuous software process improvement to read: 'If continuous software process improvement isn't engrained in the organization, it will never happen'.

'Engraining' or 'institutionalizing' the process improvement behaviour into the organization will not happen without an effective infrastructure to support the process. Investing in the software process infrastructure is a critical factor if an organization is serious about building a culture of continuous software process improvement. Management decision to invest in the infrastructure illustrates a commitment to software process improvement. I have seen many an organization and many senior managers who are ready to pay lip service to the process culture. But when it comes to authorizing investment for building a support infrastructure, the enthusiasm evaporates.

Building an effective support infrastructure to support and emphasize process improvement activities and behaviour is one of the main mechanisms that help in embedding and engraining process improvement behaviour in the organization.

An effective infrastructure should cover:

- roles and responsibilities for process ownership
- roles and responsibilities for process training and knowledge dissemination
- enforcement procedures to ensure adherence to the process standards
- feedback mechanisms for the collection and analysis of feedback data on the process performance
- tools and technologies to support and enable the above roles and procedures.

This chapter describes the main components of the software process infrastructure, covering organizational and management as well as the technical aspects.

6.1.2   WHAT IS SOFTWARE PROCESS INFRASTRUCTURE?

Infrastructure is an important concept. The word 'infrastructure' is defined in the *Little Oxford Dictionary of Current English* as the 'structural foundations of a society or an enterprise; roads, bridges, sewers etc., regarded as countries' economic foundations'. In the context of an organization, infrastructure can be defined as: 'the underlying framework of an organization or system, including organizational structures, policies, standards, training facilities, and tools, that support its ongoing performance' (Paulk *et al.*, 1994).

In general the role of the infrastructure is to provide support and guidance to the process activities and provide the channels and tools through which the process activities are to be performed and monitored. In the software process context, we can define the software process improvement infrastructure as follows: 'software process infrastructure is the underlying framework of organizational and technical foundations that support the ongoing software process improvement activities including process definition, process modelling, process training, process monitoring, process enforcement, and ongoing feedback on the process performance'.

6.1.3 A MODEL FOR THE SOFTWARE PROCESS

INFRASTRUCTURE

The software process infrastructure should provide the roles and responsibilities necessary for supporting an effective process environment. Figure 6.1 illustrates the roles and flow of activity that needs to be supported by the process infrastructure. The implementation of these roles and activities should cover all the relevant organizational levels (for example, corporate, project, team and personal processes). These roles and mechanisms should cover all the key areas for the software process. An effective infrastructure for the software process improvement environment should span across two domains, organizational and management roles and responsibilities, and technical environment. When designing a software process infrastructure we have to bear in mind these two domains:

- *The organizational domain:* organizational levels that the infrastructure needs to support (for example, corporate, project, team, and personal level)
- *The process domain:* key process categories that the infrastructure will support (for example, software engineering processes, management processes, support processes and so on).

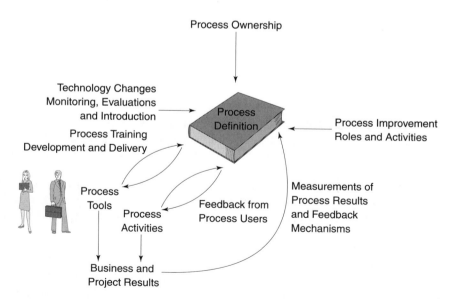

Figure 6.1   Roles and mechanisms for the software process infrastructure

Table 6.1 Mechanisms for an effective process support infrastructure

Process characteristics	Infrastructure mechanism
Defined	Process documentation
Owned	Process group
Trained	Process training
Supported	Process tools
Followed	Process enforcement
Monitored	Feedback activities
Continuously improving	Continuous process improvement roles and activities

Some of the mechanisms illustrated in Figure 6.1 are static and some are dynamic:

- static components holding the process definitions and measurement data
- dynamic feedback mechanisms and process activities.

An infrastructure that supports these activities and feedback mechanisms should provide the technical facilities that will adequately support the static element of the model, and the organizational roles and responsibilities that will drive the dynamic element of the model. For the infrastructure to support effective process performance, it should provide roles and mechanisms that will lead to the process displaying the characteristics summarized in Table 6.1.

6.1.4   ROLES AND MECHANISMS

The infrastructure should support roles and mechanisms to cover the following functions:

- *Process ownership:* This covers ownership, maintenance and dissemination of the software process definition. These are realised through roles and responsibilities for ownership of the process documentation, plus tools to enable storage and retrieval of the process documentation and data.
- *Process training:* This covers the development and provision of the software process training. For this to happen the infrastructure should define roles and tools to cover all aspects of process training, such as what, when, where, who and why. It should also cover the collection of feedback data on process training.
- *Performance monitoring*: This covers monitoring of the performance of software process activities. For this to happen the infrastructure should cover aspects such as what to monitor, where to direct the feedback, how to monitor the actions, to whom should the actions be reported and so on.

- *Process enforcement:* Enforcement of the software process standards and practices, for which the infrastructure should define and provide the measurement tools, enforcement roles and mechanisms, correction and escalation actions.
- *Process support:* Support of the ongoing process activities, for which the infrastructure should provide the latest tools and supporting technology through monitoring of the technological development and continuous alignment with business goals.
- *Technology introduction:* Intercepting, evaluating and introducing new software engineering technologies, selecting appropriate technologies and planning their introduction into the organization.

The software process infrastructure fulfils these functions through its two domains:

- *Management and organizational infrastructure:* to specify, establish and support the roles and responsibilities required for supporting the process.
- *Technology and tools infrastructure:* to specify, establish and support the automation of process activities, collection of process performance activities, retrieval of the process definitions and so on.

These two types of infrastructure components should extend their support to cover the different organizational levels that may exist in the organization (for example, corporate, project, team and personal level). A case study describing process support infrastructure roles and responsibilities as well as the supporting technology is described in Zahran (1996).

Figure 6.2 illustrates an example of the organizational levels that may exist in most organizations (corporate level, project level and personal level), the type of process at each level, and the main objective of the process at that level.

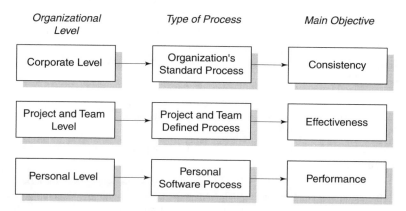

Figure 6.2 Organizational levels for the process infrastructure

6.1.5   ORGANIZATIONAL LEVELS FOR INFRASTRUCTURE

SUPPORT

Both organizational and management infrastructure and technical infrastructure should enable and enhance the roles and functions across three organizational levels. The nature and focus of the infrastructure support at each of these levels could vary along the following lines.

Corporate level

At the corporate level, the process infrastructure comprises the organization's process assets which incorporate the 'organization's standard process'. Some of the main objectives for the process resources at the corporate level are as follows:

- Providing support to and ensuring consistency of the process activities throughout the organization
- Providing direction and guidance to the process improvement activities throughout the whole organization
- Ensuring visibility of and support for the process focus at a corporate level and throughout the organization
- Encouraging the adoption of best practices across projects, and promoting the process discipline across the organization.

Project/team level

At the project/team level, process infrastructure comprises the process assets for the project or the team. There could be more than one team in the project sharing common tasks and objectives that need a specific process for that team. The common project process is referred to as the 'project's defined process', and a team's process could similarly be defined as the 'team's defined process'. Whether it is a team's process or a project's process, the main objectives of the process are:

- To ensure the effectiveness of the process in terms of its impact on the project or the team's progress
- To provide support and guidance to the project personnel and to team members
- To support project management in monitoring the project's progress by reporting the status of the project's activities, and providing feedback from the project's experience and process performance results to the organization-level process.

Personal level

At the personal level, the process infrastructure comprises the process assets available to support the individual software engineers in performing their software engineering activities. This is referred to as the 'personal software process (PSP)', a term coined by Watts Humphrey (Humphrey, 1995). The main objectives of the process resources at this level are the following:

- To support the automation of mundane tasks and activities
- To monitor the personal performance of individual software engineers by reporting on the status of their personal software engineering activities
- To provide guidance and help to software engineers in improving their personal software process.

6.2 ORGANIZATIONAL AND MANAGEMENT INFRASTRUCTURE

6.2.1 REQUIREMENTS

Alignment with business objectives

The main objective of an organizational and management infrastructure is to support the software engineering groups' effort to produce software in an efficient, systematic and continuously improving manner. Such infrastructure could have an impact on the following: process effectiveness, product quality, software engineer productivity, accuracy of cost/time estimations, effectiveness of project planning and project tracking, management visibility of project progress, consistency of processes across the different projects, developers' and top management acceptance, shifting the culture and behaviour from fire fighting to continuous improvement, and the establishment of a learning organization's culture across the software engineers and project managers. Ultimately all these factors should lead towards the achievement of the quality, cost and functionality goals of the software projects in a consistent and repeatable manner across the organization.

In order to achieve success in '(trans)planting' the process into the organization, a number of important factors should be taken into consideration when planning and implementing a software process improvement environment. The following factors will have an impact on the effectiveness of the process infrastructure:

- existing organizational culture (potential resistance to change)
- existing organizational structure and hierarchy (restrictive management practices)
- current roles and responsibilities (acceptability of new roles)

- potential sources of support (deviating resources from existing projects)
- potential sources of resistance (the gurus and the traditionalists).

This is why understanding the organizational context is critical for achieving alignment between the process infrastructure and the current organization.

Process support roles

The following recommendations should help achieve a process culture and alignment between the process infrastructure and the existing organizational structure:

- The software support roles should enable the process activities to run smoothly and effectively throughout the organization.
- New and redesigned software processes must be supported by appropriate new or redefined roles, responsibilities and procedures across the different levels within the organization.
- The software process support roles and responsibilities must be embedded into the organization's culture at all relevant organizational strata.

Degree of flexibility

Modern organizations are often complex and span across national borders. An organization may comprise a multitude of autonomous units with varying degrees of coordination. The following questions should be considered when designing the process infrastructure:

- What degree of flexibility (or rigidity, as the case may be) do we need to build into the infrastructure without losing consistency across the corporation? Flexibility may be necessary to accommodate the local characteristics and conditions of the different parts of the business.
- What degree of uniformity (or autonomy) do we want to build across the different organizational entities without losing consistency?

Relevance to the projects and benefits to the business

A disciplined software process should help software projects to achieve their goals of quality, cost and schedule. The process infrastructure should be designed with this primary goal in mind, that is to help projects achieve (and possibly exceed) their target goals. Helping the projects succeed is the bridge between the creation of an effective software process and benefits to the business. Process discipline is a way of enhancing the process effectiveness. An effective process is the way to ensure that the project achieves its quality, cost and schedule goals, thus leading to improved products and services.

Creating a process infrastructure should never be treated as a theoretical exercise or an experiment performed by a small team, isolated in an ivory tower. Rather it should be considered as a strategic initiative by all those involved in software development and in the quality of products and services that depend on software. The business benefits expected out of improved quality of the products and services should be easy to establish. An effective way to justify investment in software process improvement is to establish a link between an effective process environment and the improved quality of the resulting products and services.

There are other potential business benefits of an effective software process. They could be just as important as improved product quality. Examples of such benefits are:

- Reduction of project cost and duration. This is especially important in the area of big custom projects, where the margins are very tight and the risk factor is rather high.
- Increasing the competitiveness and effectiveness as a result of the increased predictability that an effective process could bring. This should have a positive impact on time to market, value for money, and customer satisfaction.
- Minimizing the risk through a reusable, repeatable process that has been proven to work in other projects. This provides proof of the organization's software capability, which should increase its competitiveness.
- Increased flexibility. This results in being better able to respond to the requirements of a diverse and demanding market and the variations of customer requirements.
- Availability of proof of credibility. This takes the form of the track record of process performance data and metrics collected from past projects, considered proof of the process repeatability.

All such benefits collectively should assist in raising the company's profile and increasing its competitiveness.

6.2.2 ORGANIZATIONAL AND MANAGEMENT ENABLERS

Enablers for process change

Software process improvement actions are likely to impact on the organizational structure, working policies and procedures, as well as skills, roles and responsibilities of human resources. Effectively everyone in the organization involved with software or software engineering activities is likely to be affected by the process organization and management infrastructure. Such involvement could take the form of one or more of the following roles:

- user of the process infrastructure
- performer of the process activities
- recipient of process training
- provider of feedback on process performance
- participant in process improvement activities.

In his book titled *Process Innovation*, Thomas Davenport (Davenport, 1993) lists a number of organizational and human resource enablers of process change. The following is a list of potential change enablers for software process improvement and their main focus:

- *Organizational enablers.* Focus: structure and culture. These include the organizational roles and responsibilities needed to support the process and process improvement. These include roles and responsibilities for management sponsorship, the corporate software engineering process group and software process improvement teams.
- *Cultural enablers.* Focus: empowerment and open participation in decision making. These include organizational policies and procedures. The objectives are to empower the corporate software engineering process group, empower the software process improvement teams, encourage and reward feedback on the process performance and encourage and reward creative suggestions of process improvement.
- *Human resource enablers.* Focus: process competency. These include process training, motivation and enforcement. The objective is to get software engineering staff:
  - trained in the process
  - motivated to follow the process
  - rewarded for over-achieving the process goals
  - incentivized for their contribution to process improvement activities.

These enablers should be mapped and assigned to the following roles necessary for supporting the software process infrastructure:

- sponsorship roles
- management roles
- coordination and enforcement roles
- process improvement roles.

In summary we stress the importance of considering software process improvement actions primarily as a change process. They aim at changing the habits and behaviour of software engineers and project managers. Table 6.2 summarizes the organizational and management enablers for software process improvement.

Special role of the SEPG

Although all the roles mentioned above are important for spreading and emphasizing the process discipline, two of these roles are of paramount importance. These are the executive sponsorship and the software engineering process group (SEPG). The importance of executive sponsorship is clear enough and is necessary for the success of any major change programme. The role of the SEPG is specific to software process changes. A number of authors have addressed the SEPG roles and responsibilities (Fowler and Rifkin, 1990; Dorsey and McDonald, 1996). According to Fowler and Rifkin (1990) the

Table 6.2 Organizational and management enablers for software process improvement

Type of enabler	SPI enablers and mechanisms
Organizational	• Executive sponsor for software process improvement • Corporate software process group (SEPG) • Software process improvement teams (software PITs) • Project-level software process coordinator
Cultural	• Empowerment of software process group (SEPG) • Empowerment of software process improvement teams
Human resources	• Career paths for software process group (SEPG) members • Compensation and rewards for participants in software process improvement activities • Compensation and rewards for projects and individuals who conform with the new process and prove its effectiveness and impact on the business results

SEPG is the focal point for process improvement: 'Composed of line practitioners who have varied skills, the group is at the centre of collaborative effort of everyone in the organization who is involved with software engineering improvement'.

More discussion of the SEPG is provided later in this chapter. Table 6.3 summarizes the SEPG's special role, objectives and tasks in a software process improvement programme. Practical lessons in and experiences of the formation and performance of SEPGs by organizations who pioneered software process improvement have been described by Dorsey and McDonald (1996) and Reed (1996).

6.2.3 MANAGEMENT ROLES AND RESPONSIBILITIES

The software process organization and management infrastructure could be defined as 'an organizational schema with defined roles and assigned responsibilities capable of handling the software process management and process improvement activities'.

To support the effective operation of such an organizational schema, the following need to be defined:

• Roles and their respective responsibilities sufficiently documented
• Deliverables of each role
• For every deliverable, templates and/or quality control checklists where applicable.

Some examples of the functions that need to be fulfilled by the process improvement roles and responsibilities are as follows.

Table 6.3 Objectives and tasks of the software engineering process group (SEPG)

Objective	SEPG task/activity
Leadership and keeping the SPI momentum	• Obtains and maintains the support of all levels of management • Provides overall direction for the SPI programme • Ensures involvement of all software engineers and project managers
Facilitating the change	• Works with line managers whose projects are affected by changes in software engineering practice, providing a broad perspective of the improvement effort and helping them set expectations • Maintains collaborative working relationships with software engineers, especially to obtain, plan for and install new practices and technologies
Process training and consultancy	• Arranges for any training or continuing education related to process improvements • Provides process consultation to development projects and management
Process assessment and improvement planning	• Facilitates software process assessments • Transforms the process assessment into process improvement plans • Drives and coordinates the process improvement plan
Monitoring process performance and collecting feedback	• Encourages, facilitates and collects feedback on process performance • Tracks, monitors and reports on the process performance • Analyses the process metrics, publishes results and feeds them into process improvement plans
Defining the process	• Facilitates the creation and maintenance of process definitions, in collaboration with the software process improvement teams (software PITs) • Maintains a process database • Encourages the managers and engineering staff to participate in the software PITs' activities
Coordinating software process improvement teams	• Coordinates the software PITs' activities • Secures management sponsorship for software PIT members' activities

- *Consolidated allocation of resources for software process improvement activities:* Unavailability of resources for process improvement activities is one of the most serious factors that could impede the progress of software process improvement activities. The most common excuse is that all software engineering resources are busy with project work. Such an attitude could jeopardize the success of software process improvement.

- *Cost/time estimation of the software process improvement activities:* This is especially relevant at the time of business justification, and preparing a return on investment case for software process improvement.
- *Managing software process improvement activities as proper projects:* Software process improvement activities should be managed in the same way as a development project. They should have the disciplines of project management, project planning, project monitoring, project metrics, and so on.
- *Quality control and coordination of interdepartmental activities:* Management should monitor the quality of process improvement activities. For actions shared across more than a single function, management should allocate ownership and responsibility of such interdepartmental activities, otherwise ownership could be lost among the different departments involved.
- *Feedback on software process improvement activities:* Possible roles for management could include receiving feedback information, analysing feedback data, and planning improvement actions for the software process improvement plan itself.
- *Planning of necessary training for the software process improvement teams and the SEPG*: Some software process improvement actions are different from software engineering activities (for example, the design of new processes). This may require special training for those involved in these activities. Management has to plan for and authorize such training.
- *Motivating the software process improvement teams:* This is necessary to ensure the continuous enthusiasm and commitment to software process improvement.

When designing the organizational schema for the software process infrastructure, you should define and allocate roles and assign responsibilities to the appropriate level of authority. These should be sufficiently documented, and the appropriate commitment gained from those concerned.

6.2.4 ORGANIZATIONAL MODEL

Figure 6.3 illustrates a model for the process organizational and management infrastructure with its components and feedback mechanisms. The model is based on the architecture suggested in Fowler and Rifkin (1990). The entities shown are:

- Executive sponsor
- Steering committee
- Corporate Software Engineering Process Group (SEPG)
- Process Improvement Teams (software PITs)
- Projects.

Now follows a description of the roles and responsibilities specific to process improvement.

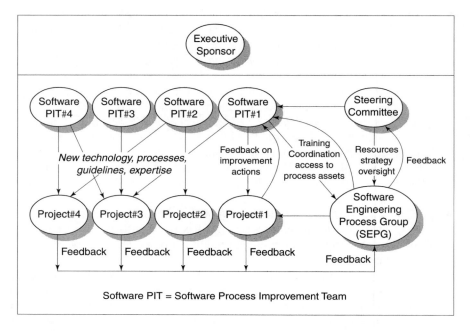

Figure 6.3 A model for software process organization and management infrastructure

Executive sponsor and leader

Role

There should be an overall sponsor of the software process improvement programme. Such a programme could be part of a bigger corporate initiative, for example, a total quality management (TQM) initiative or a business process re-engineering (BPR) initiative. Usually the sponsor is a senior executive at a corporate level (as opposed to departmental or project level). He or she is expected to adopt a vision for the long-term business objectives of the process improvement programme, and assume leadership towards achieving these objectives.

Responsibilities
- Authorization of funding for the software process improvement programme
- Ensuring the management commitment and continuous sponsorship of the process improvement effort in the organization
- Ensuring the coordination between the software process improvement programme and related corporate programmes, for example total quality management (TQM) or business process re-engineering (BPR)

- Authorization of any software process enforcement measures which may require changes/additions to corporate policies and procedures
- Acting as the driving force behind the overall programme for software process improvement and injecting enthusiasm about continuous software process improvement throughout the organization.

Steering committee

Role

The steering committee (also sometimes called Process Improvement Council, or Executive Improvement Team) is a policy-making body of a group of senior and line managers who develop the organization's overall strategy for software process improvement and monitor its progress. The SPI steering committee meets periodically to translate corporate policies into actions and align the SPI programme priorities and direction accordingly.

Responsibilities

- Setting strategic direction for SPI activities
- Reviewing the results of the software process assessments
- Approving the formation of the software process improvement teams (PITs)
- Approving the operating plans of, and setting priorities for, the various software PITs
- Monitoring and overseeing the progress of the software PITs
- Helping obtain sponsorship and resourcing for the software PITs
- Conducting ongoing policy oversight, resource and process management
- Negotiating with higher levels of management and corporate planning organizations
- Coordination and consensus building across different software PITs.

Software engineering process group (SEPG)

Role

The SEPG is a corporate level group tasked with the coordination and support of all software process improvement teams and activities across the whole organization. The SEPG should act as the central driving force for software process improvement, and the focal point for process improvement effort across the organization. Owing to its significant role in software process improvement, special attention should be given to the formation of the SEPG (Dorsey and McDonald, 1996) in terms of its organizational structure, membership and responsibilities. Table 6.4 summarizes some of the issues that need to be addressed when forming an SEPG.

Responsibilities

- Coordinating all process improvement activities across the organization, and obtaining and maintaining the support of all levels of management
- Nominating and recruiting members of the software process improvement teams (software PITs), and coordinating their activities. (The SEPG does

Table 6.4 Typical SEPG issues

Aspect	Issues
Organizational structure	• Inside or outside the software engineering organization? • At what organizational authority level? • Separate department or virtual group? • Reporting channel? • What to report? • Organizational relationships?
Membership	• How many people? • Full time or part time? • Period of membership? • Qualifications for membership? • Nominations procedures?
Responsibilities	• Specific roles, tasks and functions? • Example areas of responsibilities: assessments, recommendations, implementation of improvement actions, process consulting, communications, training, metrics, technology introduction, and so on?
SEPG internal process	• Mission statement? • Operational procedures? • Mechanisms and tools to assist/automate SEPG tasks?

not have to perform all the process improvement activities itself, but should provide support and coordination to the process improvement teams.)
• Acting as the 'keepers' of the process, with responsibility for maintaining the process assets, encouraging/soliciting feedback from process users, planning and driving the process improvement efforts, coordinating the process improvement activities and assuring synergy across the various software process improvement teams (software PITs)
• Assuming responsibility for developing/selecting/installing process-related methods, techniques and tools within the corporation
• Maintaining collaborative working relationships with software engineers and project managers. This is especially important to design, plan for and install new practices and technologies.

Software process improvement teams (software PITs)

Role
These are teams of software engineers that give part of their time to process improvement, focusing on a specific process area (for example requirements management, project planning, project tracking, and so on). Every key process area should be allocated a process improvement team (PIT). Each team takes

on responsibility for and ownership of the improvement efforts for that key process area. Membership of each PIT would vary according to the nature and boundaries of the key process area. For example, membership of a Requirements Management Process Improvement Team (RM-PIT) should include representatives of the customers, the project management, the subcontractors and user representatives of the whole system of which the software is a component.

Responsibilities

The general responsibility of a software PIT is implementing the software process improvement actions for the key process area allocated to the team. Specific activities could cover a wide variety of areas such as:

- Documentation, analysis and redesign of current processes
- Redesign of the processes under consideration
- Documenting the new processes
- Evaluating, selecting methods, techniques and tools in support of the new processes (for example, configuration management techniques and tools, design methods and tools, and so on)
- Developing and conducting process training
- Liaison with the SEPG to coordinate with related software PITs responsible for related key process areas, for example coordination between the Configuration Management PIT and the Software Quality Assurance PIT to design common change control and review procedures
- Designing procedures for monitoring the process performance, and specifying the feedback mechanisms that should be in place to collect feedback and the tools for analysis of the feedback data.

Process owners

Role

A process without ownership could easily decay and turn into 'shelfware'. Without explicit ownership everyone will be busy in his or her daily activities. Explicit ownership is essential if the process is to be kept alive and in alignment with business goals. The process ownership role could come under the banner of the SEPG, but we believe that the process ownership is quite different from the mainly coordinating role of the SEPG. Also ownership could vary depending on the nature of the key process area.

Responsibilities

- Acting as the ultimate authority for that process and leading the process improvement team for that process
- Taking responsibility for process design for that specific key process area and for coordinating the process improvement team for that process
- Assuming responsibility for ensuring that the total process is effective and efficient
- Providing vision, strategy and leadership to the process improvement team

- Ensuring that the process is followed, monitoring the feedback on the process performance, and driving any resulting improvement actions
- Anticipating business changes and their impact on the process.

6.2.5 SOFTWARE PROCESS IMPROVEMENT TEAMS (SOFTWARE PITS)

A software PIT should take on the responsibility for one or more of the key processes. One PIT could be assigned one key process area or a number of interrelated key process areas. A software PIT will usually consist of four to twelve professionals, and will be responsible for designing and continuously improving its allocated key process area. The acronym PIT was first used by James Harrington in the context of business process improvement. In his book *Business Process Improvement* (Harrington, 1991) he (amusingly) describes PIT as the most appropriate acronym for the process improvement teams, because in his own words:

> The pit is the centre of many of the delicious fruits we eat. It is the seed that brings about new life, new growth, and increased productivity. The PIT is also the centre of our improvement activity. . . . As with the pit in a peach or palm, proper nurturing of the PITs will bring about new growth for your organization and increased effectiveness, efficiency, and profits.

Following are some examples of software PITs (Figure 6.4):

- *Requirements Management PIT:*   To be responsible for designing, tracking and improving the Requirements Management Key Process Area.
- *Project Planning and Project Tracking PIT:* To be responsible for designing, tracking and improving the Project Planning and Project Tracking Key Process Area.
- *Software Subcontract Management PIT:*   To be responsible for designing, tracking and improving the Software Subcontract Management Key Process Area.
- *Software Quality Assurance PIT:* To be responsible for designing, tracking and improving the Software Quality Assurance Key Process Area.
- *Software Configuration Management PIT:*   To be responsible for designing, tracking and improving the Software Configuration Management Key Process Area.

Every PIT will have a team leader who could also take the role of the process owner for the key process area allocated to the team. Coordination of the different software PITs is the responsibility of the SEPG. The SEPG will be responsible for the overall corporate software process improvement programme. The programme should be divided into discrete process

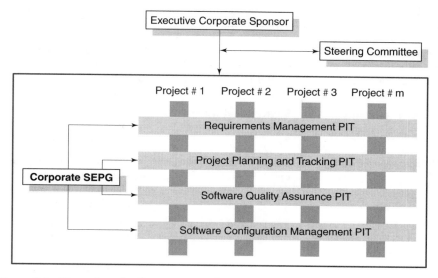

Figure 6.4 Examples of software process improvement teams (software PITs)

improvement projects, that are assigned to the software PITs and other groups if necessary. Membership of the SEPG should be on a permanent basis, as opposed to membership of the software PITs that could be on a 'rotating basis' and/or a part-time basis. This will give the opportunity for as many software engineers as possible to become involved in process improvement activities.

Ongoing role of the SEPG and the software PITs

Both the SEPG and the software PITs should not be just transient phenomena in the life of the organization. Although they may not have permanent membership, they should remain in place as organizational entities for as long as software development is critical for the business. Table 6.5 summarizes the ongoing responsibilities (Fowler and Rifkin (1990)).

6.2.6 LEADERSHIP ROLE AND EXECUTIVE SPONSORSHIP

Establishing a software process organization and management infrastructure will involve many parts of the organization that cross the organizational boundaries. Local management sponsorship may not be enough to push and enable SPI actions across organizational boundaries. Sponsorship in its traditional way of being limited to authorization of budgets may not be enough. Additional to this, software process improvement requires leadership and commitment. This is evident in a number of well-publicized early success

Table 6.5 Responsibilities of the process organizational and management infrastructure entities

Infrastructure entity	Level	Ongoing responsibilities
Executive sponsor	Strategic	• Policy • Funding
Steering committee	Strategic and tactical	• Strategy • Oversight • Feedback to sponsor
Process group (SEPG)	Strategic, tactical and operational	• Maintaining action plan • Disseminating reports • Coordinating process improvement activities
Software PITs	Tactical and operational	• Documenting, analysing, and redesign of current processes • Tracking and evaluating process performance • Acquiring new methods, technologies and tools to support the process
Projects	Tactical and operational	• Piloting new processes and technologies • Providing feedback on the process effectiveness

stories of software process improvement. Two of these came from Hughes Aircraft (Humphrey *et al.*, 1991) and Raytheon (Dion, 1993). Leadership is more than management. Leadership has the following ingredients (Bennis, 1989; Kennedy, 1996; Humphrey, 1996):

- *Guiding vision and establishing direction:* The leader has a clear idea of what he or she wants to do and the strength to persist in the face of setbacks, even failures.
- *Passion:* A leader of software process improvement should have a passion about the case of SPI, should love what he or she does and love doing it.
- *Integrity and self-discipline:* Integrity means self-knowledge and maturity. An SPI leader will be promoting messages on process maturity, discipline and continuous improvement. If he or she does not exhibit these attributes, the messages will be no more than 'vapour ware'. Soon the staff will realize that management commitment to process improvement is no more than 'lip service', and faith in it will soon disappear.
- *Taking risks:* The leader is willing to take risks, experiment and try new things. Software process improvement involves change, and every change

carries with it some risks. Leaders take risks. They do not worry about failures, but embrace errors, knowing that they will learn from them.

- *Motivating, inspiring and aligning people:* A leader of software process improvement should keep people moving in the right direction despite major political, bureaucratic and resource barriers to change.

As in the case of any change programme, leadership is essential for the success of software process improvement. In spite of being very important, leadership is not tangible. An organizational schema will not usually have a box labelled leadership. Leadership could materialize at more than one level: strategic, tactical or operational. The ideal scenario is that leadership is evident at the top of the organization. It will then disseminate to other levels in the organization. The majority of failures of change programmes could be attributed to absence of leadership and lack of management commitment. While management skills and resources are abundant, true leadership is rare and hard to get. It is worth spending a moment to compare the attributes and behaviour of managers versus those of leaders. Table 6.6 contrasts a selection of attributes and behavioural traits of managers with those of leaders.

Table 6.6 Managers versus leaders

The manager	The leader
Administers	Innovates (leading the way to a vision for software process improvement effort in the organization)
Focuses on systems and structure, and stresses the status quo (stresses current processes)	Focuses on people, has his eye on the horizon, and challenges the status quo (leading the way to changing the current status of the software processes towards a continuously improving process)
Relies on control (of software engineering activities)	Inspires trust (into the software process improvement teams)
Has a short term view (the current projects)	Has a long-range perspective (the future project and future business direction)
Asks how and when (to apply current processes)	Asks what and why (what needs improvement and why it will add value to the business)
Focuses on control and problem solving (fire fighting)	Energizes people to overcome problems (defect prevention)
Does the right thing (by stressing the current processes)	Does the right thing (by starting a software process improvement programme to move the organization from a fire fighting culture to a defect prevention culture)
Follows	Sets the direction

It is important to emphasize that we are not trying to devalue management at the expense of leadership. Leadership, management sponsorship and staff buy-in are the most critical factors that determine the success or failure of a software process improvement. The importance of management sponsorship is only paralleled by the importance of staff buy-in. These two aspects are strongly interdependent:

- Having management sponsorship in place should succeed in passing the management message on software process improvement to software engineers and project managers and ensuring their buy-in and commitment. Without such sponsorship, the software process improvement is likely to fail.
- In the same way, securing executive sponsorship is essential for getting the staff buy-in and gaining their commitment. As evidence has shown, it is very easy for a project manager to stop his staff participation in software process improvement activities at the first sight of a fire fighting battle.

In summary, the following three factors are all important and interlinked:

- Leadership provides vision and direction.
- Management provides control and focus.
- Staff commitment enables all these to happen.

The absence of any of these factors could put the software process improvement in jeopardy:

- In the absence of leadership, software process improvement activities are likely to be considered by project managers as an overhead, and by software engineers as a secondary non-core activity. If this is the case, the forces of resistance to change will prevail due to the inertia of the current organization, and the software process improvement programme will gradually fade in the background.
- In the absence of management commitment, software engineers are not likely to be released from their project work for participating in the activities of the software process improvement teams. The time and effort spent by software engineers in process improvement will not be valued as much as the time spent in the project activities. This attitude will ultimately dissuade the software practitioners from participation in the software PITs' activities.
- In the absence of staff buy-in, there will be resistance to implementing new process changes. The new processes could be ignored (under one excuse or another). Staff participation in the software process improvement teams is likely to dwindle.

6.2.7 NEED FOR ORGANIZATIONAL FIT

The exact definition of the roles suggested above will vary according to the specific situation within the organization. The introduction of these roles into the organization could occur gradually and in steps. The risks of introducing these roles prematurely are non-trivial. They could jeopardize the probability of success for software process improvement activities.

Software process improvement experience is growing rapidly. The number of practical lessons and case studies published in the literature is on the increase. One of the shared lessons is the need to carefully consider soft factors. These include factors such as resistance to change and cultural drivers (Myers, 1996; Dorsey and McDonald, 1996; Jones *et al.*, 1996). Taking these factors into consideration, and being sensitive to your organization's internal rhythm, you should be able to define an effective organizational and management infrastructure to support the software process improvement.

Matching the organizational context

A process organizational and management infrastructure covers the roles and responsibilities for establishing, promoting, monitoring and enforcing the process discipline. It should match and be aligned with the corporate culture and corporate organization. Any misalignment could lead to the creation of organizational stress. Misalignment with corporate cultural drivers could lead to resistance to software process improvement. Cultural drivers manifest themselves as patterns of behaviour that seem to be driven by pre-existing mental models that become 'engrained' within the organizational fabric. A recent paper (Jones *et al.*, 1996) summarizes experiences in introducing software process improvement in defence organizations, and highlights the potential conflict between new insights and deeply held internal images of how the world works. These shape the cultural drivers which can be, quite often, the enemies of 'change agents'.

On the other hand, alignment between process roles and responsibilities and the organizational structure could facilitate acceptance of the process by managers and software engineers into the organization. As an example, a multinational corporation would require corporate-level, country-level and project and team-level process roles and responsibilities, as well as personal-level process roles and responsibilities. For the software process to be effective, it needs to be introduced effectively and uniformly into the organization's texture in a consistent manner.

6.3   PROCESS TECHNICAL INFRASTRUCTURE

6.3.1   ARCHITECTURE

The technical infrastructure should provide support to the software process activities at all organizational levels (corporate level, project and team level, and personal level). It enables the establishment and management of the organization's process assets. A software process technical infrastructure includes the technical facilities, computing platforms and tools that support the software engineering process group and process improvement teams in performing their process-related activities. Generally the process technical infrastructure covers two areas (Figure 6.5):

- process support tools
- organization's software process assets.

It should provide support at the following organizational levels:

- *Corporate level:* The technical infrastructure should support process-related functions at the corporate level. Infrastructure users at corporate level include the executive sponsor, the steering committee and the SEPG.
- *Project and team level:* The technical infrastructure should support process-related functions at the project and team level. Infrastructure users at the project and team level include project managers, project controllers, team leaders and the software engineers working on the project.
- *Personal level:* The technical infrastructure should support the process-related activities at the personal level. Software engineers will use the infrastructure facilities at the personal level for improving and monitoring their personal software process (PSP).

Having an effective and flexible technical process infrastructure is essential for achieving process effectiveness. Ownership of the process definitions and use of the infrastructure elements should be specified at all these levels, along the lines discussed in the previous sections. Managing the infrastructure itself could be part of the management of the total IT infrastructure of the corporation. In this section we discuss the functionality required for such infrastructure in order to effectively support the software process activities.

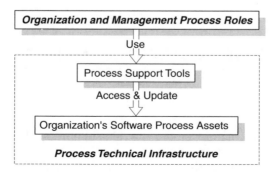

Figure 6.5 Areas covered by the software process technical infrastructure

Requirements of the process technical infrastructure

The software process roles and responsibilities should be supported by a set of tools to enable the effective performance of the process activities. Figure 6.6 highlights the types of tools required to support the process activities.

The technology infrastructure should provide tools and facilities to support the corporate level, the project level and the personal level as summarized in Table 6.7.

The process technical support infrastructure at the corporate level should be flexible enough to allow individual projects to build their own technical process support environment. A project-specific process should match the project's special features or specific requirements. Having an effective technical infrastructure for the process is essential for achieving the effectiveness of the process. The process technical infrastructure encompasses all the components of the organization's process assets.

6.3.2   THE ORGANIZATION'S STANDARD SOFTWARE

PROCESS ASSETS

The elements of the process definitions and documentation plus the supporting tools and platforms are collectively known as the organization's software process assets. These are defined as follows: 'Software process assets are a collection of entities maintained by an organization for use by projects in developing, tailoring, maintaining, and implementing their software processes' (Paulk *et al.*, 1994).

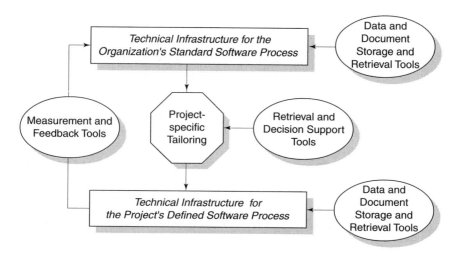

Figure 6.6   Process-support technical infrastructure

Table 6.7   Functions of process support tools

Type of tool	Functions
Data and document storage and retrieval tools	*Corporate level* • To assist the software engineering process group (SEPG) to store and modify the organization's standard process models, definitions and measurement data *Project level* • To enable project managers and the project's software process coordinators to retrieve the organization's standard process models, definitions and performance data • To enable project managers to submit feedback data on the performance of the project's defined software process • To enable project managers and the project's software process coordinators to store, modify and retrieve the project's defined software process models, definitions and performance data *Personal level* • To enable software engineers to retrieve the project's defined process • To enable software engineers to store, modify and retrieve personal software process models, definitions and performance data • To enable software engineers to submit feedback data on the performance of their personal software process
Retrieval and decision support tools	*Corporate level* • To assist the SEPG to retrieve, analyse and evaluate information on the project's defined software process *Project level* • To enable the project managers to access the organization's standard process definitions, models and data plus the tailoring guidelines • To assist the project managers in simulating various scenarios for tailoring the organization's standard process to match the specific requirements and characteristics of the project *Personal level* • To assist software engineers to retrieve, analyse and evaluate information on their personal software process performance
Process modelling and simulation tools	*Corporate level* • To enable the SEPG to model and simulate the organization's standard process; to store, retrieve and update these models *Project level* • To enable the project managers and the project process controller to model and simulate the project's defined process; to store, retrieve and update these models *Personal level* • To enable software engineers to model and simulate their personal software process (PSP); to store, retrieve and update these models

Figures 6.7 and 6.8 illustrate the main components of the organization's standard software process and software process assets. Such architecture is described as a conceptual framework for the software process capability (Paulk *et al.*, 1994).

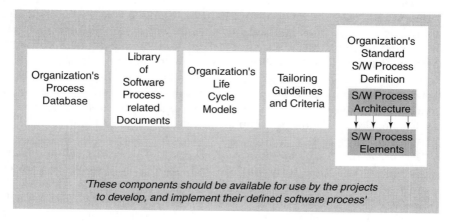

Figure 6.7 An architecture for the organization's standard software process

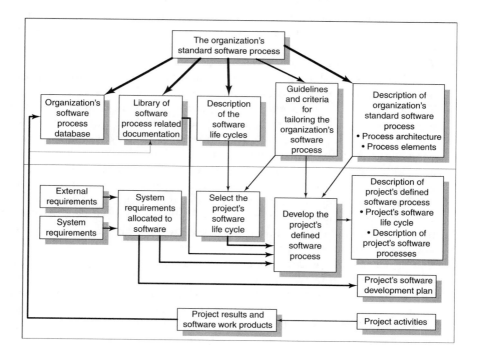

Figure 6.8 Software process assets at the organization and project levels

The actual instances of these assets should cover all the key process areas for software engineering, for example the Requirements Management Process, the Project Planning Process, the Project Tracking Process, the Software Quality Assurance Process and the Configuration Management Process.

The organization's software process assets may appear in different formats and use a variety of media (for example, electronic data and information stored in a database, physical documents or document images, or standard templates). Collectively these assets represent the corporate memory that contains the collective project experiences. It can be used as evidence to indicate the organization's software capability. The corporate software engineering process group assumes the overall responsibility for the organization's software process assets. The organization's software process assets comprise the following components (as illustrated in Figure 6.7):

- *The organization's standard software process:* This covers definitions and descriptions of the software process architecture and the software process elements. A process modelling tool may be used to generate and store the process descriptions in textual and/or diagrammatic form, and to make them available for retrieval, in a variety of formats, by the software engineers and managers.
- *Approved software lifecycles:* This covers descriptions of the lifecycles approved by the organization for use by the projects. This may take the form of lists and descriptions of these lifecycles, plus (a reference or pointer to) the detailed technical documentation and available training for these lifecycles.
- *Tailoring guidelines:* These specify guidelines and criteria for tailoring the organization's standard process. Such tailoring is necessary to make the organization's standard process usable and applicable to a specific project. The tailoring guidelines could be either general across the board, or specific to a key process area. For example, the general guidelines may cover how to select a lifecycle for the project out of the approved lifecycles, what project characteristics influence the choice of the lifecycle, what lifecycle is compatible with specific standards and so on. An example of the specific guidelines is the guidelines for tailoring the corporate definition of the configuration management process in order to generate a project-specific configuration management plan. Such guidelines may vary from one key process area to another, and they could be attached to the description of the key process area concerned.
- *The organization's process database*: As an essential component of the process infrastructure, the process database holds the process definitions and the process performance measurements. The organization's standard process database (also referred to as the corporate process database) holds all the process-related data. It holds the organization's standard process descriptions. Another example of its contents is the measurement data collected on the performance of the projects' processes, the final products, and the overall organization's process. The measurement data should cover

the product quality, project performance and process performance. The measurement data should be made available for analysis and used for a number of purposes including understanding, evaluation, control and prediction.

The SEI definition of the organization's process database is as follows:

> The process database is a central collection of files containing all critical information on the process and product aspects of software development and maintenance. It is maintained by the process group. Using simple definitions, the measurement portion of the database should contain a few indicative, useful measures of the products and processes. In addition to a quantitative database, the process group should maintain a file of process improvement lessons learned. (Fowler and Rifkin, 1990)

- *The library of software process-related documents*:   This is sometimes called the process assets library (PAL). This is a library where all process-related documents resulting from the completed software projects are stored. These documents represent the process experiences of the projects, and together with the measurements data stored in the organization's process database, they indicate the process capability of the organization.

   John Baumert describes some practical lessons gained while establishing and populating a corporate-wide process asset library (Baumert, 1996). The contents of a process asset library are summarized in Table 6.8. These assets should be 'owned' and maintained by the SEPG. They should be available for use by the projects to develop and implement their project-defined software process. They collectively represent the corporate process memory.

Attributes of the organization's standard software process assets

The organization's standard software process should be used extensively by all project managers as a source for process information and tailoring guidelines that will help them define their project's defined software process. It should save them time and effort since the standard process descriptions provided will help projects 'jump start' the definitions of their project-specific processes. For example, the effort required for tailoring a standard configuration management process is much less than the effort required for creating a new document from scratch. The organization's process database plays another important role. It should be the primary mechanism for ensuring consistency of the processes used by the various projects across the organization. Table 6.9 lists some of the essential attributes that should be considered when designing the organization's standard process database.

Table 6.8 Example contents of the organization's process asset library (PAL)

Library subject area	Example contents
Process definition assets	• Process definitions • Process models • Process methods and techniques • Process products • Process standards • Process roles • Process policies • Selection and tailoring criteria
Process implementation and support assets	• Product templates • Samples of process products • Training resources • Tool information
Evaluation support assets	• Industry reference model descriptions (e.g. CMM, ISO 9000) • Evaluation criteria and assessment methods • Cross-reference mappings between the organization's process and industry reference models
Historical project and service data	• Project/product characteristics and metrics • Project/product metrics • Lessons learned • Project and product quality profiles
Project and product quality improvement data	• Appraisal and audit (and assessment) results • Process improvement plans • Action plans • Status reports • Pilot assets
Process feedback data	• Problem reports • Enhancement requests • Feedback from process users

Use of the organization's standard software process database

The organization's standard process database is effectively the corporate memory for process experiences and learning. It is the main input to any process improvement plans or activities. When analysed, the information stored in the process database should enable its users to perform the following functions:

- *Show the trends in product quality.* These could be indicators of what improvements or otherwise have occurred to the quality of the software products. The statistical trends could be unveiled through tracking the changes in the number of defects and effort expended in rework.

Table 6.9 Attributes of the organization's standard process

Infrastructure component	Attributes
Process definition and documentation	Scope, format, media, coverage (process architecture and process elements), availability, dissemination mechanisms, friendliness, ownership, topicality, change control, feedback, relevance, flexibility, security
Lifecycles	Relevance, completeness, availability, flexibility, scalability, customizability, coverage
Customization guidelines	Coverage, flexibility, clarity, enforceability, authority, ownership, topicality
Library of process documents (feedback from projects)	Coverage, relevance, comparability, conformance to standards, scalability, ownership, security
Process and product measurements	Coverage, relevance, accuracy, dependability, conformance to standards, usability, dissemination, format, quality

- *Show the trends in project performance.* Trends can be revealed by analysing the variance between the original and actual estimates of time, cost and quality for the projects completed over a period of time.
- *Show the trends in process performance.* Examples of process performance indicators are the productivity per software engineer, productivity per project, deviations from the original estimates and effectiveness of specific processes. Every process should have a number of key performance indicators for measuring its performance. For example, the key performance indicator for the requirements management process could be the number of changes to the original requirements and the ratio of accepted versus rejected changes.
- *Point to the weak spots that need attention.* This points to candidate areas for improvement. They result from analysing the performance figures and trends for the key process areas. A record of the analysis of these trends can be used as proof of the organization's software capability. This in turn could lead to the organization's winning competitive bidding for contracts that require evidence of the organization's software capability.

Access control

There is a need to control access to the information on the corporate process database. Some of the questions that could be asked when defining a strategy for the corporate process database are:

- To whom do we want to disseminate the process model?
- To whom do we want to allow access to the process performance data, or product quality trends?
- How do we control access to the process performance data, and to the project's process documentation?
- What is the policy for restricting access to specific data in the process database? Who sets this policy? Who enforces this policy?

Use of measurement data

The measurement data stored in the organization's standard database can be used in a number of ways (Humphrey, 1989):

- *Understanding:* To learn about a particular item or process
- *Evaluation:* To determine if a process, product or activity meets acceptance criteria
- *Control:* To set limits and goals for process activities
- *Prediction:* To develop rate and trend parameters for project planning.

6.3.3   MAINTAINING THE ORGANIZATION'S STANDARD SOFTWARE PROCESS DATABASE

The process database should be owned and maintained by the process group. The definition of the contents of the process database should be a collective and collaborative effort among the following:

- *The corporate software engineering process group (SEPG):*   To define the process definitions (structure and levels of detail) that should be recorded into the process database.
- *Software process improvement teams (software PITs):*   To define the metrics to be collected on the process performance and product quality.
- *Steering committee:*   To determine policies on what the process database will contain and how it will be used, for example who the authorized users are and what access constraints should be imposed.
- *Project managers:*   To submit feedback on the performance of their project's defined process and on the resulting quality of the product, and to submit project documentation related to the software process that could be of value to future projects.

Role of the public process models and standards

Public process models and standards, such as the CMM, ISO 9000, ISO/IEC 15504 and MIL-STD-498, can be used as role models and guidelines when designing your organization's standard process. Usually such models and standards have associated with them a defined set of tailoring guidelines as depicted in Figure 6.9.

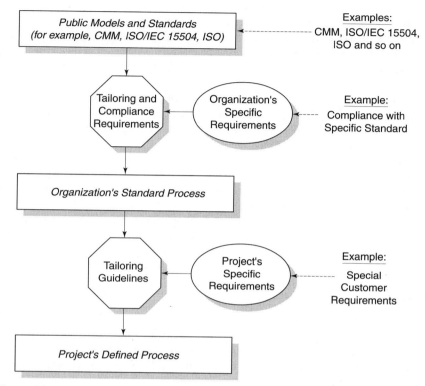

Figure 6.9 Using public process models and standards to develop the organization's standard process

In some cases, an organization may be required to illustrate compliance with a specific standard. Such a case will define which standard should be used as the basis for defining the organization's standard process. A similar tailoring process takes place when project managers specify the project's defined process based on the organization's standard process and its associated tailoring guidelines.

6.3.4 PROCESS SUPPORT TOOLS

Functions

The architecture described above represents a conceptual model for an organization's process assets. It needs physical implementation to make it happen. The physical implementation of the infrastructure is achieved through technology and tools that should provide the following:

- Facilities to enable the collection, storage and retrieval of data in the process database. For example, a database management system (DBMS) and its associated facilities. These could cover access control, physical distribution, integrity checks or more sophisticated process modelling tools that enable the storage and presentation of the process architecture and process elements.
- Facilities to enable the dissemination and presentation of the process database contents to authorized users. This could be assisted by an existing communication network plus the database management system and its associated software facilities.
- Facilities to enable the selection, retrieval and abstraction of particular classes of data stored in the process database. These could be used for management reporting, trend analysis, decision support systems and management support systems.
- Facilities to enable the storage, archiving and retrieval of the library of software process documentation. Examples of these facilities include electronic document management (EDM) and imaging systems.

Types

The tools provide support for the process groups and process users in fulfilling their roles and responsibilities. Figure 6.10 illustrates possible types of tools. It is likely that some of these tools could already be in existence as part of the overall IT infrastructure serving the organization. Types of process support tools include the following.

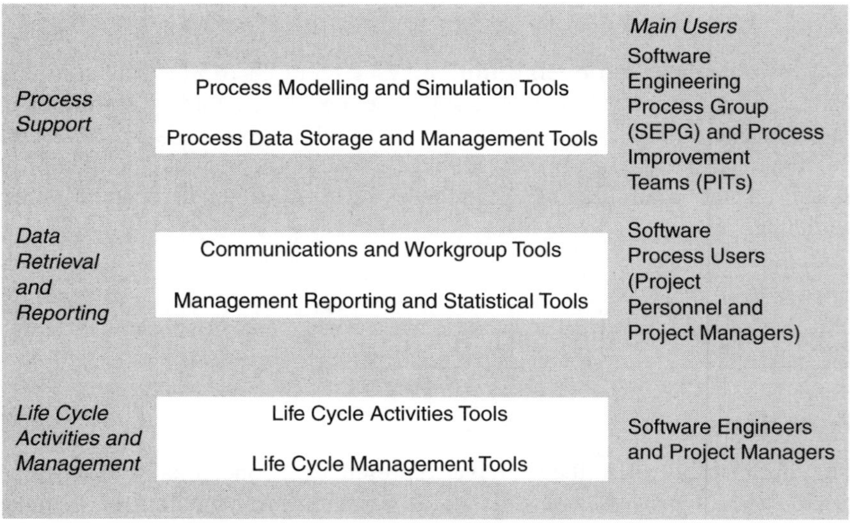

		Main Users
Process Support	Process Modelling and Simulation Tools Process Data Storage and Management Tools	Software Engineering Process Group (SEPG) and Process Improvement Teams (PITs)
Data Retrieval and Reporting	Communications and Workgroup Tools Management Reporting and Statistical Tools	Software Process Users (Project Personnel and Project Managers)
Life Cycle Activities and Management	Life Cycle Activities Tools Life Cycle Management Tools	Software Engineers and Project Managers

Figure 6.10   Process support tools

Tools for storing and managing process definitions and process data

- *Process modelling and simulation tools:* These enable the storage and retrieval of graphical presentation of the process architecture and process elements.
- *Process data storage and management tools:* These could be database management systems for storing and managing the process definitions and process data.

Tools for retrieval and distribution of the process definitions and process data

- *Communications and workgroup tools:* These manage access and dissemination of the process database contents.
- *Management reporting and statistical tools:* These present summaries and analyse trends of the information stored in the corporate process database, and assist in further analysis and decision making.

Tools to support the software activities and process management activities

- *Lifecycle activities tools:* These are tools that support lifecycle activities. They are usually dedicated to supporting one or more phases of the lifecycle. They should be integrated with other lifecycle tools to form what is sometimes referred to as integrated project support environment (IPSE). There are some integration tools that act as middleware that pass information from one tool to another. Examples of these tools are:
  - requirements management tools
  - systems analysis tools
  - systems design tools
  - code generation tools
  - testing tools
  - integration tools
- *Lifecycle management tools:* These are tools that support the management activities of the software development lifecycle. Examples of these tools are:
  - project planning and tracking tools
  - configuration management tools
  - contract financial management including project personnel time recording, tracking and optimizing resource utilization
  - skill selection to help project managers select the right resources that are viable and have the skills that match the project requirements.

6.3.5 PROCESS ENFORCEMENT MECHANISMS

Process enforcement mechanisms are necessary to prevent the process from being ignored and turning into ineffective 'shelfware'. Assume that you had a team of disciplined professionals in one project that followed the process. Without enforcement there is no guarantee of extending such a discipline across all projects or even across all generations of workers on the same project. An interesting view is to look at organizations as a set of permanent processes, while management and employees are transient phenomena that pass through these processes to serve and enable them, and then leave to be replaced by others.

Enforcement procedures and mechanisms will ensure the effectiveness of the process. Process enforcement is particularly important at the initial stages of introducing a new process or changes to a new process. A new process or changes in a current process mainly involve changing people's behaviour. This can prove difficult for some individuals, especially at the initial stages of introducing such change, hence the need for enforcement mechanisms in order to ensure that the new process is followed.

The type and extent of the enforcement mechanism vary according to the nature of the new process or the new changes in the process. In some cases, effective enforcement could take the form of organizational procedures and management practices to monitor compliance with the process. In some other cases, the enforcement could be applied through automated tools. For example, enforcing the traffic laws used to be mainly through traffic police, but in some places speed cameras are used to monitor compliance with the law.

It should be noted that automated tools on their own are not enough for enforcing the process. Rather they have to be part of management procedures that will define the activities for monitoring the feedback resulting from the enforcement tools. A process enforcement tool can also be used to capture and record violations of the process, and can collect statistics that will show the trends of conformance with the process. Process assessors/auditors can refer to such statistics as an evidence of the process discipline or lack of it.

6.4 AN EXAMPLE OF A SOFTWARE PROCESS SUPPORT INFRASTRUCTURE

Let us take the Configuration Management (CM) process as an example key process area. The scenario assumes the existence of a number of software process improvement teams (software PITs), one of which is a team which focuses on defining and improving the configuration management process across all projects within the organization. What are the components of the infrastructure that need to be in place to support such a CM PIT, and to support CM activities across and within the projects? The CM support infrastructure at corporate, project and personal levels should cover the following:

- *Organizational and management infrastructure:* the roles and responsibilities for sponsoring, managing, coordinating, defining and improving the CM processes followed across the organization and within the projects.
- *Technical infrastructure:* the CM tools, CM libraries, communication and documentation facilities used by the CM team, plus any other technical facilities that support the CM process team activities.

6.4.1 ORGANIZATIONAL AND MANAGEMENT INFRASTRUCTURE FOR THE CM PROCESS

For each of the organizational levels (corporate, project and personal), CM process-related procedures for the following roles should be defined and responsibilities allocated. Some of these roles are relevant only to the corporate and project levels.

- *Sponsorship role:* A senior executive should ensure continued sponsorship of the CM process team.
- *Management role:* A CM process team leader should be appointed to manage the activities of the CM process team.
- *Coordination role:* The CM process team should allocate responsibility for coordination with the SEPG and other process improvement teams.
- *Process improvement role:* The CM process team should devise, plan and implement process improvement actions to improve the effectiveness of the CM process as used by the projects and individual software engineers.

Table 6.10 summarizes the possible roles and responsibilities at the different levels.

The functions for the roles at the different levels could be defined as follows.

Corporate level

At corporate level the following functions need to be fulfilled by the corporate software engineering process group (SEPG):

Table 6.10 Roles for supporting configuration management process

Process-support role	Corporate level	Project level	Personal level
Sponsorship	Corporate SPI executive sponsor	Project sponsor	Project manager
Management	Corporate SPI steering committee	Project manager	Project CM coordinator
Coordination	Corporate software engineering process group (SEPG)	Project SPI coordinator	Project CM team
Process improvement	Corporate CM process improvement team	Project CM team	Project software engineers

- *Defining:* corporate guidelines and procedures for CM
- *Allocating:* the responsibility for these guidelines to a corporate resource or function to own these guidelines (usually this will be part of the corporate software engineering process group, SEPG)
- *Organizing:* CM training and awareness events across the organization
- *Drawing up:* corporate guidelines and recommendations for CM tool selection and acquisition
- *Encouraging and collecting:* feedback and metrics on the usability and effectiveness of the corporate CM guidelines
- *Analysing:* the feedback and monitoring the effectiveness of the corporate CM guidelines
- *Planning and implementing:* CM process improvement actions, based on the feedback from the users of the corporate CM guidelines results of process assessments and advances in the changes in CM standards and advances in technology.

Project level

At the project level the following functions need to be fulfilled by the project manager or the process-support roles for the project:

- *Defining and documenting:* the project CM plan
- *Allocating:* the responsibility for CM activities to a CM project resource or function
- *Organizing:* CM training and awareness events for members of the project
- *Selecting and acquiring:* a CM tool for the project (according to the corporate guidelines and recommendations for CM tool selection and acquisition)
- *Documenting and analysing:* feedback data from project members on the effectiveness of the project's CM process
- *Planning and implementing:* CM process improvement actions, based on the feedback from the users of the corporate CM guidelines, results of process assessments and changes in CM standards and advances in technology
- *Providing:* feedback and metrics on the usability and effectiveness of the project's defined CM process and the corporate CM guidelines to the corporate software engineering process group (SEPG).

Personal level

At the personal level the following functions need to be fulfilled:

- *Defining:* a personal CM plan
- *Receiving training:* on the CM tool selected for the project
- *Following:* and adhering to the project's CM process and change procedures
- *Collecting:* metrics and feedback information on the effectiveness of both the CM tool and procedures, and submitting feedback to the project manager, the CMPIT and the corporate process group

- *Analysing:* personal feedback data and taking actions for improvements as necessary.

Table 6.11 summarizes the components of the process infrastructure to support a configuration management process at the different organizational levels.

6.5 MAKING THE INFRASTRUCTURE EFFECTIVE

6.5.1 COVERAGE OF ALL ORGANIZATIONAL LEVELS

In order to ensure the effectiveness of the software process infrastructure at all organizational levels, it is useful to start with a list of the required functions and attributes for each level. These attributes should reflect the organization's overall business requirements and should be taken into consideration when specifying the infrastructure components at each level. To ensure that all such attributes have been covered, the list of attributes could be presented in a matrix listing similar to the one shown in Table 6.12.

6.5.2 PROCESS INFRASTRUCTURE AND THE LEARNING ORGANIZATION

The architecture described so far in support of the software process also facilitates the creation of a 'learning organization' culture amongst software engineers. This is possible because the process infrastructure supports the following learning mechanisms at both the corporate level and the project level:

- *Repository of experiences:* The organization process components represent a repository of the feedback from the different projects on their process experiences. This is in effect a repository of knowledge that should be shared across the projects, hence the process learning of one project is made available for future projects.
- *Corporate memory:* The organization's process database together with the library of process-related documents represent the corporate memory which stores the lessons and experiences and makes them available for future projects. The more experiences stored in the corporate memory, the more mature the organization should become.
- *Learning mechanism:* The main learning mechanism is feedback from project experience and the extent to which project managers and project personnel make use of this feedback to learn the relevant lessons and increase the chances of success for their projects.

Table 6.11   Software process infrastructure components to support a configuration management process

Component	Corporate level	Project level	Personal level
Process definition	Corporate guidelines and procedures on CM	Project configuration management (CM) plan	Personal CM guidelines
Process ownership	CM process team (part of the software engineering process group, SEPG)	Project manager or a project CM responsible (for example a dedicated CM team for the project)	Individual software engineer
Process training	Training/awareness of project managers and others in the corporate CM process and in tailoring guidelines	Training of project personnel in the project's configuration management plan, standards, procedures and tools	Training of individual software engineers in configuration management procedures and tools
Process tools	Guidelines to project managers on the selection and acquisition of configuration management tools	Selection and acquisition of a configuration management tool for the project	Competency in usage of the available configuration management tool
Feedback from process users	CM team (part of the SEPG) seeks feedback from project managers and project personnel on the usability of the corporate guidelines on configuration management	Project manager seeks feedback from project personnel on the effectiveness of the project's configuration management plans, procedures and tools, and feeds the feedback to the corporate SEPG	Software engineers collect metrics and provide feedback on the effectiveness and usability of the project's configuration management plan, procedures and tools, and feed measurements to the project manager or directly to the SEPG
Measurements of the process results	Corporate CM team (part of the corporate SEPG) collects measurements on the effectiveness of the organization's standards and guidelines on configuration management and records them in the organization's process database	Project managers collect measurements on the effectiveness of the project's configuration management plan, procedures and tools and feed them back to corporate CM process team (part of the SEPG)	Individual software engineers collect metrics on the effectiveness and performance of the personal CM process and feed measurements back to the project manager or directly to the corporate CM team (part of the SEPG)

(continued)

Table 6.11 (*continued*)

Process improvement roles and responsibilities	Corporate CM team (part of the SEPG) analyses the feedback from project managers and software engineers, studies advances in CM tools and standards, and tunes the corporate CM guidelines to achieve improvement	Project manager (or project's CM responsible) analyses the feedback from project personnel to modify the project's CM plan and procedures to improve their effectiveness, and/or to upgrade the project's CM tool to improve its usability, or refresh CM training for the project personnel	Software engineers analyse the feedback on the usability of the CM tools and procedures, and provide suggestions for improvement or refreshment of their own CM training

Table 6.12 Example of a matrix listing of the functions/attributes of the process infrastructure at the various organizational levels

Infrastructure function/attribute	Corporate level	Project level	Personal level
Scope of the process to be defined			
Boundaries and coverage			
Accessibility and usability			
Process support functions			
Consistency with other levels			
Feedback and metrics collection mechanisms			
Automation of process activities			
Automation of process management activities			
Supporting tools and technology			

6.5.3 MEASURING THE EFFECTIVENESS OF THE PROCESS INFRASTRUCTURE

As discussed in Part 1, the effectiveness of the process is ultimately measured through monitoring its impact on the business results. The effectiveness of the process infrastructure is measured through monitoring its impact on the process effectiveness. The following questions and answers provide example indicators of how effective the process infrastructure is:

- *Question:* Does the process infrastructure enable or obstruct the process activities (software engineering and project management activities)?
- *Answer:* An example: sometimes the use of a tool can be so complicated that manually performing the task is more effective. The tool turns from an enabler to a 'disabler' of the process activities. (Some of the staff time recording tools used in IT projects wasted much valuable time and effort of software engineers. They hated filling out time sheets and did not believe in the value of the data they entered. They never received any feedback on how these data were used.)
- *Question:* Is the method of retrieving and presenting process-related data to users and managers user-friendly and reliable or is it complicated and unreliable?
- *Answer:* An example: some data retrieval tools are inflexible and out of date, are rigid and not responsive to user needs, are text based and do not support graphical interfaces. In other cases tools operate only in batch mode rather than on-line. (A configuration management tool is of little use if it does not support on-line queries on the status of configuration items.)

6.5.4 ATTRIBUTES OF AN EFFECTIVE PROCESS INFRASTRUCTURE

Attributes of an effective organizational and management infrastructure

An effective process organizational and management infrastructure should be completely aligned with the requirements of the process it supports and its users. It should provide the following:

- Support for the roles and activities at the appropriate level of the organization (for example corporate, multinational, national, divisional, project, personal)
- Adaptability to changes in the business structure (for example to cope with mergers between functional groups, departments or companies)
- Support for all the process roles and responsibilities shown in the model for an effective software process environment (for example process owners, project managers, executive sponsors, process users, software engineers, process groups)
- Explicit assignment of the high level sponsorship and leadership role of the process efforts in the organization
- Flexibility to allow for sharing of roles and responsibilities across functions (for example, project personnel should be made available to participate in the process improvement activities).

Attributes of an effective process technical infrastructure

An effective process technical infrastructure should satisfy the requirements of the process it supports and its users. It should provide the following:

- Support for the storage and retrieval of the organization's process definitions and data
- Support for process flexibility (for example process changes to accommodate new methods, new techniques or new technologies)
- Support for the communication and feedback mechanisms shown in the model proposed for an effective software process environment (for example feedback from, and communicating process data to, process users, project managers, executive sponsors and so on)
- Coverage across the organization's physical distribution (for example multi-location, transnational, global and so on)
- Flexibility and ability to adapt to any major changes in the organization's business strategy or geographical distribution.

SUMMARY

The need for infrastructure to support the process

The process cannot be sustained or improved without an effective support infrastructure – imagine trying to enforce the traffic laws without having working traffic lights, good roads and up-to-date road signs.

A process without supporting infrastructure is 'vapour ware'

In the absence of a supporting infrastructure the following symptoms will be noticeable: roles not defined, ownership vague, tools non-existent, no follow-up procedures, no feedback mechanisms, and so on. Would you call this an effective process?

The process infrastructure should cover organizational and technical aspects

The process support infrastructure should cover organizational roles and responsibilities, as well as the tools and technical resources dedicated to supporting the process users, process owners and process 'guardians'.

The infrastructure should extend its support to all the organizational levels

The process support infrastructure should support the various organizational levels. It should support the corporate software engineering process group (SEPG), the project managers, and the project-level process-support resources as well as the software engineers.

The infrastructure should allow flexibility

The process support infrastructure should be flexible to:

- cover different sizes of projects
- cover different project and product requirements
- adapt to varying customer needs
- adapt to varying standards requirements.

Need for organizational and management infrastructure

- Process discipline cannot be sustained without assigned and dedicated roles and responsibilities.
- Without a process support infrastructure, software process improvement could be no more than just lip service by management.
- Without committed resources, everyone will be busy doing their day-to-day activities with no one looking after the process.

Need for executive sponsorship

- Without executive sponsorship and organizational commitment, process improvement cannot survive organizational changes.
- Without continuing executive sponsorship, software process improvement resources are likely to be reassigned to project work at the first sign of resource shortage for the projects.
- Starting software process improvement without management sponsorship is often a false start. It will very likely be shelved at the next business reorganization or downsizing. False starts can damage the morale of the software engineering staff.

Need for a dedicated software engineering process group (SEPG)

- The SEPG should be staffed by full-time professionals who should mainly take the role of coordinators rather than engineers – they should not try to be jacks of all trades. They should coordinate the activities of the software PITs.

- Generally the SEPG should operate at the corporate level as opposed to the divisional level. This will depend on the number of levels in the organization's hierarchy.

Need for software process improvement teams (software PITs)

- Software engineering practitioners, working within development projects, should form the bulk of the software process improvement teams (software PITs). There are several benefits that can be gained as a result, such as getting their buy-in into software process improvement and getting their specialized knowledge and experience through participation in process design and specification activities.
- The selection of members of the various software PITs depends on the nature of the process assigned to the team concerned. For example, a requirements management PIT should have representation from the customer, the project manager, the legal and contracts department and so on.

Software process change enablers

- There are a number of enablers for software process change in an organization. The main types of enablers are organizational, cultural and human resources enablers.
- There are risks to the software process improvement if the process change enablers are not in place.
- The availability and effectiveness of these enablers will ensure that software process improvement behaviour and practice are 'engrained' into the texture of the organization. Continuous process improvement will be part of the normal way of doing business.

Requirements of a technical infrastructure to support the software process

- Without an adequate technical infrastructure, a process is not likely to achieve the necessary levels of effectiveness and efficiency.
- The process technical infrastructure should support the activities of the SEPG, the project managers, the software engineers, and the process improvement teams.
- The process technical infrastructure should match the requirements of all the organizational levels associated with the process, the corporate level, the project level and the personal level.
- The technical infrastructure is necessary for facilitating the task of the SEPG and enabling other process-related activities.

Need for tools to support the organization's software process assets

- The organization's software process assets are the primary mechanism that will assure consistency of the processes used by the projects across the organization.
- The organization's standard process database represents the corporate process memory. It can be used to process lessons and experiences of the software projects across the organization, that will be used for improving the process.
- Tools are not substitutes for the organization and management infrastructure, which defines how the tools will be used, by whom and for what purpose.

Process support tools

Possible functions of process support tools include:

- process modelling and simulation
- storing process documentation
- dissemination of the process definition
- measuring and reporting the process results
- monitoring and enforcing the process.

These are in addition to tools to support software engineering activities, such as configuration management tools, software quality assurance tools and computer-aided software engineering (CASE) tools.

CHAPTER 7

Process improvement roadmaps

7.1 LEARNING FROM THE QUALITY GURUS

7.1.1 MODELS FOR QUALITY IMPROVEMENT

Software process improvement should be a lifetime habit of software organizations. Watts Humphrey reflects this in his frequently mentioned quotation that 'software process improvement is not a destination, it is a journey'. Once an organization goes through a complete cycle of software process improvement, it should begin the next one and repeat this continuously.

In order to make continuous software process improvement a reality in an organization, the process culture needs to be institutionalized in that organization. To achieve the status of continuous software process improvement, process awareness, attitudes and behaviours need to be ingrained in the organization culture. In his popular book *Quality is Free*, Phil Crosby realized this: 'If quality isn't ingrained in the organization, it will never happen' (Crosby, 1980).

Software process maturity has its roots in the quality movement. The software process movement has adopted many of the concepts developed by the quality gurus and adapted them for the software development process. To trace these roots the following sections summarize some of the most well-known approaches to continuous quality improvement. Let us try to learn from the quality gurus how the concept of continuous process improvement progressed over the years.

- Identify Opportunities for Improvement
- Develop Plan for Improvement
- Take Corrective Action on Common Causes
- Pursue Continuous Improvement

Figure 7.1   Shewhart's quality cycle 'Plan–Do–Check–Act'

7.1.2   SHEWHART'S IMPROVEMENT CYCLE

Back in the late 1930s Walter Shewhart proposed a 'Plan–Do–Check–Act' cycle for quality improvement (Shewhart, 1931). Shewhart's early work on statistical quality control is still an inspiration to most of the work on quality. Shewhart's cycle (see Figure 7.1) has influenced most of the current approaches to quality and process improvement.

7.1.3   JURAN'S FOUR STEPS

Joseph Juran suggests a systematic approach to controlling and improving quality (Juran, 1981). He emphasizes the management of quality at all phases in the product lifecycle. His tripartite approach of quality planning, quality control and quality improvement is reflected in his recommended four steps (see Figure 7.2).

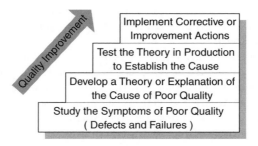

Figure 7.2   Juran's steps to controlling and improving quality

Juran's approach has been successfully adopted and proven by major organizations worldwide, especially in Japan and the USA.

7.1.4   DEMING'S WAY 'OUT OF THE CRISIS'

Edwards Deming's focus is on the need for management's long-term commitment to new learning and new philosophy in order to achieve transformation. He predicts that in the absence of such commitment, 'the timid and the fainthearted, and the people that expect quick results, are doomed to disappointment' (Deming, 1982).

Deming's methodology has transformed Japanese industry and is still applied in many of the largest corporations today. Deming's work was an inspiration for Watts Humphrey's work on software process maturity (Humphrey, 1987). Humphrey applied Deming's concepts on quality to software. While recognizing important differences between one industry and another, Humphrey argues that the concepts of statistical process control are just as applicable to software as they are to industry: 'A software-development process that is under statistical control will produce the desired results within the anticipated limits of cost, schedule, and quality' (Humphrey, 1988).

Edwards Deming suggested the following fourteen-point plan for achieving the transformation towards continuous improvement (Deming, 1982):

1   Create constancy of purpose for improvement of product and service.
2   Adopt the new philosophy.
3   Cease dependence on inspection to achieve quality.
4   End the practice of awarding business on the basis of price tag.
5   Improve constantly and forever every process for planning, production and service.
6   Institute training on the job.
7   Adopt and institute leadership.
8   Drive out fear.
9   Break down barriers between staff areas.
10   Eliminate slogans, exhortations and targets for the workforce.
11   Eliminate numerical quotas for the workforce and numerical goals for management.
12   Remove barriers that rob people of pride of workmanship. Eliminate the annual rating of the merit system.
13   Institute a vigorous programme of education and self-improvement for everyone.
14   Put everybody in the company to work to accomplish the transformation.

7.1.5   CROSBY'S QUALITY MATURITY GRID

Phil Crosby stresses the importance of involvement and motivation for everyone in the organization. In *Quality is Free*, Crosby (1980) describes the fire fighting attitudes in some organizations and argues that 'Fire fighting would have to be replaced with defect prevention. Quality would have to be recognized as a genuine first among equals'. Crosby highlighted the factors that represent the cost of quality and of non-conformance and suggested a Quality Management Maturity Grid that specifies five stages of maturity and their measurement categories (Figure 7.3). The five stages are Uncertainty, Awakening, Enlightenment, Wisdom and Certainty. These five stages present a stepped approach which describes the 'long, long way from Uncertainty to Certainty. But travelling that road is what the fun of management is all about.' Crosby's model has its parallels with the five maturity levels of the Capability Maturity Model (CMM) for software.

The behaviour of management and staff in an organization is the main indicator of the stage of the organization. Table 7.1 summarizes some examples of such behaviour for the various stages of maturity.

Measurement Category	Stage I: Uncertainty	Stage II: Awakening	Stage III: Enlightenment	Stage IV: Wisdom	Stage V: Certainty
Management Understanding and Attitudes					
Quality Organization Status					
Problem Handling					
Cost of Quality as % of Sales					
Quality Improvement Actions					
Summation of Company Quality Posture					

Figure 7.3   Crosby's quality management maturity grid

Table 7.1 Symptoms and behaviours at the various maturity stages

Stage	Stage name	Symptoms and behaviours
Stage 1	Uncertainty	• Management is confused and uncommitted. • Management has no knowledge of quality as a positive management tool. • Problems with quality are considered to be the fault of not being tough enough on the 'bad guys'.
Stage 2	Awakening	• Management is beginning to recognize that quality management can help, but is unwilling to devote the time and money to make it happen. • Management has not awakened enough to recognize that quality management takes more than understanding the technical aspects of a product or service. • Inspection and testing are performed more often, and problems are identified earlier in the production cycle, though long-range solutions are not considered seriously. • Awakening relies heavily on motivation of employees. This could work for a while, then people will soon tire and go back to what they were doing before. • Employees and management will realize that the company has to offer constant quality in service and product alike or its very life will be threatened.
Stage 3	Enlightenment	• Management decides to continue along the quality path. • With the establishment of a regular quality policy, and the admission that 'we cause our own problems', management enters the stage of enlightenment. • A new approach to problem resolution is adopted. Instead of blaming individuals, the organization rather develops a smoothly functioning system for resolving these problems. • Task teams are formed to take up responsibility for both resolving a current problem and preventing it in the future. • Quality improvement is now headed up by an official quality team, and the quality team feels confident that there is light at the end of the tunnel.
Stage 4	Wisdom	• Cost reductions are in effect. • When problems appear, they are handled and they disappear. • Incisive, in-depth reviews must continually be conducted on a 'no mercy' basis. • Now the company finds that quality control is real, and people may expect too much too soon.
Stage 5	Certainty	• Attitude in the Certainty stage is summed up in one sentence: 'We know why we do not have a problem with quality'. • A company at the Certainty stage considers quality management to be an absolutely vital part of company management. • Certainty's prevention system is such that very few significant problems ever actually occur.

7.2 SOFTWARE PROCESS IMPROVEMENT MODELS

7.2.1 WATTS HUMPHREY'S ORIGINAL SOFTWARE PROCESS IMPROVEMENT MODEL

The influence of Shewhart, Juran, Deming and Crosby can be traced easily in the work published on software process improvement. Although many people have contributed to the development of the software process maturity movement, most of the credit goes to one individual: Watts Humphrey. His pioneering work in applying the quality concepts to the software process laid the foundations for the development of the Software Engineering Institute's Capability Maturity Model (CMM).

Watts Humphrey's basic thesis is that 'if the development process is under statistical control, a consistently better result can be achieved only by improving the process. If the process is not under statistical control, sustained progress is not possible until it is' (Humphrey, 1988). Watts Humphrey's pioneering paper entitled 'Characterizing the software process: a maturity framework' (Humphrey, 1988) and his follow-on book titled *Managing the Software Process* (Humphrey, 1989) have ignited the spark that popularized the interest in the software process and its maturity. He still leads the way through his new crusade on the personal and team software process (Humphrey, 1995, 1996, 1997).

In his early work Humphrey suggested the following steps for organizations to improve their software capabilities:

1 Understand the current status of their development process or processes.
2 Develop a vision of the desired process.
3 Establish a list of required process improvement actions in order of priority.
4 Produce a plan to accomplish these actions.
5 Commit the resources to execute the plan.
6 Restart at step 1.

7.2.2 AN EXAMPLE OF APPLYING QUALITY CONCEPTS TO SOFTWARE PROCESS IMPROVEMENT

Applying the principles of quality improvement and process management, an organization can effectively come up with a model for software process improvement. The literature is full of such models with varying implementations and different interpretations of public quality improvement models and process management principles. An example of a 'home grown' model is the three-phase process-improvement paradigm adopted by Raytheon (Dion, 1993) for their programme of software process improvement. It is mentioned here as an example of specifying a local model for software process improvement based on published work. An organization can go this way, rather than adopting a readily available model, if they are ready to put in the extra effort necessary for developing such a model. Raytheon's paradigm for software process improvement is based on a three-phase cycle of stabilization, control and change, which applies the principles of Deming and Juran. The model is illustrated in Figure 7.4.

The three phases of the cycle are:

1 *Process stabilization:* The emphasis is on distilling the elements of the process actually being used (achieving visibility) and progressively institutionalizing it across all projects (achieving repeatability).
2 *Process control:* The emphasis shifts to 'instrumenting' projects. The purpose is to gather significant measurement and to analyse the data to understand how to control the process.
3 *Process change:* The emphasis is on determining how to adjust the process as a result of measurement and analysis. Adjusting the process is done first on pilot projects to confirm the findings. Then the emphasis moves to how to diffuse the new methods and technology among practitioners.

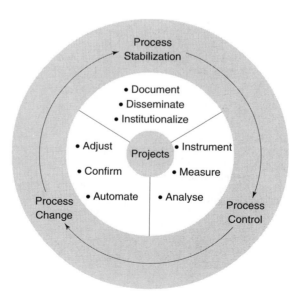

Figure 7.4 Raytheon's model for software process improvement

After the third stage, process improvement becomes continuous; completion of the third phase signals a beginning of the first.

7.2.3   REQUIREMENTS OF A SOFTWARE PROCESS
IMPROVEMENT ROADMAP

Since an improvement cycle is likely to be repeated, you need consistency across the various iterations. This can be achieved only if you base the different improvement cycles on a consistent model for process improvement that defines a roadmap for improving the process. Such a roadmap will point the way forward and act as a yardstick for measuring process improvement. The most popular roadmap for software process improvement is the Capability Maturity Model for software developed by the Software Engineering Institute. It is described in detail in Part 4 of this book. Here we provide a summary of the original five maturity levels proposed by Watts Humphrey in his early work on characterizing the software process (Humphrey, 1988). In his work, the yardstick for measuring process improvement is a model of five maturity levels. The five levels represent logical steps for progressing from a chaotic process environment (where 'fire fighting' is the norm) to a continuously improving process environment (where 'defect prevention' is the norm). The five levels are illustrated in Figure 7.5.

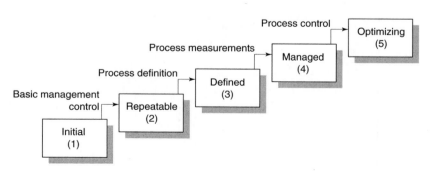

Figure 7.5   The five levels of software process maturity (Humphrey, 1988)

The five levels as originally defined in Humphrey's paper are:

Level 1 – Initial: Until the process is under statistical control, no orderly progress in process improvement is possible.

Level 2 – Repeatable: The organization has achieved stable process with a repeatable level of statistical control by initiating rigorous project management of commitments, cost, schedule and changes.

Level 3 – Defined: The organization has defined the process, to ensure consistent implementation and provide a basis for better understanding of the process. At this point, advanced technology can usefully be introduced.

Level 4 – Managed: The organization has initiated comprehensive process measurements, beyond those of cost and schedule performance. This is when the most significant quality improvements begin.

Level 5 – Optimizing: The organization now has a foundation for continued improvement and optimization of the process.

Since its initial inception by Watts Humphrey, the original software process maturity model has been developed and refined to become the Capability Maturity Model (CMM). This was developed by the Software Engineering Institute (SEI) and described in detail in Paulk *et al.* (1994). The CMM has become the most popular model so far for software process improvement.

7.3   STAGED VERSUS CONTINUOUS

ARCHITECTURE FOR SPI MODELS

With the increasing popularity of software process improvement, the number of models proposed has been increasing year by year. As well as providing coordination and leadership, the Software Engineering Institute treats its own approach, the CMM, as a continuously improving paradigm with inputs from industry and from leading software process improvement practitioners. With the increasing interest from industry and lack of international standards, the International Standards Organization (ISO) launched its SPICE project. SPICE resulted in an international standard for software process assessment and improvement (ISO/IEC 15504). It is noteworthy that both models, the CMM v1.1 and SPICE, adopt two different (though not contradictory) architectures. These are known as the 'staged' architecture and the 'continuous' architecture (Paulk *et al.*, 1996). They can be described as based on a staged model and a continuous model respectively.

7.3.1   STAGED MODELS

The staged model comprises a number of maturity levels, each process area being fixed to a particular level. For example, the CMM level 2 (repeatable) has six key process areas attached to it. These are Requirements Management,

Project Planning, Project Tracking, Subcontractor Management, Software Quality Assurance, and Software Configuration Management. CMM level 3 (Defined) has seven key process areas, level 4 (Managed) has two and level 5 (Optimizing) has three. The key process areas themselves are staged. The logic is that each key process area is the foundation for the next process areas, and each level represents the foundation for the next maturity model. The result of an assessment against such models could usually can be expressed as a calibration of the organization's maturity. The result can be expressed as a specific level of maturity. The Capability Maturity Model (CMM) is a well-known example of a staged model.

7.3.2 CONTINUOUS MODELS

In the continuous model, individual processes progress continually along the maturity scale independently of each other. For example, in an organization or a project the project management process could be at a high maturity level, while the configuration management process could be at a lower maturity level. The result of an assessment against such models usually takes the form of a profile for the assessed processes. The ISO/IEC 15504 model is an example of a continuous model.

The two approaches (summarized in Table 7.2) are not completely contradictory. A staged model can be layered onto a continuous architecture. A further analysis of the strengths and weaknesses of both approaches is provided in Paulk *et al.* (1996).

Table 7.2 Staged versus continuous architectures for software process improvement models

Aspect of comparison	Staged architecture	Continuous architecture
General focus	• Building organizational capability	• Building process capability for each process
Model focus	• Focus on the few issues that need attention to progress organizational capability	• A reference model for rating individual processes (process capability)
Nature of the model	• Describes a roadmap for process improvement • Describes organizationl capability	• Describes the terrain of process management • Describes the evolution of individual processes

7.4 STANDARDS AND MODELS FOR SPI

There are a number of software process improvement roadmaps that are publicly available. The most notable are the Capability Maturity Model (CMM), ISO 9001 with its associated guide ISO 9000-3, the ISO/IEC 15504 initiative and ISO/IEC 12207. There are also a number of public standards that specifically address software engineering activities. The most notable of these are the DoD Standard MIL-STD-498 (which superseded DoD Standards 2167A, 7735A and 1903 (NS)), and the V-Model (Software Development Standard for the German Federal Armed Forces).

7.4.1 STANDARDS

Standards are usually developed under the auspice of the International Standards Organization (ISO) or national standards organizations (general or industry-specific). The main characteristics of standards are:

- Standards define the minimum that has to be achieved.
- A standard measures compliance in 'pass or fail' terms.
- Conformance is inspected through a certification process (third-party assessment) by an external organization (by trained and registered auditors).
- The organization's quality procedures are judged against the standard.
- The organization is audited to check that, in practice, it complies with its own quality system and that the quality system is effective.
- Passing the audit usually results in a certificate of compliance being issued to the organization.
- Failing the audit usually results in a list of corrective actions to be completed and verified before the certificate is issued.
- An audit against the standard can be one of these types:
  - *First-party audit:* when an organization carries out an internal audit. Usually this is done before any third party is invited to carry out a formal compliance audit.
  - *Second-party audit:* when a customer audits an organization's products and processes. Usually this is used by purchasing organizations to audit their suppliers.
  - *Third-party audit:* when an organization at its own request and expense has an audit carried out by an external, impartial body referred to as a certification body, which is not a direct customer. A third-party audit evaluates the full range of a supplier's activities and capability within an agreed certification scope.
- Standards are owned and maintained by the International Standards Organization or national standards organizations.
- Standards goals include encouraging predictability of product quality and maximum productivity, and promoting a repeatable process.

7.4.2 MODELS

Most of the popular software process improvement models have been developed by specialized organizations and industry consortia. The main characteristics of models are:

- Models are flexible and can be customized according to guidelines issued by the developers.
- They are usually developed through sponsorship by a large 'buyer' organization, or through an initiative by a body of companies.
- Depending on the scope and focus, they are owned and maintained by an industry consortium or a specialized institution.
- Assessment against the model can take one of the following types:
  - *Self assessment:* This is when the assessment is performed internally by an internal assessment team (independently or assisted by an external facilitator).
  - *Capability evaluation:* This is when external assessors are used to perform the assessment in order to evaluate the organization's capability to fulfil specific contract requirements.
  - *Capability determination:* This is when the assessment is performed by an independent third-party organization in order to verify the organization's ability to enter contracts or produce software products.

7.4.3 CHOOSING STANDARDS AND MODELS

All public models and standards are available as general sources of information available for organizations to use and adapt for specifying their own software process improvement roadmaps. However, there are some factors that are likely to influence the choice of a process model or a standard as the basis for an organization's software process improvement roadmap, for example:

- Is the model or standard imposed by customers for a specific project (for example DoD standards imposed by the US Department of Defense for specific contracts)?
- Is there an international business standard adopted at the corporate level that the SPI initiatives need to comply with? For example, an organization that opts for ISO 9000 certification across the board for its total business would choose ISO 9001 for its software development activities.
- How stable and popular is the model or standard? More popularity will provide confidence in the approach. The more an approach has been applied in real life, the more benchmarking information will be available.

Owing to the difference in their nature and role, there are variations that distinguish standards from models. The following section discusses examples of such variation.

7.4.4   USE OF SOFTWARE PROCESS IMPROVEMENT

ROADMAPS

Process improvement models and standards have many uses. The following are some of the most common.

Basis for software process improvement programme

Process improvement roadmaps are useful tools and can be used as the foundation for a programme for software process improvement. They have many types of uses. At least the following three classes of users can be identified:

- *Software development organizations (suppliers, vendors):*   They can use the process improvement standards and models as input to developing their programmes for software process improvement.
- *Customers (purchasers, acquirers):*   These include organizations which purchase software or contract software development. They can use the process improvement roadmap (standard or model) as a basis for qualifying their software subcontractors. This is likely to result in minimizing the risk through using only those subcontractors who pass the qualification procedures.
- *Quality auditors and process assessors:*   These users assess or audit software development units against the improvement roadmap.

Design of the organization's software processes

- Due to the generic nature of software process public standards and models, they usually have to be tailored in order to match specific requirements of an organization or the special nature of projects or applications.
- One of the most effective uses of public models and standards is as inputs to the activity of designing and documenting an organization's standard software process. There are some critical factors that need to be considered when designing an organization's standard process. These include business requirements, business constraints, business strategy, the nature of application domains, and the main business line of the organization (for example customer, supplier or contractor).

Similar tailoring processes could be followed when defining a project's specific process based on the organization's standard process. Figures 7.6 and 7.7 illustrate the above point. Please note that the organization's defined process in Figure 7.6 is the same organization's standard process in Figure 7.7.

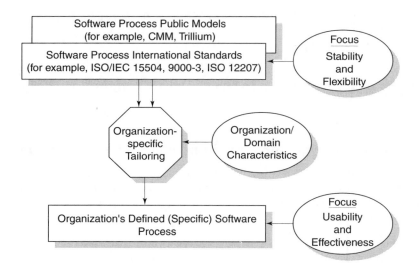

Figure 7.6 Tailoring international standards and public models to develop an organization's defined process

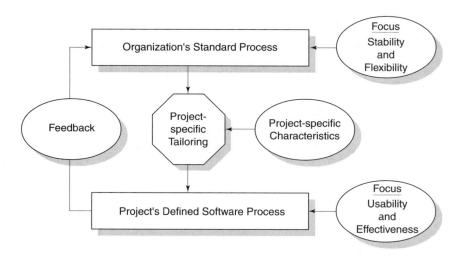

Figure 7.7 Tailoring the organization's standard process to develop a project's defined process

SUMMARY

Impact of the quality movement on the software process movement

- Quality management concepts and trends are the roots of the software process maturity and improvement models.
- The concepts of quality preached by the quality gurus Deming, Juran and Crosby have influenced the software process improvement approaches.

Watts Humphrey pioneered and popularized software process maturity

- Watts Humphrey pioneered the adaptation of the general quality approaches (developed by Deming, Juran and Crosby) for software engineering.
- Watts Humphrey's efforts led to the development of the Software Engineering Institute's Capability Maturity Model (CMM).

Software process models and standards

- Currently there are a number of software process improvement models and emerging standards developed by international organizations, industry consortia, large software purchasers and software developers.
- So far, the most popular model for software process improvement is the Capability Maturity Model (CMM).
- The international standard ISO/IEC 15504 was developed by the International Standards Organization (ISO) for software process improvement under the acronym SPICE.

Use of software process models and standards

Software process improvement models and standards have many potential users, including software purchasers (acquirers), vendors, developers (suppliers), and software process auditors and assessors. Their potential uses include the following:

- Software process improvement roadmaps can be the basis for software process assessments, software process audits, capability evaluations and certification of software subcontractors as well as self-improvement programmes.
- Organizations without in-house software development capability can use the standards and models as a basis for developing subcontractor evaluation and selection criteria for qualifying their software subcontractors.
- Organizations which do have in-house software development capability can use the standards and models to design their own software processes

(the organization's standard process and the projects' defined processes), and to develop a self-assessment method. This can be used for assessing the organization's software processes and developing a programme for software process improvement.

- Prime contractors who lead a consortium for responding to, a specific contract can use the standards and models to develop subcontractor evaluation and selection criteria for qualifying their software subcontractors. They can also use them to assess, audit and evaluate the process maturity of their subcontractors, and to assess their own software processes and develop plans for software process improvement.

- Subcontractors and suppliers who develop packages, subsystems or components of a system as part of a consortium have similar uses to customer organizations which have in-house development.

CHAPTER 8

Fundamentals of software process assessment

8.1 DEFINITIONS OF ASSESSMENT

8.1.1 WHAT IS AN ASSESSMENT?

A software process assessment is an appraisal or review of an organization's software process. The primary drive for software process assessment has come not from the software development industry, but rather from acquirers of large, critical, software-intensive systems – notably in the defence and telecommunications sectors. Defence organizations have pioneered initiatives and methods for software process improvement. Examples of such pioneering organizations include the US Department of Defense, the UK Ministry of Defence and the German Federal Armed Forces. On the telecommunications side, pioneering organizations include Bell Canada and British Telecom.

Software process assessment has a wide variety of definitions in the literature. In the following we discuss a selection of the most popular definitions. ISO documentation defines process assessment as 'the disciplined examination of the processes used by an organization against a set of criteria to determine the capability of those processes to perform within quality, cost and schedule goals'. It defines its goal as 'to characterize current practice, identifying strengths and weaknesses and the ability of the process to control or avoid significant causes of poor quality, cost and schedule performance' (ISO/IEC JTC1/SC7, 1992). BOOTSTRAP documentation defines assessment as 'a pre-requisite for process improvement. It determines the current state of the software process and the constraints of the improvement path' (Kuvaja *et al.*, 1994). The SEI defines software process assessment as 'an appraisal by a trained team of software professionals to determine the state of an organization's current software process, to determine the high-priority software process-related issues facing an organization, and to obtain the organizational support for software process improvement' (Paulk *et al.*, 1994). The ISO/IEC 15504 glossary of terms defines process assessment as 'a disciplined evaluation of an organization's software processes against process model or variant model' (ISO, 1997). It is important to always remember that the assessment is not an end in itself, rather it is a tool to help in an overall software process improvement effort.

8.1.2 ASSESSMENT VERSUS AUDIT

An important point of clarification is the need to recognize the difference between an assessment and an audit. In one of the early works on software assessment Roger Pressman defines the assessment as 'a structured investigation of the current state of the software engineering practice'. Pressman relates the assessment to an audit by positioning the audit as a primary mechanism for the assessment (Pressman, 1988). The IEEE has a specific definition of an audit: 'Audit – An independent examination of a work product or set of work products to assess compliance with specifications, standards, contractual agreements, or other criteria' (IEEE-STD-610). In reality the term 'audit' is associated with more formal inspections and certification performed by external resources (like a financial audit). Using the word 'audit' to refer to software process assessment can create a mental barrier between the assessment team and the assessment participants. ISO documents define the concepts of certification and audit as follows: 'Certification, or third party assessment (referred to as registration in some countries), is carried out by an independent organization against a particular standard' (ISO 9000-3). Watts Humphrey's view is that 'a software process assessment is not an audit but a review of a software organization to advise its management and professionals on how they can improve their operation' (Humphrey, 1989).

8.1.3 TYPES OF ASSESSMENTS AND AUDITS

Three types of assessment

Generally there are three different types of assessment depending on who plays the main role in an assessment:

- *Self-assessment:* Also known as first-party assessment. This refers primarily to a situation where the assessment is performed internally inside the software development organization, mainly by its own personnel. The main objective is to identify the organization's own software process capability and initiate an action plan for software process improvement. First-party assessment can also be performed as guided first-party assessment where external assessors act as assessment methodology facilitators and coaches for the internal assessment team.

- *Second-party assessment:* Also known as capability determination. This is an assessment where external assessors are used to perform the assessment. The main objective is to evaluate the organization's capability to fulfil specific contract requirements.
- *Third-party assessment:* Also known as capability determination. This is performed by an independent third-party organization. The main objective is to verify the organization's ability to enter contracts or produce software products, and sometimes to provide the fulfilment of certification according to a selected standard.

Three types of audit

This classification is consistent with the British Standards Institution's classification of an audit (BSI, 1995). In BSI's terms an audit can be first, second or third party:

- *First-party audit:* When an organization carries out an internal audit, the procedure is referred to as first-party audit. It is vitally important for an organization to perform internal audit and thus check its quality procedures before any third party is invited to carry out a formal compliance audit. (An internal audit is equivalent to self-assessment.)
- *Second-party audit:* A second-party audit is an audit of an organization's relevant products and processes by a customer (acquirer). The product or quality system standards are typically selected by the customer and specified as part of the contract. Second-party audits may be relatively narrow in scope because the purchasing organization examines only those elements and activities that relate to the products and services being purchased. The pre-contract survey is an example of a second-party audit.
- *Third-party audit:* This is an audit of an organization at its own request and expense by an external, impartial body referred to as a certification body, which is not a direct customer. The third-party audit is invariably performed against the requirements of a national or international standard such as ISO 9001.

8.1.4 APPROACHES TO ASSESSMENTS

The following is a summary of possible approaches to both self-assessments and independent assessments (Figure 8.1).

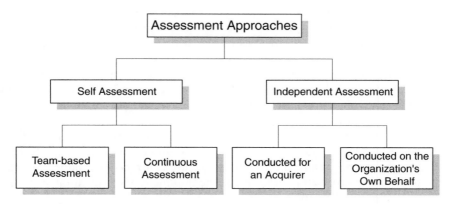

Figure 8.1   Different approaches to the assessment

Self-assessment

A self-assessment is used by an organization to assess the capability of its software process. The sponsor of a self-assessment is usually internal to the organization. A self-assessment may be either team-based or continuous assessment.

Team-based assessment
This approach establishes an assessment team from within the organization. An external expert may be brought into an organization for one or more of the following purposes:

● to assist the assessment team with the assessment
● to help the organizational unit understand the concepts expressed by the standard
● to explain how to use assessment instruments and tools.

Continuous assessment
This approach involves the use of an assessment instrument that supports automated or semi-automated collection of data in the assessment of an organizational unit's process capability. The assessment instrument could then be used continuously throughout the software development lifecycle at defined milestones for one or more of the following purposes:

● to measure adherence to the process
● to measure process improvement progress
● to gather data to facilitate a future assessment.

When using the continuous assessment approach there may not be an assessment team as there is for a team-based assessment.

Independent assessment

An independent assessment is an assessment conducted by an assessor who is independent of the organizational unit being assessed. An independent assessment may be taken up by an organization as independent verification that its assessment programme is functioning properly or by an acquirer who wishes to have an independent assessment output. The sponsor of an independent assessment will generally be external to the organizational unit being assessed. The degree of independence, however, may vary according to the purpose and circumstances of the assessment. When the independent assessment is conducted for an acquirer, the sponsor is external to the organization being assessed. If the assessment is being conducted by the organization on its own behalf, however, the sponsor is likely to belong to the same organization as the organizational unit being assessed.

8.1.5   A GENERIC DEFINITION FOR SOFTWARE PROCESS

ASSESSMENT AND ITS OBJECTIVES

Assessment definition

Taking into consideration these definitions and the models and concepts described in this book for software process improvement, we can define software process assessment and its objectives as follows: 'A software process assessment is a disciplined examination of the software processes used by an organization, based on a process model. The objective is to determine the maturity level of those processes, as measured against a process improvement roadmap. The result should identify and characterize current practices, identifying areas of strengths and weaknesses, and the ability of current practices to control or avoid significant causes of poor (software) quality, cost and schedule. The assessment findings can also be used as indicators of the capability of those processes to achieve the quality, cost and schedule goals of software development with a high degree of predictability.'

Assessment objectives

Generally a primary assessment objective is to identify the highest priority areas for improvement and to provide guidance on how to make these improvements. Assessment has some fallout benefits such as enrolling the organization's opinion leaders in the change process, and increasing the process awareness. Assessment takes place in different forms according to the specific situation. According to Part 4 of ISO/IEC 15504, process assessment is applicable in the following circumstances:

- By or on behalf of an organization with the objective of understanding the state of its own processes for process improvement

- By or on behalf of an organization with the objective of determining the suitability of its own processes for a particular requirement or class of requirements
- By or on behalf of one organization with the objective of determining the suitability of another organization's processes for a particular contract or class of contracts.

We can summarize the main objectives of a software process assessment as follows:

1 To understand and determine the organization's current software engineering practices, and to learn how the whole organization works.
2 To identify strengths, major weaknesses and key areas for software process improvement.
3 To facilitate the initiation of process improvement activities, and enrol opinion leaders in the change process.
4 To provide a framework for process improvement actions (usually based on a process model that defines an improvement roadmap).
5 To help obtain sponsorship and support for action through following a participative approach to the assessment.

8.2 ASSESSMENT PRINCIPLES AND CRITICAL SUCCESS FACTORS

8.2.1 ASSESSMENT PRINCIPLES

Watts Humphrey (1989) identified three main factors for successful software process assessments:

- competent team
- sound leadership
- cooperative organization.

These should translate into a set of principles that should be adopted by the organization and all those involved in software process improvement. There are several lists in the literature that suggest principles for assessment (Pressman, 1988; Humphrey, 1989; Olson *et al.*, 1989; Kuvaja *et al.*, 1994; Paulk *et al.*, 1994; ISO, 1997). Table 8.1 provides a list and a discussion of a consolidated selection of these principles.

There is another important aspect that you need to consider for assessment – that is, to avoid confusing assessment with rating. Some people are obsessed with getting a single digit to label their organization at a specific maturity level ('We are at level 2, or level 3', and so on). The objective of an assessment is not to determine a rating but mainly to discover the problems with the current processes and point to the way forward. Watts Humphrey puts this point in clear and unambiguous terms: 'With SEI assessments, we at one point seriously considered eliminating a rating so people would not be distracted. The key objective is to get the organization as a whole to see their problems, to recognize their importance, and to agree they have to fix them. An SEI assessment is thus not abstract data, but a real slap in the face. It takes engineers, managers, and executives by the scruff of their necks and shakes them. The CMM structure, and the questionnaires are only tools to help them' (Watts Humphrey, private communication, 1997).

8.2.2 ASSESSMENT CRITICAL SUCCESS FACTORS

Software process improvement is about changes to the organization, to the roles, to the procedures and methods and to the behaviour and activities of software engineers and project managers alike. As in any programme for change, there are some critical factors that need to be considered in order to avoid (or minimize) resistance to change. Such factors are essential for a successful process assessment. The following is a selected list of these factors.

Commitment

Both the sponsor and the owner should commit themselves to the objectives established for an assessment to provide the authority to undertake the assessment within an organization. This commitment requires that the necessary resources, time and personnel are available to undertake the assessment. The commitment of the executive sponsor is fundamentally important to ensuring that the business objectives are met.

Motivation

The attitude of the organization's management, and the method by which the information is collected, have a significant influence on the outcome of an assessment. The organization's management, therefore, needs to motivate participants to be open and constructive. An assessment should be focused on the process, not on the performance of individuals implementing the process. The intention is to make the outcome more effective in an effort to support the defined business goals, not to allocate blame to individuals.

Providing feedback and maintaining an atmosphere that encourages trust and open discussion about findings during the assessment helps to ensure that the assessment output is meaningful to the organizational unit. The organization needs to recognize that the participants are a principal source of knowledge and experience about the process and that they are in a good position to objectively identify potential weaknesses.

Table 8.1 Basic principles for software process assessment

Principle	Definition	Comments
Sponsorship	Management sponsorship that would: • Ensure the funding for the assessment • Ensure the availability of adequate resources • Ensure the organization's commitment to the results of the assessment.	The assessment demands time and effort not only by the assessment team but also by project managers and software project personnel. Without senior management support, project activities will have a higher priority that could push the assessment activities down the priority scale. Management sponsorship should be visible and the sponsor should personally get involved in the assessment and follow-up activities.
Confidentiality	Assessment results should be in general form, and should not be traceable to specific individuals (or to specific projects unless the assessment is for that project).	The assessment is an attempt to find the true state of an organization's software process. The truth will only be revealed if honest, open and accurate information is revealed by the assessment participants. In most cases this will not happen unless confidentiality is assured. (It is vital that the assessment participants feel they can speak in confidence.)
Collaboration and teamwork	Everyone in the software development organization should feel involved. The assessment teams and software engineers should work together.	Collaboration is especially important for self-assessment, when the assessment team is from the organization itself. A successful assessment is a collaborative effort. Collaboration can occur on several levels: • Within the assessment team members • Between the assessment team and the assessment participants • Between those involved in the assessment and the rest of the software organization.
Action orientation	The assessment should focus on finding areas for improvement actions. It should not be considered as an opportunity for exchanging the blame and finding scapegoats for current failures.	Assessment is just one link in the chain of software process improvement. Action orientation should reflect on the assessment findings' focus on identifying problem areas facing the organization and recommendations on how to overcome them. These findings should be input to a wider SPI programme, which sets improvement goals and business expectations.

(continued)

Table 8.1 (*continued*)

Process framework	The assessment should not be an end in itself; it is a means to an end, and the end should be expressed in the benefits of improving the software process.	An assessment implies that the status of current processes will be compared against a standard or roadmap for improvement. Such a roadmap should provide a basis for orderly exploration as well as a means for establishing improvement priorities. The intent of standard roadmaps is to maximize objectivity of the assessment process, and thereby ensure the repeatability and comparability of the assessment results.

Action orientation

Motivation without action is just 'hot air', or 'lip service'. I have seen so many of these 'lip service' initiatives that were a complete waste of time, and damaged the credibility of the whole process improvement initiative. It is of vital importance for the success of any process improvement initiative that everyone knows from the beginning that it will result in change. Creating high expectations of the software process initiative and then not following the actions through is a recipe for demotivating your staff. This could destroy the chances of future SPI programmes.

Confidentiality

Respect for the confidentiality of the sources of information gathered and personal opinions expressed during assessment is essential. If discussion techniques are utilized, consideration should be given to ensuring that participants do not feel threatened or have any concerns regarding confidentiality. Some of the information provided might be proprietary to the organization or confidential to the project. It is therefore important that adequate controls are in place to preserve such confidentiality.

Relevance

The organizational unit members being assessed should believe that the assessment will result in some benefits that are relevant to their jobs. Alignment with and focus on the business and management objectives should be explicit and should be restated throughout the assessment. Everyone should feel that the assessment is relevant to his or her job.

Credibility

The sponsor and the management and staff of the organizational unit must all believe that the assessment will deliver a result that is objective and representative of the assessment scope. It is important that all parties involved feel confident that the team selected to conduct the assessment has the following attributes:

- adequate experience in assessment
- adequate understanding of the organizational unit and its business
- sufficient impartiality.

Team building

The worst team is the one in which everyone is an opinionated guru. The assessment team should work as a team, and hold a common set of beliefs regarding the need of the assessment, the seriousness of the software process improvement effort, and its relevance to the business strategy. The team should have mutual trust and should be at a high level of maturity to ensure that the confidentiality is strictly observed and that collaboration prevails.

8.3 ASSESSMENT DOMAINS

8.3.1 SCOPING THE ASSESSMENT

It is an important step before starting an assessment that you should understand the business objectives of the software process assessment. This will help to position the assessment within the right context as follows:

- If the assessment is one component of an overall programme for software process improvement, then relate it to the overall business objectives of that programme.
- If the assessment is the step towards getting the buy-in for launching a more comprehensive SPI programme, then position its objectives within the overall strategy of the SPI programme.
- If the assessment is a step towards capability evaluation, or certification, by a potential customer for a specific contract, then relate it to that contract.

The scope of the assessment should be based on the business objectives. For example, the scope could cover one of the following scenarios:

- All software processes in the whole organization and the software process environment. In such case the assessment could cover the organization's software process assets, the feedback roles and mechanisms, the management sponsorship, process training, process enforcement and performance measurement.

- A subset of the software processes that is selected for capability evaluation requested by a customer.
- One specific project that needs to be assessed, or reassessed, as part of the project contract.

The scope of the assessment will have an impact on the following:

- The assessment approach (for example manual or computer-assisted)
- The assessment steps (for example the preplanning, the report production and so on)
- The choice of the assessment instruments (for example the design and use of the questionnaire or interviews)
- The level of sponsorship (for example Executive, Senior Business Manager, Project Manager)
- The budget and availability of resources.

The boundaries of the assessment could be one of the following:

- *Organization-wide:* In such case the overall scope of the assessment could cover all the process domains within an organization including the process culture and the process infrastructure.
- *Project-specific:* In some cases the boundaries of the assessment could be only a subset of the total software development organization, for example one specific project or one software engineering team.
- *Personal software process:* If the objective of the software process improvement programme is to improve the personal software process (PSP) of the individual software engineer, then the boundaries of the assessment could be all the software engineers or an adequate sample.

For the purpose of our discussion here, we will assume that assessment is performed for the whole organization. The coverage of the assessment could follow the model suggested in this book for an effective process environment. The model is described in earlier chapters (see Figure 5.1). It covers the process documentation, the process training and the feedback on the process performance. Also one of the aspects to be considered is the assessment scope and coverage of the process culture and process infrastructure. Figure 8.2 illustrates the possible domains for an organization-wide process assessment, which are further discussed below.

8.3.2 ASSESSING THE PROCESS CULTURE

Assessing a culture is a difficult task. You cannot touch culture. Culture is not a material thing that is documented, taught and improved, though it is a very important indicator within an organization that reveals whether people in the organization really believe in the importance and relevance of the process for their business. At a project level it shows whether the project manager and staff

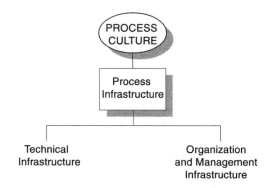

Figure 8.2   Possible domains of an organization-wide process assessment

really believe in the process focus. The assessment team should be looking for the following indicators in order to understand the culture of the organization being assessed:

- When something goes wrong, do managers jump to blame individuals? In such cases does the blame culture take over, or is a rational analysis done to try to uncover the causes of the errors, and rectify the causes?
- Is the reward policy related to process performance, or is it based on the individual judgement of managers, without relevance to the results and goals of the processes?
- Is following the process considered a liability or is it the 'natural way' of performing the software development activities?
- Are there any penalties imposed on those who ignore the process and follow their own way of performing their duties?
- Are successes attributed to the organization's disciplined process publicized and documented?
- Is process knowledge common across the whole software development community or is it restricted to only a few?

8.3.3   ASSESSING THE PROCESS INFRASTRUCTURE

Assessment of the process infrastructure should aim to establish the presence and effectiveness of the infrastructure components at the organizational level, the project level and the personal level. The process infrastructure should support the process activities at all three levels (Figure 8.3).

For each of these three levels of process assets, the assessment should cover the main components that establish and institutionalize the process. The main components that should be covered are:

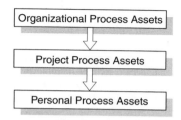

Figure 8.3 Possible domains for assessing the software process infrastructure

- *Process definition and documentation:* Are processes defined and documented and what form does the process documentation take (for example hardcopy, electronic and so on)? How do you measure its relevance and effectiveness?
- *Process training:* Is the process training in place? How often does it happen? When did it last happen? How do you measure its effectiveness? Is there a training schedule? Is it followed?
- *Process ownership:* Who owns the processes? Who is authorized to change the process? Is process ownership a defined role within the organization?
- *Process enforcement:* What are the mechanisms for enforcing the process? What actions are taken if the process is not followed? What exceptions are permitted?
- *Process results:* What mechanisms or roles and responsibilities exist for inspection of the process results? What are the measurements taken to indicate the process performance? What actions are taken as a result of analysing the process performance results?
- *Process feedback:* Is there a mechanism for encouraging and capturing feedback from process users on how helpful or obstructive the process is? Does the feedback result in process improvement? Is there ownership of such feedback?
- *Process improvement:* Is responsibility for process improvement defined?
- *Process effectiveness:* Is there a defined way to track the impact of the process discipline on the business results? Are the indicators of process effectiveness defined?

Table 8.2 lists some of the attributes that could be targeted in the assessment of the organizational process assets.

8.4 ASSESSMENT GENERIC PHASES

8.4.1 A GENERIC CYCLE FOR THE ASSESSMENT

The assessment process is in most cases one phase of a bigger programme or business plan, for example a software process improvement initiative or a software capability evaluation. Prior to the assessment there is a need for

Table 8.2 Target attributes for assessment of the organization's process infrastructure

Infrastructure component	Attributes to be assessed
Organization's process definition and documentation	Scope, format, media, coverage (process architecture and process elements), availability, dissemination mechanisms, user friendliness, ownership, topicality, change control, feedback, relevance, flexibility, security, etc.
Lifecycles	Relevance, completeness, availability, clarity, enforceability, authorship, ownership, topicality
Customization guidelines	Coverage, flexibility, clarity, enforceability, authority, ownership, topicality
Library of process documents (feedback from projects)	Coverage, relevance, comparability, conformance to standards, usability, dissemination, format
Project's defined process definition and documentation	Scope, format, media, coverage, availability, dissemination mechanisms, user friendliness, ownership, topicality, change control, feedback, relevance, flexibility, security
Project's lifecycle	Relevance, completeness, coverage, availability, flexibility
Organization's and project process measurements	Coverage, relevance, accuracy, dependability, conformance to standards, usability, dissemination, format

pre-assessment or pre-planning to understand the business objectives of the assessment and the business constraints, and to secure management commitment and sponsorship for the assessment. This is followed by the assessment cycle beginning with planning followed by fact finding, fact analysis and reporting. The assessment should be followed by a post-assessment phase. The nature of this phase will depend on the wider programme of which the assessment is one component, as a process improvement programme, a software capability evaluation, and so on. The generic phases for assessment are pre-planning, planning, fact gathering, fact analysis, reporting and post-assessment.

Figure 8.4 illustrates the main phases of this generic cycle for the assessment. These phases are further described in the rest of this section.

8.4.2 THE PRE-ASSESSMENT AND PRE-PLANNING PHASE

Pre-assessment: understanding the business and organizational context

This phase should take place before a decision for an assessment is made. It aims to investigate the business needs and assess the feasibility for conducting

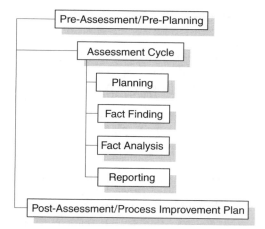

Figure 8.4 Generic phases of the assessment

an assessment. This helps understand the business drivers for the assessment. Some of the advantages of understanding the business and organizational context before planning an assessment are as follows:

- It can help the assessment team to understand why things are the way they are.
- It will enable the assessment team to present their findings in a way that is relevant to the business goals and makes sense in the business context.
- It will assist the assessment team in understanding the organizational territory they are concerned with, hence they can better identify the assessment participants.

Understanding the corporate culture is so important. It determines whether the people working in the organization are defensive or open, able to handle change or likely to resist change, and the amount of risk they are willing to take. How will the software development resources fit within the overall organization? How critical is software to the business strategy?

Pre-planning: defining a strategy for the assessment

This stage starts after a business decision to conduct the assessment has been made. At this stage the business objectives would have been identified. It involves the following tasks:

- Defining the scope and boundaries of the assessment
- Defining terms of reference for the assessment
- Defining whether the assessment will be conducted by internal or external resources (or a hybrid team with both external and internal staffs)
- Appointing a business sponsor for the assessment who will fund and authorize the assessment and ultimately have ownership of the results and recommendations of the assessment.

8.4.3 THE ASSESSMENT PHASE

This phase specifies the methods and activities involved in the actual conduct of the assessment. Although different approaches are proposed for this phase, they all fit within the following generic steps:

- *Planning:* This involves defining the assessment activities, resources, time scale and logistics. The assessment plan should be like any development project plan, for example with defined deliverables, milestones, quality plan and so on.
- *Fact gathering:* This involves gathering the data and information about the current state of the software process and practices as they exist in the organization. Also it involves gathering the views of individuals, for example software engineers and project managers, on possible areas for improvement.
- *Fact analysis:* This involves analysing the facts gathered in order to identify strengths and weaknesses based on an accurate picture of the current state of the software process.
- *Reporting:* This involves summarizing the findings and recommendations and presenting them back to the sponsor.

8.4.4 THE POST-ASSESSMENT PHASE

This phase will vary depending on the business context of the assessment. Usually the assessment will be conducted as part of a software process improvement programme. In such cases the following stage will be the actual implementation of the software process improvement recommendations as discussed in the next chapter.

The assessment generic cycle phases and activities are summarized in Table 8.3.

8.5 MAPPING ASSESSMENT APPROACHES TO THE GENERIC CYCLE

Figures 8.5 to 8.8 illustrate mappings between the generic assessment phases and some of the well-known assessment methods. This could assist in illustrating the coverage and comparability of these approaches. Further discussion of these approaches is provided in later chapters.

Figure 8.5 illustrates a mapping between ISO/IEC 15504 assessment stages and the generic cycle phases.

Table 8.3 Generic phases and activities of software process assessment

Phase	Sub-phase	Main activities
Pre-assessment	Pre-planning	• Understanding of business context and justification, objectives and constraints • Securing sponsorship and commitment
Assessment	Planning	• Selection of assessment approach • Selection of improvement roadmap • Definition of assessment boundaries • Selection of assessment team • Launching the assessment • Training the assessment team • Planning fact gathering, fact analysis and reporting activities
	Fact gathering	• Selecting a fact gathering approach, for example questionnaire, interviews, and group discussion • Defining the target interviewees • Distributing and collecting questionnaire responses • Conducting the interviews
	Fact analysis	• Analysis of questionnaire responses • Analysis of facts gathered in the interviews • Analysis of the evidence gathered • Collective analysis of the data gathered • Calibration of the findings against the roadmap • Identifying strengths and weaknesses and areas of improvement
	Reporting	• Documenting the findings: strengths and weaknesses • Documenting the recommendations
Post-assessment	Action plan for process improvement	• Implementing the process improvement actions • Managing and monitoring the process improvement plan

Figure 8.6 illustrates a mapping between SEI assessment stages and the assessment generic cycle phases.

Figure 8.7 illustrates a mapping between BOOTSTRAP assessment stages and the assessment generic cycle phases.

Figure 8.8 illustrates a mapping between the assessment stages proposed by Watts Humphrey (Humphrey, 1989) and the assessment generic cycle phases.

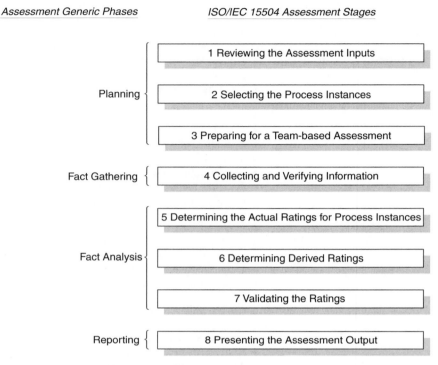

Assessment Generic Phases   *ISO/IEC 15504 Assessment Stages*

Planning
- 1 Reviewing the Assessment Inputs
- 2 Selecting the Process Instances
- 3 Preparing for a Team-based Assessment

Fact Gathering
- 4 Collecting and Verifying Information

Fact Analysis
- 5 Determining the Actual Ratings for Process Instances
- 6 Determining Derived Ratings
- 7 Validating the Ratings

Reporting
- 8 Presenting the Assessment Output

Figure 8.5   Mapping ISO/IEC 15504 assessment stages to the generic assessment cycle

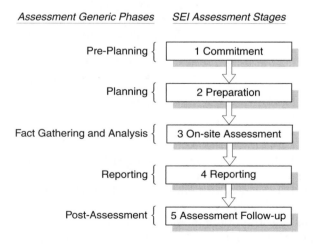

Assessment Generic Phases   *SEI Assessment Stages*

Pre-Planning
- 1 Commitment

Planning
- 2 Preparation

Fact Gathering and Analysis
- 3 On-site Assessment

Reporting
- 4 Reporting

Post-Assessment
- 5 Assessment Follow-up

Figure 8.6   Mapping SEI assessment stages to the generic assessment cycle

Assessment
Generic Phases   *BOOTSTRAP Assessment Stages*

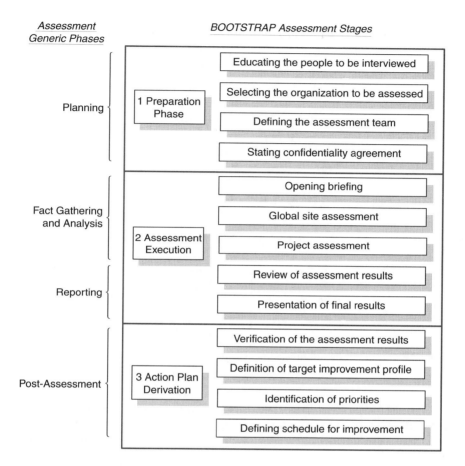

Figure 8.7 Mapping BOOTSTRAP assessment stages to the generic assessment cycle

SUMMARY

Assessment is a launch pad for software process and improvement

The assessment can provide the business justification for software process improvement plans. It is essential for starting software process improvement. It provides the foundation for any software process improvement plans.

If you do not know where you are, any road will do! The results of the assessment will be the basis for deciding which direction you should take to improve your software process.

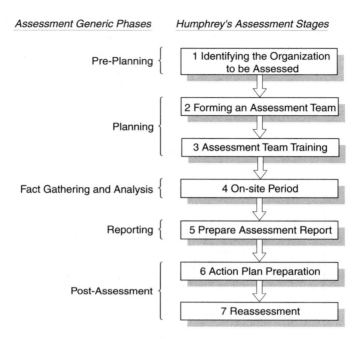

Figure 8.8 Mapping Humphrey's assessment stages to the generic assessment cycle

Get the buy-in for software process improvement. The assessment provides a good opportunity to gain buy-in and commitment of the software engineering staff and management to the value and need for software process improvement.

If you are not prepared to take action, do not assess. The assessment is a weapon with two edges. It could alienate your staff if no action has been taken as a result of the assessment.

Assessment should fit within the overall business context

Understanding the business of objectives is necessary to fit the assessment within the overall business context. Assessment is not an end in itself, rather it is a means to an end. The end point is to achieve continuous software process improvement, leading to improved quality of products and services, and increased competitiveness of business.

CHAPTER 9

Software process improvement action plan

9.1 CREATING A SOFTWARE PROCESS IMPROVEMENT ACTION PLAN

9.1.1 REQUIREMENTS OF A PROCESS IMPROVEMENT ACTION PLAN

The fourth aspect of the framework for software process improvement is the process improvement plan. The assumption is that you already know the current status of your software process through conducting an assessment. Also you should have adopted a roadmap for measuring software process improvement that gives you an indication of the target status of your software processes. In this chapter we discuss the various aspects of the software process improvement action plan. The steps necessary to convert the assessment findings into an improvement action plan are proposed and the roles and responsibilities for software process improvement are defined. Also some examples from real-life improvement initiatives are summarized. The software process improvement action plan should satisfy the following criteria and objectives in order to increase its chances of success.

Realistic approach

The recommendations should cover all aspects that may have an impact on the software process performance. Some of these aspects could be outside the organizational boundaries of the software development groups. In order that the action plan be realistic, it could very well leave out some of the recommendations that are outside the scope of the software process. Such recommendations should be referred to the executive sponsor to deal with.

Sensitivity to the organization

The action plan should be sensitive to the organization's current roles and responsibilities. This is to reduce the potential resistance to change, and avoid the creation of conflict. A conflict may lead to an organizational stress that could impede the progress of the process improvement activities. In some cases such conflict may be inevitable, but should be recognized and properly managed. The other aspect that should be considered is the organization's readiness for change. The action plan should take this into consideration, for example through proposing a phased approach to introducing major changes, or focusing on areas that could lead to quick wins and early achievements to convince the doubters.

Availability of resources

The resources involved in the improvement actions are different from the assessment teams. For example, those participating in the various software process improvement teams are mostly software engineers working on projects. The action plan should be sensitive to the business pressure on the projects to deliver results. In many situations unavailability of resources is the bottleneck that could inhibit the progress of the improvement plan.

Risk assessment

Inevitably there will be risks associated with the changes resulting from the improvement actions. Potential risks should be identified, assessed and evaluated. A risk mitigation strategy should be outlined for every major risk. The action plan should make this information available to the improvement projects.

9.1.2 CREATING AN ACTION PLAN FROM THE ASSESSMENT FINDINGS

Organizations should follow a structured approach to converting the software process assessment findings into an improvement action plan. There are a number of different approaches and methods that specify the steps to be followed to develop an action plan for software process improvement. Assessment findings should highlight the strengths and weaknesses of the current software process and its supporting infrastructure. These findings are

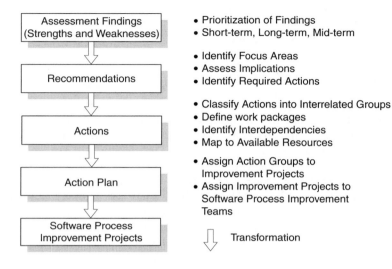

Figure 9.1 Transforming the assessment findings into process improvement projects

usually expressed in general terms that may not have all the details necessary for action planning. In most cases the assessment findings will require further analysis, review and consideration of resource availability and business priorities before arriving at a set of improvement actions. The improvement actions should be classified and grouped into work packages. Developing an improvement action plan out of the assessment findings could be achieved in a series of steps as follows:

1 Converting the assessment findings into recommendations.
2 Converting the recommendations into actions.
3 Grouping the actions into action plans/work packages.
4 Allocating the action plans to software process improvement teams.

Figure 9.1 illustrates the steps for converting the assessment findings into a process improvement action plan.

An assessment finding is the unit of analysis and is defined as 'an observation or collection of observations that have been accepted by the assessment team as valid. A finding includes strengths, weaknesses, evidence of alternative practices, and evidence of non-applicable practices. A set of findings should be accurate, corroborated, and consistent within itself' (Masters and Bothwell, 1995). Usually assessment findings are expressed in a brief way that may require further analysis and investigation to convert them into improvement actions. The following sections elaborate on the steps for converting the assessment findings into improvement action plans. For each step the following is discussed: why it is needed, who is involved, and how it is done. This is followed by practical examples to reinforce the concepts discussed.

9.1.3 CONVERTING ASSESSMENT FINDINGS INTO RECOMMENDATIONS

Why it is needed

- The assessment findings are usually expressed in general terms, which means that they may not be directly translatable into recommendations. In such cases they will require further analysis and review to come up with realistic recommendations.
- The assessment findings could cover a wider area of the organization beyond the software process. In some cases the findings relating to wider organizational issues are escalated to higher levels of management, and are virtually taken out of the software process improvement domain.
- Some of the assessment findings could be for future information only and may not necessarily be convertible into recommendations – for example, the need to create a new capability or to transfer to a new technology in the long term.

Who is involved

Usually the assessment team performs this task as the final step of the assessment. They could involve the sponsor, project managers or other resources as may seem relevant to the specific area of discussion.

How it is done

You should consider the following aspects for each of the major findings:

- What should be done about the weaknesses? Is the potential solution technical, people related or organizational? What are the business implications if nothing is done?
- What should be done about the strengths? Are they localized? How do we preserve the strengths? How do we spread the effective practices across the whole organization? How do we get the buy-in from other groups?
- What should be done about building and maintaining the organization's process infrastructure? One of the main goals of the process improvement plan should be to establish and maintain an effective software process infrastructure. If one of the findings concerns the lack of an effective infrastructure, the following aspects should be considered. What aspects of the infrastructure need to be improved (organizational or technical)? What are the interdependencies across the infrastructure components?
- What should be done about promoting process thinking and spreading process discipline? This is a cultural change that may involve other groups. The following aspects should be considered: what other groups should be involved in achieving this change? What additional management sponsor-

ship may we require for achieving this successfully? What time frame can this take, and how will it fit with the timeframe of other recommendations?

An example of an assessment finding

- The assessment team has uncovered inconsistency in applying the organizational standard for quality reviews across all projects.

This finding could be converted into the following recommendations:

- A management directive should be issued by senior management to all project managers stressing the importance of implementing quality reviews for all projects.
- Monitoring procedures with allocated responsibility should be established to monitor conformance with the quality review procedures.
- A procedure for escalating non-compliance should be defined, announced and put in place.

9.1.4   CONVERTING RECOMMENDATIONS INTO ACTIONS

Why it is needed

The recommendations are usually not specific enough. They are not expressed in such details as to enable identifying what actions should be taken and by whom. For example, 'It is recommended that a standard process should be defined at the corporate level'. The corresponding action could be 'A project team is to be set up with the responsibility of defining and establishing an organization's standard process. The project leader is ABC, and the project members will be selected from the following organizational units and projects.' The actions are more focused towards the solution, while recommendations are more focused towards the problem.

Who is involved

The assessment team role usually ceases after the assessment report has been prepared and passed to the sponsor and the software engineering process group (if it exists). The sponsor should form a task team that should review the assessment recommendations and convert them into actions. Membership of such a team could vary depending on the areas of recommendations. It could involve business managers, project managers, software engineers, project support personnel, and so on.

How it is done

You should consider the following aspects for each area of recommendations:

- What is the real goal behind this recommendation? What actions can be taken to achieve this goal?
- What are the consequences of implementing the recommendations? Are the consequences long term or short term? What are the consequences of not following these recommendations?
- What are the interdependencies between the recommendations? Is there a sequence in which they should be implemented?
- What are the steps necessary for achieving the recommendations? Can these steps translate into actions? Are the actions sequential?
- What level of effort is required for implementing the recommendations? What demand on the time of these resources do the actions require? Can the resource involvement be part-time or does it need full-time involvement?
- What is the availability of resources required to implement the recommendation? How can conflicts with project and business be resolved? What level of management authority is required to resolve such conflict?

An example of a recommendation

- Monitoring procedures with allocated responsibility should be established to enforce the quality review procedures.

This recommendation could be converted into the following actions:

- A task team (software PIT) will be formed to define the monitoring procedures. The following should be defined for every such team: team members with list of names; team leader with leader's name; operational budget for the task team; time scale for achieving the results; and management sponsor for the team.
- The task team will report the progress and results to the designated manager or to the software engineering progress group (SEPG).

9.1.5   GROUPING THE ACTIONS INTO ACTION PLANS OR WORK PACKAGES

Why it is needed

The actions resulting from the recommendations could be diverse. One recommendation could result in a number of actions with nothing in common except that they have the same goal. Some aspects could vary from one action to another, for example ownership, sponsorship, skills and knowledge required, time frame, coverage and impact. Because of these factors there is a need to assess the actions and group them into a number of action plans or work packages with consistent ownership, sponsorship and skill set.

Who is involved

The software engineering process group (SEPG) will ensure that this activity takes place and should facilitate it. A management steering group, or the equivalent of what is called in this book the Executive Improvement Team (EIT), should be involved in the grouping of the actions into action plans. They are the ones that should assume management responsibility and provide sponsorship for the resources that will implement these plans.

How it is done

You should classify the actions into interrelated groups according to chosen criteria. Candidate criteria for grouping the actions are:

- Boundaries of the process improvement actions, for example:
  - organizational level process improvement actions
  - project and team level process improvement actions
  - personal level process improvement actions
- Subject area of the improvement actions, for example actions relating to:
  - process technical infrastructure
  - process organizational roles and responsibilities
  - process redesign and improvement
  - process culture, awareness and training
- Priority; for example, prioritization could be decided on the basis of any of the following:
  - relevance to the business goals and pressure from customers
  - feasibility, impact, risk and urgency of the actions
  - complexity, resources, benefits and interdependencies
  - tactical versus strategic.

Other examples of criteria for grouping actions are:

- Actions relating to a specific key process area. For example, all actions for the requirements' management process are allocated to a 'Process Redesign Project'.
- Actions relating to the process infrastructure. For example, actions for creating an organization's process database, for selecting, acquiring and introducing a process modelling tool are allocated to a 'Software Process Infrastructure Project'.
- Actions relating to training. For example, actions for developing and introducing process training and lifecycle techniques training are allocated to a 'Process Training Project'.

An example of grouping actions into action plans/work packages

After an assessment of the effectiveness of a software process, the actions can be grouped into the following categories:

- *Action plan/work package for process coverage:* These cover actions for designing and launching some new processes.
- *Action plan/work package for the process infrastructure:* These cover actions for establishing some missing components of the process infrastructure, some missing roles and responsibilities, introducing some process tools, and so on.
- *Action plan/work package for the process awareness and process culture:* These cover actions for starting a corporate awareness campaign to emphasize the need for process discipline and its relevance to business success, and to illustrate top management sponsorship to process improvement activities.
- *Action plan/work package for the process enforcement:* These cover actions for establishing organizational policies and management procedures for enforcing the process discipline, and establishing the roles and responsibilities for monitoring process discipline and defining escalation procedures for resolving non-conformance issues.

9.1.6 ALLOCATING THE ACTION PLANS TO SOFTWARE PROCESS IMPROVEMENT TEAMS

Why it is needed

Action plans need to be converted into proper projects. A process improvement project should have a project manager, a project plan, activity schedules, milestones, project resources, and so on. This should bring a focus to the improvement actions and make them mainstream activities. The danger of leaving them afloat with no accountability or ownership is that they will get pushed down the priority scale under the pressure of ordinary business and project activities.

Who is involved

The software engineering process group (SEPG) should ensure that this activity takes place and should facilitate it. The software process improvement team leaders should be involved since they will take responsibility for the software process improvement projects. The SEPG should coordinate the different projects and synchronize them to form a coherent programme and resolve any conflicts.

How it is done

Every action plan or work package should be allocated to a software process improvement team (software PIT). Every software PIT should perform a number of actions along the following lines:

- Decompose the action plan or work package into discrete implementation tasks with defined deliverables
- Assign the implementation tasks to implementation resources with appropriate skills (organize training for missing skills if necessary)
- Organize the implementation tasks as a project plan with deliverables and milestones
- Treat the improvement project like any other software development project. Such a project should have a schedule, budget, resources, risk, quality management, interdependencies, and so on.

An example of software process improvement teams

In a particular software process improvement plan the following process improvement teams were formed: Requirements Management Process Team, Project Planning and Tracking Process Team, Software Quality Assurance Process Team, and Software Configuration Management Process Team. For every team the following were defined: team leader, team members, management sponsor (member of the Executive Improvement Team), timescale and budget. In order to ensure consistency the teams were asked to follow a common format for process design and documentation. Process design covered the following: Purpose, Goals, Activities, Commitment Policy Statements, Abilities and Training, Measurements, Verification, and Feedback Form. Sometimes there could be improvement actions across the key process areas, for example those actions concerned with the process culture and process infrastructure. Separate process improvement teams were formed to own these actions. Examples of these teams in one of the process improvement programmes included a team for process training and awareness, a team for process support infrastructure, a team for process competency recognition and awards, and a team for process culture campaign.

9.2   ALLOCATING RESPONSIBILITIES

FOR IMPLEMENTING SPI ACTIONS

Often software process improvement is not a part-time job for members of the SEPG. It may require many full-time individuals, depending on the size and complexity of the organization. It is of critical importance that a conscious effort should be made to define the roles required to drive and sustain software process improvement effort across the organization and in the projects, and to allocate these roles to competent individuals, training them if and as necessary. Training may be expensive, but not as expensive as not training. In this section we investigate what roles and responsibilities should exist to drive and sustain a software process improvement programme.

Roles for software process improvement implementation can be classified in one of these categories:

- sponsorship roles
- management roles
- coordination roles
- process improvement roles.

These categories can be mapped onto the roles identified in Chapter 6 for the software process improvement roles and change enablers.

The main roles directly involved in software process improvement are:

- Executive sponsor
- Executive Improvement Team (EIT) (or Steering Committee)
- Software engineering process group (SEPG)
- Software PITs (sometimes called action teams or task teams (TTs))
- Software PIT team leaders (with the overall responsibility for a specific group of software process improvement actions)
- Software process owners
- Software process improvement implementation manager (the overall programme manager for software process improvement implementation).

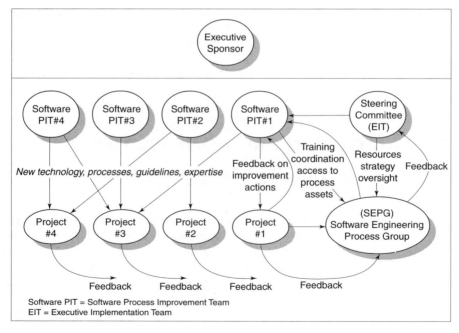

Figure 9.2 Main roles and responsibilities involved in software process improvement

Figure 9.2 illustrates the software process improvement roles and responsibilities. Many of these roles are new to software engineers and project managers. To ensure the success of achieving the objective of each of these roles, you need to perform the following actions:

- define the terms of reference for each role
- define the boundaries of the authority and responsibility for each role
- allocate the software process improvement implementation actions to the people fulfilling such roles.

Different organizations may use different names for such roles. Reed (1996) provides an example of the roles for implementing process improvement after assessment. He uses the terminology Task Working Group (TWG) to refer to what we call Software PIT, and Management Steering Group (MSG) to refer to what we call Executive Improvement Team (EIT).

Table 9.1 summarizes the process improvement responsibilities of the software process roles.

Table 9.1   Summary of software process improvement roles and responsibilities

Role	Main responsibilities
Executive sponsor	• Providing top management credibility and support for the software process improvement programme • Relating the software process improvement effort to the overall business vision and strategy • Communicating the software process improvement actions
Executive improvement team (EIT)	• Monitoring the progress of software process improvement activities • Supporting the SEPG and the software PITs • Ensuring the necessary resources for software process improvement are available in a timely manner • Forming the SEPG and establishing its terms of reference and responsibilities • Establishing the software PITs and populating them by software engineers and technical professionals • Removing any blocking factors that may prohibit the progress of software process improvement actions • Overseeing the activities of the SEPG and the software PITs • Reviewing and assessing the business benefits of software process improvement

(continued)

Table 9.1 (*continued*)

Role	Main responsibilities
Software engineering process group (SEPG)	• Coordinating the overall implementation of the software process improvement action plan • Dividing the software process improvement actions into implementation projects • Forming software PITs to implement the software process improvement projects, and facilitating their work • Appointing team leaders for the software PITs • Acting as the focal point for all software process improvement activities across the whole organization • Facilitating the improvement effort across all the software PITs • Facilitating the establishment of the process support infrastructure (both organizational and technical) at all levels: corporate, project and individual • Maintaining the organization's standard software process assets • Reviewing the progress of all the software process improvement activities across all software PITs and reporting back to the EIT • Establishing and monitoring the feedback mechanisms, definition of the process metrics, initiating the collection and analysis of software process metrics, and using these to improve the processes • Promoting process awareness and process thinking across the organization • Providing consultancy on the software process methods and techniques • Monitoring the business benefits of software process improvement across all the projects
Software process improvement teams (software PITs)	• Assuming the overall responsibility for one or more software process improvement projects (a collection of software process improvement actions that relate to a specific process area) • The software process improvement projects may include developing software process definitions (process redesign), developing standards and procedures, evaluating and suggesting technologies for specific processes, and so on • Reporting progress of software process improvement actions to the SEPG and the EIT, and reporting any problems that they may face in implementing software process improvement actions • Identifying the training necessary to successfully implement software process improvement activities and developing training plans for process and methods training

9.3 GUIDANCE FOR ACTION PLANNING (GAP) – AN EXAMPLE OF AN ACTION PLANNING METHOD

9.3.1. BACKGROUND

Guidance for Action Planning (GAP) has been developed by the ISPI (Institute for Software Process Improvement) and is summarized here as an example of an action planning method. According to ISPI literature, GAP addresses 'the transition between the assessment and the actual planning of the improvement programme' (ISPI, 1995). It fills the gap and reduces the time between the assessment and the action plan.

GAP is meant to help organizations prioritize the activities or actions that they want to take and provide a starting point for those who will create the action plans. The output of GAP is a planning roadmap that is input directly to the process improvement action plan. Table 9.2 summarizes the main outputs of the GAP method (ISPI, 1995). The latest information on GAP should be available from ISPI (address provided in the References list).

Table 9.2   GAP output – planning roadmap

Step no.	Main task	Main output
1	Goals	Vision/purpose/scope of improvement activity
2	Expectations	Benefits/measures of success – what results can managers and practitioners expect to see?
3	Improvement tasks	Major activities to be performed
4	Dependency flowchart	Graph of interrelationships within and across focus area improvement tasks
5	Early achievements	Significant accomplishments that can be achieved in near-term to show value of, and to maintain commitment for, the PI effort to ensure: • management willingness to provide scarce resources • practitioners' willingness to bear added burdens

(continued)

Table 9.2 (*continued*)

Step no.	Main task	Main output
6	Involvement/ level of effort	Who, by name or by function, needs to be part of the improvement activity and how much time they would be expected to contribute
7	Technology transfer	Preparation, resources, and so on that will improve the probability of successful implementation of a new process
8	Dependencies/ risks/ constraints	Those factors outside the PI programme that will impact on it, for example existing improvement activities, organization restructuring, business environment
9	Timetable/ schedule	A rough/preliminary estimate of what the improvement effort might be expected to achieve given the availability of the 'right' people at the indicated levels of effort: • short term activities (9 months) • medium term (18 months) • long term goals (2–3 years)

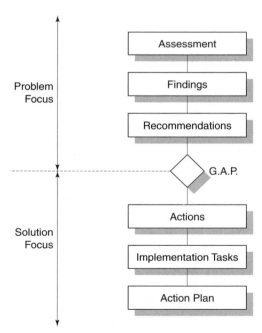

Figure 9.3 Moving from Problem Focus of the Assessment to Solution Focus of the Action Plan

9.3.2. JUSTIFICATION

Moving from assessment to improvement planning and implementation is often difficult for many organizations due to one or more of the following factors:

- Management expectations are not properly set for the time and effort required to create an action plan
- Management involvement is not at the right level
- Trying to address too many problems at once
- Lack of skills or training of software improvement teams for their new roles.

GAP provides guidelines on how the software process improvement teams should be established and trained, how the improvement tasks should be planned, and what tasks should be performed to develop, pilot and institutionalize processes. Figure 9.3 illustrates how GAP translates the problem focus of the assessment into a solution focus for planning and implementation.

SUMMARY

Assessment is a starting point and not an end

Assessment should lead to an action plan for implementing software process improvement. Once the action plan has been implemented, mechanisms should be put in place in order to achieve the process institutionalization. This means that the process discipline becomes embedded into the organization's software practices. In this chapter we discussed the different stages of implementing software process improvement.

Convert the assessment findings to process improvement projects

The assessment findings themselves are not an action plan as such. They are too general and can cover an area wider than the software process. You should perform further review and analysis to convert these findings into recommendations, and further to convert the recommendations into actions, action plans/work packages, and improvement projects to be assigned to process improvement teams with full responsibility for the projects.

Roles and responsibilities are the enablers for software process improvement

Process improvement is not about producing shelfware, rather it is about commitment and improved process discipline. The process discipline will be ensured as continuous process improvement is achieved. This can only happen if there is ownership of process improvement actions, and if these actions are assigned to specific roles and responsibilities, for example a management executive improvement team (EIT) and process improvement teams (PITs). These roles and responsibilities should be supported by organizational policies and procedures to enforce and support the process improvement activities.

PART 3

Making software process improvement happen

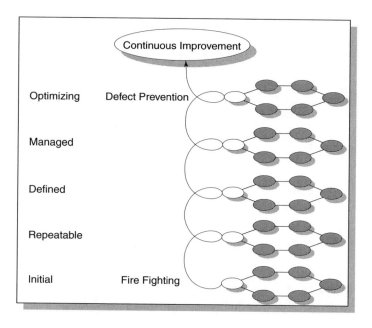

This part describes the steps and techniques for successfully implementing software process improvement. These cover launching software process improvement in the organization, implementing the improvement action plan, and finally monitoring the process performance and measuring the business benefits. It summarizes a number of approaches that could help organizations successfully plan and implement software process improvement.

CHAPTER 10

Launching software process improvement

10.1 STAGES FOR MAKING SOFTWARE PROCESS IMPROVEMENT HAPPEN

The approach we suggest for making software process improvement happen entails five stages:

- *Launching:* Concerned with introducing the concept of software process improvement to managers and technical staff and convincing them of the benefits of improving the software process. This is essential for setting the software process improvement effort on the right track.
- *Implementing:* Concerned with adopting a strategy for software process improvement, conducting the assessment, and implementing the action plan resulting from the assessment.
- *Institutionalizing:* Concerned with ensuring that software process improvement is continuous and is embedded in the organization's culture.
- *Measuring:* Concerned with measuring the benefits and ensuring the alignment between the software process activities and the business goals.
- *Improving:* Concerned with assessing the measurements resulting from the 'measuring' stage, and devising plans to improve the process in order to enhance the benefits of the process discipline and preserve the alignment between the software process and the business goals.

These stages are illustrated in Figure 10.1 and further discussed in the rest of this chapter.

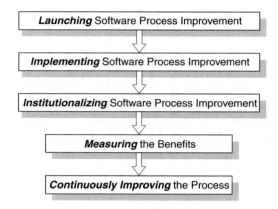

Figure 10.1   Stages for making software process improvement happen

10.2   LAUNCHING SOFTWARE PROCESS IMPROVEMENT

10.2.1   VISION, STRATEGY, ALIGNMENT, MOTIVATION AND IMPLEMENTATION (VSAMI)

Most successful change programmes pass through the five phases of Vision, Strategy, Alignment, Motivation and Implementation. These phases make a commonsense scenario as follows:

- *The vision phase:*   Vision sets the future direction and points the way forward. It takes into consideration future developments and expected changes in technology, economy, politics, the marketplace and the business segment.
- *The strategy phase:*   Strategy draws the roadmap towards the vision, and the practical steps necessary for achieving that vision.
- *The alignment phase:*   Alignment mobilizes the current workforce and resources for working out and implementing tactical and operational plans for implementing the strategy.
- *The motivation phase:*   Motivation keeps the momentum, monitors the success of the strategy, and enforces the alignment.
- *The implementation phase:*   Implementation makes the strategy a reality, otherwise it will be no more than wishful thinking. Many change programmes fall through at the implementation phase. It is at this phase that all the management of change skills should be utilized.

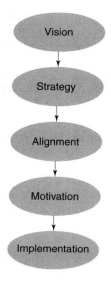

Figure 10.2 Main steps for change programmes

Software process improvement, being a change programme itself, should follow similar phases to those mentioned above. These phases are illustrated in Figure 10.2 and are further discussed below.

10.2.2 CREATING A VISION

In most organizations, senior management has a vision for the business. If this is not the case, then a 'visioning' exercise may be necessary to create such a vision. A vision is important since it paints a picture of the future and points to the future direction that the business should take. It is important that the senior management vision for the business is passed down the organization to be the driver of business strategies and change programmes. Software process improvement is in essence a change programme, and must be tuned and aligned to the management vision of the business. Misalignment between the business vision and the objectives of the software process improvement programme will incur several risks.

A vision for a software process improvement programme should be created in support of the business vision. An example of a business vision could be 'to gain market leadership by diversifying the product range through mergers and acquisitions'. A corresponding vision for the software process improvement programme could be 'to create a flexible and adaptable software process that will cater for different product ranges, and will accommodate methods and techniques that may come through the acquired organizations'.

A software process improvement vision should relate to the business vision, not directly but probably through a vision for the role of software in the business. A software process improvement programme could easily be interrupted or cancelled if the business unexpectedly changes direction in such a way as to jeopardize the business benefits of software process improvement. Senior management must communicate their vision down the organizational hierarchy in such a way that everyone in the organization can understand how their daily tasks can support that vision. An SPI vision must clearly reflect how the SPI effort will support the business vision. There are some approaches and techniques that could facilitate 'vision design' and initiate 'vision thinking', for example asking senior management questions about the shape of their business in the future, and how this relates to the possible shape of the market, the competition, the political and economic climate, and so on. Without a vision a company will be walking in the dark, often in a reactive 'fire-fighting' mode.

10.2.3 DEFINING A STRATEGY

Once you have a vision for the business, the next step is to devise workable strategies for achieving that vision. There could be more than one way of achieving the vision, hence there could be alternative strategies. The choice between these strategies would normally be dictated by the realities in the organization. This could impact on the availability of resources, the degree of change that the organization can sustain, and so on.

A similar scenario could be true for software process improvement. Once you have created a vision for SPI you could then define the strategy for achieving that vision. The strategy considers the real situation in terms of what is feasible and what is not feasible. A vision is usually long term, while a strategy could be defining the route via short term, mid term, and long term phases towards achieving that vision. Figure 10.3 illustrates a possible scenario relating software process improvement vision to the business vision.

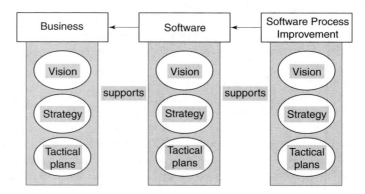

Figure 10.3 Software process improvement should be aligned with the business vision and strategy

An essential element in the strategy should be how to secure senior management commitment to the SPI effort. Senior management sponsorship is critical for the success of process improvement. Such sponsorship should be visible and should be re-emphasized frequently in order to show the right level of commitment. Sponsorship must cascade down through the management levels to the practitioners, and this should continue throughout the SPI programme. Commitment should be secured, not only from management, but also from all stakeholders. Stakeholders are individuals who have interest in the success of the SPI programme. Examples of SPI stakeholders are the quality manager, the systems engineering manager, and business manager.

10.2.4 ALIGNMENT WITH THE BUSINESS

For a software process improvement programme to be successful (in supporting the business) it must be aligned with the organization's business objectives. It should reflect the priorities of, and interdependencies between, the business objectives. Also an SPI programme should fit within the overall business context. It should be sensitive to business constraints and ability to accommodate change. This requires an understanding of the business and organizational context. Let us look at what we mean by organizational context.

In the general sense a context is defined as the set of all social and technical aspects of an environment. It includes everything that surrounds the organization in which software process improvement will be implemented. Understanding the organizational context is of paramount importance for the success of a software process improvement programme. Viewing organizations like living organisms, they perform functions and have organizational 'organs' to perform those functions. Introducing a new process is like transplanting a new organ into the organization. If the new process does not match the organization culture, it will be rejected by the 'organizational' body.

10.2.5 IMPLEMENTATION PLANNING TO MATCH THE

ORGANIZATIONAL CONTEXT

Implementation planning is the most critical activity for succeeding with software process improvement. The implementation plan should be in alignment with the current organization. There are many benefits of understanding and analysing the organizational context before starting the implementation of software process improvement. It can help to achieve the following:

- Clarify potential sources of support for and against the proposed changes
- Identify potential champions for change (change agents)
- Align the pace of introducing the changes with the organization's readiness to accept change

- Devise a strategy for long-term goals, ongoing change and continuous process improvement.

Generally an organizational context has many facets. Some of these may not necessarily be relevant to software process improvement. In order to facilitate understanding and analysis of the organizational context of software process improvement, a number of levels of the organizational context should be considered before introducing changes to the software processes and practices (see Figure 10.4). Within each of these levels there are a number of focus areas that should be considered when planning an SPI programme, as follows:

Corporate and organizational context

- *Financial status and budgeting practices:*   For example, is the organization able to sustain investment in SPI? What level of management authorization is necessary to authorize SPI budget?
- *Economic and business conditions:*   This should indicate whether the organization is in a survival mode. Does the organization have higher business priorities? Is the organization in a growth phase? Is the SPI considered strategic for that growth?
- *The corporate organizational structure:*   This should indicate how the software engineering groups would best fit within the overall organization, for example centralized, decentralized, distributed, full-time, contractors, or part time. This also should give an indicator of the number of levels required for process monitoring and control.
- *The geographical spread of the software engineering groups:*   This should give an indication of the travel effort for the software assessment activities, the influence and diversity of local culture, and the degree of coordination necessary across the sites.
- *The extended enterprise (customers, partners and suppliers):*   This should indicate whether there are standards restrictions imposed by the customers, or imposed on suppliers, plus any requirements for interoperability of applications across the organization and its customers and/or suppliers.

Figure 10.4   Levels of organizational context for software process improvement

- *The corporate culture:* This should indicate whether there is a common corporate culture, any conflicts with local culture, and acceptability of change.

Departmental or project or team context

- *Managerial style:* This indicates whether the management is too autocratic to accept changes to the existing culture.
- *Reward system:* This should indicate how rewards for software process improvement can fit in as part of the rewards policy.
- *Technological environment (hardware and software):* This should reveal the details of software development platforms, CASE tools, and hardware facilities available for the software engineers.
- *Network and system software infrastructure:* This indicates the degree of connectivity across the software engineering groups, and the availability of workgroup facilities that connect the software engineering groups together.
- *Development standards:* This should indicate standards used across the development department or within a specific project.
- *Prevailing development methodologies:* This should indicate software development lifecycle, development methods and techniques used across a department or by a specific project.
- *Software engineering tools:* This should indicate tools recommended as corporate standard and used across the department or within a specific project.

Personal or individual software engineers context

- *Homogeneity of staff:* This should indicate the degree of commonality of experience and background and compatibility of professional practices.
- *Education and training of software engineers:* This should indicate how up-to-date the training is and how comprehensive its coverage.
- *Experience and knowledge of software engineers:* This should indicate how knowledgeable they are in the software process, in modern software engineering methodologies, and so on.
- *Acceptability of change:* This should indicate the staff and management reaction to the last change programme in terms of the degree of acceptance or resistance.
- *Process awareness:* This should indicate whether any process training has been organized for software engineers, what level of process discipline is in place, what degree of management commitment to process discipline, and so on.

Analysing the organizational, social, economic and technical contexts of software development is necessary for developing the most appropriate strategy and realistic plans for implementing the software process improvement activities. It helps identify the dominant frames of reference that need to be addressed directly in the process improvement plan. Planning for introducing changes to current processes or introducing new processes resembles planning for a surgical or an organ-transplant operation. The surgeon has to analyse the physical conditions and state of the patient's body and prepare it before the transplant, otherwise the body could reject the transplanted organ. Similarly if the new process or process changes are not sensitive to the organizational context, the new improvements could be rejected through the focus of inertia and resistance to change by both management and staff. The pace of introducing the new changes should match the willingness of the organization to accept the change. The management of change issues will be discussed further in the next chapter.

Some organizational, social and technical aspects within the organization fall outside the realm of software process improvement but may have to be considered in planning for implementing process changes. For example, corporate-wide constraints that cannot be changed locally could have a strong influence on the local implementation of the software process improvement plan.

10.3 ADOPTING A SOFTWARE PROCESS IMPROVEMENT MODEL

10.3.1 DEFINING THE BOUNDARIES FOR SOFTWARE PROCESS IMPROVEMENT

Software process improvement should be aligned with the business strategy, and should be targeted to implement and achieve the business goals and management objectives. An ideal scenario is that the software process improvement activities cover the whole corporation. Usually the target boundaries for software process improvement vary in terms of organizational boundaries and/or process boundaries.

The following question helps define the organizational boundaries of software process improvement: 'Does the software process improvement effort aim to improve the software process throughout the whole corporation, within one division, or for one project?'

For process boundaries the question could be: 'What critical processes should be the focus of our software process improvement effort?'

Having a clear definition of both the organizational and process boundaries for the software process improvement effort will help achieve the following:

- Identifying the stakeholders at an early stage
- Focusing the effort and plans for software process improvement on target improvement areas and target audience
- Identifying the level of management sponsorship and leadership required to support the software process improvement effort
- Identifying the roles and responsibilities necessary to sustain the activities of software process improvement
- Identifying the implications of introducing the change, thus helping to develop the most appropriate strategy for managing the change.

10.3.2 NEED FOR AN IMPLEMENTATION MODEL FOR SOFTWARE PROCESS IMPROVEMENT

An implementation model for software process improvement could serve as a generic step-by-step guide to defining an SPI programme. Ideally such a guide should cover enough detail and specify milestones to help you answer the following questions:

- How to prepare a business justification for investing in software process improvement. Such a justification could be used to monitor alignment between the software process improvement and the business goals.
- How to gain commitment and sponsorship from senior management. Such sponsorship should ensure the continuing provision of budgets and resources to the software process improvement activities.
- How to launch a software process improvement programme in your organization. Such a programme should take into consideration the organization culture and acceptability of change.
- How to get buy-in for software process improvement from software engineers, project managers and middle managers.
- What are the components of the overall plan for the software process improvement programme? Does it specify software process infrastructure, software process improvement roadmap, software process assessment, and a process improvement action plan?
- What are the roles and responsibilities required to support the software process improvement activities?
- How is a software engineering process group (SEPG) formed? How are software process improvement teams (software PITs) formed?
- How are the changes introduced by software process improvement managed? How is software process improvement institutionalized in the organization?

An example of an implementation model for software process improvement is the framework approach developed by the software engineering institute (SEI) referred to as the IDEAL approach. It is summarized in the following chapter.

10.4 HUMPHREY'S PROCESS CHANGE REQUIREMENTS

Watts Humphrey suggests a set of requirements for software process change (Humphrey, 1989). The following is a summary of these requirements supported by discussions and comments relating them to practical experiences.

10.4.1 SELL TO TOP MANAGEMENT

Management support is essential for the success of any major change programme. Software process improvement results in changes and its implementation is essentially a change programme. It requires top management support if it is to succeed. Software process improvement implementation requires new priorities, additional resources and consistent support. Senior management will not provide such backing unless they are convinced that the improvement programme makes sense in the business context. The approach we advocate for achieving this is through alignment of the software process improvement vision and strategy with the business vision and strategy. Monitoring and reporting the business benefits resulting from software process improvement should prove the effectiveness of investing in SPI. Many SPI programmes have been doomed to failure once the executive sponsor left the organization or changed job.

10.4.2 GET TECHNICAL SUPPORT

Ultimately the changes brought about by a software process improvement programme will affect the professional practices followed by the technical staff and software engineers. Their support for software process improvement is essential for the new changes to be effective. One effective way to achieve such support is through the technical opinion leaders. These are the few technical professionals whose opinions are widely respected. They should be convinced first that the proposed improvements address their key concerns, then they will generally convince the others. The approach we advocate for achieving this is through involving technical staff in software process improvement activities through software process improvement teams (software PITs). These teams will drive the implementation of all process improvement activities under the guidance and coordination of the software engineering process group. Without the support of the technical staff and software engineers, the software process improvement actions are not likely to be carried out. The recent focus on the personal software process (PSP) is a good vehicle to get the buy-in from software engineers to process improvement effort.

10.4.3 INVOLVE ALL MANAGEMENT LEVELS

Project managers and middle managers usually have delivery schedules and commitments that take top priority. Many of them would consider software process improvement activities a divergence from their delivery targets. They may refuse to release their technical staff to participate in software process improvement activities. Lack of middle managers' commitment and involvement could threaten the software process improvement programme. When they do not support the SPI plan, their priorities will not be adjusted, and progress will be painfully slow or non-existent. Support from all management levels is necessary if you are serious about establishing a process focus throughout.

10.4.4 ESTABLISH AN AGGRESSIVE STRATEGY AND A

CONSERVATIVE PLAN

A strategy reflects a long term vision. It may demand higher levels of resources than are currently available. In the meantime, an implementation plan should be realistic and should match the current levels of resources. An aggressive and ambitious strategy may attract senior managers, but middle managers will be attracted to a realistic plan that they know how to implement. It is thus essential for a software process improvement programme to be aggressive at the strategy level and realistic at the implementation planning level. The strategy sets the direction and strategic goals, but the plan provides frequent achievable steps toward the strategic goals. Striking a balance between strategy and tactics could prove a critical factor for the success of the SPI programme.

10.4.5 STAY AWARE OF THE CURRENT SITUATION

Being divorced from reality is a recipe for failure of software process improvement. It is essential that the software process improvement plan is based on an assessment of the current situation, and stays in touch with reality. This is because changes are inevitable and continuous, and solutions to outdated problems may no longer be pertinent. While important changes take time, the plan must keep pace with current needs. Even if the SPI programme starts in perfect alignment with the business goals, unless it is continuously re-aligned to match changes in the business goals and objectives, it could lose its effectiveness.

10.4.6 KEEP PROGRESS VISIBLE

Any change programme could fail because of lack of motivation. In order to keep the level of interest and motivation high, you should publicize and celebrate successes of software process improvement. Make the evidence of progress visible in order to broaden the buy-in and support for software process improvement. Organize forums and events that will bring together members of the software process improvement teams, software engineering process groups, software engineering teams, project managers and business managers. Advertise success, periodically reward the key contributors, and maintain enthusiasm and excitement. These activities will broaden the interest and encourage involvement in SPI. A dangerous sign of an SPI programme is when its activities are restricted to a small team in a locked room while no-one is aware of the SPI activities.

10.5 INGREDIENTS FOR SUCCESSFUL SOFTWARE PROCESS IMPROVEMENT

Success with software process improvement requires senior management vision, middle management commitment, staff enthusiasm and alignment with business goals. Careful consideration and planning of critical success factors for the software process improvement effort are very important.

The following lists summarize a number of critical factors (CSFs) which represent essential ingredients for successful implementation of software process improvement. Each factor is followed by a number of suggested actions. These could be used as a checklist when planning a programme for software process improvement.

CSFI: Alignment with the business strategy and goals

- Create a vision for SPI in support of the business vision.
- Create a strategy for SPI to realize the vision, and help achieve the business goals.
- Preserve the alignment between the SPI effort and the business goals.

CSF2: Consensus and buy-in from all stakeholders

- Organize awareness events.
- Promote process thinking.
- Enlist the support of process champions (evangelists).

CSF3: Senior and middle management support

- Secure executive sponsorship, to provide support, budget, vision, motivation and sponsorship, and to sell SPI at senior management level (for example, board of executives).
- Gain management commitment, to release staff for SEPG and software PIT activities, and to participate in the executive improvement team (EIT) steering committee.
- Form an Executive Implementation Team (EIT) which comprises a group of senior and middle managers to oversee software process improvement.

CSF4: Dedicated resource to manage the implementation and coordinate the process improvement activities

- Form a software engineering process group (SEPG).
- Define terms of reference for the SEPG.
- Specify the role and terms of reference for the software engineering group.
- Form as many software process improvement teams (software PITs) as necessary.
- Monitor the progress of the software PITs.

CSF5: Sensitivity to the organizational context

- Avoid imposing an alien process, not aligned with the business strategy.
- Resolve conflicts between day-to-day activities and process improvement tasks.
- Promote what benefits the software professionals would get out of the SPI success, and try to sell the benefits.

CSF6: Management of change

- Plan the implementation of software process improvement as a proper change programme. Use the services of a change management expert at the planning stage.
- Gain support for software process improvement through the stages of vision, strategy, alignment, motivation and implementation.
- Identify potential risks and roadblocks and plan an avoidance strategy. (Examples of potential roadblocks are resistance to change, failure to support business goals, lack of management commitment, and lack of staff buy-in.)

CSF7: Prioritization of actions

- Prioritize actions. Do not try to do too much at the same time, especially if you do not have adequate resources dedicated to SPI implementation.
- Possible criteria for prioritization could be impact, urgency, interdependencies, benefits, resources, risks, complexity and coverage.
- Differentiate between tactical and strategic actions (for example, tactical is one year, strategic is 3–5 years).

CSF8: Creation of the support infrastructure

- Define the infrastructure required to support software process improvement efforts.
- Gain management sponsorship for creating and maintaining the process support infrastructure.
- Create the software process improvement support infrastructure, including organizational and management as well as technology and tools infrastructure.

CSF9: Monitoring the results of software process improvement

- Define the critical performance indicators which need to be monitored to ensure that the process performance is on track.
- Establish and enable process monitoring and feedback mechanisms.
- Use the feedback data to establish the business value of software process improvement and to keep the momentum.

CSF10: Learning from the feedback results

- Analyse the feedback results and extract the main lessons learned.
- Take into consideration the lessons learned when planning the next cycle of software process improvement.
- Make software process improvement part of the organization's culture.

The points discussed above are not exhaustive but are useful as a checklist. Before starting a programme for software process improvement, you should do the following:

- Compile a similar list of critical success factors and potential blocking factors
- Use the critical success factors and the list of blocking factors as an input to your software process improvement plan. This should enhance the chances of success.

SUMMARY

Selling the benefits

Launching software process improvement is an important step for putting the software process improvement programme on the right path. It should start with selling the benefits and gathering the support and commitment of senior management, middle management and technical staff.

Vision and strategy

Devise a vision and strategy for software process improvement in support of the business vision and strategy. Follow a general approach that covers the steps of Vision, Strategy, Alignment, Motivation and Implementation.

Business and organizational context

Understand the business and organizational context. Such understanding should make your plan compatible with the organization's culture and enhance acceptability of change.

Define software process improvement boundaries

Defining the boundaries for your software process improvement effort should help you identify the stakeholders and enlist their help, focus on the target business areas, better utilization of the SPI resources, and so on. Both organizational boundaries and process boundaries should be defined.

Adopt an implementation model

Adopt a software process improvement implementation model as a basis for your software process improvement programme. The model should match your organization's specific requirements.

Critical success factors

Think of the critical success factors and potential roadblocks in the context of your business and organization and devise an avoidance strategy as part of your software process improvement plan. Revisit the ingredients for success and Watts Humphrey's process change requirements.

CHAPTER II

Implementing and institutionalizing software process improvement

II.I IMPLEMENTATION AND INSTITUTIONALIZATION PHASES

This chapter discusses two phases of the cycle for making software process improvement happen: the implementing phase and the institutionalizing phase. To start the implementation phase, the assumption is that:

- launch and planning for software process improvement have been completed (as described in the previous chapter), and
- software process assessment has been completed and resulted in recommendations for improvement.

Generally the implementation phase starts after the assessment with the objective of implementing the assessment recommendations for improvement. The general flow of implementation activities is described in the following paragraphs.

II.I.I CREATING A SOFTWARE PROCESS IMPROVEMENT ACTION PLAN

This involves using the recommendations resulting from the assessment as the basis for working out an action plan to implement the recommendations of the assessment. This chapter describes a number of approaches to action planning.

11.1.2 ALLOCATING RESPONSIBILITIES FOR SPI

The action plan should be the basis for defining and starting a software process improvement project, or number of projects. These are different from the conventional software engineering projects, and there may very well be a need for new roles and responsibilities to implement the software process improvement actions. This chapter summarizes the roles and responsibilities that should be established to support the implementation of the software process improvement activities. Although it is recommended to get almost everyone in the organization involved in software process improvement one way or the other, defining the roles and responsibilities will encourage and persuade management and technical staff to participate.

11.1.3 IMPLEMENTING SPI ACTIONS

Those involved in the implementation of software process improvement actions will have to perform some activities that may be different from conventional software engineering (for example process redesign, process infrastructure specification and so on). This chapter provides examples of actions that the software process improvement action plan may cover.

11.1.4 INSTITUTIONALIZING SPI

Once the first cycle of software process improvement has been completed, there will be a need to repeat the whole exercise regularly. The second, and following, cycles of software process improvement should be easier than the first, since the process thinking and process discipline should be common across technical staff and managers.

Figure 11.1 illustrates these stages and the following sections discuss them in more detail.

11.2 PRINCIPLES FOR IMPLEMENTING AND INSTITUTIONALIZING SPI

SPI implementation is about introducing and managing change

- You need a change model and a plan to make change happen.
- People resist change, so identify potential sources of resistance.
- People change behaviourally, intellectually and emotionally.
- Managing change is key to effective process improvement.

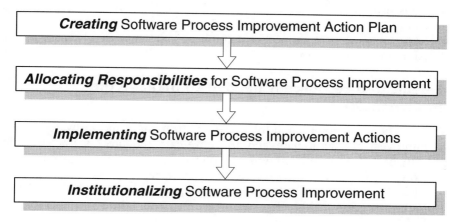

Figure 11.1 Stages of implementing and institutionalizing software process improvement

Software process improvement is not a destination, it is a journey

- Software process improvement should not be a one-off exercise. Rather it should be a continuous effort that is practised by everyone involved in software development activities.
- Chaotic forces will continuously try to degrade the process. Once you stop improving the process, it will deteriorate.
- Organizational structure should be established to sustain the process improvement effort.

Start with an assessment

- Improvement actions should be based on the status of the current processes. This is revealed by the assessment.
- Assessment should be sensitive to the current organizational context.
- Assessment is not an end in itself, it is a catalyst for change.
- Assessment will do more harm than good if it is not followed by an action plan.

Process behaviour needs to be embedded into the organization

- Ultimately, it is people's behaviour that we want to change to improve the process.
- Roles, responsibilities and ownership are the mechanisms that embed process behaviour into the organization.

- Consensus and buy-in from stakeholders is vital for creating process culture.
- Senior management support, commitment and active involvement are of paramount importance.

A dedicated resource is needed to manage the implementation

- You should appoint a full-time resource to manage the software process improvement action plan and to coordinate the process improvement activities. This is in addition to software process improvement teams (software PITs) who will execute the improvement actions.
- This is necessary to ensure ownership and accountability of the implementation action plan (such resource could be a member of the SEPG).

Management sponsorship and staff commitment are vital

- Software process improvement activities cost time and resources. Without management sponsorship, project managers and technical staff will be inclined to be busy performing their daily activities with no time to spare for improvement activities.
- You should create management roles and responsibilities to ensure continuing management commitment and involvement, and to resolve any conflict between day-to-day activities and improvement activities.
- Examples of management roles are the sponsor and the executive improvement team (EIT).

11.3 IMPLEMENTING SPI ACTIONS AND MANAGING THE CHANGE

11.3.1 PROCESS IMPROVEMENT ACTIONS

What would a software PIT be doing? What process improvement tasks could the software PIT be performing within a software process improvement project? An important task for the software process improvement actions could take the form of a redesign or improvement of current processes, design of new processes, or design or improvement of the process environment. The ultimate objective of software process improvement effort is to create a process infrastructure and a process culture, so that process thinking and process behaviour become a natural way of doing things (performing the business).

The process improvement tasks are grouped into software process improvement projects allocated to the relevant software process improvement teams (software PITs). A software PIT takes the responsibility of one or more software process improvement project, and implements the software process improvement actions. The following is a discussion of some of the main types of improvement actions that a software PIT could find themselves responsible for.

11.3.2 PROCESS DESIGN/REDESIGN

It is always useful and helpful for a software PIT, when faced with a process design or redesign task, to follow a model for process design (which specifies all the components that a process definition should include). The literature discussing process modelling describes a number of process models. An approach that I have found most useful and have used in the design or redesign of software processes is the one developed by the SEI as a template for interpreting the CMM key process areas and described in Paulk *et al.* (1993b). The process template identifies the components of a key process area shown in Figure 11.2. It starts with the purpose and goals followed by five common features: Activities Performed (Activities), Commitment to Perform (Commitment), Ability to Perform (Abilities), Measurement and Analysis (Measurement) and Verifying Information (Verification). Common features comprise a set of practices which contribute to achieving the process goals.

The practices in the 'Activities Performed' common feature describe what must be implemented to establish a process capability. The other practices taken as a whole form the basis by which an organization can institutionalize the practices described in the Activities Performed common feature.

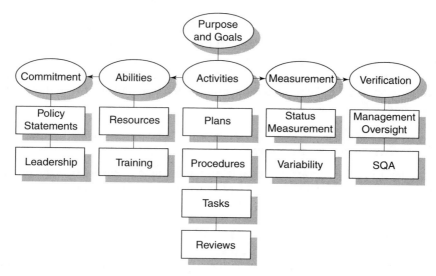

Figure 11.2 The SEI template for key process area design specification

The SEI template for process design is one of the most comprehensive models for process design. In most process literature the process definitions focus on the activities. They ignore other important aspects such as those included in the CMM process 'institutionalization' common feature. Components of the SEI template for key process areas are defined as follows (Paulk *et al.*, 1995).

Goals

Following a statement of the purpose of the key process area, a list of goals should summarize the key practices of a key process area that can be used to determine whether an organization or project has effectively implemented the key process area. The goals signify the scope, boundaries and intent of each key process area. Discussion of the process goals could address questions such as: How does the process contribute to achieving the business and/or the project goals? How can we measure and manage the process performance? How can we align the process goals in support of the project and business goals? How can we enhance the coverage and scope of the process (for example to make it an end-to-end process)? For the goals to be effective they should satisfy the SMART criteria (S = specific, M = measureable, A = attainable, R = relevant, T = traceable).

Activities performed

This describes the activities, roles and procedures necessary to implement a key process area. They typically involve establishing plans and procedures, performing the work, tracking it, and taking corrective actions as necessary. Discussion of the process activities could address questions such as: What are the tasks and activities that have to be performed in order to realize (achieve) the process goals? Also, the software PIT should hunt for process improvement opportunities, such as analysis of current process activities with the objective of uncovering and eliminating non-value-adding activities (NVAs), eliminating redundancy and duplication, and identifying the mundane tasks candidates for automation.

Commitment to perform

This describes the actions the organization must take to ensure that the process is established and will endure. They typically involve establishing organizational policies and leadership. The software PIT could discuss ways of enhancing current organizational policies and procedures in order to support and emphasize the process discipline. Commitment covers questions such as: How can we ensure that the process will endure (survive) after those who originally designed it have left the company? What procedures and regulations are in place in order to enforce the process?

Ability to perform

This describes the preconditions that must exist in the project or organization to enable staff and management to implement the software process competently. This typically involves resources, organizational structures and training. A software PIT could be responsible for defining what training, retraining or awareness events are necessary to enhance the process knowledge and discipline. What skills are required for those who will be performing the process activities in order to make them competent? What training should they go through before they are asked to perform the process activities?

Measurement and analysis

This describes the basic measurement practices that are necessary to determine status related to the process. These measurements are used to control, monitor and improve the process. They typically include examples of the measurements that should be taken and the analysis performed on them. The software PIT could be specifying the process measurements and analysis (for example what and/or who to measure; analysis of process measurements). What are the measurements that should be taken to measure the process performance? What are the process characteristics that need to be monitored which are indicative of the process performance or will impact on the product quality? The measurement should relate to the goals specified for that process.

Verifying implementation

This describes the steps that should be taken to ensure that the activities are performed in compliance with the process that has been established. This typically encompasses reviews and audits by management and software quality assurance. This protects the process from being corrupted. The software PIT should be specifying external verification procedures to protect the process from corruption or decay and to identify risks of not having external verification. Examples of areas to be covered when specifying verification are: What external verification is necessary to ensure that the process is properly performed? Define what is to be verified. Define who is responsible for the verification. To whom should the results be sent? What possible actions should be taken as a result, for example escalation procedures? External verification protects the process from corruption.

Design/improvement of process environment and process infrastructure

Good process design is not enough. The environment within which the process operates should be supportive of the new processes and new process features. A process could be disabled if its environment or its infrastructure does not support it. The process feedback mechanisms are especially important since they indicate the process performance through the measurement and feedback mechanisms and highlight areas for improvement (for example where the process is underperforming). The process infrastructure covers both the organizational and the technical infrastructure which support the process activities, process definition, process feedback and any other process-related activities.

II.3.3 MANAGING THE CHANGE

The objective of software process improvement is to create a process culture and process infrastructure for the organization. Creating a process culture will involve creating new roles and responsibilities, continuing management sponsorship, introducing new organizational policies and procedures, and establishing the measurement and enforcement mechanisms. The management of change is of critical (if not the most critical) importance for the success of implementing software process improvement. One of the main reasons for its criticality is that it involves a wide spectrum of domains that may need to be changed, for example:

- cultural changes
- behavioural changes
- organizational changes
- technological changes
- environmental changes.

Change has many issues, most notably sponsorship, communication, corporate culture, intergroup cooperation, current organizational status, and acceptability of or resistance to change.

The instinctive human reaction to change is usually a rejection of the new change and preference for the status quo. The literature is full of models for change management and the human reaction to the changes. An example of these approaches is provided in Table 11.1 which illustrates four stages of

Table 11.1 Stages of human adoption to process changes

Stage	Description
Installation	Initial installation of the methods (new processes) and training in their proper use
Practice	People learn to perform the methods (new processes) as instructed
Proficiency	The traditional learning curve as people gradually improve their efficiency
Naturalness	The methods (new processes) are so ingrained that they are performed without intellectual effort (the processes are internalized)

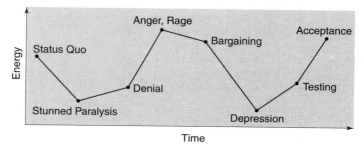

Figure 11.3 Typical human response to change (source: Software Engineering Institute)

human adoption of a new process or changes to an existing process (Humphrey, 1989).

There is generally a mapping between these stages and the typical response to change illustrated in Figure 11.3.

Potential sources of resistance to change

As in the case of most change programmes, software process improvement implementation could face many forms of resistance. It is the duty of those who are planning the implementation of the software process improvement to think of potential sources of resistance to change, and include in their plans means and actions to minimize and eliminate resistance to change. Viewing the software process improvement implementation primarily as a programme for change, the Software Engineering Institute (SEI) has a team dedicated to the study of the management of change and has published some literature and models for managing the change brought about by software process improvement implementation. Charles Myers (1996) summarizes the SEI experiences in implementing software process improvement with organizations worldwide as follows:

'Over the course of time we (the SEI) have seen spectacular success, disappointing failure, and many shades of grey between these two extremes. We have also seen some common factors that seem to contribute to success and failure.' (Myers, 1996)

Table 11.2 summarizes some factors that could lead to the failure of implementing software process improvement.

Table 11.2 Some possible causes of failure with software process improvement

Source of failure	Possible causes of failure
Sponsorship	• Short-term commitment • Unrealistic expectations • Belief in 'silver bullets'
Culture	• Underestimating the power of status quo • Assuming that changing the culture is a trivial matter • 'Undiscussable' assumptions, 'sacred cows'
Transition	• Lack of planning the transition, 'hope rather than plan' • Lack of managing the transition • Expecting short-term results, 'demand immediate productivity increase' • Lack of linking rewards to the new behaviours
Resistance to change	• Not recognizing resistance, 'forcing resistance underground' • Ignoring/denying feedback you don't want to hear • Not involving people who will have to change
Change agent	• Being alienated from the organization • Taking setbacks personally • Working harder rather than smarter • Committing to aggressive, optimistic schedules

II.3.4 STRATEGIES FOR IMPLEMENTING ORGANIZATIONAL CHANGE

Introducing changes is not an easy task. The skill and cleverness is in the approach you may adopt to introduce and implement the change. In the following we will briefly discuss a number of strategies for implementing such a change.

Many would consider the idea and practice of managing changes as boring, often painful and only occasionally exciting. The question is how to bring about successful change to maximize effectiveness and minimize pain. There are many books, articles and studies on dealing with change. The project manager managing the implementation of the software process improvement plan should decide a strategy for managing the changes introduced as part of the software process improvement implementation action plan. One of the most interesting articles on strategies for organizational change (Furnham, 1994) suggests that managers choose different strategies with different consequences. Furnham summarized seven strategies, each with its features and risks (see Table 11.3).

Table 11.3 Strategies for implementing organizational changes

Strategy for managing the change	Main features	Risks
The Fellowship Strategy	• Reliance on interpersonal relations. • Use of seminars, dinners and events to announce and discuss what needs to be changed and how.	• The change process may have serious problems as a consequence of the 'warm and fuzzy' approach. • This strategy is averse to conflict, it can miss crucial issues, and even waste time.
The Political Strategy	• Targeting the power structure by attempting to influence the official and unofficial leaders. • Seeking to identify and persuade those who are most respected and who have large constituencies.	• Political bargaining, flattery and compromises can destabilize the organization. • Maintaining credibility can be difficult because the strategy is obviously 'devious'.
The Economic Strategy	• Driven by the belief that money is the best persuader. • Based on the rational approach that assumes that people's logic is based on economic motives.	• 'Buying people off' can be costly and the effect short term. • This strategy also ignores emotional issues and all questions besides bottom-line profits.
The Academic Strategy	• Based on the assumption that if you present people with enough information and the correct facts they will accept the need to change. • Usually leads to commissioning studies and reports from employees, experts and consultants.	• Difficult to mobilize energy and resources after the analysis phase. • May lead to 'paralysis by analysis' because the study phase lasts too long and the results and recommendations are often out of date.
The Engineering Strategy	• Assumes that if the physical nature of a job is changed, enough people will be forced to change. • Strong emphasis on the structural aspects of problems leads to a sensitivity to the environment (which is particularly helpful in unstable situations).	• The concern over channels of communication can prompt structural change, but fails to commit most people. • Most people do not like being treated as machines and hence do not feel committed. • Such change can also break up happy and efficient teams.

(continued)

Table 11.3 *(continued)*

Strategy for managing the change	Main features	Risks
The Military Strategy	• Reliance on brute force and sometimes ignorance. • Used at times by the military and the police, students, pressure groups and political parties. • The emphasis is on learning to use the weapons for the fight. • Physical strength and agility are required and following the plan is rewarded.	• The change-enforcer cannot relax, in case the imposed change disappears. • Furthermore, force is met by force and the result could be ever-escalating violence. • Focus too narrow and could miss recognizing the real reasons behind resistance to change.
The Confrontational Strategy	• Based on the assumption that if you can arouse and then mobilize anger in the people to confront the problem, they will change. • Much depends on the strategist's ability to argue the points, as well as being able to stir up anger without promoting violence.	• This is a high-risk strategy. • Encourages people to confront problems they would prefer not to address but tends to focus too much on the problem and not on the solution. • Anger and conflict tend to paralyse people and can cause a backlash.

Normally you could mix and match strategies within the same change programme.

Few of these strategies occur in isolation, but they do have different basic assumptions about who to influence, how to proceed and what to focus on. Each tends to be effective at addressing certain change problems but very bad at dealing with others.

The fellowship strategy could be too lenient, the engineering strategy is too narrow, the military strategy is too harsh, the confrontational strategy is too risky and the political strategy has problems with credibility, the economic approach with maintaining change, and the academic with implementing findings. A mix of the above approaches could help software process improvement implementation teams achieve success in implementing process improvement action plans depending on the nature and maturity of the organization (Furnham, 1994).

II.4 INSTITUTIONALIZING SOFTWARE PROCESS IMPROVEMENT

II.4.1 SYMPTOMS OF AN INSTITUTIONALIZED PROCESS

One of the main goals of a process improvement implementation programme is to institutionalize the process in the organization.

Process institutionalization is defined in Paulk *et al.* (1994) as follows:

'Institutionalization: The building of infrastructure and culture that support methods, practices, and procedures so that they are the ongoing way of doing business, even after those who originally defined them are gone.'

Process improvement is not a one-shot deal, it is a way of working. After the first cycle of process improvement, senior management must periodically review process improvement in the organization and initiate reassessment and corrective actions as necessary to ensure that process discipline perseveres. Process groups must bring critical process problems to the attention of management. In a process-focused organization, where the process has been institutionalized, one can identify the following symptoms:

- Following the process is the natural way of performing activities.
- Not following the process is the unnatural way of performing the activities.
- There are strong induction and training of new joiners.
- Management enable the process by providing the necessary resources, commitment and training.
- Performance is judged by the process results, rather than by the performance of individuals.
- Process improvement teams are a common phenomenon, and most of the technical staff have participated in such teams at one time.

Process institutionalization is achieved through stages as shown in Figure 11.4.

When planning for the implementation of software process improvement, the implementation teams should be made aware of the stages towards achieving the institutionalization.

II.4.2 MECHANISMS FOR SOFTWARE PROCESS INSTITUTIONALIZATION

To reach the status of process institutionalization, roles and mechanisms for monitoring and feedback of the process performance should be in place and

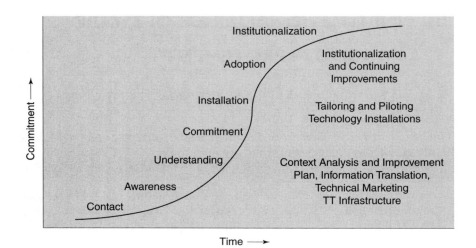

Figure 11.4 Stages towards process institutionalization (source: Software Engineering Institute)

working effectively. Such mechanisms are shown in Figure 11.5 which illustrates the model adopted for an effective process environment.

Process enforcement mechanisms and roles have been discussed in earlier chapters, and the following chapter will discuss how and what to measure in order to monitor the process performance. Process measurements are taken through feedback mechanisms, process feedback and ownership. Process institutionalization can be stressed and emphasized through management policies and organizational procedures. Examples of organizational policies to enforce process institutionalization are:

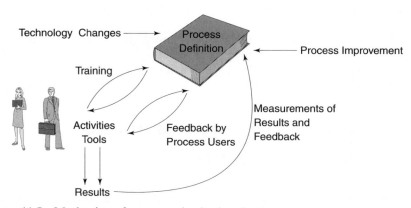

Figure 11.5 Mechanisms for process institutionalization

- Rewards for process achievements
- Rules for process enforcement
- Penalties for not following the process
- Process training and retraining.

Examples of management practices to enforce process institutionalization are:

- 'Walk the talk' (managers, staff and executives)
- Process talk is the natural way of communication
- Executive briefings
- Keep your eyes on the ball (the bottom line).

11.4.3   TOWARDS CONTINUOUS SOFTWARE PROCESS IMPROVEMENT

The intention is that the software process improvement programme is an ongoing programme. A software process improvement cycle could start as a senior management initiative to the improvement effort, and then go through the phases of assessment, recommendations, action plan, and improvement implementation, then back to reassessment (Figure 11.6). After the completion of one process improvement cycle, SPI practices will have been institutionalized into the organization. The software process improvement team will have earned credibility, and there will be a sustained interest in and commitment to SPI effort.

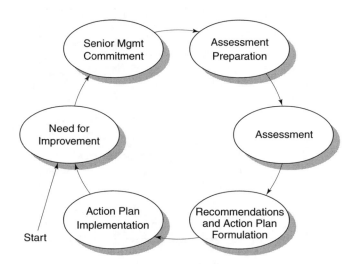

Figure 11.6   A software process improvement cycle

The improvement opportunities will be identified through the process assessment and monitoring of process performance through feedback mechanisms. The types of feedback mechanisms that could help measure the process performance and identify improvement opportunities include feedback mechanisms from:

- process users (How the process helps them)
- process owners (How the process achieves its goals effectively)
- process groups (How simple or complicated is the process)
- project managers (How the process helps them manage the staff)
- business managers (How effective is the process in achieving the business goals).

Every cycle of software process improvement should progress the process discipline and maturity of the process infrastructure along the chosen process improvement roadmap. Every process improvement cycle could take from six to eighteen months depending on the scope and boundaries of the improvement and on the size of the organization undergoing improvement. The process improvement activities should become embedded in the organization's culture, and should not be looked on as an overhead but rather considered to be as important to the success of the business as core activities. Software process improvement cycles should result in progressing the maturity of the software process and its infrastructure along a process improvement roadmap such as the Capability Maturity Model (as illustrated in Figure 11.7).

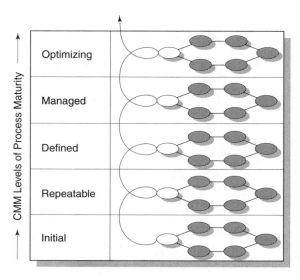

Figure 11.7 Software process improvement cycles move process maturity up the maturity roadmap

11.5 THE SEI IDEAL MODEL – AN EXAMPLE OF AN SPI IMPLEMENTATION MODEL

The Software Engineering Institute has developed an implementation approach for software process improvement that describes the necessary phases, activities and resources needed for successful process improvement effort. The approach is referred to as the IDEAL model, and the following is a summary of IDEAL as described in the SEI literature and in Peterson (1995). For more information on IDEAL and other SEI material, contact Customer Relations at the Software Engineering Institute, Carnegie Mellon University, Pittsburgh, PA 15213-3890, USA.

11.5.1 IDEAL STAGES

The Software Engineering Institute has developed the IDEAL model to answer the following question: 'What should I do, once I have been assessed, to start an improvement program and what activities will the program entail?' (Peterson, 1995).

The IDEAL model is meant to depict the activities of a process improvement programme, and present a consistent view of what is involved in transitioning the CMM into an organization's practice. Although the model is explicitly linked to the CMM, I believe its concepts are generic enough to make them useful for defining SPI implementation programmes using other software process improvement roadmaps.

The IDEAL model addresses the needs of software organizations in various areas of quality improvement. It encompasses five stages of a software process improvement cycle. IDEAL is an acronym that comprises the initials of these five phases:

- I: Initiating
- D: Diagnosing
- E: Establishing
- A: Acting
- L: Leveraging

The main purpose of each of these phases is summarized in Table 11.4.

The intention is for IDEAL to present a single picture – a view that is easy to remember and utilize of what to do to establish a successful improvement programme and infrastructure to address the results of an assessment. The five IDEAL phases are illustrated in Figure 11.8 and briefly described in the following sections.

Table 11.4 Purpose of IDEAL stages

Acronym	Stage	Main purpose
I	Initiating	Starting the improvement programme
D	Diagnosing	Assessing the current state of practice
E	Establishing	Setting the implementation strategy and action plans for the improvement programme
A	Acting	Executing the plans and recommended improvements
L	Leveraging	Analysing the lessons learned and the business results of the improvement effort, and revising the approach

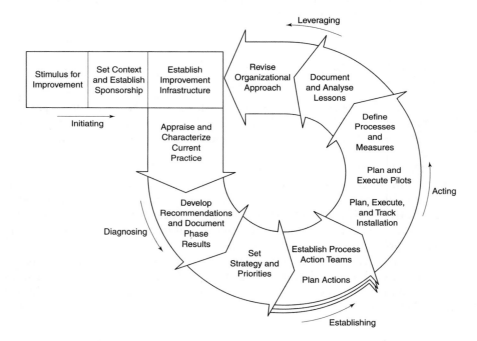

Figure 11.8 IDEAL[SM] SEI's approach to software process improvement (Peterson, 1995)

II.5.2 THE INITIATING PHASE

- Stimulus for improvement (business justification)
- Set context and establish sponsorship (awareness and buy-in)
- Establish improvement infrastructure (assessment team readiness)

The first phase of the IDEAL model establishes the business reasons for undertaking a software process improvement effort. It identifies high-level concerns in the organization that can be the stimulus for addressing various aspects of quality improvement. Communication of these concerns and business perspectives is needed during the Initiating phase in order to gain visible executive buy-in and sponsorship at this very early part of the improvement effort.

Sponsorship implies more than simply deciding to pursue the effort and allocate resources to do the work. Sponsorship has an element of leadership. As stressed in this book, software process improvement represents a major change in the way most organizations perform their software development. It is imperative that key leaders thoroughly understand what SPI is about and firmly believe that it is the right thing to do. This kind of commitment will provide the impetus for the change and the long-term staying power needed to see a major improvement effort through to completion.

During the Initiating phase, the start-up infrastructure necessary to get the software process improvement effort underway and supported should also be put in place. Key players are identified and assigned to the effort, perhaps with some changes to the organization to facilitate new roles and the necessary relationships to the sponsor of the improvement effort. Those sponsoring and supporting the improvement effort must begin to communicate to others about the improvement effort and to build additional support at all levels of the organization.

11.5.3 THE DIAGNOSING PHASE

- Appraise and characterize current practice (assessment findings)
- Develop recommendations and document results (assessment recommendations and final report)

The second phase of the IDEAL model is used to baseline, through an assessment, your organization's software process maturity. This baseline will build a common understanding of the current process of the organization, especially the strengths and weaknesses of those current processes. It will also help you to identify priorities for improving your software processes.

In the context of a software process improvement programme, the Diagnosing phase will help determine how well the organization is prepared to manage, support and fund the SPI programme. Finally, the Diagnosing phase will result in recommendations of specific SPI actions for the organization to undertake.

11.5.4 THE ESTABLISHING PHASE

- Set strategy and priorities (prioritized action list)
- Plan actions (SPI action plan and improvement projects)
- Establish action teams (SEPG and software PITs)

The third phase of the IDEAL model finalizes the strategy and supporting plans for the software process improvement programme. It sets the direction and guidance for the next three to five years, including the following:

- An organization's strategic plan
- A software process improvement strategic plan
- Long-term (three to five years) and short-term (one year) goals of the software process improvement programme
- The tactical plans for selected software process improvement actions.

II.5.5 THE ACTING PHASE

- Define processes and measures (design/redesign processes)
- Plan and execute pilots (pilot improvement actions)
- Plan, execute and track installation (monitor process performance through feedback)

The fourth phase takes action to effect changes in organizational systems which should result in improvements in these systems. These improvements are made in an orderly manner and in ways that will cause them to be sustained over time.

Techniques used to support and institutionalize change include:

- defining software processes
- defining software measurements
- pilot testing of new processes and measurements
- installation of new processes and measurements throughout the organization.

The software process improvement effort is managed and tracked in order to ensure its success. Also, information on the improvement effort is gathered and recorded for use in enhancing the organization's future implementation of software process improvements.

II.5.6 THE LEVERAGING PHASE

- Document and analyse lessons (analyse feedback)
- Revise organizational approach (time SPI processes and infrastructure)

The fifth phase of the IDEAL model completes the process improvement cycle. Lessons learned from the pilot projects and from the improvement efforts are documented and analysed in order to improve the process improvement programme for the future. The business needs that were determined at the beginning of the cycle are revisited to see if they have been met. Sponsorship for the programme is visited and renewed for the next software process improvement cycle.

The intention is that the software process improvement programme is an ongoing programme. At the completion of one process improvement cycle, SPI practices will have been institutionalized into the organization. The software process improvement team will have earned credibility, and by now there should be a sustained interest in and commitment to software process improvement effort.

SUMMARY

Implementing software process improvement is a change programme

The ultimate objective of a software process improvement programme is to improve the practices of software engineers and project managers, hence it is mainly a change programme. All the management of change strategies and techniques are applicable and relevant to software process improvement implementation. In this chapter we discussed the main issues of the management of change and reviewed some approaches and strategies for managing the change. Software process improvement teams should take these approaches into consideration.

Process institutionalization leads to continuous process improvement

The ultimate goal is for the organization to succeed in achieving process institutionalization. This should lead to the creation of a process culture in which process discipline prevails. Adherence to the process becomes the natural way of performing software engineering activities. The management practices and reward systems are all geared towards emphasizing and enhancing the process discipline.

Resistance to change could impede the implementation of SPI

As in the case of any change programme, the implementation of a software process improvement most likely will face resistance. Identifying potential sources of resistance and planning ways to overcome and minimize the resistance is important for the success of software process improvement.

The SEI IDEAL model

The SEI IDEAL model is a good change management model and could be adapted to define the main phases and steps necessary for introducing software process improvement into your organization, and to establish the infrastructure to support your SPI programme.

Management of change

Remember that implementing SPI is essentially a change management programme. Follow all the change management rules. Identify potential stakeholders and enlist their support. There are different strategies for change. You should define which strategy is most effective for your SPI effort.

Continuing management sponsorship

Ensure the continuity and visibility of senior management sponsorship and commitment to the software process improvement programme. This is important since SPI is not a 'one-off' shot, rather it is a continuing effort.

CHAPTER 12

Measuring the benefits of software process improvement

12.1 MEASURING SOFTWARE PROCESS PERFORMANCE

One of the major obstacles to the adoption of software process improvement is the reluctance of business management to invest in SPI because they do not have convincing evidence of the return on investment. There is a general lack of reliable information on the business benefits of software process improvement. Hence there is a need for more hard evidence of satisfactory return on investment (ROI) from software process improvement. This chapter provides a summary of evidence of the business benefits of software process improvement. The material for the case studies summarized is publicly available. Readers interested in more details of the approaches and results of those case studies are advised to refer to the original references. The chapter also discusses issues relating to measurement of software process performance and outlines a method developed in Europe for starting a programme for software process measurement. This is presented as an example of approaches to measuring software process performance.

12.1.1   WHY DO WE NEED TO MEASURE SOFTWARE

PROCESS PERFORMANCE?

Most areas of business and industry use quantitative approaches to managing staff and business performance. Look at manufacturing industry, for example. It is unimaginable that a factory can run effectively without measuring product quality, workforce productivity, reliability of the machinery, cost and time of production, and customer satisfaction. On the other hand, in the software industry most software engineers whom I have worked with clearly state that 'they hate measurement'. However, measurement is necessary to managers in order to be able to monitor the performance and efficiency of their staff. There is a commonsense rule 'what you cannot measure, you cannot manage'. Within the context of software process improvement it is equally true that 'what we cannot measure we cannot improve'. If you do not measure your SPI results, your SPI effort could be addressing the wrong issue.

With measurement in place in a software project, a project manager should be able to think in quantitative terms, and know what is going on in objective terms. Examples of quantitative measurements include the following: how much longer will a project activity take? How many errors have been detected? How much has the project cost so far?

With the personal software process (PSP) concept taking off in the software engineering community (Humphrey, 1995) measurement should be the concern of not only managers but also individual software engineers. Watts Humphrey has an elegant argument to persuade software engineers of the need to measure their process performance: 'A defined process permits you to gather data on the time you spend on each software task and track the number of defects you introduce and remove in each process step. These data can then help you to analyse your process, to understand its faults, and to improve it' (Humphrey, 1995).

One of the main objectives of software process maturity is to improve management visibility of the software process and achieve statistical control of the quality of both the product and the process. The software process assessment itself is a kind of qualitative measurement of how effective is your current process. With feedback mechanisms in place, you should be able to get quantitative indicators of how well your process is performing, and then you can base your improvement targets (in quantitative terms) on the current performance.

Measuring the performance of the software process provides the feedback loop necessary for any system to improve. A feedback loop is necessary for any system to stabilize and adjust with its environment. Within a software process environment, a feedback loop is necessary to reach the state of continuous process improvement. Such a feedback loop will carry information on process performance, (which should result in improvement in product quality).

The software industry is not completely alien to the concept of measurement, thanks to pioneers who advocated the need for quantitative statistical control of the software process (Humphrey, 1989) and of the quality of software products (Boehm, 1981; Putnam and Myers, 1992). Many companies start measurement on a small scale by creating a database of project costs and sizes, and setting a goal of improving project estimates based on past experiences.

12.1.2 WHAT DO WE NEED TO MEASURE?

Metrics and measurement are quite a controversial subject to many software engineers. The number of failures in metrics programmes exceeds the number of successes. One reason is that organizations which start measuring performance in a chaotic, non-disciplined environment are likely to fail, since the measurements will be non-indicative and unreliable. The lack of a consistent and standard process is likely to yield uncomparable metrics. It is of paramount importance for organizations to relate any metrics initiative to the level of their process maturity and link their metrics programmes with software process improvement programmes.

When deciding to collect quantitative measurements, you should be careful in deciding what to measure. Usually no single measure can adequately characterize a complex product, rather a balanced set of indicators should be used. Care should be taken when deciding what measures are to be used as quality and performance indicators. Too many measures can often be confusing, and too few measures could present a distorted view of the total picture. The quality literature is full of proposed lists of the quality attributes and quality indicators for software products. Table 12.1 lists some examples of process-related measures that can also be used as indicators of the process performance.

Process measurement should be related to process goals. Using the CMM process design template, there should be a statement of purpose and a list of goals as part of every process definition. The goals defined for the process should reflect:

- alignment between the process and the business goals
- parameters for managing the process
- key indicators for measuring the process performance
- should be SMART (S = specific, M = measurable, A = attainable, R = relevant, T = traceable)

A measurement programme should focus on measuring the progress goals.

12.2 PRINCIPLES OF SOFTWARE PROCESS MEASUREMENT

Measurements are important, but they can easily misfire and result in a reverse effect. The following are principles and guidelines that should be observed

Table 12.1 Examples of process-related measures

Class	Example measures
Process-related	Number of change requests
	Amount of rework
	Number of process defects (and analysis)
	Number of process problems/faults
	Number of subcontractors' problems
	Cycle time measures
	Productivity trends
	Quality trends
	Effectiveness of the process (degree of achieving its goals)
	Cost of non-quality
	Maturity level
Project-related	Project development time
	Slippage
	Work completed
	Effort expended
	Funds expended
	Completion of milestones
	Deviation of costs (actual versus estimates)
	Amount of rework
	Deviation of resources (actual versus estimates)
	Staff productivity
	Staff turnover
	Project development effort
	Resource usage
	Staffing profile
	Project type
	Number of changes
	Number of failures
	Test coverage
Product-related and customer-related	Number of defects (and causal analysis)
	User-reported bugs
	Usage problems
	Availability problems
	Usability problems
	Customer satisfaction
	Source code size
	System size
	Number of document pages
	Cyclomatic number
	Structure metric
	Number of product faults

when implementing a measurement programme. They should help in achieving the success of the process measurement programme.

Define clear objectives of your measurement programme

A measurement programme without a clear objective would result in mountains of unused data. It could be very demoralizing to the staff when they discover that the measurement data they have been submitting results in no action. Process performance data gathered should have a specific objective. The objectives of a process measurement programme should be closely related to the objectives of the software process improvement programme and ultimately to the business goals and management objectives.

The measurement programme must have management support

Process measurement should be part of an overall programme for software process improvement. It requires resources, time and money. Management support and involvement are necessary. Hence it should enjoy a high level of senior management sponsorship and commitment. Management support is also important to ensure the availability of the required resources, and the alignment between the measurement programme and the business goals.

Measurement roles and responsibilities must be allocated

Process measurement tasks and responsibilities should be allocated to specific roles. Some of the roles identified for software process improvement could take up some of the process measurement responsibilities.

Examples of assigning measurement responsibilities to the roles identified for software process improvement are as follows:

- *Software PITs* assigned to *specific processes* could be assigned the task of defining the measures required to monitor the performance of those processes.
- *Software PITs* assigned to the process *technical infrastructure* could be assigned the task of devising data-gathering mechanisms that would collect and disseminate process performance data.
- *The Software Engineering Process Group (SEPG)* could be assigned the tasks of analysing the process performance data and reporting quality and productivity trends to the sponsor and the Executive Improvement Team (EIT).

Measurements should cover both the process and the product

A good process is the one that will ultimately produce a good product. Measurement should monitor key performance indicators of the process, as well as key quality characteristics of the final product. The software process performance could then be assessed in terms of both key product characteristics and key process performance indicators.

12.3 ISSUES WITH SOFTWARE PROCESS MEASUREMENT

Many people believe that it is difficult to conduct experiments in a difficult discipline such as software engineering. However, claims of significant improvements in quality and productivity should be backed by hard empirical evidence. Intuition should not be a substitute for evidence. In the meantime the lack of hard knowledge regarding the effectiveness of software process improvement could be blamed on 'poor experimental designs and lack of adherence to proper measurement principles' (Fenton, 1993).

Generally there is difficulty in measuring software processes and comparing results consistently across organizations. Also, quantifying the return on investment from investing in software process improvement is a challenging task. The challenge is that effective and meaningful measurements could only happen in a disciplined process environment, whereas you may need to conduct the measurement of a non-disciplined process performance. Measurements of chaotic processes will not be comparable across organizations, nor across processes with different maturity levels. James Herbsleb and his co-authors (Herbsleb *et al.*, 1994) listed a number of issues that must be confronted and addressed when attempting to quantify the impact of a particular software process improvement. Table 12.2 summarizes issues for measuring the results of software process improvement.

12.4 AN EXAMPLE OF A SOFTWARE PROCESS MEASUREMENT METHOD

12.4.1 *ami* BACKGROUND

In October 1990 a consortium of European companies started a two year project aimed at improving the uptake and exploitation of measurement techniques within the software community. This was the start to the *ami* project (application of metrics in industry). The approach used by the project was 'to make the technology and techniques of metrics and measurement available in a simple, straightforward and understandable form that could be easily implemented' (Pulford *et al.*, 1996).

Table 12.2 Issues in measuring the results of software process improvement

Category	Issues
Selecting measures	How to define the key performance indicators for the process that we need to track, for example • financial • customer satisfaction • efficiency and effectiveness • innovation? How to ensure the relevance of the measures to our business and project goals, for example • GQM (Goal–Question–Metric) paradigm (Basili and Selby, 1991)
Process and product measurements (Baumert and McWhinney, 1992; Florac, 1992)	How to accurately reflect the business and engineering objectives of the organization, for example • resources expended on software process improvement • resources and time taken to execute the process • size and quality of the products resulting from the process?
Quantitative business benefits (Rozum, 1993; Curtis and Statz, 1996; Zahran, 1996; Herbsleb *et al.*, 1994)	How to measure the business value or return-on-investment of the software process improvement effort in quantitative terms, for example • increased productivity • early error detection and correction • improved maintainability • process simplification • cost of software process improvement?
Qualitative benefits (Rozum, 1993; Curtis and Statz, 1996; Zahran, 1996; Herbsleb *et al.*, 1994)	How to measure qualitative benefits, for example • product availability (mean time between failures, mean time to repair) • customer satisfaction • employee morale • motivation • staff turnover • disciplined culture • quality of work life • improved communication?

The *ami* consortium (representing nine companies from six European countries) comprised both experts in software measurement and users applying quantitative approaches to the management of their projects. The result was the *ami* handbook and the *ami* method (Pulford *et al.*, 1996). The *ami* method is claimed to be firmly grounded on common sense and well-tried practice.

The project was motivated by the growing awareness in the software industry of the benefits of using quantitative goals, and by the increasing popularity of software process focus. The first version of the SEI process maturity questionnaire has been adopted by the project for the assessment phase of *ami*.

12.4.2 *ami* APPROACH

The *ami* approach adopts what is described as 'goal-oriented measurement' (Pulford *et al.*, 1996). The application of goal-oriented measurement in an organization requires a structured method. Each organization, because it is different from all other organizations, must construct its own measurement framework. Without a generic common method, it is not possible to build a coherent framework that suits all organizations. The *ami* approach provides a commonsense framework for quantifying software projects. This framework comprises four activities:

- *Assessment* of the project environment: the objective is to define primary goals for measurement and link measurement to objectives.
- *Analysis* of the assessment conclusions and of the primary goals: in order to derive sub-goals and identify the most suitable metrics. This analysis is formalized as a goal tree with a corresponding set of questions to which these metrics are linked. The participants affected by the metrication goals will generally carry out the activity. Examples of such participants include the metrics' promoter, project managers and quality engineers.
- *Metrication* by implementing a measurement plan and then processing the collected primitive data into measurement data. The metrics' promoter should write the measurement plan and coordinate its implementation.
- *Improvement* as you exploit the measurement data and implementation actions. The participants affected by the goals start to use the measurement data and implementation actions. Comparison of the measurement data with the goals and questions in the measurement plan will guide you towards achievement of your immediate project goals. When your measurements show that you have achieved a goal, you have improved enough to reassess your primary goals.

The relationships among the four activities are illustrated in Figure 12.1.

The method itself consists of a 12-step sequence (Figure 12.2) with a series of support tools. These steps are described in detail in the *ami* handbook (Pulford *et al.*, 1996).

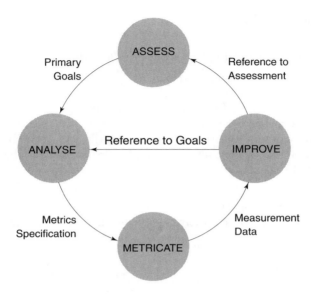

Figure 12.1 The *ami* activities for process measurement

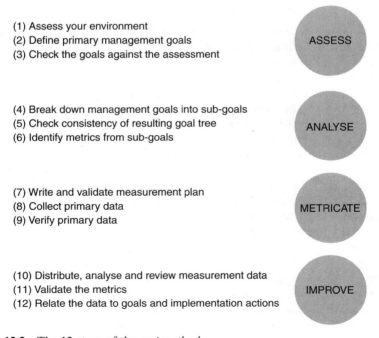

(1) Assess your environment
(2) Define primary management goals
(3) Check the goals against the assessment

(4) Break down management goals into sub-goals
(5) Check consistency of resulting goal tree
(6) Identify metrics from sub-goals

(7) Write and validate measurement plan
(8) Collect primary data
(9) Verify primary data

(10) Distribute, analyse and review measurement data
(11) Validate the metrics
(12) Relate the data to goals and implementation actions

Figure 12.2 The 12 steps of the *ami* method

12.4.3 *ami* METRICS

The *ami* methodology distinguishes metric from primitive metric as follows:

- A metric is a measurable attribute of an entity. For example, attribute 'projecteffort' is a measure (i.e. metric) of project size. To be able to calculate this metric you would need the time-sheet bookings for the project.
- A primitive metric is a raw data item that is used to calculate a metric. In the above example the time-sheet bookings are the primitive metrics. A primitive metric is typically a metric that exists in a database but is not interpreted in isolation.

Each metric is made up of one or more collected primitive metrics. Consequently, each primitive metric has to be clearly identified and the collection procedure defined. Metrics are identified using a predefined template as shown in Table 12.3.

12.4.4 *ami* MEASUREMENT ROLES AND RESPONSIBILITIES

Roles defined in the *ami* method could be mapped to the roles and responsibilities involved in software process improvement. Table 12.4 summarizes such mapping.

The *ami* reference material provides the following guidelines for starting a software process metrics programme.

1 Managers must be involved. Management must take the lead in initiating measurement, defining goals and asking for the feedback information.
2 Measurement tasks must be clearly allocated and budgeted so that all those concerned will be able to put in the required effort.
3 There must be a metrics promoter to write and implement the measurement plan and to organize the presentation and distribution of the information. His or her main role is to keep everyone involved in the metrication process. The analysis of measurement data should relate to the needs of participants affected by the goals (project managers, designers, and so on).
4 There must be a work environment in which goal-oriented measurement is feasible. The essential criterion is not project size or maturity level, but continuity of management strategy. There is little point in investing in improvement or measurement programmes if there is no continuity or conformity across projects.
5 Staff training. Measurement in the workplace is an emotive issue for all members of staff. Resistance to measurement could come from several sources and in many disguises. Typical sources of resistance to measurement include common fear of having the normal software working practices subjected to scrutiny and laid bare to criticism. A measurement programme is likely to stand or fall by the collaboration and commitment of the staff.

Table 12.3 *ami* metrics and primitive metrics definition and analysis procedure

Metric attribute	Description
Name	Name of the metric and any known synonyms
Definition	The attributes of the entities that are measured using this metric, how the metric is calculated, and the primitive metrics from which it is calculated
Goals	List of goals and questions related to the metric. You should include some explanation of why the metric is being calculated
Analysis procedure	How the metric is intended to be used. Preconditions for the interpretation of the metric (for example valid ranges of other metrics). Target trends of the metric values. Models or analysis techniques and tools to be used. Implicit assumptions (for example of the environment or models). Calibration procedures.
Responsibilities	Who will collect and aggregate the measurement data, prepare the reports and analyse the data
Training required	What training is required for application and interpretation of this metric

Primitive metric attribute	Description
Name	Name of the primitive metric
Definition	Unambiguous description of the metric in terms of the project's environment
Collection procedure	Description of the collection procedure. Data collection tools and form to be used. The points in the lifecycle when data are collected. The verification procedure to be used. Where the data will be stored, its format and precision
Responsibilities	Who is responsible for collecting the data. Who is responsible for verifying the data. Who will enter the data into the database. Who has access to modify the data

Table 12.4 Mapping between *ami* roles and SPI roles

ami role	Role in the context of SPI
Manager who initiates measurements	SPI sponsor
Metrics promoter (to write the measurement plan and coordinate its implementation)	Software engineering process group (SEPG)

(*continued*)

Table 12.4 (*continued*)

ami role	Role in the context of SPI
Participants affected by the goals (including senior executives, middle-level managers, engineers, customers)	Project managers and software engineers. Also the executive sponsor and the executive improvement team (EIT)
Metrics team	Software process improvement teams (software PITs)

SUMMARY

People don't like measurement

Measurement is quite a sensitive subject. Most people have gone through a metrics programme that failed to provide useful results.

Why measure?

Measurements are important because they provide the feedback for improvement. Any system without a feedback loop is likely to become unstable.

What to measure

Measuring the product quality and the process performance are both important. When designing processes you should specify the process goals and tie the measurement to those goals.

You can't measure chaos

Measuring the performance of a chaotic process will lead to inconsistent results. Organizations which start their improvement from a chaotic level do not have a baseline against which to compare the process improvement results.

Measurement must be supported by top management

As in any corporate programme, measurement will impact on the activities of all those involved in the software process. Because it requires an added effort from individuals, it is likely to face resistance. To overcome potential resistance, the measurement programme must get management support.

Measurements take time and effort

The measurement programme must be allocated resources. If not it will be pushed down the list of priorities, and may never happen.

PART 4

Current models and standards for software process improvement

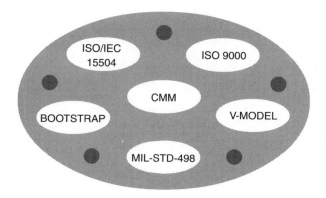

Part 4 describes some of the most significant models and standards for software process assessment and improvement. These include the Software Engineering Institute's Capability Maturity Model (CMM) and CMM-based assessments, the International Standards Organization's ISO/IEC 15504 and ISO/IEC 15504 Guide for Assessments, and the BOOTSTRAP Assessment Method. It also discusses other initiatives and models including ISO 9001, MIL-STD-498, Trillium and the V-Model.

CHAPTER 13

The Capability Maturity Model (CMM)

13.1 OVERVIEW OF THE CAPABILITY MATURITY MODEL

13.1.1 BACKGROUND AND HISTORICAL OVERVIEW

Definition of the CMM

This chapter provides an overview of the Capability Maturity Model for software and reflects Version 1.1. Specifically, it describes the process maturity framework of five maturity levels, the structural components that comprise the CMM, how the CMM is used in practice, and the potential changes for CMM Version 2.0. This chapter is intended to help readers understand the overall structure of the CMM and appreciate the value of using the CMM as a basis for software process improvement.

The CMM is a commonsense application of process management and quality improvement concepts to software development and maintenance. It describes how software organizations mature as they improve their software process. It is 'formally' defined as follows:

'Capability Maturity Model: A description of the stages through which software organizations evolve as they define, implement, measure, control and improve their software processes.' (Paulk *et al.*, 1994)

Organizations can use the CMM to determine their current process capabilities and to identify the issues most critical to software quality and process improvement.

Historical background

The Capability Maturity Model (CMM) was developed by the Software Engineering Institute. It is based on Watts Humphrey's work on the characterization of the software process (Humphrey, 1988).

The CMM is based on knowledge acquired from software process assessments and extensive feedback from both industry and government. By elaborating the maturity framework, a model has emerged that provides organizations with more effective guidance for establishing process improvement programmes.

The CMM can be used as the foundation for systematically building a set of tools, such as a maturity questionnaire, which is useful in software process assessment and improvement. The essential point to remember is that the model, not a questionnaire, is the basis for improving the software process.

Table 13.1 lists the organizational roles and responsibilities defined in the CMM.

Multitudes of CMMs

The initial focus of the CMM was the software process. It was soon clear that the generic concepts of the CMM were applicable to other disciplines. Konrad *et al.* (1996) describes the SEI effort in developing 5 CMM-based models: CMM for Software (SW-CMM); Software Acquisition CMM (SA-CMM); Systems Engineering CMM (SE-CMM); Integrated Product Management CMM (IPM-CMM); People CMM (P-CMM).

The focus in this book is on software CMM (SW-CMM). Every time you see the acronym CMM in the book it means the Software CMM (SW-CMM).

13.1.2 EVOLUTION OF THE CMM

According to Mark Paulk, the Capability Maturity Model (CMM) 'has evolved since its initial publication in 1987 to a reasonably detailed description of software engineering and management processes' (Paulk *et al.*, 1994). The SEI has worked with industry and government to refine and expand the CMM model. The CMM is continuously evolving and improving to reflect refinements and feedback from the practitioners using the CMM as a basis for their software process improvement efforts.

The development of the CMM goes as far back as August 1986. The effort was initiated in response to a request to provide the US federal government with a method for assessing the capability of their software contractors. Figure 13.1 shows the milestone events in the history of the CMM's development and evolution.

Table 13.1 Organizational roles and responsibilities defined in the CMM

Organizational role	Responsibilities
Manager	• Providing technical and administrative direction and control to those performing tasks within his/her area of responsibility. • Traditional functions include planning, organizing, directing and controlling work.
Senior manager	• Fulfilling a management role at high level where the primary focus is on the long-term vitality of the organization. • Typically, would have the responsibility for multiple projects. • Provides and protects budgets and resources for long-term improvement of the software process.
Project manager	• Has total business responsibility for an entire project and is ultimately responsible to the customer. • Directs, controls, administers and regulates a project to build a software or hardware/software system.
Project software manager	• Has total responsibility for all the software activities for a project. • Controls all the software resources for a project and is accountable to the project manager for all software commitments.
First-line software manager	• Direct management responsibility for the staffing and activities of a single organizational unit.
Software task leader	• Leader of a technical team for a specific task. • Has technical responsibility and provides technical direction to the staff working on the task.
Staff, software engineering staff, individuals	• The staff are the individuals, including task leaders, who are responsible for accomplishing an assigned function but who are not managers. • The software engineering staff are the software technical people (e.g. analysts, programmers and engineers) who are not managers. • The term 'individuals' is bounded by the context in which it appears.

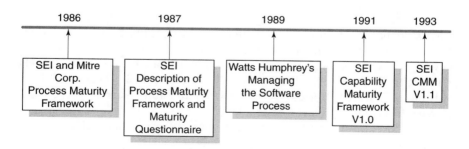

Figure 13.1 Milestones in the history of the Capability Maturity Model (CMM)

1986: In November 1986, the Software Engineering Institute (SEI), with assistance from the Mitre Corporation, began developing a process maturity framework that would help organizations improve their software process. This effort was initiated in response to a request to provide the US federal government with a method for assessing the capability of its software contractors.

1987: In June 1987, the SEI released a brief description of a software process maturity framework (Humphrey, 1988). This was followed in September 1987 by the release of a preliminary maturity questionnaire (Humphrey and Sweet, 1987). The SEI intended the maturity questionnaire to provide a simple tool for identifying areas where an organization's software process needed improvement. Unfortunately, the maturity questionnaire was too often regarded as 'the model' rather than as a vehicle for exploring process maturity issues.

1991/1992: After four years of experience with the software process maturity framework and the preliminary version of the maturity questionnaire, the SEI evolved the software process maturity framework into the Capability Maturity Model for Software (CMM) (Paulk et al., 1991; Weber et al., 1991). The initial release of the CMM, Version 1.0, was reviewed and used by the software community during 1991 and 1992.

1992/1993: A workshop was held in April 1992 on CMM v1.0, which was attended by over 400 software professionals. The CMM, Version 1.1, is the result of the feedback from that workshop and ongoing feedback from the software community.

1997/1998: As a result of the practical experience gained through extensive use of the CMM Version 1.1 by the software industry worldwide, feedback was sought from industry, evaluated, piloted and incorporated in CMM Version 2.0. Beside its use as a software process maturity framework, the generic model of the CMM is used by the SEI as a basis for developing capability maturity in other disciplines (see 13.1.1).

13.1.3   THE SOFTWARE ENGINEERING INSTITUTE

The Capability Maturity Model has been developed by the Software Engineering Institute (SEI). The SEI is a federally funded research and developed centre established in 1984, and affiliated to Carnegie Mellon University in Pittsburgh, Pennsylvania, USA. The SEI is managed by the Advanced Research Project Agency (ARPA) and administered by the US Air Force's Electronic Systems Center.

The SEI was established because of several factors that included:

- rising cost of software development and maintenance;
- need for improved quality of software products;

- increasing delay of software projects. A general belief in the software industry is that 'a typical software project is a year late and double the budget'.

The SEI mission is: 'To provide leadership in advancing the state-of-the-practice of software engineering to improve the quality of systems that depend on software'. The SEI vision is: 'To bring engineering discipline to the development and maintenance of software' (Paulk, 1995b).

This book is dedicated as a small step towards the realization of this vision.

13.2 MATURITY LEVELS OF THE CMM

13.2.1 FIVE LEVELS OF PROCESS MATURITY

The CMM as a roadmap for improvement

The CMM provides a roadmap for moving from a 'fire fighting', *ad hoc* or chaotic process culture to a culture of process discipline and continuous process improvement. In doing this an organization will be continuously improving its process maturity. The CMM specifies the major steps along this road and defines what practices need to be in place in order to make this journey. Continuous process improvement is based on both small, evolutionary steps and revolutionary innovations.

Process maturity levels

The CMM provides a framework for organizing these evolutionary steps into five maturity levels that lay successive foundations for continuous process improvement. These five maturity levels define an ordinal scale for measuring the maturity of an organization's software process and for evaluating its software process capability. The levels also help an organization prioritize its improvement efforts.

Five maturity levels

A maturity level is a well-defined evolutionary plateau towards achieving a mature software process. Each maturity level provides a layer in the foundation for continuous process improvement. Each level comprises a set of process goals that, when satisfied, stabilize an important component of the software process. Achieving each level of the maturity framework establishes a different component in the software process, resulting in an increase in the process capability of the organization.

Organizing the CMM into the five levels prioritizes improvement actions for increasing software process maturity (Figure 13.2). The labelled arrow

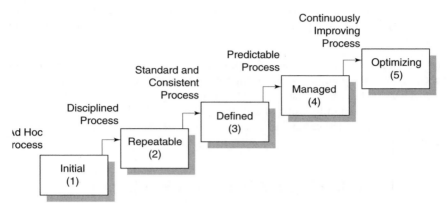

Figure 13.2   The five maturity levels of the CMM

illustrates the type of process capability being institutionalized by the organization at each step of the maturity framework.

The higher the process maturity, the lower the risk is, and the higher productivity and quality become. Each of these maturity levels has its own challenges that organizations should focus on to move up their process maturity and consequently increase productivity and improve quality (Figure 13.3).

13.2.2 CHARACTERIZING THE MATURITY LEVELS

The following characterizations of the five maturity levels highlight the primary process changes that need to be made at each level.

Level 1: the Initial Level

At this level the software process is characterized as *ad hoc*, and occasionally even chaotic. Few processes are defined, and success depends on individual effort. At the Initial Level, the organization is typically characterized by the following behaviours:

● The organization lacks sound management practices, does not provide a stable environment for developing and maintaining software and is characterized by ineffective planning and reaction-driven commitment systems.
● During a crisis, projects typically abandon planned procedures and revert to coding and testing.
● Success depends entirely on having an exceptional manager and a seasoned and effective software team.

MATURITY LEVEL/KEY CHALLENGES

Level	Characteristics	Key Challenges	Result
5 Optimizing	Improvement fed back into process	Still human intensive process Maintain organization at optimizing level	Productivity and quality
4 Managed	(Qualitative) Measured process	Changing technology Problem analysis Problem prevention	
3 Defined	(Qualitative) Process defined and institutionalized	Process measurement Process analysis Quantitative quality plans	
2 Repeatable	(Intuitive) Process dependent on individuals	Training, testing Technical practices and reviews Process focus, standards and processes	
1 Initial	(Ad hoc/chaotic)	Project management and planning Configuration management Software quality assurance	Risk

Figure 13.3 Higher process maturity leads to higher productivity and quality

- Occasionally, capable and forceful software managers can withstand the pressures to take shortcuts in the software process; but when they leave the project, their stabilizing influence leaves with them.
- Even a strong engineering process cannot overcome the instability created by the absence of sound management practices.

The software process capability of a Level 1 organization is unpredictable because the software process is constantly changed or modified as the work progresses (i.e., the process is *ad hoc*). Schedules, budgets, functionality and product quality are generally unpredictable. Performance depends on the capabilities of individuals and varies with their innate skills, knowledge and motivation. There are few stable software processes in evidence, and performance can be predicted only by individual rather than organizational capability.

Level 2: the Repeatable Level

At this level, basic project management processes are established to track cost, schedule and functionality. The necessary process discipline is in place to repeat earlier successes on projects with similar applications. The software process capability of Level 2 organizations can be characterized as disciplined because planning and tracking of the software project is stable and earlier successes can be repeated. Effective management processes are institutionalized for software projects, which allow organizations to repeat successful practices developed on earlier projects, although the specific processes implemented by the projects may differ.

At the Repeatable Level, the organization is typically characterized by the following behaviours:

- The organization establishes policies and procedures for managing software projects and installing basic software management controls. Planning and managing new projects is based on experience with similar projects.
- Software project standards are defined and faithfully followed.
- Realistic project commitments are based on the results observed on previous projects and on the requirements of the current project.
- The software project managers track software cost, schedule and functionality. Problems in meeting commitments are identified when they arise.
- Baseline software requirements are defined and the work products developed to satisfy them, and to control their integrity.
- The software project works with its subcontractors, if any, to establish a strong customer–supplier relationship.

The final result is that the project's process is under the effective control of a project management system, following realistic plans based on the performance of previous projects.

Level 3: the Defined Level

At this level the software process for management and engineering activities is documented, standardized and integrated into a standard software process for the organization. All projects use an approved, tailored version of the organization's standard software process for developing and maintaining software. The software process capability of Level 3 organizations can be characterized as standard and consistent because both software engineering and management activities are stable and repeatable.

At the Defined Level, the organization is typically characterized by the following behaviours:

- The organization documents the standard process for developing and maintaining software across the organization. This covers both software engineering and management processes. This standard process is referred to throughout the CMM as the organization's standard software process. It is an essential component of the software process infrastructure. The software process infrastructure is discussed in Part 2 of this book.
- Processes established at Level 3 are used (and changed, as appropriate) to help the software managers and technical staff perform more effectively.
- The organization is continuously exploiting effective software engineering practices when standardizing its software processes.

- There is a group that is responsible for the organization's software process activities, i.e. a software engineering process group (SEPG).
- An organization-wide training programme is planned and implemented to ensure that the staff and managers have the knowledge and skills required to fulfil their assigned roles.
- Projects tailor the organization's standard software process to develop their own defined software process, which accounts for the unique characteristics of the project (see Part 2 of this book).

The final result is that management has good insight into technical progress on all projects. Cost, schedule and functionality are under control, and software quality is tracked.

Level 4: the Managed Level

At this level the software process capability of Level 4 organizations can be characterized as predictable because the process is measured and operates within measurable limits. Detailed measures of the software process and product quality are collected. Both the software process and products are quantitatively understood and controlled. At the Managed Level, the organization is typically characterized by the following behaviours:

- The organization sets quantitative quality goals for both software products and processes.
- The organization measures productivity and quality for important software process activities across all projects as part of an organizational measurement programme.
- The organization uses an organization-wide software process database to collect and analyse the data available from the projects' defined software processes.
- The organization uses the measurements to establish the quantitative foundation for evaluating the projects' software processes and products.
- The variation in the projects' process performance is narrowed. This helps in achieving control over the performance of their products and processes to fall within acceptable quantitative boundaries.
- The risks involved in moving up the learning curve of a new application domain are known and managed.

At this level software products are expected to be of predictably high quality.

Level 5: the Optimizing Level

Continuous process improvement is enabled by quantitative feedback from the process and from piloting innovative ideas and technologies. The software process capability of Level 5 organizations can be characterized as continuously improving. Improvement occurs both by incremental advancements in the existing process and by innovations using new technologies and methods. At the Optimizing Level, the organization is typically characterized by the following behaviours:

Table 13.2 Behavioural characterization of the maturity levels

CMM level	Nature of the process	Process characteristics
Level 5: Optimizing	Continuously improving	• Process improvement is institutionalized
Level 4: Managed	Predictable	• Product and process are quantitatively controlled
Level 3: Defined	Standard and consistent	• Software engineering and management processes are defined and integrated
Level 2: Repeatable	Disciplined	• Project management system is in place • Performance is repeatable
Level 1: Initial	*Ad hoc*	• Process is informal and *ad hoc* • Performance is unpredictable

- There is a focus on continuous process improvement.
- There is proactive identification of process weaknesses and strengths, with the goal of preventing the occurrence of defects.
- New technologies and proposed changes to the organization's software process are assessed through cost–benefit analyses using data on the current effectiveness of the software process.
- Innovations that exploit the best software engineering practices are identified and transferred throughout the organization.
- Defects are analysed to determine their causes. Software processes are evaluated to prevent known types of defects from recurring, and lessons learned are disseminated to other projects.

A description of a Level 5 organization, the Space Shuttle On-board Software, is provided in Paulk *et al.* (1994). Table 13.2 summarizes the behavioural characterization of processes at the different maturity levels.

13.2.3 PROCESS MATURITY AND PROCESS CAPABILITY

Definition of process capability

The assumption is that the higher the level of the process maturity of an organization, the higher its process capability. Process capability is defined as 'The range of expected results that can be achieved by following a process' (Paulk *et al.*, 1994).

Another definition of capability is given in the Trillium documentation as 'The ability of a development organization to consistently deliver a product or an enhancement to an existing product, that meets customer expectations, with minimal defects, for the lowest life-cycle cost, in the shortest time' (Trillium, 1994).

Benefits of higher process capability

Process capability leads to increased predictability of performance. The maturity of an organization's software process helps to predict a project's ability to meet its goals. Higher process capability can yield many benefits for both the customer organizations (internal or external) and the development organization. For the customer organizations, a higher capability means that:

- the development organization is more responsive to customer and market demands;
- lifecycle cost of the product(s) is minimized; and
- end-user satisfaction is maximized.

For the development organization, a higher capability means:

- lower development and maintenance costs;
- shorter cycle time and development intervals;
- an increased ability to achieve cost and schedule commitments owing to effective project risk analysis and effort estimation; and
- increasing ability to meet quantifiable design and quality objectives.

Impact of process maturity level on schedule, cost and quality

Projects in Level 1 organizations experience wide variations in achieving cost, schedule, functionality and quality targets. As illustrated in Figure 13.4 three improvements in meeting targeted goals are observed as the organization's software process matures.

1 As maturity increases, the difference between targeted and actual results decreases across projects. This is because higher maturity organizations use a carefully constructed software process. Such a process will be operating within known parameters. The selection of the target date is based on the extensive data the projects possess about their process and on their performance in applying it. This is illustrated in Figure 13.4 by how much of the area under the curve lies to the right of the target line.

2 As maturity increases, the variability of actual results around targeted results decreases. This narrowed variation occurs at the highest maturity levels because virtually all projects are performing within controlled parameters approaching the organization's process capability for cost, schedule, functionality and quality. This is illustrated in Figure 13.4 by how much of the area under the curve is concentrated near the target line.

3 Targeted results improve as the maturity of the organization increases. That is, as a software organization matures, costs decrease, development time becomes shorter, and productivity and quality increase. In a low

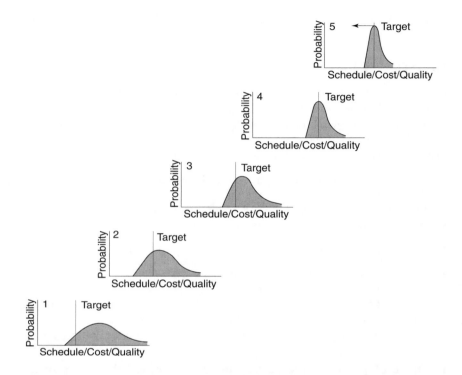

Figure 13.4   Impact of maturity on predictability of schedule/cost/quality (Paulk *et al.*, 1995)

maturity organization, development time can be quite long because of the amount of rework that must be performed to correct mistakes. In contrast, high maturity organizations practise continuous process improvement and defect prevention techniques. The purpose is to increase process efficiency and eliminate rework, allowing development time to be shortened. This is illustrated in Figure 13.4 by the horizontal displacement of the target line from the origin.

In a mature organization earlier detection of defects contributes to the project stability and performance. This is achieved by eliminating the rework during later phases. Risk management is an integral part of project management in a mature process environment. In some cases a mature process means that 'failed' projects are identified early in the software lifecycle and investment in a lost cause is minimized. In summary the higher the process maturity of an organization, the more predictable are their projects, and the higher the product quality and the staff predictability.

13.3 INTERNAL STRUCTURE OF THE CMM

13.3.1 KEY PROCESS AREAS (KPAs)

The five maturity levels represent the highest level of the CMM structure. The substructures below the five levels comprise what are called 'key process areas' (KPAs). Each maturity level is composed of several key process areas, and a key process area is assigned to one and only one maturity level. The substructure below the key process areas is called 'common features'. Each key process area is organized into five sections called common features (these will be discussed in the next section). The common features specify the key practices that, when collectively addressed, accomplish the goals of the key process area. Figure 13.5 illustrates the main components of the CMM internal structure.

The following paragraphs define the main components of the CMM internal structure.

Maturity levels

A maturity level is a well-defined evolutionary plateau towards achieving a mature software process. Each maturity level indicates a level of process capability. For instance, at Level 2 the process capability of an organization

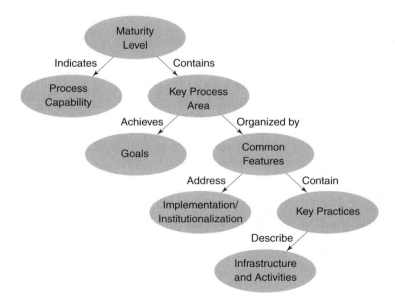

Figure 13.5 The internal structure of the Capability Maturity Model

has been elevated from *ad hoc* to disciplined by establishing sound project management controls.

Key process areas

Except for Level 1, each maturity level is decomposed into several key process areas that indicate the areas an organization should focus on to improve its software process. The key process areas of the CMM represent one way of describing how organizations mature. These key process areas were defined based on many years of experience in software engineering and management and on over five years of experience with software process assessments and software capability evaluations.

Key process areas identify the issues that must be addressed to achieve a maturity level. Each key process area identifies a cluster of related activities. When performed collectively, these activities achieve a set of goals considered important for enhancing process capability. The key process areas have been defined to reside at a single maturity level as shown in Figure 13.6.

The CMM does not describe all the process areas in detail that are involved with developing and maintaining software; rather it focuses on the 'key' areas that contribute most to process capability. Although other issues influence process performance, the key process areas were identified because of their effectiveness in improving an organization's software process capability. They may be considered as the requirements for achieving a maturity level.

Goals

Every key process area is assigned a set of goals. The goals signify the scope, boundaries and intention of each key process area. All the goals of a key process area must be achieved for the organization to satisfy that key process area. When the goals of a key process area are accomplished on a continuing basis across projects, the organization can be said to have institutionalized the process capability characterized by that key process area. To achieve a maturity level, the key process areas for that level must be satisfied. To satisfy a key process area, each of the goals for the key process area must be satisfied. The goals can be used to determine whether an organization or project has effectively implemented the key process area.

Practices

The specific practices to be executed in each key process area will evolve as the organization achieves higher levels of process maturity. For instance, many of the project estimating capabilities described in the Software Project Planning key process area at Level 2 must evolve to handle the additional project data available at Levels 3, 4 and 5. Integrated Software Management at Level 3 is the evolution of Software Project Planning and Software Project Tracking and Oversight at Level 2 as the project is managed using a defined software process.

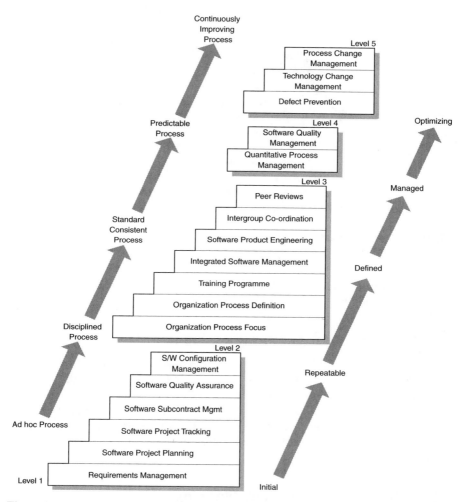

Figure 13.6   The CMM (v1.1) key process areas by maturity level

The following sections describe the key process areas associated with Maturity Levels 2 through 5. The paragraphs are numbered to show the Maturity Level number where the key process area is located, and the sequence of that key process area within that level. For example $L_2/KPAI$ refers to the first key process area of maturity level number 2.

13.3.2   LEVEL 2 KEY PROCESS AREAS

The key process areas at Level 2 focus on the software project's concerns related to establishing basic project management controls. Figure 13.7 illustrates the key process areas associated with Maturity Level 2, 'Repeatable'.

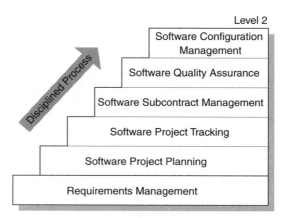

Level 2

Figure 13.7   Key process areas of maturity level 2, 'Repeatable'

The purpose and a brief description of each of the key process areas for Level 2 are given below.

L2/KPA1 Requirements Management

- *Purpose:*   To establish a common understanding between the customer and the software project of the customer's requirements that will be addressed by the software project.
- *Brief description:*   This common agreement with the customer is used as the basis for planning and managing the software project. Control of the relationship with the customer depends on following an effective change control process.

L2/KPA2 Software Project Planning

- *Purpose:*   To establish reasonable plans for performing the software engineering and for managing the software project.
- *Brief description:*   These plans are the necessary foundation for managing the software project. Without realistic plans, effective project management cannot be implemented.

L2/KPA3 Software Project Tracking and Oversight

- *Purpose:*   To establish adequate visibility into the actual progress of the project.
- *Brief description:*   This visibility enables management to take effective actions when the software project's performance deviates significantly from the software plans.

L2/KPA4 Software Subcontract Management

- *Purpose:* To select qualified software subcontractors and to manage them effectively.
- *Brief description:* The software subcontract management KPA combines the following concerns which are related to controlling the subcontractor and monitoring the progress of the subcontract:
  - Requirements Management for controlling changes to the requirements
  - Software Project Planning, and Software Project Tracking and Oversight for basic management control
  - Software Quality Assurance for the necessary coordination
  - Configuration Management, for configuration control.

L2/KPA5 Software Quality Assurance

- *Purpose:* To provide management with appropriate visibility into the process being used by the software project and of the products being built.
- *Brief description:* Software Quality Assurance is an integral part of most software engineering and management processes. It is of paramount importance to continuously assure the quality of the software product being developed and to address and resolve process-related issues and concerns.

L2/KPA6 Software Configuration Management

- *Purpose:* To establish and maintain the integrity of the products of the software project throughout the project's software lifecycle.
- *Brief description:* Software Configuration Management is an integral part of most software engineering and management processes. It assures the integrity of the product.

13.3.3 LEVEL 3 KEY PROCESS AREAS

The key process areas at Level 3 address both project and organizational issues, as the organization establishes an infrastructure that institutionalizes effective software engineering and management processes across all projects. Figure 13.8 illustrates the key process areas associated with Maturity Level 3, 'Defined'.

The purpose and a brief description of each of the key process areas for Level 3 are given below.

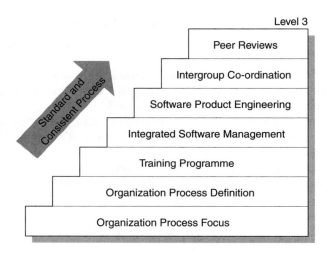

Figure 13.8 Key process areas of maturity level 3, 'Defined'

L3/KPAI Organization Process Focus

- *Purpose:* To establish the organizational responsibility for software process activities that improve the organization's overall software process capability.
- *Brief description:* The primary result of the Organization Process Focus activities is a set of software process assets, which are described in the Organization Process Definition. These assets are used by the software projects, as described in Integrated Software Management.

L3/KPA2 Organization Process Definition

- *Purpose:* To develop and maintain a usable set of software process assets.
- *Brief description:* These assets improve process performance across the projects and provide a basis for cumulative, long-term benefits to the organization. They provide a stable foundation that can be institutionalized via mechanisms such as training, which is described in Training Program.

L3/KPA3 Training Program

- *Purpose:* To develop the skills and knowledge of individuals so they can perform their roles effectively and efficiently.
- *Brief description:* Training is an organizational responsibility, but the software projects should identify their needed skills and provide the necessary training when the project's needs are unique.

L3/KPA4 Integrated Software Management

- *Purpose:* To integrate the software engineering and management activities into a coherent, defined software process for the project.
- *Brief description:* The project's defined software process is tailored from the organization's standard software process and related process assets, which are described in Organization Process Definition. This tailoring is based on the business environment and technical needs of the project.

L3/KPA5 Software Product Engineering

- *Purpose:* To consistently perform a well-defined engineering process that integrates all the software engineering activities to produce correct, consistent software products effectively and efficiently.
- *Brief description:* Software Product Engineering describes the technical activities of the project, including requirements analysis, design, coding, integration and testing.

L3/KPA6 Intergroup Coordination

- *Purpose:* To establish a means for the software engineering group to participate actively with the other engineering groups. This makes the project better able to satisfy the customer's needs effectively and efficiently.
- *Brief description:* Intergroup Coordination is the interdisciplinary aspect of Integrated Software Management that extends beyond software engineering. Not only should the software process be integrated, but the software engineering group's interactions with other groups must be coordinated and controlled.

L3/KPA7 Peer Reviews

- *Purpose:* To remove defects from the software work products early and efficiently.
- *Brief description:* An important corollary effect is to develop a better understanding of the software work products and of the defects that can be prevented. Peer review is an important and effective engineering method that can be implemented via inspections, structured walkthroughs or a number of other review methods.

13.3.4 LEVEL 4 KEY PROCESS AREAS

The key process areas at Level 4 focus on establishing a quantitative understanding of both the software process and the software work products being built. Figure 13.9 illustrates the key process areas associated with Maturity Level 4, 'Managed'.

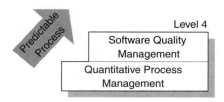

Figure 13.9   Key process areas of maturity level 4, 'Managed'

The two key process areas at this level, Quantitative Process Management and Software Quality Management, are highly interdependent. The purpose and a brief description of each of these key process areas are given below.

L4/KPA1 Quantitative Process Management

- *Purpose:*   To control the process performance of the software project quantitatively. Software process performance represents the actual results achieved from following a software process.
- *Brief description:*   The focus is on identifying special causes of variation within a measurably stable process and correcting, as appropriate, the circumstances that drove the transient variation to occur. Quantitative Process Management implies a comprehensive measurement programme.

L4/KPA2 Software Quality Management

- *Purpose:*   To develop a quantitative understanding of the quality of the project's software products and achieve specific quality goals.
- *Brief description:*   Software Quality Management applies a comprehensive measurement programme to the software work products described in Software Product Engineering.

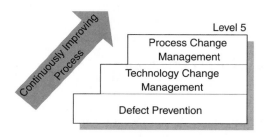

Figure 13.10   Key process areas of maturity level 5, 'Optimizing'

13.3.5 LEVEL 5 KEY PROCESS AREAS

Figure 13.10 illustrates the key process areas associated with Maturity Level 5, 'Optimizing'. They cover the issues that both the organization and the projects must address to implement continuous and measurable software process improvement. The purpose and a brief description of each of the key process areas for Level 5 are given below.

L5/KPAI Defect Prevention

- *Purpose:* To identify the causes of defects and prevent them from recurring. This should lead to continuous evolutionary improvement of the software process.
- *Brief description:* The software project analyses defects, identifies their causes, and changes its defined software process, as described in Integrated Software Management. Process changes of general value are transferred to other software projects, as described in Process Change Management.

L5/KPA2 Technology Change Management

- *Purpose:* To identify beneficial new technologies (including tools, methods and processes) and transfer them into the organization in an orderly manner. The procedures to introduce the changes are as described in Process Change Management. Innovative technologies could lead to revolutionary process improvement.
- *Brief description:* The focus of Technology Change Management is on performing innovation efficiently in an ever-changing world of the software processes used in the organization. The intention is to improve software quality, increase productivity and decrease the cycle time for product development.

L5/KPA3 Process Change Management

- *Purpose:* To improve continually the software processes used in the organization with the intention of improving software quality, increasing productivity and decreasing the cycle time.
- *Brief description:* Process Change Management takes the incremental improvements of Defect Prevention and the innovative improvements of Technology Change Management and makes them available to the entire organization.

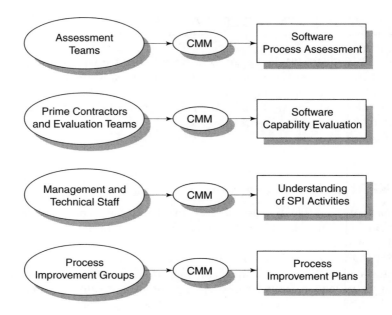

Figure 13.11   Potential users of the CMM

13.4   USES OF THE CMM

13.4.1   USING THE CMM FOR PROCESS ASSESSMENT,

EVALUATION AND IMPROVEMENT

The CMM is a framework representing a path of improvements recommended for software organizations that want to increase their software process capability. This operational elaboration of the CMM is designed to support the many ways it will be used. At least four groups of users of the CMM are supported (Figure 13.11):

1   **Assessment teams** can use the CMM as basis for their assessment of the existing processes in the organization to identify the process strengths and weaknesses (relative to the CMM process definitions).
2   **Evaluation teams** can use the CMM to identify the risks of selecting among different contractors for awarding business and to monitor the progress of contracts. This could be achieved by identifying the missing critical practices of the key processes on the side of contractors, and evaluating the potential risk that these could cause.

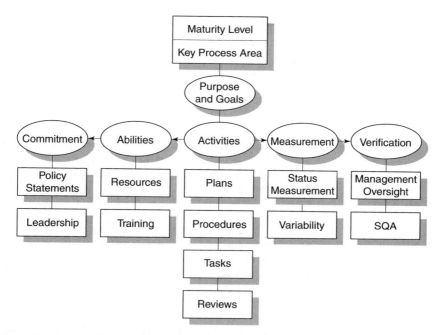

Figure 13.12   The CMM model for software process design

3   **Managers and technical staff** can use the CMM to understand the activities necessary to plan and implement an improvement programme for the software process in their organization. This could be achieved by using the CMM as an improvement roadmap.

4   **Process improvement groups**, such as an SEPG, can use the CMM as a guide to help them define and improve the software process in their organization. This could be achieved by using the CMM process architecture and descriptions as the target for their process improvement and process redesign activities.

Because of the diverse uses of the CMM, it must be decomposed in sufficient detail so that actual process recommendations can be derived from the structure of the maturity levels. This decomposition should be at the appropriate level of detail that suits each type of CMM user. Uses of the CMM by these groups are usually described respectively as CMM-based assessments, CMM-based evaluations, and CMM-based improvements. The SEI has published guidelines on tailoring the CMM (Ginsberg and Quinn, 1995).

13.4.2 USING THE CMM FOR PROCESS DESIGN

The CMM provides an excellent model for process design or redesign. It specifies a template with the components that need to be specified when

Table 13.3 Summary of the common features of the CMM's key process areas

Common feature	Definition and interpretation
Commitment to perform	• *Policy statements:* to emphasize the connection between organizational commitment and the process (for example to establish Organization Process Focus, Organization Process Definition). • *Leadership:* assignment of a leadership role or particular sponsorship necessary for institutionalizing the key process area (for example, key roles in Process Change Management, Technology Change Management).
Ability to perform	• *Organizational structures:* a particular organizational structure that supports the key process area (for example teams for QA, Configuration Management). • *Resources and funding:* for example access to special skills, adequate funding, and access to tools. • *Training:* which may include formal as well as informal training and skill transfer mechanisms. • *Orientation:* refers to less depth of skill or knowledge being transferred than would be expected via training. • *Prerequisites:* the inputs required for a key process area (for example specific documents such as the project plan, or the output of another process, or delegation of responsibility).
Activities performed	• *Activities, roles and procedures* necessary to implement a key process area and achieve its goals. • *Establishing plans and procedures*, performing the work, tracking it, and taking corrective actions as necessary.
Measurement and analysis	• *Basic measurement practices* that are necessary to determine status related to the process. • *Other measures* such as quality of training, effectiveness of management, and functionality and quality of software products.
Verifying implementation	• *Senior management oversight* on a periodic basis: to gain awareness of, and insight into, software process activities at an appropriate level of abstraction and in a timely manner. • *Project management oversight:* on both a periodic and event-driven basis at a more detailed level reflecting project management's more active involvement in the operational aspects of a project. • *Software quality assurance:* in the form of review/audit by the software quality assurance group or an independent group.

designing a software process. It also gives a jump start for the design of all the critical processes for software development. The key process area specifications in the CMM documentation should be used by software process improvement teams (software PITs) to guide them when designing or improving specific software processes. Figure 13.12 illustrates the process design template showing the components of the CMM internal structure. Also this template can be the basis for assessing the completeness of the current process specifications.

The software process improvement teams (software PITs) can use this template as a starting point for their process design and process improvement sessions. Table 13.3 summarizes the definitions and interpretations of the common features. These are the main areas that need to be covered in a process design workshop or a process specification document.

The CMM's model for process definition is one of the most comprehensive software process models. If applied properly, the resulting processes could successfully lead to the creation of a process culture and the establishment of an effective process environment. This should ultimately lead to the institutionalization of the process thinking within the software organization. To illustrate this point, the following section provides an example of the CMM specification of one key process area 'Software Configuration Management'. The CMM has similar definitions for all 18 key process areas.

13.4.3 A KEY PROCESS AREA DEFINITION

Software Configuration Management key process area

Table 13.4 is a summary of the CMM specifications of the Software Configuration Management KPA. The actual CMM documentation contains much more information than this summary. It has examples of the contents of the configuration repository, examples of the membership for the software configuration board, example functionality of support tools, example contents of the software configuration management plan, and examples of training.

Purpose

The purpose of the Software Configuration Management KPA is to establish and maintain the integrity of the products of the software project throughout the project's software lifecycle.

Goals

- *Goal 1:* Software configuration management activities are planned.
- *Goal 2:* Selected software work products are identified, controlled and available.

Table 13.4 Summary of the common features of the Software Configuration Management key process area specified in the CMM

Common feature	Key practices
Commitment to perform	• *Commitment 1:* The project follows a written organizational policy for implementing software configuration management (SCM).
Ability to perform	• *Ability 1:* A board having the authority for managing the project's software baselines (i.e. a software configuration control board – SCCB) exists or is established. • *Ability 2:* A group that is responsible for coordinating and implementing SCM for the project (i.e. the SCM group) exists. • *Ability 3:* Adequate resources and funding are provided for performing the SCM activities. • *Ability 4:* Members of the SCM group are trained in the objectives, procedures and methods for performing their SCM activities. • *Ability 5:* Members of the software engineering group and other software-related groups are trained to perform their SCM activities.
Activities performed	• *Activity 1:* An SCM plan is prepared for each software project according to a documented procedure. • *Activity 2:* A documented and approved SCM plan is used as the basis for performing the SCM activities. • *Activity 3:* A configuration management library system is established as a repository for the software baselines. • *Activity 4:* The software work products to be placed under configuration management are identified. • *Activity 5:* Change requests and problem reports for all configuration items/units are initiated, recorded, reviewed, approved and tracked according to a documented procedure. • *Activity 6:* Changes to baselines are controlled according to a documented procedure. • *Activity 7:* Products from the software baseline library are created and their release is controlled according to a documented procedure. • *Activity 8:* The status of configuration items/units is recorded according to a documented procedure. • *Activity 9:* Standard reports documenting the SCM activities and the contents of the software baseline are developed and made available to affected groups and individuals. • *Activity 10:* Software baseline audits are conducted according to a documented procedure.

(*continued*)

Table 13.4 (*continued*)

Common feature	Key practices
Measurement and analysis	• *Measurement 1:* Measurements are made and used to determine the status of the SCM activities.
Verifying implementation	• *Verification 1:* The SCM activities are reviewed with senior management on a periodic basis. • *Verification 2:* The SCM activities are reviewed with the project manager on both a periodic and an event-driven basis. • *Verification 3:* The SCM group periodically audits software baselines to verify that they conform to the documentation that defines them. • *Verification 4:* The software quality assurance group reviews and/or audits the activities and work products for SCM and reports the results.

- *Goal 3:* Changes to identified software work products are controlled.
- *Goal 4:* Affected groups and individuals are informed of the status and content of software baselines.

13.5 CMM VERSION 2.0

13.5.1 MOTIVATION

In line with their strategy of continuously improving the CMM, the Software Engineering Institute has elicited feedback from the software industry on proposed changes to CMM Version 1.1. This feedback has resulted from the extensive practical use of CMM Version 1.1 over the years by organizations worldwide. At the time of writing this book CMM Version 2.0 Draft A was in the software community review stage. Considering the information available, the main variations between Version 1.1 and Version 2.0 Draft A key process areas for levels 2 and 3 are summarized in the following points. Changes to Levels 4 and 5 key process areas will be released in Draft B (this was not released at the time of writing this book).

Another factor that impacts on the development of CMM Version 2.0 is the new standard ISO/IEC 15504, formerly SPICE (see Chapter 15) adopts a continuous architecture and the current version of CMM reflects a staged architecture. While a staged model can be mapped to a continuous architecture, it is planned that CMM Version 2.0 will support both architectures.

13.5.2 CHANGES TO KEY PROCESS AREAS

The Software Subcontract Management key process area will be renamed Software Supplier Management. This is a major expansion of Software Subcontract Management that will include off-the-shelf and customer-supplier software. CMM Version 2.0 key process areas for level 2 are likely to be:

- Requirements Management
- Software Project Planning
- Software Project Tracking and Oversight
- Software Supplier Management
- Software Quality Assurance
- Software Configuration Management.

CMM Version 2.0 key process areas for Level 3 are likely to be:

- Organization Process Focus
- Organization Process Definition
- Organization Training Programme
- Integrated Software Management
- Software Product Engineering
- Intergroup Coordination

CMM Version 2.0 key process areas for Level 4 are likely to be:

- Statistical Process Management
- Organization Process Focus
- Organization Process Performance

CMM Version 2.0 key process areas for Level 5 are likely to be:

- Defect Prevention
- Organization Process Innovation
- Organization Improvement Deployment

Future editions of this book will reflect the latest state of the CMM.

SUMMARY

The Capability Maturity Model

- The Capability Maturity Model is a roadmap defining the steps that an organization needs to take to move from a chaotic process to a continuously improving process.
- The Capability Maturity Model (CMM) is the most well-known software process improvement roadmap.

- The CMM has been developed by the Software Engineering Institute based on Watts Humphrey's early work on characterizing the software process.
- Software practitioners worldwide contribute to the evolution of the CMM through the CMM Advisory Board and through the annual SEPG Conferences.

The CMM five maturity levels

The CMM comprises five maturity levels:

- Level 1 Initial: the process is characterized as *ad hoc* or chaotic.
- Level 2 Repeatable: the process is characterized as disciplined.
- Level 3 Defined: the process is characterized as standard and consistent.
- Level 4 Managed: the process is characterized as predictable.
- Level 5 Optimizing: the process is characterized as continuously improving.

Key process areas

The key process areas (KPA) are the building blocks of the CMM. They are assigned to specific maturity levels (there are none at level 1) as follows:

- *Level 1 Initial:*   No key process areas.

- *Level 2 Repeatable:*   Level 2 has six key process areas:
  - Requirements Management
  - Project Planning
  - Project Tracking and Oversight
  - Software Subcontract Management
  - Software Quality Assurance
  - Software Configuration Management

- *Level 3 Defined:*   Level 3 has seven key process areas:
  - Organization Process Focus
  - Organization Process Definition
  - Training Program
  - Integrated Software Management
  - Software Product Engineering
  - Intergroup Coordination
  - Peer Reviews

- *Level 4 Managed:*   Level 4 has two key process areas:
  - Quantitative Process Management
  - Software Quality Management

- *Level 5 Optimizing:*   Level 5 has three key process areas:
  - Defect Prevention
  - Technology Change Management
  - Process Change Management

Use of the CMM

The CMM can be used by the following:

- Software process assessment teams as a basis for assessing their software process
- Software process improvement teams as a basis for process improvement and process design
- Technical managers and staff to understand what is required for improving the software process
- Software process capability teams as a basis for evaluation of software suppliers.

Future development of the CMM

The CMM is continuously developing through contributions from software professionals worldwide. The plans for publishing version 2.0 of the CMM are already in progress. The CMM generic model is used as the basis for developing capability maturity models to process improvement in the following domains: CMM for Software (SW-CMM); Software Acquisition CMM (SA-CMM); Systems Engineering CMM (SE-CMM); Integrated Product Development CMM (IPD-CMM) and People CMM (P-CMM).

CHAPTER 14

CMM-based software process assessment

14.1 CMM-BASED APPRAISALS

14.1.1 WHAT IS A CMM-BASED APPRAISAL?

The Capability Maturity Model (CMM) is used as the basis for different types of software process assessments. These are generically known as CMM-based appraisals (CBA). CMM-based appraisals are any assessments based on the Capability Maturity Model's key process areas and the SEI questionnaire (Zubrow *et al*, 1994) (or a customized version of both).

Generally, an assessment has a number of essential components:

- A process model (against which to assess the current state of your process)
- An assessment method that specifies the phases and steps of the assessment
- One or more assessment tools to assist in the activities of fact gathering, fact analysis and reporting.

In CMM-based assessments, the process model and improvement road map used is the CMM, the assessment method contains the phases described below, and the assessment tool is the SEI maturity questionnaire. The CMM or a tailored version of it has been used as the basis for process models by a number of assessment methods (for example Trillium). It influences nearly all the other assessment methods.

In this chapter we review two approaches based on the CMM: one for SEI-assisted assessments (Olson *et al*, 1989) and the other for software capability evaluations (Humphrey and Sweet, 1987). Then we provide some guidelines on using the CMM as a basis for developing your own approach to self-assessment.

Within the context of software process improvement, the main objectives of assessments are 'to understand the state of the practice of the software process in an organization, to identify key areas for improvement, and to initiate actions that facilitate those improvements' (Olson *et al.*, 1989).

14.1.2 CONTEXT OF CMM-BASED ASSESSMENTS

The SEI has developed and is continuously refining a methodology for assessing the software process. The discussions below aim to provide an example of an assessment approach based on the CMM. The latest information on the SEI methodologies and the SEI process programme can be obtained by contacting the SEI Customer Relations Office.

The SEI assessment methodology uses the CMM as a framework for software process maturity, and uses a maturity questionnaire (MQ) as a fact-gathering tool to be used by the assessment team. In ISO/IEC 15504 terminology, the questionnaire is an 'assessment instrument'. The questionnaire is structured to reflect the key process areas of the CMM. It can be used in any of the three contexts of assessments summarized in Table 14.1.

The context of using the questionnaire will affect the way it is used, the freedom to customize it, and the degree of SEI involvement. Additional to the uses listed above, the CMM is used at workshops, conferences, tutorials and symposiums in which the SEI describes software process assessments, software capability evaluations and the assessment methodology. These events also enable the SEI to receive feedback on the quality of the maturity questionnaire and to gather industry-profile data from the questionnaire.

In the following sections we will discuss in detail each of the two contexts of SEI-assisted assessment and SEI capability evaluations. First, let us review the structure and contents of the maturity questionnaire that is the main assessment instrument for CMM-based assessments.

14.2 THE SEI MATURITY QUESTIONNAIRE

14.2.1 THE QUESTIONNAIRE

One of the main instruments of the CMM-based assessments is the process maturity questionnaire (MQ) developed by the SEI (Zubrow *et al.*, 1994). The questionnaire is an assessment instrument that is used in the Fact Gathering phase. Other fact-gathering instruments are interviews, workshops, group discussions, observation, and so on. The 1994 version of the questionnaire is based on the CMM version 1.1 and reflects the following features:

- The questionnaire focuses solely on process issues, derived from the CMM.
- The questionnaire is organized by CMM key process areas (KPAs), and covers the 18 KPAs of CMM Version 1.1.
- The questionnaire addresses the goals of each KPA, but not all of the key practices. It contains from six to eight questions per KPA.
- The questionnaire includes a glossary of terms and KPA descriptions to assist respondents who may be unfamiliar with CMM terminology.
- Ample space is provided beneath each question to allow respondents to provide additional information regarding their answers, i.e. further explanation of their answers or references to supporting documentation.
- There is room for customizing the questionnaire by adding more questions to cover more of the key practices.

An example of the questions in the SEI maturity questionnaire for the Software Configuration Management key process area is shown in Table 14.2.

Table 14.1   Contexts of CMM-based assessments

Context	Definition and scope
SEI-assisted assessments	• These are software process assessments conducted by a trained team of software professionals from both the SEI and the organization being assessed. • The scope of an SEI-assisted assessment is usually a section or division of an organization or possibly an entire site (i.e. one location of an organization).
Software capability evaluations	• The Software Capability Evaluation (SCE) method is a subset of an assessment. (The SEI does not perform evaluations, but it does offer training in conducting software capability evaluations.) • These are evaluations conducted as part of the Department of Defense (DoD) software acquisition process (or conducted by any other acquirer). • They may also be used by software organizations to evaluate subcontractors.
Self-assessment	• These are software process assessments conducted by a team of software professionals from the same organization undergoing the assessment. • The SEI trains in-house assessment teams to conduct self-assessments of their organization. • The scope of the self-assessment may be a division of an organization, an organizational site, or the entire organization. • Self-assessments provide a way for an organization to examine its own software process and monitor process improvement.

Table 14.2   Example of the questions in the SEI questionnaire (questions for Software Configuration Management key process area)

- Are software configuration management activities planned for the project?
- Has the project identified, controlled, and made available the software work products through the use of configuration management?
- Does the project follow a documented procedure to control changes to configuration items or units?
- Are standard reports on software baselines (i.e. software configuration control board minutes and change request summary and status reports) distributed to affected groups and individuals?
- Does the project follow a written organizational policy for implementing software configuration management activities?
- Are project personnel trained to perform the software configuration management activities for which they are responsible?
- Are measurements used to determine the status of activities for software configuration management (for example effort and funds expended for software configuration management activities)?
- Are periodic audits performed to verify that software baselines conform to the documentation that defines them (for example by the SCM group)?

14.2.2 USE OF THE QUESTIONNAIRE

In a CMM-based assessment the SEI process maturity questionnaire serves primarily to identify issues to be explored further through further interviews and discussions. Analysis of the response to the questionnaire provides focus areas for further discussion and fact finding activities, and highlights areas about which to request supporting information.

The SEI maturity questionnaire is intended for those interested in performing and learning about software process appraisals. The questionnaire is a tool for use in the context of process assessment. The descriptions for use of the maturity questionnaire for each appraisal method are completely addressed in the documentation for that method.

Organizations wishing to use the maturity questionnaire are strongly recommended to contact the SEI for information about the CMM-based appraisal methods. These methods include more specific guidance. It is important that you know that the questionnaire on its own is not a process assessment method, rather it is just one component of the whole assessment process. The questionnaire should be filled in by the assessment participants. They should be briefed on the structure and contents of the questionnaire and on the guidelines for answering the questions. The answer to each question can be one of four possible responses: Yes, No, Does Not Apply or Don't Know. Table 14.3 summarizes when each response is used. One response has to be checked for each question, and all the questions should be answered.

Table 14.3 Possible responses to the SEI process maturity questionnaire

Response	When to check the response
Yes	The practice is well established and consistently performed: 'The practice should be considered well established and consistently performed as a standard operating procedure.'
No	The practice is *not* well established or is inconsistently performed: 'The practice may be performed sometimes, or even frequently, but it is omitted under difficult circumstances.'
Does Not Apply	You have the required knowledge about your project or organization and the question asked, but you feel the question does not apply for your project: 'For example, the entire section on Software Subcontract Management may not apply to your project if you don't work with any subcontractors.'
Don't Know	You are uncertain about how to answer the question.

14.2.3 BENEFITS OF USING THE QUESTIONNAIRE

Using the questionnaire to start an assessment has several benefits, for example:

- The responses to the questionnaire will provide a detailed framework for identifying key issues for discussion later in the assessment.
- The questionnaire narrows the focus of the assessment team to selected key process areas, and helps the team to focus on areas most important to the organization.
- The questionnaire identifies areas about which to request supporting information.
- The questionnaire responses quickly establish an initial rating of an organization's software process maturity level.
- The questionnaire is used as a 'springboard' to start the software process improvement programme and set it in the right direction.
- The assessment provides a baseline for the current state of the software process in the organization. This baseline will provide the foundation upon which to base the improvement actions.
- Using consistent assessment tools and models (such as the SEI maturity questionnaire and the CMM) across assessments is likely to produce ratings and results in a reliable, consistent and repeatable manner.
- The questionnaire provides an entry point through which the assessment team can get to the truth about what really goes on in the software organization.

14.2.4 CUSTOMIZING THE SEI QUESTIONNAIRE

When using the SEI questionnaire for self-assessment, an organization may choose to customize the questionnaire. Usually the objective of such customization is to make the questions more aligned to one or more of the following:

- Objectives of the assessment
- Overall direction of the software process improvement programme
- Business and software environment (for example in-house development for business applications)
- Package acquisition strategy – 'Commercial-off-the-shelf' (COTS) strategy, and so on.

Customizing the questionnaire could involve one or more of the following actions:

1 Adding more questions to cover additional key practices in a key process area.
2 Adding more questions to cover non-process aspects, for example organizational, management or technology.
3 Customizing the number of key process areas covered by the questionnaire, for example by taking out the questions relating to a key process area that is not relevant to the organization being assessed. If the organization does not use software subcontractors, for example, the questions on software subcontract management are taken out of the questionnaire.
4 Also the CMM focuses solely on process-related issues. Sometimes it may be desirable to include other domains such as the organization or the technology. This means adding more questions to cover these areas. For example, in the questions on software configuration management listed in Table 14.2, an additional question could be about the CM tools used in the project. The same could be done for other key process areas.

14.3 THE SEI-ASSISTED ASSESSMENT

PROCESS

14.3.1 OBJECTIVES AND PHASES OF THE SEI-ASSISTED

ASSESSMENT

The SEI-assisted assessment is an assessment conducted jointly by members of the SEI staff and of the organization being assessed. It takes place under a legal agreement with the SEI. An SEI-assisted assessment has the following features:

- Uses the CMM as a process maturity framework
- Uses a questionnaire as a tool for the assessment team

Objectives of SEI-assisted assessments

SEI-assisted assessments have the following specific objectives:

- To determine the current state of the software process that is practised on a day-to-day basis in an organization.
- To identify the high-priority key areas for software process improvement on which the organization should focus its improvement efforts.
- To enrol key software practitioners in the software process improvement and change process.
- To help an organization focus on monitoring and improving its software process.
- To identify areas of strength and spread them across the organization.
- To send a copy of the assessment report back to the SEI to be stored in the assessments database.

Phases of SEI-assisted assessment

SEI-assisted assessments are typically conducted in six stages, as illustrated in Figure 14.1 and described in further detail in the following sections. In the figure, the assessment stages are mapped to the generic assessment phases described earlier in Chapter 8.

14.3.2 PRE-PLANNING

This phase takes place in two stages of the SEI-assisted assessments, selection and commitment, as follows.

Selection phase

This phase involves identifying an organization as a candidate for assessment and setting up an executive-level briefing. The SEI uses a number of guidelines in selecting candidate organizations for SEI-assisted assessments. The SEI considers the following factors:

- DoD priorities and needs
- The level of activity and affiliation between the SEI and the organization
- The extent to which the assessment and the data collected will be of value to the SEI
- The level of commitment of the organization's management to the assessment.

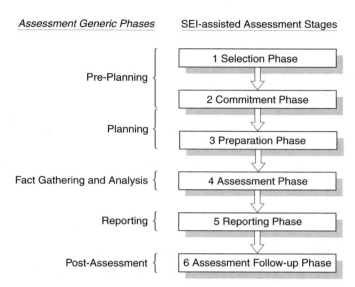

Assessment Generic Phases   SEI-assisted Assessment Stages

Pre-Planning
- 1 Selection Phase
- 2 Commitment Phase

Planning
- 3 Preparation Phase

Fact Gathering and Analysis
- 4 Assessment Phase

Reporting
- 5 Reporting Phase

Post-Assessment
- 6 Assessment Follow-up Phase

Figure 14.1   SEI-assisted assessment process phases mapped to the generic assessment cycle

Commitment phase

In this phase, the organization commits to the full assessment process. An assessment agreement is signed by senior representatives of the organization and the SEI. This commitment includes the personal participation of the senior site manager, site representation on the assessment team, and agreement to take action on the assessment recommendations. This phase includes a number of activities:

- Conducting an executive-level briefing
- Signing the assessment agreement
- Selecting the assessment team.

14.3.3 PLANNING

This phase takes place in one stage of the SEI-assisted assessments, that is the preparation phase, as follows.

Preparation phase

The third phase is devoted to preparing for the on-site assessment. An assessment team, composed of members from the SEI and the organization being assessed, receives training. In addition, the on-site assessment is planned. The assessment participants are selected and briefed about the assessment process, including times, duration, and purpose of their participation. The questionnaire can also be filled in at this time. This phase includes a number of activities:

- Pre-assessment team training
- Project selection criteria
- Organizational briefing
- Assessment team training. Typical contents of such training are:
  - Process management overview
  - Organizational briefing
  - Assessment process overview
  - Maturity questionnaire
  - Review of project responses
  - Assessment discussions
  - Team-building exercises
  - Assessment findings
  - Final report preparation
  - Planning for the assessment
- Preparing for the on-site period. This includes the following activities:
  - Selecting the assessment participants, for example to include representatives from software quality assurance and release, software integration and test, coding and unit test, requirements and high-level design
  - Briefing the assessment participants to prepare them for the assessment. This briefing could cover the following: assessment principles, assessment overview and a detailed schedule for the on-site period
  - Filling out the questionnaire by project representatives of the selected projects.

14.3.4 ASSESSMENT

The activities in this phase are grouped in two categories, fact gathering and analysis, plus reporting. We will consider each of them separately.

Fact gathering and analysis – assessment phase

These activities take place in one stage of the SEI-assisted assessments, that is the on-site assessment phase. At this phase the on-site assessment is conducted. It takes a minimum of four days; most assessments take 5–8 days (Weber *et al.*, 1991). The on-site assessment is structured as follows (Figure 14.2 illustrates the flow of the main activities of the on-site period):

- On the first day: senior management and assessment participants' briefings. They are briefed as a group about the objectives and activities of the assessment. The project representatives complete the assessment questionnaire (if they have not done so previously). The resulting data and information are reviewed and analysed by the assessment team. The team then holds discussions with each project.

- On the second day, the team conducts discussions with the key software practitioners, who provide further insight into the software process.
- Over the course of the third day, the assessment team formulates findings based upon the information that has been collected on the previous days and gets feedback from the project representatives.
- On the fourth and last day, the findings are reviewed with the project representatives to help ensure that the assessment team understands the issues correctly. The findings are revised, if necessary, and presented to the assessment participants and senior site management.
- The assessment ends with formulation of the recommendations that address the findings.

Reporting – reporting phase

The fifth phase is concerned with the final formulation and communication of assessment findings and specific recommendations that address those findings. The assessment team prepares a formal written report, which is given to the organization along with a formal presentation of the recommendations. Presentation of the assessment findings would usually include the following: scope of the assessment, how the assessment was conducted, composite organizational status, examples of any strengths found, summary of the findings, and next steps. This is followed by formulating the recommendations and getting the assessment team's consensus on what goes on in the final report. Some guidelines used by the assessment team for formulating recommendations are:

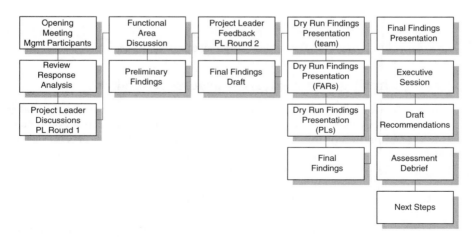

Figure 14.2 The SEI-assisted assessment on-site period

- Address each key finding.
- Limit the number of recommendations.
- Make recommendations specific and concise.
- Prioritize the recommendations.
- Focus on 'what' the recommendations are, not 'how' they will be implemented.
- Make the recommendations realistic. Be sensitive to the impact of the recommendations on the organization's resources. For example, if there are ten recommendations, the highest priority recommendations (say three) are grouped together into priority group one. Then other recommendations are grouped into other priority groups.

Following the on-site assessment phase, the assessment team prepares a final report of the assessment findings and recommendations. The purpose of the final report is to document the assessment, describe the key findings, and make specific recommendations to the organization based on these findings. The final report is the only permanent record of the assessment and will be used as a reference for the action plan formulation and execution. It should be written carefully.

The final report is reviewed for quality by the SEI. The report should contain the following sections: Executive Summary, Organizational Status, Key Findings, Recommendations, Appendices. After the final report is completed, the assessment team leader gives a presentation summarizing the main findings to the senior site manager, his or her immediate staff, the assessment team members, and the assessment participants. The main purpose of this presentation is to provide an overview of the recommendations to senior management and to deliver the final report.

14.3.5 POST-ASSESSMENT

This phase covers the activities needed to transform the assessment findings and recommendations into an action plan, plus any continuing support and guidance required from the SEI. These activities take place in the assessment follow-up phase.

Assessment follow-up phase

In the final phase, an action team composed entirely of professionals from the assessed organization is assembled and charged with formulating an action plan and facilitating its implementation. Developing the action plan is most effective when done as a team effort involving all organizational units involved in implementation.

An action plan should be sufficiently detailed to provide a clear guide for execution by including the following:

- What recommendations will be implemented (action tasks)
- What recommendations will not be implemented, and why
- How each action task will be implemented
- Resources required to implement each action task
- Person responsible for each task
- Action task schedule.

The action plan should be reviewed with senior management and it should also specify regular checkpoints for periodic management reviews.

Typically, there is also some continuing support and guidance from the SEI. After approximately 18 months, a reassessment or self-assessment is done by the organization to determine progress. This also motivates the continuation of the cycle of software process improvement. This follow-up assessment has the following purposes:

- To assess the progress that has been made
- To establish a target for completion of the most important actions
- To establish new priorities for continued improvement.

After receiving the final report, the organization spends three to six months developing an action plan. Implementation of the software process improvement actions begins when the plan is approved by senior management. Eighteen months later, the organization may be ready to conduct a self-assessment to evaluate progress and determine the new status of its software process.

14.4 SEI SOFTWARE CAPABILITY EVALUATION (SCE)

14.4.1 INTRODUCTION

Software capability evaluation is sometimes referred to in the literature as capability determination. The following is a review of various definitions of software capability evaluation or determination.

ISO/IEC 15504 defines Process Capability Evaluation as 'a systematic assessment and analysis of selected software processes within an organization against a target capability, carried out with the aim of identifying the strengths, weaknesses and risks associated with deploying the processes to meet a particular specified requirement' (ISO, 1997).

Note that SPICE, the forerunner of ISO/IEC 15504, used the word 'determination' in place of 'evaluation'. In this book we will take the liberty of using either of these two words to refer to the same thing.

SEI defines software capability evaluation as 'an appraisal by a trained team of professionals to identify contractors who are qualified to perform the software work or to monitor the state of the software process used on an existing software effort' (Paulk *et al.*, 1994).

The SEI developed a method for software capability evaluation with the abbreviation SCE based on the Capability Maturity Model (CMM). SCE is a method for evaluating the software process of an organization to gain insight into its software capability. As in the case of software process assessment, the insight gained through SCE also can be a valuable input to process improvement activities.

The processes evaluated by the SCE focus on the management aspects of the project management, engineering and technical support processes (for example project management, peer reviews, integration, and test). The SCE team evaluates the organization's software project development practices against the key process areas (KPAs) of the CMM, in order to determine whether the organization follows a stable, predictable software process.

Although a mature process does not guarantee a successful product, the likelihood of success should increase as the software processes mature. SCE is a model-based method that provides a structure for collecting information resulting from investigating the practices within the key process areas of the CMM relating them to the goals of that KPA.

14.4.2 PHASES OF SOFTWARE CAPABILITY EVALUATION

The SCE method consists of five phases: Evaluation, General and Specific Preparation, Site Data Collection, and Findings (Humphrey and Sweet, 1987) (as illustrated in Figure 14.3). These are summarized as follows.

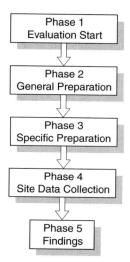

Figure 14.3 Phases of the SEI Software Capability Evaluation (SCE) method

Phase 1 – Evaluation Start

Activities in this phase are performed by the sponsoring or procuring organization. It comprises the following activities:

- Determining the attributes of the desired software product and the project required to produce it
- Determining the process capability that is most applicable for the planned development
- Selecting the SCE team.

Phase 2 – General Preparation

Activities in this phase are performed by the SCE team. It comprises the following activities:

- Identifying areas where the development organization lacks experience
- Defining the scope of the SCE to be investigated.

Phase 3 – Specific Preparation

Activities in this phase are performed by the SCE team. It comprises the following activities:

- Selecting projects for evaluation
- Preparing specific topics corresponding to the sub-process areas for evaluation
- Coordinating preparation for the site data collection activities.

Phase 4 – Site Data Collection

Activities in this phase are performed by the SCE team. It comprises the following activities:

- Visiting the site and investigating each critical sub-process area in enough depth to determine their strengths, weaknesses and observable improvement activities
- Determining strengths, weaknesses and improvement activities through interviewing and document reviews.

Phase 5 – Findings

Activities in this phase are performed by the SCE team. It comprises the following activities:

- Consolidating the decisions made in phase 4 relating the findings to key process areas and sub-process areas
- Expressing the findings as KPA strengths and weaknesses and improvement activities
- Conclusion and completion.

14.4.3 SOFTWARE CAPABILITY EVALUATION VERSUS

SOFTWARE PROCESS ASSESSMENT

Although both can use the same process improvement model, there are some differences between software process assessment and software capability evaluation. The main differences concern focus, ownership of the results, and the composition of the teams conducting the assessment or the evaluation. Figure 14.4 summarizes some of these differences between the SEI approaches for software capability evaluation (SCE) and software process assessment (SPA).

The ISO/IEC 15504 standard differentiates between software process assessment and software capability evaluation as illustrated in Figure 14.5.

One of the main differences is that capability evaluation is performed against a target capability. The target capability is determined by the nature, scope and motivation of the capability evaluation, while the process assessment is always performed against a standard process model or a variant of such a model.

Software Capability Evaluation (SCE)	Software Process Assessment (SPA)
• Used by DoD or another major customer for selection and monitoring of software contractors or for assessing the risks associated with the procurement of a given product	• For the use of the organization to improve its software process
• Results known to DoD or the initiator of the evaluation	• Results are confidential to the organization
• Substantiates current practice	• Assesses current practice of one or more software producing units
• Assesses contractor commitment to improve/monitor a quality/capability improvement programme	• Acts as a catalyst for process improvement
• Analyses contract performance and potential	• Provides input for improvement action plan
• Findings restricted to maturity model issues	• Findings may include issues not explicit in maturity model (for example organizational issues)
• Audit-oriented – no organization members on team	• Collaborative – organization must have members on team
• Applies to performance on one specific contract	• Applies to the organization, not individual projects or contracts

Figure 14.4 Differences between the SEI's Software Capability Evaluation and Software Process Assessment

Software Process Assessment

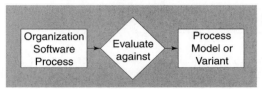

Software Process Capability Evaluation

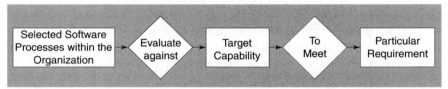

Figure 14.5 Software Process Assessment versus Software Capability Evaluation

SUMMARY

CMM-based assessments

These are assessments that use the CMM as a process model against which to assess the processes, and use the SEI questionnaire as an assessment instrument.

The SEI questionnaire

The questionnaire is an assessment instrument developed by the SEI.

- It focuses only on process related issues.
- It is structured according to the CMM key process areas.
- The questions focus on the goals of the key process areas (not the key practices).
- The response has four options: Yes, No, Does not apply, and Don't know.

Customizing the SEI questionnaire for self-assessment

The SEI questionnaire has questions that relate to the goals of the CMM key process areas. For the right reasons it could be customized to add more questions about organizational aspects, technology aspects, and so on. This should be considered as one of the attractive features of the CMM.

SEI-assisted software process assessments

SEI-assisted software process assessments differ from self-assessments in that they have the following special features:

- They are performed by joint teams from both the SEI and the organization being assessed.
- They are based on the CMM and the SEI questionnaire.
- They are controlled by an agreement between the SEI and the organization being assessed.

Software capability evaluations

These are assessments performed on behalf of an acquirer (for example the Department of Defense). The main aim is to assess the risks associated with a particular project or software supplier.

CHAPTER 15

ISO/IEC 15504 Draft Technical Report for Software Process Assessment

15.1 INTRODUCTION

15.1.1 MOTIVATION AND BACKGROUND

By the early 1990s, process improvement and capability determination methods had been developed in several countries. Some addressed just process improvement, others just capability determination, and some both. Some were targeted at large organizations, others at small ones; some were openly available while others were proprietary. Several methods had evolved from pioneering work on software process maturity carried out at the Software Engineering Institute of Carnegie Mellon University in the US. All sought to identify and assess key software processes in order to analyse strengths, weaknesses and risks. An international consensus soon began to emerge on the urgent need for a public domain standard for software process assessment. This was driven by the prospect of being able to compare the outputs of different methods, and maybe even *reuse* them for both process improvement and capability determination.

In June 1991 in London (UK), the Joint Technical Committee 1/Sub-Committee 7 (JTC1/SC7) of the International Organization for Standardization and the International Electrotechnical Commission (ISO/IEC) approved at its plenary meeting a resolution recommending the creation of a new working group (WG10) to develop an international standard on software process assessment. In January 1993, ISO/IEC JTC1 adopted the resolution and assigned the task to WG10. WG10 mandated the establishment of a special project called SPICE (Software Process Improvement and Capability dEtermination) to ensure a fast development route and to solicit the opinions of world leading experts.

A meeting in January 1993 established that a wide range of international bodies was willing to commit effort to developing a new ISO standard. An innovative approach was proposed, and the SPICE project was set up outside normal ISO structures to carry through a rapid development. The project was closely aligned with ISO/IEC JTC1/SC7/WG10, and an International Project Manager – supported by five Regional Technical Centre Managers – coordinates contributions from several experts in 20 countries representing industry, government and universities (Dorling, 1997, Barker, 1996).

The result of this effort is a suite of draft standards on software process. SPICE was inspired by numerous efforts on software process around the world including the SEI's work with the Capability Maturity Model (CMM) and Bell Canada's Trillium. As in the case of any evolving standard, ISO/IEC 15504 is continuously under review and development. The information provided in this chapter reflects the status of SPICE at the time of writing; readers interested in the most up-to-date information on ISO/IEC 15504 are advised to contact their local ISO organization.

Figure 15.1 depicts the evolution of SPICE.

15.1.2 BENEFITS OF A PROCESS STANDARD

Organizations can use the ISO/IEC 15504 draft standard in one of the following modes:

- *Capability determination mode:* To help determine the capability of a potential software supplier.
- *Process improvement mode:* To help improve their own software development process.
- *Self-assessment mode:* To help determine their ability to undertake a new project.

The benefits of an International Standard on software process assessment are numerous. It assists the following potential users to achieve the following objectives:

- *Purchasers:* To determine the capability of software suppliers and assess the risk involved in selecting one supplier over another.
- *Acquirers:* Ability to determine the current and potential capability of a supplier's software processes.
- *Software suppliers:* Ability to use one process assessment scheme instead of having to go through numerous schemes. It will provide them with the ability to determine the current and potential capability of their own software processes and to define areas and priorities for software process

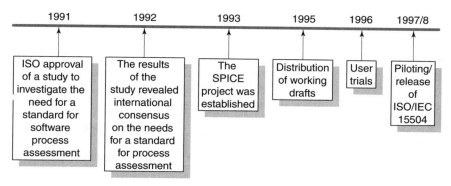

Figure 15.1 Milestones in SPICE evolution to ISO/IEC 15504

improvement, and with a framework that defines a route map for software process improvement.

- *Software development organizations:* To have a tool to initiate and sustain a continuous process improvement programme.
- *Managers:* To ensure that their software development process is aligned with and supports the business needs of the organization.
- *Assessors:* A framework that defines all aspects of conducting assessments.

15.2 ARCHITECTURE OF THE ISO/IEC 15504 DRAFT TECHNICAL REPORT

15.2.1 ISO/IEC 15504 PRODUCTS ARCHITECTURE

Figure 15.2 illustrates the set of documents initially developed by the SPICE project and currently published by the International Standards Organization as the draft ISO/IEC 15504. The following sections summarize the contents of these documents.

15.2.2 ISO/IEC 15504 DOCUMENTS

Part I: *Concepts and introductory guide* (informative)

This part is an entry point into the International Standard. It describes how the parts of the suite fit together, and provides guidance for their selection and use. It explains the requirements contained within the Standard and their

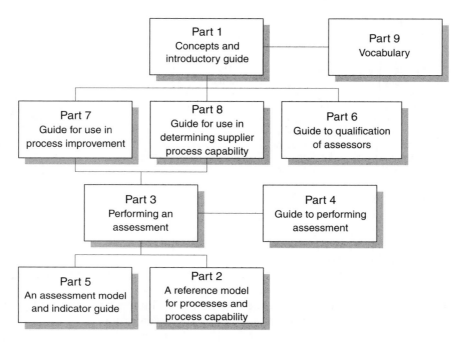

Figure 15.2 Components of the ISO/IEC 15504 standard

applicability to the conduct of an assessment, to the construction and selection of supporting tools, and to the construction of extended processes. (Extended processes are processes that include base practices additional to those defined in part 2 of the Standard, or which are entirely new processes, for example to meet industry-specific requirements.)

Part 2: *A reference model for processes and process capability (normative)*

This part of the International Standard defines, at a high level, a two dimensional reference model for describing processes and process capability used in a process assessment. The reference model defines a set of processes and a framework for evaluating the capability of the processes through assessment of process attributes structured into capability levels.

Part 3: *Performing an assessment* (normative)

This part of the International Standard defines the requirements for performing an assessment, in such a way that the outcome will be repeatable, reliable and consistent.

Part 4: *Guide to performing assessment* (informative)

This part of the International Standard provides guidance on performing software process assessments. This guidance is generic enough to be applicable across all organizations, and also for performing assessments using a variety of different methods and techniques and supported by a range of tools. It covers the selection and use of a compatible assessment; of a supportive method for assessment; and of an appropriate assessment instrument or tool.

Part 5: *An assessment model and indicator guidance* (informative)

This part of the International Standard provides an example model for performing process assessments that is based upon and is directly compatible with the reference model in ISO/IEC 15504. The assessment model extends the reference model through the inclusion of a comprehensive set of indicators of process performance and capability.

Part 6: *Guide to qualification of assessors* (informative)

This part of the International Standard describes the competence, education, training and experience of assessors that are relevant to conducting process assessments. It describes mechanisms that may be used to demonstrate competence and to validate education, training and experience.

Part 7: *Guide for use in process improvement* (informative)

This part of the International Standard describes how to define the inputs to and use the results of an assessment for the purposes of process improvement. The guide includes examples of the application of process improvement in a variety of situations.

Part 8: *Guide for use in determining supplier process capability* (informative)

This part of the International Standard describes how to define the inputs to and use the results of an assessment for the purpose of process capability determination. It addresses process capability determination both in straightforward situations and in more complex situations involving, for example, future capability. The guidance on conducting process capability determination is applicable either for use within an organization to determine its own capability, or by an acquirer to determine the capability of a (potential) supplier.

Part 9: *Vocabulary* (informative)

This part is a consolidated vocabulary of all terms specifically defined for the purposes of ISO/IEC 15504.

(ISO/IEC 15504 Part 1)

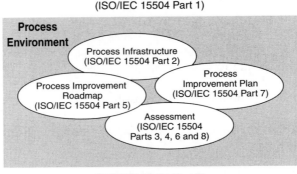

(ISO/IEC 15504 Part 9)

Figure 15.3 Applicability of ISO/IEC 15504 documents to the software process improvement framework

Figure 15.3 illustrates the applicability of ISO/IEC 15504 documents to the software process improvement framework proposed in this book and described in Part 2.

15.2.3 STRUCTURE OF ISO/IEC 15504 REFERENCE MODEL

ISO/IEC 15504 reference model architecture for processes and process capability is made up of two dimensions:

- Process dimension, which is characterized by process purposes which are the essential measurable objectives of a process, and the expected outcome of the process that indicates its successful completion.
- Process capability dimension, which is characterized by a series of process attributes, applicable to any process, and represents measurable characteristics necessary to manage a process and improve its capability to perform.

The process dimension

The reference model groups the processes in the process dimension into five process categories, according to the type of activity they address. Figure 15.4 illustrates the different ISO/IEC 15504 process categories. They are defined as follows:

1 **The Customer–Supplier process category (CUS)** comprises processes that directly impact on the customer, support development and transition of the software to the customer, and provide for its correct operation and use.
2 **The Engineering process category (ENG)** comprises processes that directly specify, implement or maintain a system and software product and its user documentation.

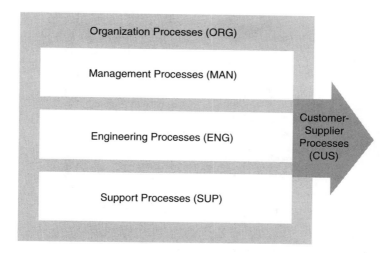

Figure 15.4 ISO/IEC 15504 process categories

3 **The Support process category (SUP)** comprises processes that may be employed by any of the other processes (including other supporting processes) at various points in the software lifecycle.

4 **The Management process category (MAN)** comprises processes that contain generic practices that may be used by anyone who manages any sort of project within a software lifecycle.

5 **The Organization process category (ORG)** comprises processes that establish the business goals of the organization and develop process, product and resource assets. When used by the projects in the organization, these processes will help the organization achieve its business goals.

   Process categories and processes provide a grouping by type of activity. Each process in the reference model is described in terms of a purpose statement. Satisfying the purpose statements of a process represents the first step in building process capability. This is equivalent to the goals of the CMM key process areas (see Chapter 13).

The capability dimension

A capability level is a set of attribute(s) that work together to provide a major enhancement in the capability to perform a process. Each level provides a major enhancement of capability in the performance of a process. The levels constitute a rational way of progressing through improvement of the capability of any process. ISO/IEC 15504 specifies six capability levels in the reference model (numbered 0 to 5). These are illustrated in Figure 15.5. The capability levels incorporate nine process attributes.

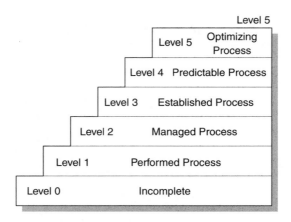

Figure 15.5   ISO/IEC 15504 process capability levels

A process capability is determined by whether the process purpose statement has been achieved. The reference model does not define how, or in what order, the process purpose statements are to be achieved. The process purpose will be achieved in an organization through the activities, tasks and practices being carried out to produce work products. These performed tasks, activities and practices, and the characteristics of the work products produced, are the indicators that demonstrate whether the specific process purpose is being achieved.

The reference model alone cannot be used as the basis for conducting reliable and consistent assessments of process capability since the level of detail is not sufficient. The descriptions of process purpose and capability attributes in the reference model need to be supported by a comprehensive set of indicators of process performance and capability. In this way, consistent ratings of process capability will be possible.

15.3   ISO/IEC 15504 PROCESS CATEGORIES

ISO/IEC 15504 provides a classification of the processes normally undertaken by organizations concerned with the development, maintenance, acquisition, supply and operation of software. The classification recognizes a number of process categories each of which contains a number of processes. The process categories and processes are strongly aligned to those defined in *ISO/IEC 12207, Software Life Cycle Process*. The five process categories are CUS (Customer–Supplier) processes, ENG (Engineering) processes, SUP (Support) processes, MAN (Management) processes, and ORG (Organization) processes.

The description of each process contains two sections: a statement of the purpose of the process, and one or more notes providing further information. The statement of purpose describes at a high level the overall objectives of performing the process, and expanded to describe in generic terms the likely outcomes of effective implementation of the process. The notes provide further information about the process, and its relation to the processes defined in ISO/IEC 12207 and to other processes in this reference model. The following sections briefly describe these process categories.

15.3.1 CUSTOMER–SUPPLIER PROCESS CATEGORY (CUS)

The *Customer–Supplier* process category, referred to as the **CUS Processes**, consists of processes that directly impact the customer. These are the processes that support development and transition of the software to the customer, and provide for its correct operation and use. There are five processes belonging to the Customer–Supplier process category: Acquire software, Manage customer needs, Supply software, Operate software, and Provide customer service. They are illustrated in Figure 15.6 and briefly described in the following sections.

CUS.1 Acquire software

- *Purpose:* To obtain the product and/or service that will satisfy the need expressed by the customer. The acquisition process is enacted by the acquirer. The process begins with the identification of a customer need and ends with the acceptance of the product and/or service needed by the customer.
- *Expected outcome:* Successful implementation of the process should lead to the development of a contract that clearly expresses the expectation, responsibilities and liabilities of both the supplier and the customer. The contract should specify a product and/or service that will be produced to satisfy the customer need. The acquisition will be managed so that specified constraints (for example cost, schedule and quality) are met.

CUS.2 Manage customer needs

- *Purpose:* To manage the gathering, processing and tracking of ongoing customer needs and requirements throughout the operational life of the software; to establish a software requirements' baseline that serves as the basis for the project's software work products and activities; and to manage changes to this baseline.
- *Expected outcome:* Successful implementation of the process should lead to the following:
  - Establishing clear and ongoing communication with the customer
  - Defining documented and agreed customer requirements and managing changes
  - Establishing customer requirements as a baseline for project use

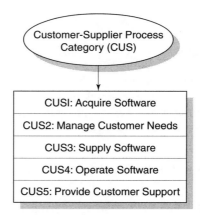

Figure 15.6 ISO/IEC 15504 customer–supplier processes

- Establishing a mechanism for ongoing monitoring of customer needs
- Establishing a mechanism for ensuring that customers are easily able to determine the status and disposition of their requests.

CUS.3 Supply software

- *Purpose:* To package, deliver and install the software at the customer site; and to ensure that quality software is delivered as defined by the requirements.
- *Expected outcome:* Successful implementation of the process should lead to the following:
  - Requirements for packaging, delivering and installing the software will be determined
  - Software will be packaged in a way that facilitates its efficient and effective installation and operation
  - Quality software as defined by the requirements will be successfully delivered to the customer and installed in accordance with the identified requirements.

CUS.4 Operate software

- *Purpose:* To support the correct and efficient operation of the software for the duration of its intended usage in its installed environment.
- *Expected outcome:* Successful implementation of the process should lead to the following:
  - Identifying and managing operational risks for the software introduction and operation
  - Running the software in its intended operational environment according to documented procedures

- Providing operational support by resolving operational problems and handling user enquiries and requests
- Providing assurance that software (and host system) capacities are adequate to meet user needs.

CUS.5 Provide customer service

- *Purpose:*   To establish and maintain an acceptable level of service to the customer to support effective use of the software.
- *Expected outcome:*   Successful implementation of the process should lead to the following:
  - Identifying the customer support service needs on an ongoing basis
  - Ongoing assessment of customer satisfaction with both the support services being provided and the product itself
  - Meeting customer needs through delivery of appropriate services.

15.3.2 ENGINEERING PROCESS CATEGORY (ENG)

The *Engineering* process category, referred to as the **ENG Processes**, consists of processes that directly specify, implement or maintain a system and software product and its user documentation. In circumstances where the system is composed totally of software, the Engineering process deals only with the construction and maintenance of such software. There are seven processes belonging to the Engineering process category: Develop system requirements and design, Develop software requirements, Develop software design, Implement software design, Integrate and test software, Integrate and test system, and Maintain system and software. They are illustrated in Figure 15.7 and briefly described in the following sections.

ENG.1 Develop system requirements and design

- *Purpose:*   To establish the system requirements (functional and non-functional) and architecture identifying which system requirements should be allocated to which elements of the system and to which releases. This process should be achieved by a group of people representing the diverse components of the system. Examples of those who should be involved are users, operators, hardware experts, software engineers, and so on.
- *Expected outcome:*   Successful implementation of the process should lead to the following:
  - Development of requirements of the system that matches the customer's stated and implied needs
  - Proposing an effective solution that identifies the main elements of the system
  - Allocating the defined requirements to each of the system's main elements

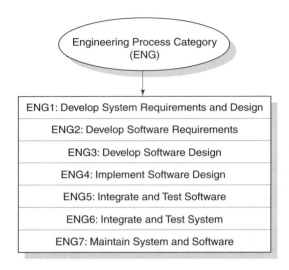

Figure 15.7 ISO/IEC 15504 engineering processes

- Developing a relevant release strategy that defines the priority for implementing system requirements
- Communicating the requirements, proposed solution and their relationships to all affected parties.

ENG.2 Develop software requirements

- *Purpose:* To establish the requirements of the software component of the system.
- *Expected outcome:* Successful implementation of the process should lead to the following:
  - Defining the requirements allocated to software components of the system and their interfaces to match the customer's stated and implied needs
  - Developing analysed, correct and testable software requirements
  - Understanding the impact of software requirements on the operating environment
  - Developing a relevant software release strategy that defines the priority for implementing software requirements
  - Approving the software requirements and updating them as needed
  - Communicating the software requirements to all affected parties.

ENG.3 Develop software design

- *Purpose:* To define a design for the software that accommodates the requirements and can be tested against them.

- *Expected outcome:* Successful implementation of the process should lead to the following:
  - Developing an architectural design that describes major software components that accommodate the software requirements
  - Defining internal and external interfaces of each software component
  - Developing a detailed design that describes software units that can be built and tested
  - Establishing traceability between software requirements and software designs.

ENG.4 Implement software design

- *Purpose:* To produce executable software units and to verify that they properly reflect the software design.
- *Expected outcome:* Successful implementation of the process should lead to the following:
  - Defining verification criteria for all software units against software requirements
  - Producing all software units defined by the design
  - Accomplishing verification of the software units against the design.

ENG.5 Integrate and test software

- *Purpose:* To integrate the software units with each other producing software that will satisfy the software requirements.
- *Expected outcome:* This process is accomplished step by step by individuals or teams. Successful implementation of the process should lead to the following:
  - Developing an integration strategy for software units consistent with the release strategy
  - Developing acceptance criteria for aggregates that verify compliance with the software requirements allocated to the units
  - Verifying software aggregates using the defined acceptance criteria
  - Verifying integrated software using the defined acceptance criteria
  - Recording test results
  - Developing a regression strategy for re-testing aggregates or the integrated software should a change in components be made.

ENG.6 Integrate and test system

- *Purpose:* To integrate the software component with other components, such as manual operations or hardware, producing a complete system that will satisfy the user's expectations expressed in the system requirements. This process is managed step by step, by a group of people including a software expert.
- *Expected outcome:* Successful implementation of the process should lead to the following:

- Developing an integration plan to build system unit aggregates according to the release strategy
- Defining acceptance criteria for each aggregate to verify compliance with the system requirements allocated to the units
- Verifying system aggregates using the defined acceptance criteria
- Constructing an integrated system demonstrating compliance with the system requirements (functional, non-functional, operations and maintenance)
- Recording test results
- Developing a regression strategy for re-testing aggregates or the integrated system should a change in components be made.

ENG.7 Maintain system and software

- *Purpose:* To manage modification, migration and retirement of system components (such as hardware, software, manual operations, network if any) in response to user requests. The origin of requests might be a discovered problem or the need for improvement or adaptation. The objective is to modify and/or retire existing systems and/or software while preserving the integrity of organizational operations.
- *Expected outcome:* Successful implementation of the process should lead to the following:
  - Defining the impact of organization, operations and interfaces on the existing system in operation
  - Updating specifications, design documents and test plans
  - Developing modified system components with associated documentation and tests that demonstrate that the system requirements are not compromised
  - Migrating system and software upgrades to the user's environment on request
  - Retiring software and systems from use in a controlled manner that minimizes disturbance to the users.

15.3.3 SUPPORT PROCESS CATEGORY (SUP)

The *Support* process category, referred to as the **SUP Processes**, consists of processes that may be employed by any of the other processes (including other supporting processes) at various points in the software lifecycle. The Support process category comprises eight processes: Develop documentation, Perform configuration management, Perform quality assurance, Perform work product verification, Perform work product validation, Perform joint reviews, Perform audits, and Perform problem resolution. They are illustrated in Figure 15.8 and briefly described in the following sections.

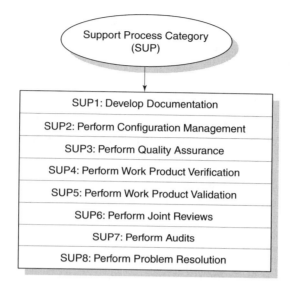

Figure 15.8 ISO/IEC 15504 support processes

SUP.I Develop documentation

- *Purpose:* To develop and maintain documents recording information produced by a process or activity within a process.
- *Expected outcome:* Successful implementation of the process should lead to the following:
  - Identifying all documents to be produced by the process or project
  - Specifying the content and purpose of all documents, and their production, planned and scheduled
  - Identifying the standards to be applied for development of documents
  - Developing all documents published in accordance with identified standards and in accordance with nominated plans
  - Maintaining all documents in accordance with specified criteria.

SUP.2 Perform configuration management

- *Purpose:* To establish and maintain the integrity of all of the work products of a process or project.
- *Expected outcome:* Successful implementation of the process should lead to the following:
  - Identifying, defining and baselining all relevant items generated by the process or project

- Controlling modifications and releases
- Recording and reporting the status of the items and modification requests
- Ensuring the completeness and consistency of the items
- Controlling storage, handling and delivery of the items.

SUP.3 Perform quality assurance

- *Purpose:* To ensure that work products and activities of a process or a project comply with all applicable standards, procedures and requirements.
- *Expected outcome:* Successful implementation of the process should lead to the following:
  - Identifying, planning and scheduling quality assurance activities for the process or project
  - Identifying quality standards, methodologies, procedures and tools for performing quality assurance activities
  - Identifying resources and responsibilities for the performance of quality assurance activities
  - Ability of those responsible for performing quality assurance activities to carry out their duties independently of the management and performers of the process assured
  - Performing the identified quality assurance activities in line with the relevant plans and schedules.

SUP.4 Perform work product verification

- *Purpose:* To confirm that each work product of a process or project properly reflects the requirements for its construction.
- *Expected outcome:* Successful implementation of the process should lead to the following:
  - Identifying criteria for verification of all required work products
  - Performing required verification activities
  - Finding and removing defects efficiently from products produced by the project.

SUP.5 Perform work product validation

- *Purpose:* To confirm that the specific requirements for a particular intended use of the work product are fulfilled.
- *Expected outcome:* Successful implementation of the process should lead to the following:
  - Identifying criteria for validation of all required work products
  - Performing required validation activities
  - Providing evidence that the work products as developed are suitable for their intended use.

SUP.6 Perform joint reviews

- *Purpose:* To maintain a common understanding, with the customer, of the progress against the objectives of the contract and what should be done to help ensure development of a product that satisfies the customer.
- *Expected outcome:* Successful implementation of the process should lead to the following:
  - Evaluating the status and products of an activity of a process through joint reviews between the customers, suppliers and other stakeholders (or interested parties)
  - Planning and scheduling the joint reviews to be performed
  - Tracking to closure action items resulting from reviews.

SUP.7 Perform audits

- *Purpose:* To confirm independently that the products and processes employed conform with the specific requirements defined.
- *Expected outcome:* Successful implementation of the process should lead to the following:
  - Determining compliance with requirements, plans and contract as appropriate
  - Arranging the conduct of audits of work products or process performance by an appropriate independent party.

SUP.8 Perform problem resolution

- *Purpose:* To ensure that all discovered problems are analysed and removed, and trends are identified.
- *Expected outcome:* Successful implementation of the process should lead to the following:
  - Providing a timely, responsive and documented means, to ensure that all discovered problems are analysed and resolved
  - Providing a mechanism for recognizing and acting on trends in problems identified.

15.3.4 MANAGEMENT PROCESS CATEGORY (MAN)

The *Management* process category, referred to as **MAN Processes**, consists of processes that contain practices of a generic nature that may be used by anyone who manages any sort of project or process within a software lifecycle. The Management process category comprises four processes: Manage the project, Manage quality, Manage risks, and Manage subcontractors. They are illustrated in Figure 15.9 and briefly described in the following sections.

MAN.I Manage the project

- *Purpose:* To define the processes necessary to establish, coordinate and manage a project and the resources necessary to produce a product.
- *Expected outcome:* Successful implementation of the process should lead to the following:
  - Defining the scope of the work for the project
  - Sizing, estimating, planning, tracking and measuring the tasks and resources necessary to complete the work
  - Identifying and managing interfaces between elements in the project, and with other projects and organizational units
  - Taking corrective action when project targets are not achieved.

MAN.2 Manage quality

- *Purpose:* To manage the quality of the project's products and services and to ensure that they satisfy the customer. The process involves establishing a focus on managing the quality of product and process at both the project and the organizational level.
- *Expected outcome:* Successful implementation of the process should lead to the following:
  - Establishing quality goals, based on the customer's quality requirements, for various checkpoints within the project's software lifecycle
  - Defining and using metrics that measure the results of project activities, at checkpoints within the project's lifecycle, to assess whether the quality goals have been achieved
  - Systematically identifying good practices for software engineering and integrating them into the software lifecycle models employed
  - Performing the identified quality activities and confirming their performance
  - Taking corrective action when quality goals are not achieved.

MAN.3 Manage risks

- *Purpose:* To continuously identify and mitigate the project risks throughout the lifecycle of a project. The process involves establishing a focus on management of risks at both the project and organizational levels.
- *Expected outcome:* Successful implementation of the process should lead to the following:
  - Determining the scope of the risk management to be performed for the project
  - Identifying risks to the project as they develop
  - Analysing the risks and determining the priority in which to apply resources to manage these risks
  - Defining, implementing and assessing appropriate risk management strategies

Figure 15.9 ISO/IEC 15504 management processes

- Defining and applying risk metrics and assessing them to measure the change in the risk state and the progress of the management activities
- Taking corrective action when expected progress is not achieved.

MAN.4 Manage subcontractors

- *Purpose:* To select qualified subcontractor(s) and manage their performance.
- *Expected outcome:* Successful implementation of the process should lead to the following:
  - Establishing a statement of the work to be performed under subcontract
  - Qualifying potential subcontractors through an assessment of their capability to perform the required software function
  - Selecting qualified subcontractors to perform defined portions of the contract
  - Establishing and managing commitments to and from the subcontractor
  - Regularly exchanging information on technical progress with the subcontractor
  - Assessing compliance of the subcontractor against the agreed standards and procedures
  - Assessing the quality of the subcontractors' delivered products and services.

15.3.5 ORGANIZATION PROCESS CATEGORY (ORG)

The *Organization* process category, referred to as **ORG Processes**, consists of processes that establish the business goals of the organization and develop process, product and resource assets that, when used by the projects in the organization, will help the organization achieve its business goals. Although organizational operations in general have a much broader scope than that of software process, software processes are implemented in a business context. For these processes to be effective, they require an appropriate organizational environment.

These organizational processes build organizational infrastructure, take advantage of the best of what is available in any one part of the organization (effective processes, advanced skills, quality code, good support tools) and make it available to all. The Organization process category contains five processes: Engineer the business, Define the processes, Improve the processes, Provide skilled human resources, and Provide software engineering infrastructure. They are illustrated in Figure 15.10 and briefly described in the following sections.

ORG.I Engineer the business

- *Purpose:* To provide the individuals in the organization and projects with a vision and culture that empowers them to function effectively. Although business re-engineering and Total Quality Management have a much broader scope than that of software process, software process improvement occurs in a business context, and to be successful it must address business goals.
- *Expected outcome:* Successful implementation of the process should lead to the following:
  - Defining a vision, mission, objectives and goals for the business, and making them known to all employees
  - Challenging every individual to ensure that his or her job is defined and performed to contribute effectively to the realization of the business's vision.

ORG.2 Define the processes

- *Purpose:* To build a reusable library of process definitions (including standards, procedures and models) that will support stable and repeatable performance of the software engineering and management process (all the processes covered in this reference model).
- *Expected outcome:* Successful implementation of the process should lead to the following:
  - Existence of a well-defined and maintained standard set of processes, along with an indication of each process's applicability
  - Identifying the detailed tasks, activities and associated work products of the standard process, together with expected performance characteristics
  - Existence of a deployed specific process for each project, tailored from the standard process, in accordance with the needs of the project
  - Existence and maintenance of a library of information and data related to the use of the standard process for specific projects.

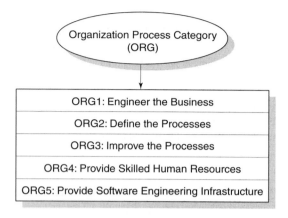

Figure 15.10   ISO/IEC 15504 organization processes

ORG.3 Improve the processes

- *Purpose:*   To continually improve the effectiveness and efficiency of the processes used by the organization in line with the business need.
- *Expected outcome:*   Successful implementation of the process should lead to the following:
  - Understanding the relative strengths and weaknesses of the organization's standard software processes
  - Making changes to standard and defined processes in a controlled way, with predictable results
  - Implementing planned and monitored software process improvement activities in a coordinated manner across the organization.

ORG.4 Provide skilled human resources

- *Purpose:*   To provide the organization and projects with individuals who possess skills and knowledge to perform their roles effectively and to work together as a cohesive group.
- *Expected outcome:*   Successful implementation of the process should lead to the following
  - Identifying the roles and skills required for the operations of the organization and the projects
  - Establishing formal procedures by which talent is recruited, selected and transitioned into assignments in the organization
  - Designing and conducting training to ensure that all individuals have the skills required to perform their assignments

- Identifying and recruiting or training individuals with the required skills and competencies as appropriate to perform the organizational and project roles
- Supporting effective interaction between individuals and groups
- Making available the skills of the workforce to share information and coordinating their activities efficiently
- Defining objective criteria against which group and individual performance can be measured, to provide performance feedback and to enhance performance continuously.

ORG.5 Provide software engineering infrastructure

- *Purpose:* To provide a stable and reliable environment with an integrated set of software development methods and tools for use by the projects in the organization. The infrastructure should be consistent with and supportive of the defined process.
- *Expected outcome:* Successful implementation of the process should lead to the following:
  - The existence of a well-defined, established and maintained software engineering environment
  - Consistency with and support of the process standard, including reuse, which ensures organization and project data integrity, availability and security
  - Tailorability of the software engineering environment to the needs of the project and the project team in order to support productive performance of all project activities wherever located
  - Implementing a defined and deployed strategy for reuse.

15.4 ISO/IEC 15504 CAPABILITY LEVELS

Evolving process capability is expressed in terms of process attributes grouped into capability levels. Process attributes are features of a process that can be evaluated on a scale of achievement, providing a measure of the capability of the process. They are applicable to all processes. Each process attribute describes a facet of the overall capability of managing and improving the effectiveness of a process in achieving its purpose and contributing to the business goals of the organization. It is worth noting that ISO/IEC 15504 defines the capability per process, while the CMM version 1.1 defines the capability per organization.

   Six levels of process capability are defined below. Each level is described in terms of its main process characteristics, and the attributes used for capability measurement.

15.4.1 LEVEL 0 – INCOMPLETE

Characterization

At this level, there is general failure to attain the purpose of the process. There are no easily identifiable work products or outputs of the process. The process is not implemented, or fails to achieve its purpose.

Attributes

There are no attributes at this level.

15.4.2 LEVEL 1 – PERFORMED

Characterization

The purpose of the process is generally achieved. The achievement may not be rigorously planned and tracked. Individuals within the organization recognize that an action should be performed, and there is general agreement that this action is performed as and when required. There are identifiable work products for the process, and these testify to the achievement of the purpose.

Attributes

The following attribute of the process demonstrates the achievement of this level:

- *PA 1.1 Process performance attribute:* The extent to which the execution of the process follows the practices defined in the process definition. Such practices are initiated and followed using identifiable input work products to produce identifiable output work products that are adequate to satisfy the purpose of the process.

15.4.3 LEVEL 2 – PLANNED AND TRACKED

Characterization

The process delivers work products of acceptable quality within defined timescales and resources. Performance according to specified procedures is planned and tracked. Work products conform to specified standards and requirements. The primary distinction from the Performed level is that the performance of the process is planned and managed and progressing towards a defined process.

Attributes

The following attributes of the process demonstrate the achievement of this level:

- *PA 2.1 Performance management attribute:* The extent to which the execution of the process is managed to produce work products within stated time and resource requirements.
- *PA 2.2 Work product management attribute:* The extent to which the execution of the process is managed to produce work products. Such work products are documented and controlled to meet their functional and non-functional requirements, in line with the work product quality goals of the process.

15.4.4 LEVEL 3 – ESTABLISHED

Characterization

The process is performed and managed using a defined process based upon good software engineering principles. Individual implementations of the process use approved, tailored versions of standard, documented processes. The resources necessary to establish the process definition are also in place. The primary distinction from the Managed level is that the process of the Established level is planned and managed using a standard process.

Attributes

The following attributes of the process demonstrate the achievement of this level:

- *PA 3.1 Process definition attribute:* The extent to which the execution of the process uses a process definition based upon a standard process, that enables the process to contribute to the defined business goals of the organization.
- *PA 3.2 Process resource attribute:* The extent to which the execution of the process uses suitable skilled human resources and process infrastructure effectively to contribute to the defined business goals of the organization.

15.4.5 LEVEL 4 – PREDICTABLE

Characterization

The defined process is performed consistently in practice within defined control limits, to achieve its goals. Detailed measures of performance are collected and analysed. This leads to a quantitative understanding of process capability and an improved ability to predict performance. Performance is objectively managed. The quality of work products is quantitatively known. The primary distinction from the Established level is that the defined process is quantitatively understood and controlled.

Attributes

The following attributes of the process demonstrate the achievement of this level:

- *PA 4.1 Process measurement attribute:* The extent to which the execution of the process is supported by goals and measures that are used to ensure that implementation of the process contributes to the achievement of the goals.
- *PA 4.2 Process control attribute:* The extent to which the execution of the process is controlled through the collection and analysis of measures to control and correct, where necessary, the performance of the process. The objective is to reliably achieve the defined process goals.

15.4.6 LEVEL 5 – OPTIMIZING

Characterization

Performance of the process is optimized to meet current and future business needs, and the process achieves repeatability in meeting its defined business goals. Quantitative process effectiveness and efficiency goals (targets) for performance are established, based on the business goals of the organization. Continuous process monitoring against these goals is enabled by obtaining quantitative feedback and improvement is achieved by analysis of the results. Optimizing a process involves piloting innovative ideas and technologies and changing ineffective processes to meet defined goals or objectives. The primary distinction from the Predictable level is that the defined process and the standard process undergo continuous refinement and improvement. These are based on a quantitative understanding of the impact of changes to these processes.

Attributes

The following attributes of the process demonstrate the achievement of this level:

- *PA 5.1 Process change attribute:* The extent to which changes to the definition, management and performance of the process are controlled better to achieve the business goals of the organization.
- *PA 5.2 Continuous improvement attribute:* The extent to which changes to the process are identified and implemented to ensure continuous

improvement in the fulfilment of the defined business goals of the organization.

15.5 ISO/IEC 15504 CAPABILITY MEASUREMENTS

15.5.1 RATING PROCESS CAPABILITY

The ISO/IEC 15504 measurement model defines how to rate the process capability of any of the processes described in the above sections. Process capability is defined on an ordinal scale with six points. This enables capability to be assessed from the bottom of the scale, Incomplete, through to the top end of the scale, Optimizing. The scale represents increasing capability of the performed process from performance that is not capable of fulfilling its goals through to performance that is capable of meeting its goals and sustaining continuous process improvement. The scale therefore defines a well-defined route for improvement for each individual process.

15.5.2 RATING PROCESS ATTRIBUTES

Process attribute rating scale

A process attribute represents a measurable characteristic of any process as defined above. The rating scale defined below is used to describe the levels of achievement of the defined capability of the process attributes.

- N Not achieved: There is no evidence of achievement of the defined attribute.
- P Partially achieved: There is some achievement of the defined attribute.
- L Largely achieved: There is significant achievement of the defined attribute.
- F Fully achieved: There is full achievement of the defined attribute.

Process attribute ratings

For each process instance assessed, each process attribute, up to and including the highest capability level defined in the assessment scope, is accorded a rating using the attribute scale (NPLF).

Achievement of process capability levels

The capability level for a process instance is derived from the attribute ratings for that process instance. The attribute ratings for a process instance are calculated according to the process capability level model defined in Table 15.1.

Aggregation of capability levels

Where more than one instance of a process is assessed, the process capability levels achieved by the process instances may be aggregated to show a frequency distribution of achieved capability levels. When aggregating capability levels, the representation used identifies the process, the capability levels included in the aggregation, the ordering of the ratings within the distribution, and the number of instances included within the aggregation.

15.6 RELATIONSHIP OF ISO/IEC 15504 TO OTHER INTERNATIONAL STANDARDS

ISO/IEC 15504 International Standard is complementary to several other International Standards and other models for evaluating the capability and effectiveness of organizations and processes.

ISO/IEC 15504 incorporates the intent of the ISO 9000 series. This is to provide confidence in a supplier's quality management whilst providing acquirers with a framework for assessing whether potential suppliers have the capability to meet their needs. Process assessment provides users with the ability to evaluate process capability on a continuous scale in a comparable and repeatable way. This is rather than using the pass/fail characteristic of quality audits based on ISO 9001. In addition, the framework described in ISO/IEC 15504 provides the opportunity to adjust the scope of assessment to cover specific processes of interest, rather than all of the processes used by an organizational unit.

ISO/IEC 15504 is related in particular to the following components of the ISO 9000 series:

- ISO 9001 – 1994, *Model for quality assurance in design, development, production, installation and servicing*
- ISO 9000-3 – 1991, *Quality management and quality assurance standards – Part 3: Guidelines for the application of ISO 9001 to the development, supply and maintenance of software*
- ISO 9004-4 – 1993, *Quality management and quality system elements – Part 4: Guidelines for quality improvement.*

Table 15.1   Capability level ratings

Scale	Process attributes	Rating
Level 1	Process performance	Largely or fully
Level 2	Process performance	Fully
	Performance management	Largely or fully
	Work product management	Largely or fully
Level 3	Process performance	Fully
	Performance management	Fully
	Work product management	Fully
	Process definition and tailoring	Largely or fully
	Process resource	Largely or fully
Level 4	Process performance	Fully
	Performance management	Fully
	Work product management	Fully
	Process definition and tailoring	Fully
	Process resource	Fully
	Process measurement	Largely or fully
	Process control	Largely or fully
Level 5	Process performance	Fully
	Performance management	Fully
	Work product management	Fully
	Process definition and tailoring	Fully
	Process resource	Fully
	Process measurement	Fully
	Process control	Fully
	Process change	Largely or fully
	Continuous improvement	Largely or fully

ISO/IEC 15504, and particularly part 2, is strongly related to the following standard:

- ISO/IEC 12207-1 – 1994, *Software life cycle processes.*

Where software-based tools are developed or used to support assessments their conformance to the requirements of part 5 of ISO/IEC 15504 International Standard may be evaluated against the following requirement:

- ISO/IEC 12159 – 1995, *Software products – Evaluation and test.*

Criteria for the development and/or acquisition of software-based tools are based on the characteristics defined in ISO/IEC 9126 – 1991, *Software quality characteristics.*

SUMMARY

ISO/IEC 15504: the emerging international standard

- ISO/IEC 15504 is the emerging international standard for the software process.
- ISO/IEC 15504 adopts a continuous architecture. Staged models can be mapped to this architecture.
- ISO/IEC 15504 has benefits for software suppliers, acquirers and developers.
- ISO/IEC 15504 specifies a reference model that has two dimensions: a process dimension and a capability dimension.
  ISO/IEC 15504 architecture.
- ISO/IEC 15504 specifies a set of conformance criteria that can be used as a guideline to develop process assessment approaches in conforming with the standard.
- ISO/IEC 15504 capability profile has two dimensions, the process dimension and the capability dimension.
- ISO/IEC 15504 has five process categories: CUS: Customer–Supplier Processes; ENG: Engineering processes; SUP: Support processes; MAN: Management processes; ORG: Organization processes.
- Each process category comprises a number of processes.
  Measuring process capability.
- A process capability is assigned a number of process attributes.
- A process capability is measured in terms of its attribute ratings.
- The capability profile comprises six capability levels (0–5).
  ISO/IEC 15504 documents.
- The following documents are available through Version 1.0 standard:
  - Part 1: *Concepts and introductory guide*
  - Part 2: *A reference model for process*
  - Part 3: *Performing an Assessment*
  - Part 4: *Guide to peforming an assessment*
  - Part 5: *An assessment model and indicator guide*
  - Part 6: *Guide to qualification of assessors*
  - Part 7: *Guide for use in process improvement*
  - Part 8: *Guide for use in determining supplier process capability*
  - Part 9: *Vocabulary*.

CHAPTER 16

ISO/IEC 15504 draft guide to conducting assessment

16.1 OVERVIEW

16.1.1 ISO/IEC 15504 FRAMEWORK FOR SOFTWARE PROCESS ASSESSMENT

The ISO/IEC 15504 Guide on assessment provides overall information on the concepts of software process assessment and its use in the two contexts of process improvement and process capability determination. It describes how the parts of the suite fit together, and provides guidance for their selection and use. It explains the requirements contained within this International Standard, and their applicability to the conduct of an assessment, to the construction and selection of supporting tools, and to the construction of extended processes.

As well as defining a process model and a process capability scale, ISO/IEC 15504 provides a framework for the assessment of software processes. This framework can be used by organizations involved in planning, managing, monitoring, controlling and improving the acquisition, supply, development, operation, evolution and support of software. The Standard provides a structured approach for the assessment of software processes for the following purposes:

- By or on behalf of an organization with the objective of understanding the state of its own processes for process improvement
- By or on behalf of an organization with the objective of determining the suitability of its own processes for a particular requirement or class of requirements

● By or on behalf of one organization with the objective of determining the suitability of another organization's processes for a particular contract or class of contracts.

The context of the assessment has an impact on its plans and activities.

Based on the process model and the capability scale described in the previous chapter, the ISO/IEC 15504 framework for process assessment has the following characteristics:

● encourages self-assessment;
● takes into account the context in which the assessed processes operate;
● produces a set of process ratings (a process profile) rather than a pass/fail result;
● addresses the adequacy of the management of the assessed processes;
● is appropriate across all application domains and sizes of organization.

16.1.2 TARGET USERS

ISO/IEC 15504 as an International Standard has been designed to satisfy the needs of acquirers, suppliers and assessors, and their individual requirements from within a single source. ISO/IEC 15504 guidelines on conducting assessment are primarily aimed at the following:

● *The assessment team*, who use the document to prepare for the assessment
● *The assessment participants*, who use the document to help understand the assessment and interpret the results
● *All staff within organizations* who need to understand the details and benefits of performing process assessment
● *Tool and method developers* who wish to develop tools or methods supporting the process assessment model.

Figure 16.1 illustrates potential types of users of the ISO/IEC 15504 Guide for conducting assessment.

Also ISO/IEC 15504 can serve each of the following classes of users:

● *For acquirers:* ISO/IEC 15504 offers an ability to determine the current and potential capability of a supplier's software processes.
● *For suppliers:* ISO/IEC 15504 offers an ability to determine the current and potential capability of their own software processes, an ability to define areas and priorities for software process improvement, and a framework that defines a route map for software process improvement.
● *For assessors:* ISO/IEC 15504 offers a framework that defines all aspects of conducting assessments.

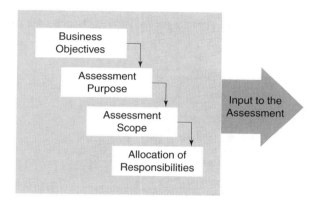

Figure 16.1 Input to the ISO/IEC 15504 assessment

16.1.3 ISO/IEC 15504 ASSESSMENT STAGES

Process assessment according to ISO/IEC 15504 consists of eight stages:

1 Reviewing the assessment input
2 Selecting the process instances
3 Preparing for assessment
4 Collecting and verifying information on practices
5 Determining the actual ratings for process instances
6 Determining derived ratings
7 Validation the ratings
8 Presenting the assessment output.

Figure 16.2 illustrates a mapping between these steps and the generic assessment phases discussed in the previous chapter (Planning, Fact Gathering, Fact Analysis, Reporting). The rest of this chapter discusses details of these steps grouped according to this mapping. The relationships between these stages are shown in Figure 16.3.

16.2 ASSESSMENT PLANNING

The first three assessment stages defined in the ISO/IEC 15504 Guide for Assessment are concerned with assessment planning. They are:

- Reviewing assessment inputs
- Selecting the process instances
- Preparing for a team-based assessment.

These stages are briefly discussed below.

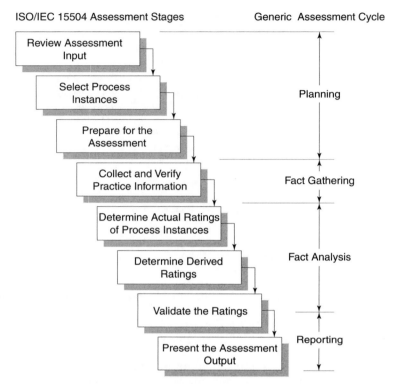

Figure 16.2   ISO/IEC 15504 assessment stages

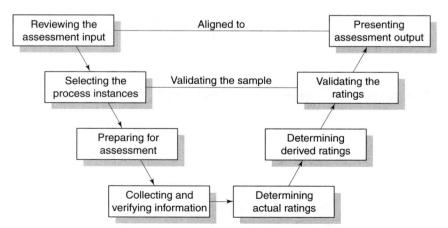

Figure 16.3   Relationship between ISO/IEC 15504 assessment stages

16.2.1 STAGE I: REVIEWING THE ASSESSMENT INPUTS

The assessment is likely to be more effective if all necessary inputs are in place. These inputs would help the assessment team in achieving the following:

- Understanding the business justification of the assessment
- Scoping the assessment
- Understanding the assessment constraints
- Allocating the roles and responsibilities for the assessment

Figure 16.4 summarizes the main tasks of this phase. These are mainly pre-planning activities that should precede the assessment. These cover items such as the business justification for the assessment, scoping the assessment, the assessment constraints, and allocation of responsibilities of the assessment. The result of all of these activities should be input to the assessment. They should be reviewed by the assessment's qualified assessor who should seek clarifications from the sponsor as appropriate. ISO/IEC 15504 defines the minimum inputs to the assessment as:

- The assessment purpose
- The assessment scope
- The assessment constraints
- The identity of the qualified assessor and any other specific responsibilities for the assessment
- The definition of any extended processes identified in the assessment scope
- The identification of any additional information to be collected to support process improvement or process capability determination.

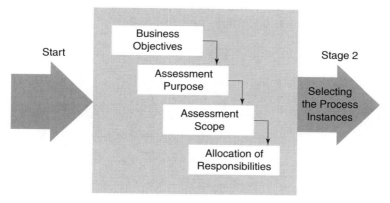

Figure 16.4   Stage 1: Reviewing inputs to the assessment

16.2.2 STAGE 2: SELECTING THE PROCESS INSTANCES

The assessment scoping activity should specify which organizational unit(s) and what process instances will be assessed. The tasks for this activity are shown in Figure 16.5 and are briefly described below.

Mapping the organizational unit processes to the process model

The process model adopted by ISO/IEC 15504 represents the software process as a whole. In order to provide a consistent basis for assessment, ISO/IEC 15504 establishes a representative process model. The organizational unit processes selected for the assessment should be mapped to the ISO/IEC 15504 process model. The mapping will have to be agreed with the sponsor. The ISO/IEC 15504 standard requires that 'The qualified assessor shall ensure that the organizational unit's processes to be assessed, as defined in the assessment scope, are mapped to the corresponding processes' (ISO/IEC 15504 – Software Process Assessment – Part 3: Rating processes, 4.3).

Process instance selection

The process instances selected for the assessment should satisfy the business objectives and the assessment purpose and scope. The assessment purpose and scope usually indicate the required depth and coverage of the assessment, and consequently the selection of the process instances to be covered by the assessment. Also the assessment constraints may affect the scope and boundaries of the assessment (this could result in particular process instances to be included or excluded). The ISO/IEC 15504 standard specifies that 'The qualified assessor shall ensure that the set of process instances selected for assessment is adequate to meet the assessment purpose and will provide outputs that are representative of the assessment scope' and that 'The assessment shall include at least one process instance of each process identified in the assessment scope'.

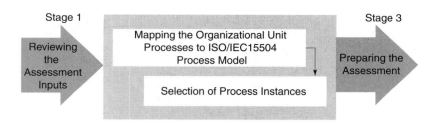

Figure 16.5 Stage 2: Selecting the process instances

16.2.3 STAGE 3: PREPARING FOR A TEAM-BASED ASSESSMENT

A team-based self-assessment is usually conducted by an assessment team from within the organization. This team could be assisted by an external expert. In such cases there are four stages that should be completed. The four stages are illustrated in Figure 16.6, and described briefly below.

Selecting and preparing the assessment team

The first stage in preparing for the assessment is the selection and preparation of the assessment team. This involves three activities as briefly summarized below (more details are in the ISO/IEC 15504 standard).

Choosing the assessment team size
The team should consist of at least two members, though the optimum size will depend on the assessment scope, the size of the organizational unit concerned, the skills and experience of available resources, and so on.

Defining the roles of the assessment team
A qualified assessor should appoint the assessment team leader and assessment team coordinator. The assessment team leader will be responsible for the overall conduct of the assessment. The assessment team coordinator will be responsible for the assessment logistics and interfacing with the organizational unit. The composition of the assessment team should ensure a balanced set of skills to meet the assessment purpose and scope.

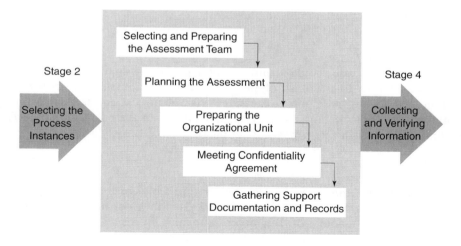

Figure 16.6   Stage 3: Preparing for a team-based assessment

Table 16.1 Potential sources of risk to the assessment

Source of risk	Brief description
Organizational	• Changes in the commitment of the sponsor • Organizational changes
Resistance to change	• Resistance or unwillingness to participate by organizational unit members
Unplanned change	• Unplanned changes to the structure of the assessment team • Implementation or changeover to new standard processes • Changes in the assessment purpose or scope
Lack of funds	• Lack of financial or other resources required for the assessment
Lack of trust	• Lack of confidentiality, either internal or external to the organization

Preparing the assessment team
Prior to the assessment, the qualified assessor should ensure that the assessment team has an understanding of the assessment inputs, purpose, constraints, output and process, and an understanding of the ISO/IEC 15504 guidelines on conducting assessments.

Planning the assessment

This phase involves the following tasks.

Identifying risk factors
The assessment team should identify to the sponsor any significant risk factors that could lead to a failure of the assessment. A suitable risk assessment technique should be adopted to conduct risk identification, assessment and mitigation. Table 16.1 lists some potential sources of the risk that should be considered at the assessment planning phase.

Selecting the assessment techniques
The assessment team should select the appropriate assessment techniques to suit the assessment purpose and scope, the skills of the assessment team and the level of understanding of the organizational unit being assessed. These techniques may include, for example, on-line expert system, interviews, individual discussions, group discussions, closed team sessions, documentation reviews and feedback sessions.

Selecting the assessment instrument
The assessment team should decide which assessment instrument will be used to assist the team in performing the assessment. The following aspects should be considered when defining the requirements for an appropriate assessment instrument:

- The type of assessment instrument required
- Support for security and confidentiality
- The level and detail of reporting
- Support for rating and analysis.

Developing the assessment plan
The assessment team should develop an assessment plan. Table 16.2 illustrates possible contents of such a plan.

   The assessment team should ensure that the assessment plan is able to meet the assessment purpose. The assessment plan should be formally accepted by the sponsor and owner. The assessment team should endeavour to ensure that the plan is acceptable to the participants and that it is realistic in terms of its impact on existing projects.

Preparing the organizational unit

This stage involves the following tasks.

Selecting the organizational unit coordinator
An organizational unit may appoint an organizational unit coordinator to represent it in the assessment. The organizational unit coordinator is responsible for supporting all assessment logistics for the organizational unit, interfacing with the assessment team and establishing the environment needed for the assessment activities.

Table 16.2 Possible contents of the assessment plan

- The assessment inputs
- Roles and responsibilities of all involved in the assessment activity
- Estimates for schedule
- Costs and resources
- Control mechanisms and checkpoints
- The interface between the assessment team and the organizational unit
- Outputs expected
- Risk factors to be taken into account and appropriate contingent and preventive actions
- The logistics that may include the rooms for discussions and presentations
- Appropriate audio-visual equipment
- Word processing facilities
- Escort requirements and access to facilities

Briefing of the organizational unit
The organizational unit should be briefed on the assessment purpose, scope and constraints, the conduct of the assessment, how the assessment outputs can be used to provide the most benefit to the organization and what arrangements exist for confidentiality and ownership of the assessment outputs.

Selecting the participants
The assessment team needs to capture information on every base practice and generic practice for each process instance to be assessed. The organizational unit should, in cooperation with the assessment team, select the participants that adequately represent the process instances chosen to ensure that the appropriate expertise will be available to allow for a satisfactory assessment.

Meeting confidentiality agreements
The assessment team should ensure that any discussions held with participants and the use of the assessment outputs are subject to any confidentiality agreement defined in the assessment constraints. The assessment team should ensure that all participants fully understand the confidentiality agreement.

Gathering support documentation and records

The assessment team may need access to support documentation and records (i.e. project plan, progress meeting minutes, deliverable review notes) on the process instances to be examined, either in advance of the assessment or to provide support during the assessment. This may be particularly important for an independent assessment.

Much of this material will be local to the organizational unit being assessed but some may be shared with other organizational units or be held centrally within the organization. If necessary the organizational unit coordinator should ensure that access to such material is considered in the assessment plan. It helps the progress of the assessment if adequate time is provided for this information to be collated off-line from any ongoing discussions.

16.3 FACT GATHERING

16.3.1 STAGE 4: COLLECTING AND VERIFYING INFORMATION

During an assessment, it is the usual practice to perform a series of information collection and analysis stages, where the scope of the information is refined and more detailed information is collected along the way. Although an assessment may be a self-assessment or an independent assessment, the principles behind the involvement of participants are the same. They are a primary source of information to be provided to the assessment team about the process instances being assessed. They may participate in informal, unstructured discussions that allow them to express their professional views about the processes in place, and any issues or problems facing the organization. They may also be involved in providing validation materials to the assessment team.

The fourth assessment stage defined in the ISO/IEC 15504 Guide for Assessment is concerned with fact gathering and analysis. The stage is concerned with collecting and verifying information. It has three main tasks:

- Collecting information
- Categorizing information
- Analysing information.

These tasks are illustrated in Figure 16.7 and briefly discussed below.

Collecting information

Collecting the information will depend on the assessment instrument and assessment techniques selected. Information has to be collected for each base practice and each generic practice for each process instance to be assessed. Certain base practices or generic practices may be implemented more than once within a single process instance, i.e. multiple reviews. In this case the assessment team must use the selected assessment instrument and their judgement to choose a representative sample.

Categorizing information

The categories of information that should be collected during an assessment include the degree of adequacy or existence of base practices, the adequacy of generic practices, and the experiences of the participants where they observed problems associated with the current processes used, i.e. ideas for process improvement. The assessment team should take adequate steps to protect any information collected that may be covered by a confidentiality agreement.

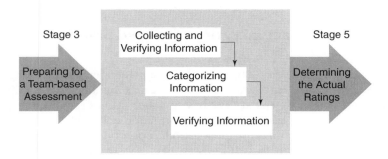

Figure 16.7   Stage 4: Collecting and verifying information

Verifying information

Support documentation and records should be used as appropriate to verify the information collected during an assessment. The amount of support documentation and records examined depends upon the assessment team's knowledge of the organizational unit, the assessment purpose, and the level of trust and confidentiality established for the assessment.

16.4 FACT ANALYSIS

Following the collection and verification of information, ISO/IEC 15504 specifies three stages to cover fact analysis and verification. They are:

- Stage 5: Determining the actual ratings for process instances
- Stage 6: Determining the derived ratings
- Stage 7: Validating the ratings.

These stages are briefly discussed below.

16.4.1 STAGE 5: DETERMINING THE ACTUAL RATINGS FOR PROCESS INSTANCES

The actual ratings, collected for every process instance assessed, are determined from the information collected about the process instance by the assessment team. ISO/IEC 15504 specifies that 'A base practice adequacy rating or a base practice existence rating shall be determined and validated for every base practice within each selected process instance for each process and/or extended process identified within the assessment scope' and that 'A generic practice adequacy rating shall be determined and validated for every generic practice within each selected process instance of each process and/or each extended process identified within the assessment scope'.

The tasks for this stage are illustrated in Figure 16.8 and briefly discussed below.

Determining the actual ratings for base practices

Base practice adequacy and existence
Base practices may be rated using either the base practice adequacy rating scale or the base practice existence scale. The same scale should be used for all base practices for a given assessment. The base practice ratings are determined for each process instance assessed from the information collected.

The base practice ratings do not constitute a part of the process profile but rather are recorded as part of the assessment record. Their purpose is to provide a clear understanding of the extent to which the process is performed. The work product indicators that are defined in the assessment instrument are

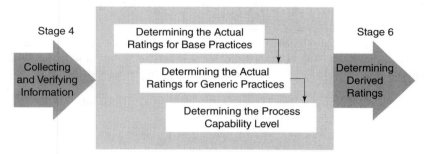

Figure 16.8 Stage 5: Determining the actual ratings for process instances

provided to indicate which points to consider to help to make consistent rating judgements. Base practice adequacy shall be rated using the following base practice adequacy rating scale:

- *N Not adequate:* The base practice is either not implemented or does not to any degree contribute to satisfying the process purpose.
- *P Partially adequate:* The implemented base practice does little to contribute to satisfying the process purpose.
- *L Largely adequate:* The implemented base practice largely contributes to satisfying the process purpose.
- *F Fully adequate:* The implemented base practice fully contributes to satisfying the process purpose.

Base practice existence shall be rated using the following base practice existence rating scale:

- *N Non-existent:* The base practice is either not implemented or does not produce any identifiable work products.
- *Y Existent:* The implemented base practice produces identifiable work products.

Base practice rating reference
ISO/IEC 15504 provides guidance as well as examples of the rating reference. In the examples provided, the rating reference is of the form PC.PR.BP [instance reference] where PC is a process category, PR is a process within that process category, BP is a base practice of the process, and [instance reference] is either the number of process instances in the rating or a complete list of the process instance references.

The ISO/IEC 15504 standard specifies that 'A unique reference shall be generated for each base practice rating that includes the process category, the process within the process category, the base practice of the process, and a process instance reference' (ISO/IEC 15504 – Software Process Assessment – Part 3: Rating processes).

Determining the actual ratings for generic practices

Generic practice adequacy

The generic practice adequacy ratings are determined for each process instance assessed from the information collected. Generic practice adequacy shall be rated using the following generic practice adequacy rating scale.

- *N Not adequate:*   The generic practice is either not implemented or does not to any degree satisfy its purpose.
- *P Partially adequate:*   The implemented generic practice does little to satisfy its purpose.
- *L Largely adequate:*   The implemented generic practice largely satisfies its purpose.
- *F Fully adequate:*   The implemented generic practice fully satisfies its purpose.

The following notes should be taken into consideration when determining the ratings. It is possible, even though the ratings for each individual base practice are fully adequate or existent, that the process is not satisfying its process purpose. This may be the result of an inability of the base practices to operate effectively as a whole, or because key base practices not included in the process model are required to achieve the process purpose in a particular context. Reference should be made to the ISO/IEC 15504 standard documentation for a fuller explanation of the ratings' algorithm.

Generic practice rating reference

The rating scheme proposed in ISO/IEC 15504 is that 'A unique reference shall be generated for each generic practice rating that includes the process category, the process within that process category, the capability level, the common feature within that capability level, the generic practice within that common feature, and a process instance reference.' Detailed examples of this rating are given in ISO/IEC 15504 manuals.

Determining the process capability level

Rating processes at a certain capability level should be calculated according to the following ISO/IEC 15504 guidance:

- 'An actual process capability level rating shall be determined for each process instance assessed by aggregating the generic practice adequacy ratings within each capability level. For each process instance, the actual process capability level ratings shall describe, for each capability level, the proportion of generic practices that were rated at each point on the generic practice adequacy scale in a clear and unambiguous way.'
- 'Equal weighting shall be applied to each generic practice adequacy rating when aggregating or deriving ratings.'

Detailed examples of this rating process are given in the ISO/IEC 15504 documentation.

16.4.2 STAGE 6: DETERMINING THE DERIVED RATINGS

The main tasks in this phase are:

- Aggregation between process instances:
  - Generic practice adequacy
  - Process capability level rating
- Aggregation across processes.

Figure 16.9 illustrates these tasks, and they are briefly described in the following paragraphs.

The ISO/IEC 15504 guideline for these steps is that 'Equal weighting shall be applied to each generic practice adequacy rating when aggregating or deriving ratings.'

The following notes should be observed by the assessment team while determining derived ratings:

- From the actual ratings, derived ratings may be determined which can help to gain further insight into the processes within the organizational unit as a whole. Derived ratings are based on sampling and are therefore subject to all the restrictions that apply to sampled ratings.
- The assessment team should decide which of the following derived ratings are useful in helping to ensure that the assessment purpose can best be fulfilled.
- Since any derived ratings are based on an aggregation of actual ratings for process instances, the assessment team has to ensure that traceability is provided from the derived ratings to the actual ratings.

Aggregation between process instances

The ratings for generic practices and process capability levels for two or more process instances may be aggregated to determine a derived rating for the process.

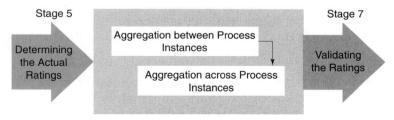

Figure 16.9   Stage 6: Determining the derived ratings

Generic practice adequacy

Actual generic practice adequacy ratings may be aggregated between two or more process instances of a specific process to derive an aggregated rating for the generic practice. A detailed example of this rating process is given in ISO/IEC 15504 documentation.

Process capability level rating

By aggregating process capability level ratings between a sample of process instances of a specific process within an organizational unit, derived ratings for the capability levels are obtained for the process. A detailed example of this process is provided in the ISO/IEC 15504 documentation.

The ISO/IEC 15504 standard specifies the following requirements for this stage: 'A set of derived process capability level ratings shall be determined for each process identified in the assessment scope by aggregating the actual process capability ratings of the process instances. These derived ratings shall be sufficiently representative of the process capability levels of each process assessed to satisfy the assessment purpose. For each process identified in the assessment scope, the derived process capability level ratings shall describe, for each capability level, the proportion of generic practices that were rated at each point on the generic practice adequacy scale in a clear and unambiguous way.' (ISO/IEC 15504 – Software Process Assessment – Part 3: Rating processes).

Aggregation across processes

Any generic practice ratings between process instances may be aggregated across different processes. The mechanism described in ISO/IEC 15504 may be used to infer ratings for the generic practices within a specific capability level of a group of processes where a derived rating from a subset of those processes suggests that the implementation of that capability level is identical across the entire group, for example because there is an organization-wide measurement programme.

16.4.3 STAGE 7: VALIDATING THE RATINGS

The ratings should be validated to ensure that they are an accurate representation of the processes assessed. The validation should include assessing whether the sample size chosen is representative of the processes assessed and that it is capable of fulfilling the assessment purpose. ISO/IEC 15504 requirements are that:

- 'A base practice adequacy rating or a base practice existence rating shall be determined and *validated* for every base practice within each selected process instance for each process and/or extended process identified within the assessment scope.'

- 'A generic practice adequacy rating shall be determined and *validated* for every generic practice within each selected process instance of each process and/or each extended process identified within the assessment scope.'

The tasks for this stage are illustrated in Figure 16.10 and summarized below. The following mechanisms are useful in supporting validation:

- Comparing results to those from previous assessments for the same organizational unit
- Looking for consistencies between connected or related processes
- Looking for proportional ratings across the capability levels, for example higher ratings for higher levels than for lower ones
- Taking an independent sample of ratings and comparing them to the assessment team ratings
- Feedback sessions of preliminary findings to the organizational unit.

16.5 PRESENTING THE ASSESSMENT OUTPUT

IEC 15504 provides guidance for presenting the assessment results which is covered in Stage 8 of its assessment model. It involves two tasks: presenting the assessment output, and reporting the assessment output. Figure 16.11 illustrates these two steps, which are briefly described below.

Preparing the assessment output

Having determined the base practice, generic practice and process capability level ratings, the assessment outputs need to be prepared. The ISO/IEC 15504 standard requires that 'The qualified assessor shall ensure that all of the information required in the assessment output is recorded in a suitable format to fulfil the assessment purpose and that it meets the requirements of this International Standard'. This task has two outputs: the process profile and the assessment record.

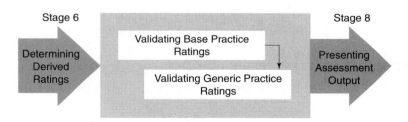

Figure 16.10 Stage 7: Validating the ratings

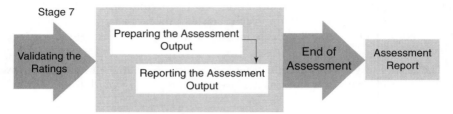

Figure 16.11 Stage 8: Presenting the assessment output

The process profile
The ratings for the assessed process instances within the assessment scope shall be recorded as the process profile consisting of the following:

- The actual generic practice ratings and process capability level ratings for each process instance
- The derived generic practice ratings and process capability level ratings for each process within the scope of the assessment.

The assessment record
Any other information that is pertinent to the assessment and which may be helpful in understanding the output of the assessment shall be compiled and recorded as the assessment record. At a minimum, the assessment record shall contain:

- The assessment input
- The assessment approach that was used
- The assessment instrument used
- The base practice ratings for each process instance assessed
- The date of the assessment
- The names of the team who conducted the assessment
- Any additional information collected during the assessment that was identified in the assessment input to support process improvement or process capability determination
- Any assessment assumptions and limitations.

The assessment output will normally be used as a basis for developing an agreed improvement plan or determining capability and associated risk as appropriate. ISO/IEC 15504 provides more guidance on how to perform this task.

Reporting the assessment output

The presentation of the assessment output might take the form of a simple presentation for an internal assessment or might be a detailed report for an independent assessment. In addition, other findings and proposed action plans may be prepared for presentation, depending upon the assessment purpose and whether this additional analysis is performed at the same time as the assessment. In some circumstances it may be desirable to compare the outputs of the assessment of two or more organizational units, or for the same organizational unit at different times. Comparisons of assessment outputs shall be valid only if their process contexts are similar.

The ratings determined for generic practice adequacy provide the input necessary for generating the process capability level ratings. The use of summary ratings, for example for a process category, in addition to the detailed findings may be used to help to understand the findings. In some circumstances it may be useful to assign a weighting to the four points on the generic practice adequacy scale, i.e. 100% for F, 75% for L, 25% for P and 0% for N. Any derived rating may then be represented as a single value rather than as a vector. This may assist with presentation of ratings at a summary level. These ratings should be used for summary purposes only and should not be used for comparison instead of the generic practice adequacy ratings. The presentation of the ratings may be in absolute terms (numbers, absolute scales) or relative terms (since last time, compared to benchmarks, compared to contract requirements, compared to business needs).

16.6 ISO/IEC 15504 GUIDANCE ON

ASSESSMENT INSTRUMENTS

The assessment team should decide which assessment instrument will be used to assist the team in performing the assessment. The following aspects should be considered when defining the requirements for an appropriate assessment instrument:

- The type of assessment instrument required
- Support for security and confidentiality
- The level and detail of reporting
- Support for rating and analysis.

ISO/IEC 15504 specifies the requirements for an assessment instrument to be ISO/IEC 15504-conformant. The standard requires that an assessment instrument that conforms to those requirements should be used to support the assessment.

It is helpful if at least one assessment team member has experience of the particular assessment techniques and assessment instrument to be used. More guidance on selecting or developing an assessment instrument is provided in ISO/IEC 15504. Some highlights of this guidance are as follows.

16.6.1 WHAT IS AN ASSESSMENT INSTRUMENT?

An assessment instrument (AI) is a tool (or set of tools) used throughout an assessment to support the evaluation of the adequacy or existence of practices. An assessment instrument aids the assessor by providing a consistent set of indicators as discriminators to help judge how well the practices have been implemented in the organizational unit's processes. An assessment instrument provides a mechanism to record the collected information from an assessment. Storage and retrieval capabilities provide the ability to maintain the results and supporting information for post-assessment analysis and improvement. Sophisticated assessment instruments may help the assessor to process the data and generate the results, thereby improving the efficiency and effectiveness of the assessment.

The ISO/IEC 15504 Standard describes a framework for an assessment instrument. An important aspect of the framework is a set of assessment indicators that are the source input data to an assessment instrument. Other elements of the framework incorporate the ability to capture and process assessment data to produce repeatable results. Different types of assessment instrument support specific assessment techniques, objectives or modes of use. This document does not prescribe a particular format for an assessment instrument (i.e. questionnaire, checklist, computer input screen): the requirements for an assessment instrument are independent of a particular design, instrument style or mode of use. Assessment tool designers and methodology providers should evaluate the intended approach to gathering data and build an assessment instrument that supports the assessment approach.

The ISO/IEC 15504 Standard does not require an assessment instrument to take any particular form or format. It may be constructed to be, for example, a paper-based instrument containing elements such as forms, questionnaires or checklists, or it may take the form of a computer-based instrument such as a spreadsheet, a data base system, an expert system or an integrated CASE tool.

16.6.2 USE AND TAILORING OF THE ASSESSMENT

INSTRUMENT

Requirements

ISO/IEC 15504 specifies a set of requirements on the use and tailoring of the assessment instrument. The following are provided as examples, and readers are advised to refer to the standards document for the full set of guidelines.

- The assessment instrument should be appropriate to the scope and purpose of assessment. Assessors should record the existence, absence or non-applicability of the indicators used in the assessment.

- The assessment instrument records of the existence, absence or non-applicability of the indicators should be provided to the assessed organizational unit upon request to allow the use of the information in subsequent process improvement planning. Assessment instrument records should be maintained by the assessor's organization as a record of the assessment.
- An assessment instrument should be capable of loading, storing and comparing process profiles. Assessors should use all the data captured in an assessment instrument about indicators, the context of the assessment and the organizational unit characteristics to support their judgements of practice adequacy or existence.

Automated ISO/IEC 15504-conformant assessment instruments are now available. An example is a portfolio of tools to assist in process assessment and process improvement marketed under the title of Process Professional, which has been developed in the UK (Process Professional, 1996).

Tailoring the assessment instrument

Regarding the tailoring of the assessment instrument, ISO/IEC 15504 specifies that within an assessment instrument, the standard set of indicators and the form of the instrument may be tailored to meet the needs of the assessment team or sponsor in the following aspects:

- The modifications of indicator format to accommodate presentation style preferences (for example, questions, sentences, tables, on-line input screens, and so on)
- The modification of indicator wording to accommodate synonym names or meanings for cultural differences
- The addition of scoping characteristics to help select the set of indicators used by process area, user, job function, application domain, software product or other predefined organizational unit or tool characteristics
- The addition of new indicators to support new work products, new technology and specific extended processes
- The adaptation of the assessment instrument to accommodate extended processes, limited scope modularity, or intended distribution of tools to collect the assessment data incrementally
- The user interface (for example, format for data input, method of recording data, and so on)
- The format of the results (presentation format and output record format, and so on)
- The overall design and format of the assessment instrument.

Tailoring the indicators shall not impair the availability of the standard set of indicators appropriate to the scope and context of the assessment. All practices within the assessment scope shall be covered by the tailored indicators.

Tailoring indicators for extended processes

The ISO/IEC 15504 Standard allows for the creation of extended processes containing additional practices to supplement those in the ISO/IEC 15504 process model. When extended processes are defined, the following shall apply:

- Corresponding indicators shall be defined and included in the assessment instrument for each additional practice in the extended process.
- A reference shall be recorded in the assessment record identifying the indictors related to the practices in extended processes.
- Indicators for the practices in extended processes shall be maintained and made available to the sponsor or the assessed organization on request.

Modular assessment instruments

A modular assessment instrument is an instrument constructed or tailored from a collection of components, each of which provides only partial coverage of the full scope of the process model. A modular assessment instrument, at a minimum, shall incorporate all standard indicators related to the processes to be assessed and all of the process management indicators.

Assessors using a modular assessment instrument shall record any limitation of the coverage of the instruments used in the assessment record.

The use of a modular assessment instrument shall not negate the rules for coverage of the practices contained within this International Standard.

A supplier of a modular assessment instrument should clearly identify the applicability of the instrument and the extent of its coverage of the process and practices of the ISO/IEC 15504 process model or of extended processes.

Capturing and processing assessment data

An assessment instrument shall have the ability to capture the data required to be used in the production of ratings as defined in the International Standard. (This means that in a paper-based instrument, for example, this could be met simply by providing a place to write the results.)

An assessment instrument shall have the ability to capture and maintain supporting information as required by the assessment sponsor and defined in the assessment input.

An assessment instrument shall support the rating of the practices being assessed, including those contained in extended processes, according to the rating scheme defined in the ISO/IEC 15504 Standard.

When an extended process is included in the scope of an assessment, the assessment instrument should enable the assessor to segregate the rating of the base practices contained in the process model from the additional base practices in an extended process.

An assessment instrument should provide a mechanism to aid the segregation of data and results between the assessment output as defined in the ISO/IEC 15504 standard.

An assessment instrument should, whenever possible, provide automated support to the assessor for the processing and aggregation of results across multiple organizational units or process instances.

16.7 USING ISO/IEC 15504 GUIDANCE FOR CONDUCTING ASSESSMENTS

16.7.1 FIELD OF APPLICATION

Depending on the business motivation of the assessment, it can take place within one of two contexts: a software process improvement or a software process capability determination. Within a context of software process improvement, process assessment provides the means of characterizing the current practice within an organizational unit in terms of the capability of the selected processes. Analysis of the results identifies strengths, weakness and risks inherent in the processes. This, in turn, leads to the ability to determine whether the processes are effective in achieving their goals, and to identify significant causes of poor quality, or overruns in time or cost. These provide the basis for prioritizing software process improvement actions. In the case of process capability determination, assessment is concerned with analysing the proposed capability of selected processes against a target process capability profile in order to identify the risks involved in undertaking a project using the selected processes.

16.7.2 USING ISO/IEC 15504 FOR DEVELOPING AN ISO/IEC 15504-CONFORMANT ASSESSMENT METHOD

As in the case of any standard, ISO/IEC 15504 is not an assessment method as such. Rather it is a set of requirements and guidelines for assessment methods. An assessment method based on and consistent with these requirements will be considered as ISO/IEC 15504-conformant. ISO/IEC 15504 defines guidelines for developing conformant assessment methods. The idea is to achieve comparability of results across different 'conformant' methods.

By its nature the ISO/IEC 15504 model is at a higher abstraction of assessment models. It can be considered as a 'meta-model' that can be used as the basis for developing process assessment models. Guidelines for the

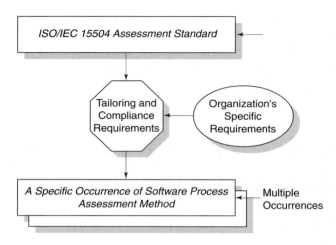

Figure 16.12 Using ISO/IEC 15504 to develop assessment methods

development of an assessment method based on the ISO/IEC 15504 standard are provided as 'Conformance Guidelines' in ISO/IEC 15504.

Figure 16.12 illustrates the use of ISO/IEC 15504 to develop a specific assessment method using the conformance guidelines and specific organization's requirements.

A central concept of ISO/IEC 15504 assessment is the concept of a conformant assessment. An ISO/IEC 15504-conformant assessment should have the following characteristics:

- It should be conducted by an assessment team that meets the requirements defined in the ISO/IEC 15504 standard.
- It should use an assessment process that at a minimum meets the requirements specified in the standard.
- It should be based on a set of practices that at a minimum include those defined in the standards for the processes assessed.
- It should use an assessment process that at a minimum contains the features specified in the ISO/IEC 15504 standard.
- It should provide results in the form of a process profile as defined in the ISO/IEC 15504 standard.
- It should retain objective evidence that demonstrates that the above conditions have been met.

The intent of conformance is to maximize the objectivity of the assessment process, and thereby to ensure the repeatability and comparability of the assessment results. This is achieved through the following:

- employing a clearly defined process;
- ensuring that the assessment team members have the necessary skills and competence to apply the rules consistently; and

- judging of process adequacy to be justified by reference to a defined set of objective indicators.

The sophistication and complexity required of a process is dependent upon its context. For instance, the planning required for a five-person project team is much less than for a fifty-person team. This context influences how a qualified assessor judges a practice when assessing its adequacy and influences the degree of comparability between process profiles.

SUMMARY

In this chapter we reviewed the main areas of ISO/IEC 15504 guidance on conducting software process assessments. The comments represent the author's interpretation of this guidance in light of his experience of the subject matter. The information provided in this chapter is based on ISO/IEC 15504 documentation, and readers must refer to the latest ISO/IEC 15504 publications for the latest version. This chapter is not a substitute for the real thing.

The author acknowledges that the ISO/IEC 15504 clauses published in this chapter are published in accordance with the ISO/IEC 15504 Terms and Conditions.

ISO/IEC 15504, the emerging international standard for software process assessment

As an international standard, ISO/IEC 15504 should bring worldwide recognition to software process assessment as a useful discipline for organizations to adopt to improve their software processes.

ISO/IEC 15504 conformance

Conformance with ISO/IEC 15504 will help consistency of assessment methods and results after the initial take-up phase. Such consistency will enhance the compatibility of the assessment results across organizations.

ISO/IEC 15504 is a meta model that can be used to develop assessment methods

The standard provides guidelines for developing assessment methods. ISO/IEC 15504 as it stands is not an assessment method as such. Organizations wishing to develop ISO/IEC 15504-conformant assessment methods should base their methods on ISO/IEC 15504 guidelines and conformance rules.

Strengthening the software process wave

ISO/IEC 15504 will help internationalize the software process assessment and software process maturity movement. ISO/IEC 15504 as an international initiative should spread the knowledge and experience in software process assessment and improvement. It should boost the popularity of the process maturity movement.

SPECIAL NOTE TO THE READERS

The extracts from ISO/IEC 15504-1, 2 and 4 have been reproduced with the permission of the International Organization for Standardization, ISO. These Draft Technical Reports are subject to change and the up-to-date versions should be obtained from any ISO member body. Copyright remains with ISO.

CHAPTER 17

BOOTSTRAP software process assessment

17.1 MOTIVATION AND BACKGROUND

17.1.1 HISTORICAL BACKGROUND

The BOOTSTRAP methodology, described in detail in Kuvaja *et al.* (1994), is the result of a European Community project (ESPRIT Project 5441). The project ran from September 1991 to February 1993. The project consisted of the development of the BOOTSTRAP model and method and about 60 trials in the industry. Since the end of the project the methodology has been further developed and marketed by the BOOTSTRAP Institute (BOOTSTRAP 1996). The BOOTSTRAP Institute maintains a database of assessment results mainly from European companies but also from others in the rest of the world.

17.1.2 SCOPE

As mentioned earlier, the mission of the BOOTSTRAP project was to study investments in technology upgrades and lay the groundwork for European technology transfer standards and common practices. The main goal was to speed up the application of software engineering technology in the European software industry. The BOOTSTRAP assessment methodology describes the assessment process developed for determining where an organization stands in terms of process maturity, identifying the strengths and weaknesses, and offering improvement guidelines. Although the original project was concluded in 1993, its members founded the BOOTSTRAP Institute (BOOTSTRAP, 1996) as a non-profit organization. The purpose is to ensure the continuous development of the BOOTSTRAP methodology, promote, support, manage and control its use, and disseminate information. Version 2.3 was released by the end of 1995 and version 3.0 is the next planned release and will conform with ISO/IEC 15504.

The BOOTSTRAP assessment method covers three dimensions:

1 *Organization:* This covers the roles of management and leadership.
2 *Methodology:* This covers the way of developing software and of conducting projects.
3 *Technology:* This covers development tools used as the means of process optimization or automation and productivity improvement.

17.1.3 CONTEXT

BOOTSTRAP can be used within an initiative for software process improvement. BOOTSTRAP not only an assessment of the current practises, but also provides guidelines for transforming the assessment results into an action plan and gives guidance on prioritizing the actions.

Within the context of software process improvement, BOOTSTRAP assessment represents one component of the overall model for software improvement environment described earlier in this book. Other components are the process infrastructure, the improvement roadmap and the improvement plan. BOOTSTRAP represents an assessment method and spreads into process improvement planning.

17.2 BOOTSTRAP PROCESS MODEL

17.2.1 THE OMT TRIAD (ORGANIZATION, METHODOLOGY AND TECHNOLOGY)

BOOTSTRAP adopts a process model which addresses processes and practices for both the SPU (software producing unit) and the project. The process areas are categorized into organization, methodology and technology (Figure 17.1). The process categories comprise process areas (sets of processes addressing the same general goal) and ultimately decompose into activities and base practices.

The Organization-Methodology-Technology Triad

Figure 17.1   BOOTSTRAP scope

17.2.2 ORGANIZATIONAL COVERAGE

The BOOTSTRAP assessment covers the whole organization to be assessed (called the software producing unit, 'SPU'), as well as its software projects. The SPU level addresses the set of policies and procedures for software development, while the project level addresses the implementation of these procedures. (In CMM terms, these are known as the organization's standard software process and the project's defined software process respectively.)

17.2.3 BOOTSTRAP PROCESS MODEL ARCHITECTURE

The BOOTSTRAP process architecture reflects a tree structure that identifies the following objects: process categories, process areas, processes and best practices. These are shown at both SPU and project levels. Figure 17.2 illustrates the BOOTSTRAP process architecture. The three main process categories are detailed below (Stienen *et al*, 1997).

Organization

The first process category is the organization processes according to the definition of ISO 9000-3. It covers personnel organization and work organization. Personnel organizational issues cover functions, roles and responsibilities, and work organizational issues cover planning, implementing and controlling software development activities. The main areas covered by the organization process are:

- Resource Management practices
- Quality management
- Resource management.

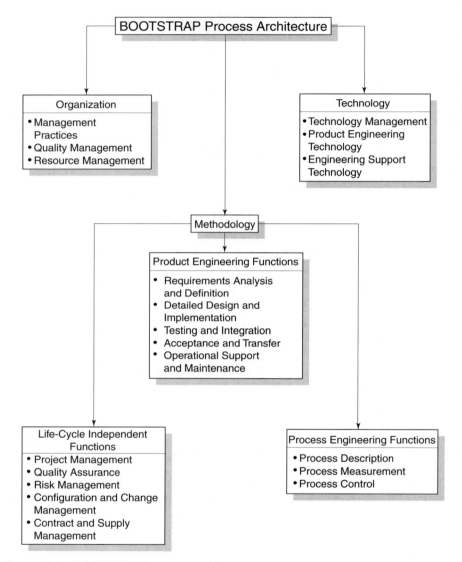

Figure 17.2 BOOTSTRAP process architecture

Methodology

The second category is the methodology processes. It is organized as three process areas:

- Process Engineering
- Product Engineering
- Engineering Support functions.

Process engineering functions
These contain process control activities such as:

- Process description
- Process measurements
- Process control.

Engineering support functions
These contain the ISO 9000-3 'supporting activities' and the 'risk avoidance and management activities'. The following processes are included:

- Project management
- Quality assurance
- Risk management
- Configuration and change management
- Contract and supply management.

Product engineering functions
This covers ISO 9000-3 and ESA PSS-05 'lifecycle activities'. The following processes are included:

- Specification and analysis
- Requirements
- Architectural design
- Detailed design and coding
- Testing and integration
- Acceptance and transfer
- Operational support and maintenance.

Technology

This process category covers the following processes:

- Technology management
- Product engineering technology
- Engineering support technology.

Figure 17.2 illustrates the overall BOOTSTRAP process architecture.

17.3 CAPABILITY SCALE AND ASSESSMENT INSTRUMENTS

17.3.1 BOOTSTRAP CAPABILITY SCALE

Although the BOOTSTRAP questionnaire is different in its coverage and focus from the SEI questionnaire, BOOTSTRAP adopts the five maturity levels of the CMM as its capability scale. The internal parameters on the scoring algorithm have been prepared on the CMM five-level maturity scale:

- Level 1: Initial
- Level 2: Repeatable
- Level 3: Defined
- Level 4: Managed
- Level 5: Optimizing.

There are some differences between the BOOTSTRAP scale and SEI:

- In BOOTSTRAP the assessment output is expressed as a profile of key attributes rather than one aggregated number.
- In BOOTSTRAP process areas are not confined to one single capability level, but cover several levels.

BOOTSTRAP defines a scoring algorithm to be used by the assessment teams when analysing the questionnaire responses. The internal parameters of the algorithm have been prepared in such a way that the key attributes are directly represented on the five-level maturity scale. The following is a brief description of the main features of the scoring algorithm; more details on the scoring method can be found in Kuvaja *et al.* (1994).

- The questionnaire is subdivided into sub-checklists.
- Sub-checklists correspond to key attributes.
- Each question in a checklist is scored on a four-point scale (absent, basic, significant, excellent) extended with the 'not applicable' option.
- The scores correspond to certain numeric equivalents, to enable calculating aggregated average scores for the key attributes.
- Evaluations of the answers give estimates for the critical process characteristics.
- Further processing is necessary to work out the overall maturity level of an SPU as described in Kuvaja *et al.* (1994).
- The assessment results can cover the three levels of SPU results, project results and industry results.

17.3.2 BOOTSTRAP QUESTIONNAIRE

The main assessment instrument used in a BOOTSTRAP assessment is a questionnaire. There are two types of questionnaires:

- Organizational level questionnaire (at the SPU level). This contains general questions about the software producing unit (SPU) and about the whole organization. This section of the questionnaire is referred to as the G-questionnaire.

- Project level questionnaire (at the project level). This contains, for each project, questions about the project profile and specific attributes. This section of the questionnaire is referred to as the P-questionnaire.

The main areas addressed by the questionnaires are shown in Figure 17.3. The figure illustrates the coverage of both questionnaires.

17.3.3 BOOTSTRAP TOOLS

BOOTSTRAP tools are meant to support individual assessment teams, and assessment participants, as well as the community of BOOTSTRAP assessors. The following tools can be used to support the assessment:

- Session Tool
- Reporting Tool
- Database Tool.

The main functions of these tools are listed in Table 17.1.

It is possible that using some tools to assist the assessment team in capturing and analysing the assessment data could be helpful, but a word of caution is necessary. Coming up with the assessment findings could be affected by qualitative rather than quantitative factors. A tool will not be able to capture the general feelings of the assessment team, nor the heuristic aspect of the analysis. A tool could support but cannot replace the individual judgement and experiences of the assessment team. Tools increase efficiency, speed up the analysis and provide the ability to prepare nearly immediate feedback. This could be very important from the customer point of view.

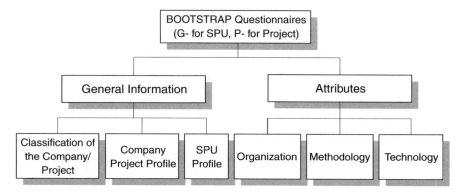

Figure 17.3 Structure of the BOOTSTRAP questionnaires

Table 17.1 Summary of the main functions of BOOTSTRAP tools

Tool	Main functions
Session Tool	*Individual support* • Selection of suitable questions • Displaying BOOTSTRAP questionnaire electronically • Capturing the questionnaire responses • Monitoring dependencies across questions • Consistency and completeness checks of the assessment session results • Allowing access/update to the session results *Group work support* • Supporting iterative completion of the questionnaire • Recording alternative expertise of different members of the assessment team • Consolidating the final conclusion
Reporting Tool	*Analysis and reporting of the questionnaire responses* • Ability to select the analysis algorithm for calculation of averages over projects • Calculating and displaying various types of profiles based on questionnaire responses • Calculating and displaying the numerical maturity level results and any relevant brief verbal comments *Analysis and reporting of the mean reference profile and maturity levels* • Ability to select the analysis algorithm • Calculating and displaying various types of profiles based on the database contents and comparison between the G and P results • Calculating and displaying the numerical maturity level results and any relevant brief verbal comments *Analysis and reporting of the process capability evolution history for the following:* • Comparison of SPUs • National industry sectors • European industry sectors
Database Tool	• Collecting and maintaining the assessment inputs • Maintaining consistency across assessment inputs • Enforcing policies of data security and change control • Maintaining evolution history of SPUs • Maintaining evolution history of the national and European industry sectors

17.4 THE BOOTSTRAP ASSESSMENT PROCESS

17.4.1 PHASES OF BOOTSTRAP ASSESSMENT

BOOTSTRAP assessment has three main phases: preparation, assessment, and action plan derivation. Figure 17.4 summarizes the main stages in these phases and maps them to the generic phases suggested in Chapter 8.

17.4.2 PRE-PLANNING

There are some start-up activities that have to be undertaken before the assessment takes place. These correspond to the pre-planning phase described

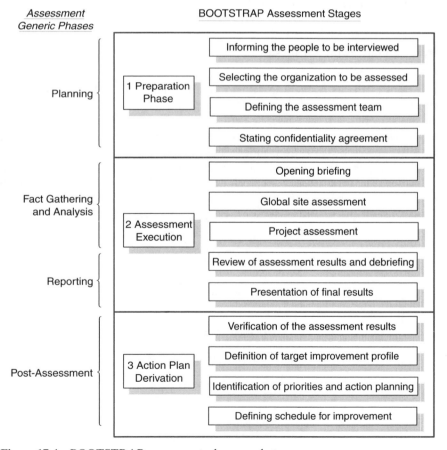

Figure 17.4 BOOTSTRAP assessment phases and stages

in the generic assessment model. It is mainly concerned with identifying the business context within which the assessment is taking place. Aspects could include, for example, the motivation behind the assessment (external or internal), gaining the management commitment, defining the organizational boundaries of the assessment, selecting the target projects, and forming the assessment team. Figure 17.5 summarizes the main pre-assessment steps that form the pre-planning phase.

17.4.3 PLANNING

The assessment is usually conducted by a joint team with members from the organization being assessed plus qualified BOOTSTRAP assessors. A typical assessment would take less than 12 weeks from project initiation to the final presentation (typically 4–6 weeks). Figure 17.6 illustrates a typical BOOTSTRAP assessment plan.

17.4.4 THE ASSESSMENT

The steps in the assessment are illustrated in Figure 17.7. The core activity of an assessment is the actual assessment week (on-site assessment). This is when the assessment team, consisting of at least two licensed assessors, conducts the actual assessment. This is usually completed during 3–4 days spent by the assessors in the organization undergoing the assessment.

The activities in a typical assessment week are shown in Figure 17.8. The actual length of the assessment week depends on the number of projects to be assessed. The typical number is four projects, but it may be more or less depending on the nature of the projects the organization usually undertakes.

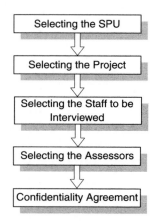

Figure 17.5 BOOTSTRAP pre-assessment steps

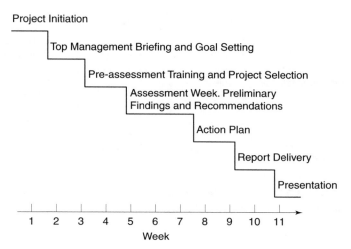

Figure 17.6   A typical BOOTSTRAP assessment plan

The purpose of the pre-meeting is to brief the local assessment team on the organization. The purpose of the opening meeting is to give a general introduction to the BOOTSTRAP model and assessment procedure, in order for all participants in the assessments to have the same starting point. There is a considerable training side-effect in this opening meeting, with regard to understanding the concepts of software best practice.

The actual detailed assessments are based on the two questionnaires, one for the organization as a whole and one for the projects. As mentioned above, the questionnaire has two parts, one for general information and one covering the BOOTSTRAP model. The latter part contains between 110–150 detailed questions.

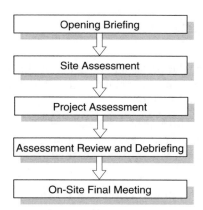

Figure 17.7   The BOOTSTRAP assessment steps

Day - 1	Day - 2	Day - 3	Day - 4
9.15-10.00 Pre-meeting	8.30-12.30 Assessment Project 1	8.30-12.30 Assessment Project 3	8.30-11.00 Evaluation and Review
10.00-12.00 Opening meeting			11.00-12.00 Final meeting
13.00-17.00 Assessment Site	13.00-17.00 Assessment Project 2	13.00-17.00 Assessment Project 4	

Figure 17.8 A typical BOOTSTRAP assessment week

The questionnaires are used to drive the interviews. Existing quality and process documentation is reviewed in connection with the interviews if deemed necessary. The answers to the questions are derived from the interviews by the assessors. The answers are given as one of five values: absent, basic, fair, extensive, and non-applicable.

The site assessment is conducted with the management at the highest possible level in the organization. It will typically be the managing director if the SPU is the entire company (or, for example, the divisional or departmental manager, the relevant quality manager, the development manager, and supporting staff). The project assessments are conducted with the participation of as many of the project management staff involved in the actual software development projects as necessary, though not more than 4–6 people. This will typically be the project manager, those responsible for quality and testing, plus one or two developers.

17.4.5 REPORTING

At the final meeting, the preliminary results of the assessment are presented. These results are subsequently further analysed and a final report is produced. The final report should include:

- process quality performance profile;
- analysis of strengths and weaknesses; and
- identified key areas for improvement suggestions for specific improvement actions.

The assessment results should cover the SPU results and the project results. The contents of the assessment report should cover the following points for both the SPU and the projects.

- *Maturity tree:* Pictorial representation of the key attributes considered in the capability assessment.
- *Organization or project profile:* All resulting methodology attributes presented in a single bar chart.
- *SPU/project profile:* A single bar chart showing all resulting main attributes of organization, methodology and technology.
- *European relative profile:* A single bar chart showing all resulting main attributes presented against the mean maturity level of the SPU's/project's industry sector across Europe.
- *National relative profile:* A single bar chart showing all resulting main attributes presented against the mean maturity level of the SPU's/project's industry sector across the country.

Detailed capability profiles are derived from the completed questionnaire. A tool is provided to support the calculation of the results, both for the SPU, and for each project or for an average of the findings for all the projects. The profiles show the maturity level for each of the defined development areas in the BOOTSTRAP model individually. A corresponding profile for the lower-level development areas is also produced. From those maturity profiles, absolute strengths and weaknesses may be derived for the SPU and for specific projects or all projects as a whole (Jonassen Hass, 1996).

It may, however, also be interesting to compare the results for the SPU and one project or to compare the results for the SPU and the average results for the projects. An example of a maturity profile for an SPU versus project is shown in Figure 17.9. From combined maturity profiles it is possible to derive strengths and weaknesses for the SPU relative to a specific project or all projects as a whole.

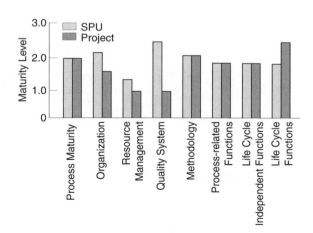

Figure 17.9 Example of a BOOTSTRAP SPU versus project maturity profile

The vertical axis in Figure 17.9 representing maturity could also be calibrated as percentage starting from 0% = absent (no criteria fulfilled) up to 100% = extensive (call criteria completely fulfilled).

A capability profile may also be presented relative to a mean score profile calculated from relevant data extracted from the BOOTSTRAP database. From profiles like this, it is possible to derive strengths and weaknesses for the SPU, for a specific project, or for all projects as a whole relative to corresponding European units.

An analysis of all the maturity profiles and additional information gathered about the organization during the assessment is performed and an analysis matrix is produced. This shows selected software development areas sorted according to how well the organization masters them and how important they are considered to be for the organization. An example of such an analysis matrix is shown in Table 17.2.

Areas where improvement actions will be of greater benefit to the organization are derived from the analysis matrix by picking areas from the upper right-hand corner working down towards the lower left-hand corner. The assessment report will contain a list of the top five improvement areas and a preliminary plan for implementing improvements in these areas in the organization.

Table 17.2 Example of an analysis matrix

Importance for company	Current status of point			
	Excellent	**Fair**	**Basic**	**Absent**
Crucial		● Risk management	● Development model ● Test	● Configuration management ● Project management
High			● Architectural design ● Contract management	● Architectural design ● QA system
Medium		● Training	● Process control	● Process management
Low				

17.4.6 POST-ASSESSMENT

The assessment itself is a means to an end, with the end being the actual software process improvement. The assessment findings and recommendations are not normally in a form that can directly be transformed into an action plan

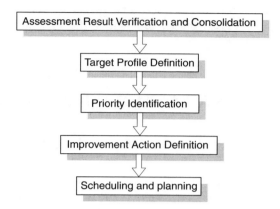

Figure 17.10 BOOTSTRAP procedures for action plan derivation

(for example the absence of priorities, dates or resources allocated). Some effort is required to transform the assessment findings and recommendations into an action plan. BOOTSTRAP defines a procedure to guide the assessment team into the derivation of such an action plan. Figure 17.10 summarizes the main steps for the action plan derivation. BOOTSTRAP documentation provides some definition and recommendations for these steps (Kuvaja *et al.*, 1994).

Actions could be grouped into software process improvement projects, each with its own plan and project manager. An overall action plan could follow a template such as the one shown in Table 17.3.

The implementation of the improvement plan in the organization is outside the scope of the BOOTSTRAP assessment and will be the responsibility of the organization (Jonassen Hass, 1996). The implementation

Table 17.3 An example template for BOOTSTRAP action planning

1 Assessment goal and purpose
2 Assessment scope and performance
4 Executive summary for top management
5 Analysis of current status
6 Overview of strengths and weaknesses
7 Additional factors of impact
8 Action plan
   8.1 Action (projects)
   8.2 Target profiles
   8.3 Priorities
   8.4 Risks
   8.5 Gantt plan
   8.6 Organization
Appendix (for projects): Project summary status and actions

should, however, be followed by a second assessment. This is necessary in order to determine the progress made, to identify the new status, and to derive continuous improvement actions.

17.5 BOOTSTRAP AND OTHER INITIATIVES

17.5.1 BOOTSTRAP AND ISO/IEC 15504 CONFORMANCE

BOOTSTRAP is being continuously enhanced by the BOOTSTRAP Institute (Bicego and Kuvaja, 1996, Messnarz, 1997) to keep it aligned with the emerging standard and state-of-the-art. The BOOTSTRAP Institute is developing a new version of BOOTSTRAP (version 3.0) to assure full ISO/IEC 15504 conformance and to align with the ISO/IEC 12207 standard. The ISO/IEC 15504 conformance will manifest itself through a conformant process model and a conformant capability dimension.

17.5.2 BOOTSTRAP AND OTHER INITIATIVES

BOOTSTRAP and the CMM

The BOOTSTRAP methodology is based on the Capability Maturity Model (CMM) developed by the Software Engineering Institute (SEI) at Carnegie Mellon University, USA. It has, however, been extended and adapted to include guidelines in the ISO 9000 family of standards and the European Space Agency software engineering standard (ESA-PSS-05). An assessment, carried out according to the BOOTSTRAP methodology, is a European assessment, though compatible with a CMM-based assessment.

Like CMM, BOOTSTRAP has a general assessment approach, based on a questionnaire. The maturity level is determined on a five-level scale equal of the CMM. The BOOTSTRAP scale is a continuous one. This is made possible by a differentiated answering scheme. BOOTSTRAP uses all questions from the CMM questionnaire published by the SEI.

BOOTSTRAP and ISO 9001

The BOOTSTRAP methodology takes into account the ISO 9001 concept of a quality system as a company-wide organization. The assessment is therefore performed at two levels: software producing unit (SPU) and projects. ISO 9001 distinguishes lifecycle-dependent and lifecycle-independent processes. This approach has been adopted in BOOTSTRAP.

BOOTSTRAP and ESA PSS-05

The ESA PSS-05 lifecycle model has been used for the product engineering functions in BOOTSTRAP in order to employ a European-wide recognized terminology. However, no specific lifecycle is recommended, or 'mandated'.

SUMMARY

Here is a reminder of the main features of the BOOTSTRAP methodology:

- BOOTSTRAP is the result of a European ESPRIT project, hence the focus on small and medium sized organizations.
- The BOOTSTRAP capability scale is based on the five maturity levels of the CMM however, key practices are not bound to one single level.
- The BOOTSTRAP process model and questionnaire accommodate ISO 9000 concepts.
- The BOOTSTRAP scope covers the software producing unit (SPU) and its software projects.
- BOOTSTRAP focuses on assessment but also extends to action planning.
- BOOTSTRAP will be ISO/IEC 15504 conformant, with assessments led by authorized assessors.
- BOOTSTRAP has tools to support an assessment team and to create a database for European benchmarking.
- BOOTSTRAP results in a capability profile for the SPU and its projects.
- Results from BOOTSTRAP assessments are stored in a central database and can be used to provide industry trends and as the basis for benchmaking.
- The BOOTSTRAP method is continuously evolving, and readers who are interested in the up-to-date versions should contact the BOOTSTRAP Institute.

CHAPTER 18

Other initiatives (ISO, MIL-STD-498, Trillium and the V-Model)

18.1 ISO 9000 QUALITY STANDARDS

18.1.1 ISO 9000 SERIES OF STANDARDS

The ISO 9000 family of standards has been developed to control the relationship between the purchaser and supplier within a contractual agreement. They specify quality systems requirements for use where a contract between two parties requires the demonstration and documentation of a supplier's capability to design and supply a product. The two parties could be an external client and the supplier, or both could be internal, for example marketing and engineering groups in a company.

Of the ISO 9000 series, ISO 9001 is the standard most pertinent to software development and maintenance. Organizations use it when they must ensure that the supplier conforms to special requirements during several stages of development, including design, development, production, installation and servicing. ISO 9000-3 provides guidelines for applying ISO 9001 to the development, supply and maintenance of software.

The relevant parts of the ISO series comprise the following standards:

Reference	Title
ISO 9000	Quality management and quality assurance standards – Guidelines for selection and use
ISO 9001	Quality systems – Model for quality assurance in design, development, production, installation and servicing

ISO 9004	Quality management and quality system elements – Guidelines
ISO 9004-4	Quality management and quality system elements – Part 4: Guidelines for quality improvement
ISO 9000-3	Quality management and quality assurance standards – Part 3: Guidelines for the application of ISO 9001 to the development, supply, and maintenance of software
ISO 8402	Quality management and quality assurance – Vocabulary

The ISO series of standards stress the following quality concepts:

- An organization should achieve and sustain the quality of the product or service produced so as to meet continually the purchaser's stated or implied needs.
- An organization should provide confidence in its own management that the intended quality is being achieved and sustained.
- An organization should provide confidence to the purchaser that the intended quality is being, or will be, achieved in the delivered product or service provided. When contractually required, this provision of confidence may involve agreed demonstration requirements.

Transforming these concepts in terms of software process improvement, they read:

- An organization should achieve and sustain continuous process improvement for the processes used for developing the product or service produced. The objective is to meet continually the business goals, product and process quality requirements and the purchaser's stated or implied needs.
- An organization should provide confidence to its own management that the intended process improvement targets are being achieved and sustained.
- An organization should provide confidence to its customers that the intended process improvement will result in an improved quality of the delivered product or service provided. When contractually required, this provision of confidence may involve agreed demonstration of capability (for example, through Process Capability Evaluation).

18.1.2 ISO 9001

The full title of ISO 9001 is 'Quality systems – Model for quality assurance in design/development, production, installation, and servicing'. This is intended for use when conformance to specified requirements is to be assured by the supplier during several stages. These stages may include design, development, production, installation and servicing. Of the ISO 9000 standards, ISO 9001 is the standard that is pertinent to software development and maintenance.

There are 20 clauses in ISO 9001. Table 18.1 summarizes these clauses, and Figure 18.1 maps ISO 9001 main clauses to the five generic process categories (Organization, Management, Engineering, Support and Customer–Supplier).

ISO 9000-3 provides guidelines for the application of ISO 9001 to the development, supply and maintenance of software. It deals primarily with situations where specific software is developed as part of a contract according to purchaser's specifications. However, the concepts described could be equally of value in other situations. ISO 9000-3 elaborates significantly on ISO 9001, and provides guidance on how to interpret ISO 9001.

Organizations typically use ISO 9000 standards to regulate their internal quality system and assure the quality system of their suppliers. The standards are also frequently used to register a third-party quality system. ISO 9000 has a certification (sometimes called registration) scheme associated with it. Such a certification can be obtained by an organization only after it undergoes an audit. Certificates of registration have a defined scope within an organization and are issued by quality-system registrars. Auditors are trained in the ISO 9000 standards, but they may not have been trained in, nor be knowledgeable about, software-specific issues.

18.1.3 ISO 9001 VERSUS THE CMM

Frequently a company may face the situation when they are required for business reasons to be ISO 9001 certified, and in the meantime they follow a CMM-based approach for software process improvement. The question they may have in mind could be whether the CMM-based software process improvement will help them achieve such registration, and whether there is an overlap with ISO 9001. This question has been tackled initially by Mark Paulk in his article 'How ISO 9001 compares with the CMM', published in *IEEE Software*, January 1995 (Paulk, 1995a). Some companies that have faced such a situation in reality have also published their lessons (Bush and La Manna, 1996). The main conclusion is that there is a strong correlation between ISO 9001 and the CMM, although some issues in ISO 9001 are not covered by the CMM and vice versa. The following is a summary of the arguments and findings resulting from comparing the CMM and ISO 9001 in the context of software improvement (Paulk, 1995a).

Common themes across ISO 9001 and CMM include:

- Emphasis on process
- Documented processes
- Practised processes
- Address the 'what', not the 'how'.

Areas of difference include the following:

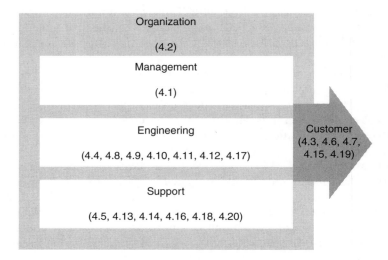

Figure 18.1 Mapping ISO 9001 main clauses (in brackets) to the generic process categories

- *Focus:* The CMM focuses on continuous process improvement, while the ISO 9001/9000-3 model aims primarily to establish an acceptable baseline for software process. It addresses only the minimum criteria for an acceptable quality system.
- *Dimensions:* ISO is a 'binary' model (either you comply or not) whereas the CMM is a staged model (to help you find out where you are, and point to where you should go).
- *Assessment and certification:* The CMM can be used for either an internal assessment or an external audit, whereas a company can only be ISO certified in an external audit.
- *Coverage:* ISO is a standard for companies producing hardware and software as well as various other services and manufactured goods, and usefully provides compatible standards for all products. The CMM focuses primarily on the software development and management activities.
- *Supplier's role:* The CMM explicitly addresses how the organization can acquire software through subcontracting with an external customer or other subcontractor (the supplier may also be a customer). ISO 9001's contract-review clause does not explicitly describe the supplier's role when it is acting as a customer to a subcontractor.
- *Level of detail:* The level of detail differs significantly. While the relevant sections in ISO 9001 and ISO 9000-3 do not exceed 25 pages, the CMM is more than 500 pages.

For a software process improvement programme, the more detailed guidance and software specificity provided by the CMM suggests that it is the better choice.

18.1.4 MAPPING ISO 9001 CLAUSES TO THE CMM KEY

PROCESS AREAS

In order to highlight areas of coverage and areas of difference between the two, it is useful to map ISO 9001 clauses to the software process infrastructure components described in Chapter 6, and the CMM key process areas. Table 18.1 summarizes the main clauses of ISO 9001 relating to the quality system requirements. It maps them to components of the model proposed for the software process infrastructure described earlier in this book and to the key process areas of the CMM v1.1.

18.1.5 ISO 9001 AND CMM: WHICH ONE TO CHOOSE?

In his article Mark Paulk (Paulk, 1995a) tries to answer the following common questions about CMM and ISO 9001:

- At what level in the CMM would an ISO 9001-compliant organization be?
- Can a CMM level 2 (or 3) organization be considered compliant with ISO 9001?
- Should my software quality management and process improvement effort be based on ISO 9001 or on the CMM?

Following a detailed discussion and mapping between ISO 9001 clauses and CMM key process areas, the following guidelines are proposed to help answer the above questions.

ISO 9001 does not address all the CMM practices

An ISO 9001-compliant organization would not necessarily satisfy all the key process areas in level 2 of the CMM, but it would satisfy most of the level 2 and many of the level 3 goals. Further, because ISO 9001 does not address all the CMM practices, a level 1 organization could receive ISO 9001 registration.

ISO certification and CMM levels

A CMM level 2 (or level 3) organization would probably be considered compliant with ISO 9001. Even a level 3 organization would need to ensure that it adequately addressed the delivery and installation process described in Clause 4.15 of ISO 9001. Also it should consider the use of included software products, as described in clause 6.8 of ISO 9000-3. With this caveat, obtaining certification should be relatively straightforward for a level 2 or higher organization.

Table 18.1 Mapping ISO 9001 main clauses to the process infrastructure components and the CMM key process areas

Clause no. in ISO 9001	Topic addressed	Corresponding infrastructure component(s) and CMM key process areas
4	Quality system requirements	The total infrastructure
4.1	Management responsibility	Ownership of the process documentation and feedback
4.2	Quality system	Process documentation
4.3	Contract review	Requirements Management process
4.4	Design control	Software Product Engineering process
4.5	Document control	Software Configuration Management
4.6	Purchasing	Software Subcontract Management
4.7	Purchaser supplied product	Integrated Software Management
4.8	Product identification and traceability	Software Configuration Management and Software Product Engineering
4.9	Process control	Software Product Engineering and Quantitative Process Management
4.10	Inspection and testing	Software Product Engineering and Peer Reviews
4.11	Inspection, measuring and test equipment	Software Product Engineering
4.12	Inspection and test status	Testing practices in the Software Product Engineering, and problem reporting and configuration status in the Software Configuration Management
4.13	Control of non-conforming product	Non-conforming products are not specifically addressed in the CMM
4.14	Corrective action	Software Configuration Management and Software Quality Assurance key process areas
4.15	Handling, storage, packaging and delivery	Replication, delivery and installation are not covered in the CMM. Acceptance testing is addressed in the Software Configuration Management and Software Product Engineering key process areas

(continued)

Table 18.1 *(continued)*

Clause no. in ISO 9001	Topic addressed	Corresponding infrastructure component(s)
4.16	Quality records	This is distributed in the CMM throughout the key process areas. Specifically the testing and peer review practices in the Software Product Engineering and problem reporting in the Configuration Management key process areas
4.17	Internal quality audits	This is covered in the Software Quality Assurance key process area
4.18	Training	Specific training needs are covered in the training practices in the 'Ability to perform' common feature. The general training infrastructure is described in the Training Program key process area
4.19	Servicing	CMM practices do not directly address the unique aspects of a maintenance environment
4.20	Statistical techniques	This is described through the measurements and analysis key practices distributed throughout the key process areas of the CMM

Use for software process improvement

Should software process improvement be based on the CMM or ISO 9001? A short answer is that an organization may want to consider both, given the significant degree of overlap. A market may require ISO 9001 certification. In such a case addressing the concerns of the CMM would help an organization prepare for an ISO 9001 audit. Conversely, CMM level 1 organizations would certainly profit from addressing the concerns of ISO 9001. Although either document can be used alone to structure a process-improvement programme, the more detailed guidance and software specificity provided by the CMM suggests that it is the better choice, although admittedly this answer may be biased.

Finally, if your organization faces the choice between an ISO approach and a CMM-based approach to software process improvement, then you should get your organization to 'focus on improvement to build a competitive advantage, not on achieving a score – whether that is a maturity level or a certificate' (Paulk, 1995a). Continuous process should be viewed within the larger business context in the spirit of Total Quality Management.

18.2 ISO/IEC 12207, 'SOFTWARE LIFE CYCLE PROCESSES'

18.2.1 BACKGROUND

In June 1989, the International Standards Organization (ISO) and the International Electrotechnical Commission (IEC) initiated the development of an International Standard, ISO/IEC 12207 on software lifecycle processes. The International Standard was published in August 1995 (ISO, 1995).

ISO/IEC 12207 establishes a common framework for software lifecycle processes that can be used by software practitioners to manage and engineer software. The International Standard contains processes, activities and tasks that are to be applied during the acquisition, supply, development, operation and maintenance of software products. It describes the architecture of the software lifecycle processes but does not specify the details of how to implement or perform the activities and tasks included in the processes.

18.2.2 LIFECYCLE PROCESSES

The lifecycle processes are grouped into three broad classes: primary, supporting and organizational (Singh, 1996). These classes are defined as follows:

- *Primary processes:* These are the prime movers and provide for conducting major functions during the lifecycle. They comprise five processes: acquisition, supply, development, operation and maintenance.
- *Supporting processes:* These are the coordinating activities that support and coordinate the development and lifecycle primary activities. A supporting process supports another process in performing a specialized function. They comprise eight processes: documentation, configuration management, quality assurance, verification, validation, joint reviews, audit and problem resolution.
- *Organizational processes:* These are the overall management and support for the total development environment. They comprise the following four processes: management, infrastructure, improvement and training.

Mapping these processes to the generic process categories (see Figure 18.1), we can see that:

- ISO/IEC 12207 Primary Processes cover both the Engineering and the Customer process categories.
- ISO/IEC 12207 Organizational Processes cover both the Organizational and the Management process categories.
- ISO/IEC 12207 Supporting Processes map to the Support process category.

In ISO/IEC 12207, each process is further designed in terms of its constituent activities, each of which is further designed in terms of its constituent tasks. A summary of the main lifecycle processes is shown in Figure 18.2.

18.2.3 RELATIONSHIP TO OTHER STANDARDS

With the proliferation of standards and models for the software process, one could easily become confused as to which one applies in what situations, and whether they all relate to each other within a bigger picture. Figure 18.3 puts forward a possible scenario that proposes a focus for each of the main standards and models. In fact, when planning and defining an improvement programme for its software process, an organization should be able to benefit from the relevant components of each of these standards. This could happen more effectively if the organization adopts an overall framework for software process improvement that supports its business strategy along the lines of the framework described in Part 2 of this book.

18.3 DOD STANDARD MIL-STD-498

18.3.1 OVERVIEW

The full title of MIL-STD-498 is 'Military Standard – Software Development and Documentation'. It supersedes DOD-STD-2167A, DOD-STD-7935A and DOD-STD-1703 (NS). The following comments summarize the background and positioning of MIL-STD-498 (DoD, 1984).

Use

MIL-STD-498 Military Standard is approved for use by all departments and agencies of the US Department of Defense.

Specification

This standard merges DOD-STD-2167A and DOD-STD-7935A to define a set of activities and documentation suitable for the development of both weapon systems and automated information systems. A conversion guide from these standards to MIL-STD-498 is provided in its appendices.

New features

New changes introduced in MIL-STD-498 include the following:

- Improved compatibility with incremental and evolutionary development models
- Improved compatibility with non-hierarchical design methods

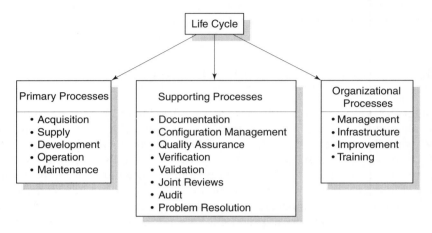

Figure 18.2 ISO/IEC 12207 International Standard Lifecycle Processes

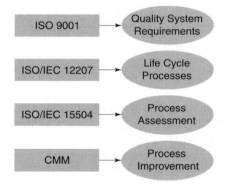

Figure 18.3 Focus areas for the main software process standards

- Improved compatibility with computer-aided software engineering (CASE) tools
- Alternatives to, and more flexibility in, preparing documents
- Clearer requirements for incorporating reusable software; introduction of software management indicators; added emphasis on software supportability; and improved links to systems engineering.

Applicability

This standard can be applied in any phase of the system lifecycle. It can be applied to contractors, subcontractors or government in-house agencies performing software development.

Terminology

For uniformity, the term 'acquirer' is used for the organization requiring the technical effort, the term 'developer' for the organization performing the technical effort, and the term 'contract' for the agreement between them. The term 'software development' is used as an inclusive term encompassing new development, modification, reuse, reengineering, maintenance and all other activities resulting in software products.

Methodology independence

This standard is not intended to specify or discourage the use of any particular software development method. The developer is responsible for selecting software development methods that support the achievement of contract requirements.

Related standards

This standard implements the development and documentation processes of ISO/IEC 12207. It interprets all applicable clauses in MIL-Q-9858A (Quality Program Requirements) and ISO 9001 (Quality Systems) for software.

Coverage

The standard includes all activities pertaining to software development. It invokes no other standards. It can be applied on its own or supplemented with other standards. If other standards are applied, the acquirer is responsible for resolving any conflicts that arise.

Tailorability

MIL-STD-498 standard and its information requirements (Data Item Descriptions (DIDs)) are meant to be tailored by the acquirer to ensure that only necessary and cost-effective requirements are imposed on software development efforts. General tailoring guidance is provided in the appropriate sections of the standard.

18.3.2 MIL-STD-498 REQUIREMENTS

MIL-STD-498 specifies two types of requirements, general and detailed. The general requirements are required to be met in carrying out the detailed requirements. The general requirements cover the software development process, methods and standards. Also they address reusable software products, handling of critical requirements and computer hardware utilization. The detailed requirements go into the details of the engineering and management processes. The MIL-STD-498 Standard uses the word 'process' to refer to all the activities that may be involved in software development. Those activities are listed below (the numbers between brackets refer to the clause number in the MIL-STD-498 standards document):

- Project planning and oversight (section 5.1)
- Establishing a software development environment (5.2)
- System requirements analysis (5.3)
- System design (5.4)
- Software requirements analysis (5.5)
- Software design (5.6)
- Software implementation and unit testing (5.7)
- Unit integration and testing (5.8)
- CSCI qualification testing (5.9)
- CSCI/HWCI integration and testing (5.10)
- System qualification testing (5.11)
- Preparing for software use (5.18)
- Preparing for software transition (5.13)
- Integral processes:
  - Software configuration management (5.14)
  - Software product evaluation (5.15)
  - Software quality assurance (5.16)
  - Corrective action (5.17)
  - Joint technical and management reviews (5.18)
  - Other activities (5.19).

Figure 18.4 suggests a mapping between the MIL-STD-498 detailed requirements and the five generic process categories.

18.3.3 MIL-STD-498 AND SOFTWARE PROCESS IMPROVEMENT

MIL-STD-498 presents the whole lifecycle as a development process. It requires that the project should assess and improve its processes. There are two paragraphs specific to the process (Table 18.2). These are Clause 4.1 which states the requirement for establishing a software development process, and Clause 5.19.7 which states the requirement for periodical assessment of the suitability and effectiveness of the development process, and improvement as necessary. These paragraphs and the overall process focus of MIL-STD-498 are likely to increase process awareness and promote focus on the process and process improvement among project managers.

18.4 TRILLIUM

18.4.1 BACKGROUND AND OVERVIEW

Trillium has been developed by a consortium of telecommunications companies, headed by Bell Canada. It is based on the Software Engineering

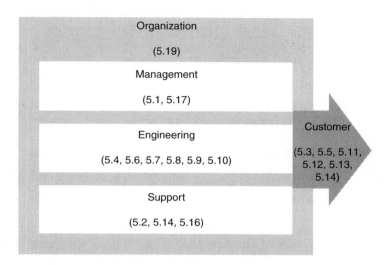

Figure 18.4 Mapping MIL-STD-498 detailed requirement clauses (in brackets) to the generic process categories

Table 18.2 MIL-STD-498 paragraphs on the software development process and its improvement

Paragraph number	Subject area	Requirements
4.1	Software development process	The developer shall establish a software development process consistent with contract requirements. The software development process shall include the following major activities, which may overlap, may be applied iteratively, may be applied differently to different elements of software, and need not be performed in the order listed below. Appendix G provides examples. The developer's software development process shall be described in the software development plan (DoD, 1994).
5.19.7	Improvement of project processes	The developer shall periodically assess the processes used on the project to determine their suitability and effectiveness. Based on these assessments, the developer shall identify any necessary and beneficial improvements to the process, shall identify these improvements to the acquirer in the form of proposed updates to the software development plan and, if approved, shall implement the improvements on the project (DoD, 1994).

Institute's Capability Maturity Model (CMM) version 1.1. The goal of the Trillium model is to provide a means to initiate and guide a continuous improvement programme. The Trillium model and its accompanying tools are not in themselves a product development process or lifecycle model. Rather, the Trillium model provides key industry practices which can be used to improve an existing process or lifecycle. Although it is oriented towards the special requirements of the telecommunications industry, it can also be generally used as the basis of a software process improvement strategy for other industries. The process model adopted by Trillium and its capability scale have similarities with other initiatives such as the CMM, ISO/IEC 15504 and ISO 9001. In addition to the CMM, Trillium incorporates the intentions of a number of national and international standards. The most notable of these are ISO 9001:1994 International Standard, ISO 9000-3:1991 Guidelines, Bellcore TR-NWT-000179 Issue 2 (June 1993), Bellcore TA-NWT-001315 Issue 1 (December 1993), relevant parts of the Malcolm Baldrige National Quality Award (1995 Award Criteria), IEEE Software Engineering Standards Collection (1993 edition), and the IEC Standard Publication 300:1984.

Trillium can be used in a variety of ways such as:

- to benchmark an organization's product development and support process capability against best practices in the industry;
- in self-assessment mode, to help identify opportunities for improvement within a product development organization; and
- in pre-contractual negotiations, to assist in selecting a supplier.

The Trillium model provides guidelines for improving an organization's capability in a competitive, commercial environment. In this context, Trillium documentation defines the capability as: 'The ability of a development organization to consistently deliver a product or an enhancement to an existing product: that meets customer expectations, with minimal defects, for the lowest life-cycle cost and in the shortest time.'(Trillium, 1994)

18.4.2 TRILLIUM MATURITY LEVELS

The Trillium model specifies five levels for process improvement (generally corresponding to the CMM five levels of process maturity) as illustrated in Figure 18.5 and summarized below:

- *Level 1: Unstructured:* The development process is *ad hoc*. Projects frequently cannot meet quality or schedule targets. Success, while possible, is based on individuals rather than organizational infrastructure. At this level the product development is 'hero-driven' and characterized as *Risk– High.*

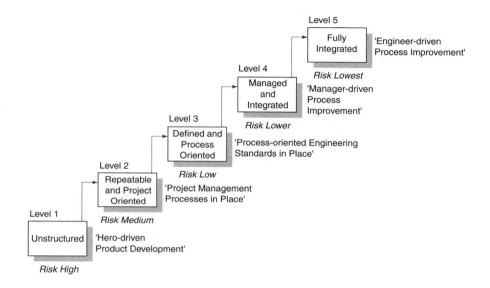

Figure 18.5 Trillium process improvement levels

- *Level 2: Repeatable and project oriented:* Individual project success is achieved through strong project management, planning and control, with emphasis on requirements management, estimation techniques and configuration management. At this level the project management processes are in place and product development is characterized as *Risk–Medium*.
- *Level 3: Defined and process oriented:* Processes are defined and utilized at the organizational level, although project customization is still permitted. Processes are controlled and improved. ISO 9001 requirements such as training and internal process auditing are incorporated. At this level the process-oriented engineering standards are in place, and product development is characterized as *Risk–Low*.
- *Level 4: Managed and integrated:* Process instrumentation and analysis are used as key mechanisms for process improvement. Process change management and defect prevention programmes are integrated into processes. CASE tools are integrated into processes. At this level the process improvement is 'manager-driven', and characterized as *Risk–Lower*.
- *Level 5: Fully integrated:* Formal methodologies are extensively used. Organizational repositories for development history and process are utilized and effective. At this level the process improvement is 'engineer-driven' and characterized as *Risk–Lowest*.

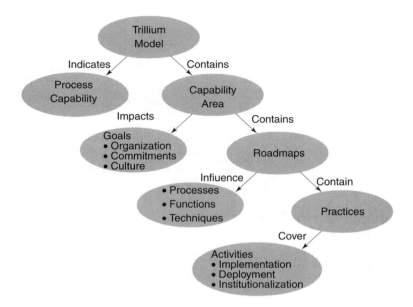

Figure 18.6   Trillium architecture

18.4.3 TRILLIUM ARCHITECTURE

The Trillium internal structure is very similar to that of the Capability Maturity Model. The main variation is introducing the concept of roadmaps instead of the key process areas in the case of the CMM. Figure 18.6 illustrates the architecture.

The five levels of maturity are similar to those of the CMM, the capability areas and their associated roadmaps span maturity levels (unlike the CMM key process areas), and the practice statements serve as assessment questionnaire.

18.4.4 CAPABILITY AREAS

There are eight capability areas in the Trillium model. Each capability area has a number of roadmaps associated with it and contains practices at multiple Trillium levels. (For example, Management spans levels 2 to 4 while Quality System spans levels 2 to 5.) Table 18.3 lists the Trillium capability areas and their associated roadmaps, and Figure 18.7 maps Trillium capability areas to the generic process categories.

Table 18.3 Trillium capability areas and roadmaps

Capability area	Roadmaps
Organizational process quality	• Quality management • Business process engineering
Human resource development and management	• Human resource development and management
Process	• Process definition • Technology management • Process improvement and engineering • Measurements
Management	• Project management • Subcontractor management • Customer–supplier relationship • Requirements management • Estimation
Quality system	• Quality system
Development practices	• Development process • Development techniques • Internal documentation • Verification and validation • Configuration management • Reuse • Reliability management
Development environment	• Development environment
Customer support	• Problem response analysis • Usability engineering • Lifecycle cost modelling • User documentation • Customer engineering • User training

Each capability area incorporates one or more roadmaps. A roadmap is a set of related practices that focus on an organizational area or need, or a specific element within the product development process. Each roadmap represents a significant capability for a software development organization.

18.4.5 CAPABILITY EVALUATION

The result of a process assessment of a development organization will take the form of a capability profile. This is a profile of the capability areas illustrating the relative areas of strengths and weaknesses. Figure 18.8 illustrates a sample profile. As can be seen in this example, organizations typically achieve some

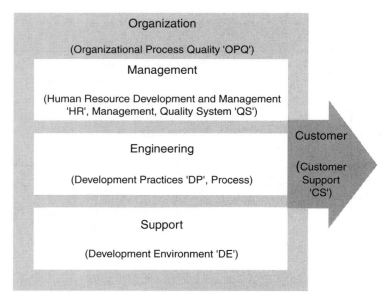

Figure 18.7 Mapping Trillium capability areas (in brackets) to the generic process categories

higher-level practices without having completed all the practices at the lower levels. To achieve a Trillium level, an organization must satisfy a minimum of 90% of the criteria (practices) in each of the eight capability areas at that level, plus all lower levels of maturity. Levels 3, 4 and 5 require the achievement of all lower Trillium levels (i.e. levels cannot be skipped).

Within a given roadmap, the level of practices is based on their respective degree of maturity. The most fundamental practices are at a lower level whereas the most advanced ones are located at the higher level. An organization matures through the roadmap levels. Lower-level practices must be implemented and sustained for higher-level practices to achieve maximum effectiveness.

Assigning practices to capability levels

Practices are assigned to a given maturity level (Table 18.4). The assignment of a practice to a maturity level is based on the following guidelines:

- Practices that are considered fundamental for the successful conclusion of a development project are assigned to level 2.
- Practices that are considered to be organization-wide in scope or fundamental to the continuous improvement of the development process are assigned to level 3.

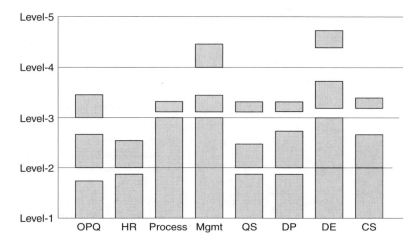

Figure 18.8 An example of Trillium profile and score

- Practices that deal with CASE technology or characterize advanced process maturity (for example change management, integration of defect prevention, statistical process control and advanced metrics) are generally assigned to level 4.
- Level 5 typically deals with advancing technology as it applies to process automation, formal methodologies and strategic utilization of organization repositories.

18.4.6 TRILLIUM VERSUS CMM

The Trillium model is based on the Software Engineering Institute (SEI) Capability Maturity Model (CMM) version 1.1. The most notable differences are:

- Trillium model architecture is based on roadmaps, rather than key process areas.
- Trillium has a wider product perspective, rather than software.
- Trillium claims a wider coverage of capability-impacting issues.
- Trillium has orientation towards customer focus, technological maturity and the telecommunications industry.

Version 3.0 of Trillium covers all SEI CMM v1.1 activities and abilities and some of the commitments, measurements and verifications. A paper at the 1996 SEPG Conference discussed the differences between the Trillium model and the CMM (Popel and Wise, 1996). The following list elaborates on the points

Table 18.4   Maturity levels practices

Level no.	Maturity level	Nature of practices assigned to this level
Level 2	Repeatable and project oriented	Practices considered fundamental for the successful conclusion of a development project
Level 3	Defined and process oriented	Practices considered to be organization-wide in scope or fundamental to the continuous improvement of the development process
Level 4	Managed and integrated	Practices that deal with CASE technology or characterize advanced process maturity (for example change management, integration of defect prevention, statistical process control and advanced metrics)
Level 5	Fully integrated	Practices which typically deal with advancing technology as it applies to process automation, formal methodologies and strategic utilization of organization repositories

discussed and includes further observations resulting from analysis of the two models.

- All the practices of the CMM Version 1.1 have been incorporated into Trillium after going through the following transformation, if applicable.
- The practice is generalized by either removing references to 'software' or replacing them by 'product and services' or 'systems'.
- The practice is generalized by either removing references to 'development', or replacing them by 'development and support'.
- References to 'group' or other specific organizational units are replaced by 'function'.
- Indirect references to specific documents are replaced by references to a process (for example 'quality plan' by 'quality planning').
- There is an added dimension of complexity for Trillium. One source of complexity is relating the maturity level to individual practices (there are 507 practices in the Trillium model).
- CMM's key process areas are replaced by roadmaps.
- CMM is more focused on software engineering and provides a clearer stepped approach.

- Trillium has added some concepts from BPR, TQM and other useful standards.
- Trillium has extended the coverage to product (as opposed to software) and to areas such as BPR and TQM.

Although Trillium has been designed to be applied to embedded software systems such as telecommunications systems, much of the model can be applied to other segments of the software industry such as Management Information Systems (MIS). (It is claimed in the Trillium literature that most of the practices in the model can be applied directly to hardware development. Although this could be taken as a positive point, it could easily dilute the focus on software issues.)

18.5 THE V-MODEL

18.5.1 BACKGROUND AND OVERVIEW

The V-Model is described in the document titled 'Software Development Standard for the German Federal Armed Forces, General Directive 250 – Software Life Cycle Process Model' (IABG, 1992). It is a standard to be applied to the entire effort of software development and generation. It is reviewed here alongside other standards and models for the software process as an example of how a national standard addresses the software process and its improvement. This should enrich the picture that readers get out of comparing and contrasting the coverage and approach followed by the variety of models and standards.

The value of a standard for software is the extent to which its use contributes towards reducing software costs of the entire lifecycle, improvement/warranty of software quality, and improvement in communication between customer and contractor. The standardization effort of the German federal authorities pursues these objectives through regulation on three levels:

1 *Procedures:*   What has to be done? Which activities have to be carried out in the process of the development of software, which results have to be produced in this process, and which are the contents that these results must have?

2 *Methods:*   How is this to be achieved? Which methods are to be followed for performing the activities and which representation means are to be used in the results?

3 *Tool requirements:*   What is used to do something? Which functional characteristics must the tools to be used in software development have?

On all levels, the standards are structured according to the following activity areas: Software Development, Quality Assurance, Configuration Management and Project Management. The V-Model is the lifecycle model and is the standard for the first level (procedure). It regulates the software

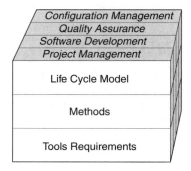

Figure 18.9   Standards architectures adopted by the German federal authorities

development process in a uniform and binding way by means of activities and products (results). These have to be taken into consideration during software development and the accompanying activities for quality assurance, configuration management and project management. This leads to a two-dimensional architecture (illustrated in Figure 18.9) for the family of standards of which the V-Model covers the lifecycle processes.

18.5.2 SUBMODELS AND BASIC CONCEPTS

Submodels

The V-Model is structured into functional parts called submodels:

- Software Development (SWD) submodel: The SWD submodel develops the system or software.
- Quality Assurance (QA) submodel: The QA submodel submits quality requirements to the SWD, CM and PM submodels. These include test cases and criteria in order to assure the products and compliance to standards.
- Configuration Management (CM) submodel: The CM submodel administers the generated products.
- Project Management (PM) submodel: The PM submodel plans, monitors and passes information to the SWD, QA and CM submodels.

These four submodels are closely interconnected and mutually influence one another through exchange of products/results. Figure 18.10 illustrates the interaction of these submodels, and Figure 18.11 maps these submodels to the generic process categories.

Basic concepts

The V-Model and its submodels describe the processes in terms of two basic concepts: Activities and Products.

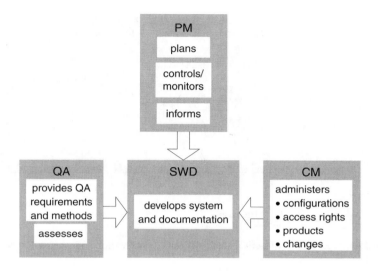

Figure 18.10   Submodels of the V-Model and their interactions

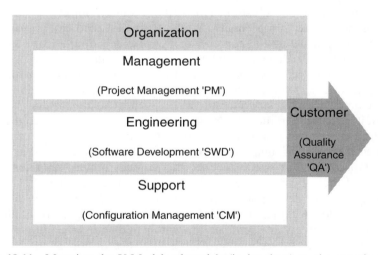

Figure 18.11   Mapping the V-Model submodels (in brackets) to the generic process categories

Activities are worksteps in the software development process. Activities may consist of a set of 'sub-activities', and at the highest level they are called 'main activities'. An activity may include the generation of a product, the change of state of a product, or the modification of the contents of a product. Activities are described in terms of activity description and activity patterns. Activity patterns consist of the following: Name of the activity, Product Flow, Handling. If an activity is to be decomposed into sub-activities, and logical

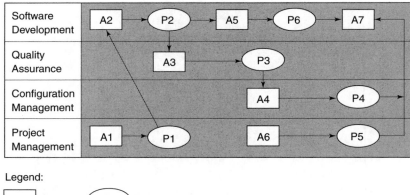

Legend:

| A | Activity | (P) Process |

Figure 18.12 Example of activity and product flow within and across the V-Model's submodels

interdependencies between sub-activities and products have to be pointed out, the activity pattern includes an activity decomposition.

Products are the results of activities (the processed objects). Products may be decomposed into 'sub-products'. Products are described in terms of product descriptions that define the contents of the product in adherence to a strict product pattern. Products may take the following states: *planned*: initial state of all the products; *being processed*: the product is under control of the developer; and *submitted*: the product is transferred to the configuration management. It is then subjected to QA assessment. If the product is rejected by QA, it is returned to the state 'being processed', otherwise it is considered as *accepted*: the product has been checked by QA and is released. It can only be modified if the version number is updated. Products are described in terms of product patterns. For every product the product pattern contains a short synopsis of the contents and also a listing of the structural items.

The software development process is represented in the form of activity and product flow within and across the four submodels. Figure 18.12 illustrates an example of activity and product flow within and across the four submodels.

The following subsections provide a brief description of the V-Model's submodels.

18.5.3 THE V-MODEL'S SUBMODELS

The Software Development (SWD) submodel

The SWD submodel regulates which activities are to be carried out during software development and when products (documents, code) are to be prepared. It comprises the nine main activities shown in Figure 18.13.

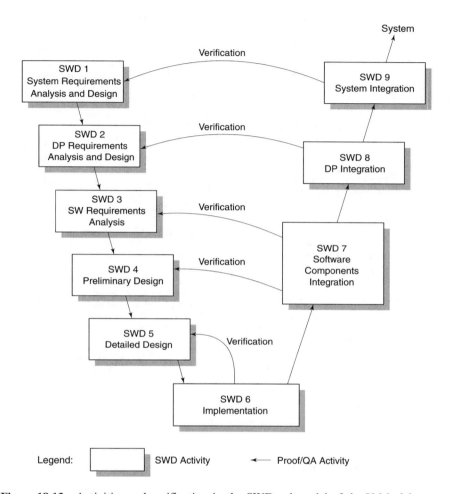

Figure 18.13 Activities and verification in the SWD submodel of the V-Model

The Quality Assurance (QA) submodel

The QA submodel regulates the tasks and functions of quality assurance within the software development process. The QA submodel ensures the fulfilment of the requirements specified in the System Requirements, DP Requirements and SW Requirements of the SWD submodel. It comprises the seven main activities shown in Figure 18.14. It is worth noting the focus on assessment on this submodel.

The Configuration Management (CM) submodel

The CM submodel ensures that all products are uniquely identifiable, that interrelations and deviations of different versions or variants of a configuration

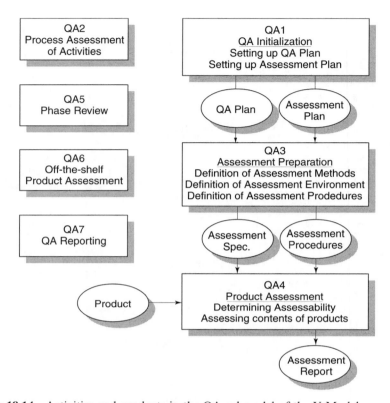

Figure 18.14 Activities and products in the QA submodel of the V-Model

remain evident and that any product changes can be made only in a controlled manner. It comprises the following five main activities:

- CM1: Initiation
- CM2: Configuration Administration
- CM3: Change Management
- CM4: Data Backup
- CM5: CM Reporting

Products of the CM submodel include:

- The CM Plan
- The Configuration Identification document
- The Data Dictionary

The Project Management (PM) submodel

The PM submodel regulates the tasks and functions. It comprises the following main activities and sub activities:

- PM1: Project Initiation
- PM2.1: Initiating the Main Activity
- PM2.2: Monitoring the Main Activity
- PM2.3: Completing the Main Activity
- PM3: Project Completion

Products of the P submodel include:

- Work order
- Project Plan
- Project manual
- Project History
- Final Report

18.5.4 ORGANIZATIONAL ROLES DEFINED IN THE V-MODEL

The V-Model defines the roles appropriate to each of the submodels and maps the roles to the main activities, where each activity can be allocated more than one role. Mapping the roles to activities takes the form of a matrix where the entries indicate the nature of the role allocated to the activity, for example Executing, Advisory, or Cooperative. Figure 18.15 summarizes the roles specified in the V-Model for the different submodels.

18.5.5 THE V-MODEL AND THE CMM

There are differences and similarities between the V-Model and the CMM as follows.

Boundaries

The V-Model addresses software development within a project rather than a whole organization.

Mapping the V-Model submodels to the CMM key process areas

The V-Model submodels cover most of CMM level 2 key process areas as illustrated in Table 18.5.

Coverage of process infrastructure

The CMM literature gives comprehensive coverage of the technical infrastructure required to support the process at the organizational level. The V-Model does not cover this aspect, but specifies the roles necessary to execute the process activities. The V-Model is more explicit in defining the roles

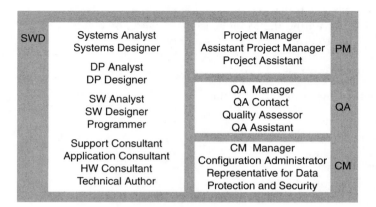

Figure 18.15   Roles and responsibilities in the V-Model

required for executing the main activities. Although similar roles are defined in the CMM, the V-Model documentation is more formal in mapping the roles to the activities, and in characterizing the roles.

Activity and product flow across submodels

The V-Model illustrates the flow of activities and products across submodels explicitly as matrices. The CMM lists them in the textual descriptions of the key process areas.

Table 18.5   Mapping between the V-Model and CMM

CMM level 2 key process area	V-Model submodel	See note
Requirements Management	Software Development (SWD)	1
Project Planning	Project Management (PM)	
Project Tracking	Project Management (PM)	2
Subcontract Management	Project Management (PM)	3
Software Quality Assurance	Quality Assurance (QA)	
Software Configuration Management	Configuration Management (CM)	

Notes
1 By treating the Requirements Management as a separate key process area, the CMM provides a strong focus on controlling the requirements. The V-Model SWD submodel includes a main activity for requirements analysis and recording.
2 Project tracking is covered in the activities of the V-Model PM submodel.
3 The V-Model does not give as strong emphasis on subcontract and supplier management as the CMM does. The CMM treats it as a separate key process area, whereas the V-Model treats it as an activity in the PM submodel.

Process modelling

The V-Model expresses the processes in terms of two main concepts: Activities and Products. The CMM definition of processes in terms of the common features is much more comprehensive in its coverage of the factors leading to the institutionalization of the process. The CMM common features group the key practices into five categories: Activities, Commitment, Abilities, Measurement and Verification (see Chapter 13).

SUMMARY

In this chapter we reviewed a number of standards and initiatives (national and international) related to the software process. They have varying degrees of focus on the software process, its maturity and improvement. They all share the objective of enhancing the control and improving the discipline of the software development process. Analyzing their features against a common framework reveals the areas of commonality and differences between these models.

Complementary rather than contradictory approaches

These standards should not be treated as contradictory, rather they are complementary in terms of having the common objective of producing higher quality software systems and products. (A war between process standards and approaches is the last thing that the software industry and the process maturity movement needs.)

Process focus could help

Process focus in your software organization should enable you to think at a level higher than any single initiative. When preparing a software process improvement strategy you should feel free to adopt the most relevant concepts out of each model and fit them in a common consistent framework.

Always think of the business objectives

Always start from, and stay aligned with, the business objectives point of view. Considering the business objectives, define an architecture for the organization's standard process, and devise a strategy for software process improvement. The strategy should ultimately lead to the creation, support and improvement of the organization's software process assets and infrastructure.

Start with an overall framework

Use available and relevant standards and models to help you design and adopt an overall framework for software process improvement. The framework should aim to create an overall infrastructure and accommodate all the organization's software process assets, technical as well as management and organizational.

SPECIAL NOTE TO THE READERS

All the standards and initiatives described here are subject to continuous change. Readers who are interested in the up-to-date versions should contact the organization concerned.

Business benefits of software process improvement

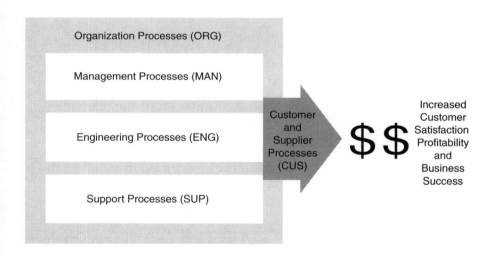

Part 5 describes the business benefits of software process improvement, and summarizes some of the case studies in Europe and the USA that come from organizations which have tracked and measured the benefits. Finally it discusses some scenarios for the future of software process improvement.

CHAPTER 19

The evidence: business benefits of software process improvement

19.1 RELATING SPI BENEFITS TO THE BUSINESS

Ultimately every investment should produce a return in terms of benefits to the business. You must try to measure the impact of software process improvement on the business. Already evidence of the business benefits of software process improvement is building up. In his speech at the SEPG conference in 1996, John Major, Senior Vice President of Motorola, reported the following benefits resulting from the software process improvement effort since 1992:

- More than 75% of product development at Software Maturity Level 3 and above
- Approaching 10 times software quality improvement rate over the last two years
- More than twice productivity improvement
- More than twice software cycle time improvement.

The median results from an SEI study of 13 software organizations reveal an average of $5.0 net business return per dollar investment in software process improvement. There is increasing evidence that in moving their processes up the maturity levels, organizations save more than they invest in improvements. The following are some of the most quoted examples of cost saving (Humphrey, 1995):

- US Air Force Logistics Command invested $4,792,527 and gained direct savings of $2,000,000.
- Hughes Aircraft invested $445,000 for a one-year saving of $2,000,000.
- Raytheon invested $1,000,000 a year for four years and gained a saving of $15,800,000.

The apparent conclusion is that process improvement pays off. Relating the software process improvement to business results can be achieved by considering some business savings and improvement factors of the business that can be traced back to software process improvement. These factors include the following:

- *Improved product quality:* This could be done through proving the impact of an improved process on the quality of the software, hence on the quality of the products and services which use the software. Improved product quality should lead ultimately to improved customer satisfaction, fewer errors in the products, fewer returned products, no disasters for the press to talk about, and so on. All of these are significant factors for business success.
- *Shorter time to market:* Through improved processes that lead to improved quality with less error and no rework, the organization should be able to deliver products to the marketplace in a much shorter time than a competitor whose processes are less mature. Also a mature process should facilitate introducing new technologies in an effective way that could speed up the inclusion of such technologies in the products to gain competitive advantage.
- *More productivity:* Fewer errors, less rework, inspection at early lifecycle phases: all these are expected from an improved process, and all of them should enhance the productivity of software engineers which translates into real benefits to the business.

The rest of this chapter summarizes the role of some leading organizations in promoting software process improvement in both the USA and Europe, and provides an overview of a number of case studies of benefits resulting from software process improvement.

19.2 EVIDENCE FROM EUROPE

19.2.1 EUROPEAN SYSTEMS AND SOFTWARE INITIATIVE (ESSI)

The European Commission launched an initiative known as the European Systems and Software Initiative (ESSI) in 1993. The ESSI sponsors a programme for research and technological development in the field of information technologies (1994–1998). Within the domain of software technologies, there is a specific subdomain dedicated to software process improvement, which is known as 'Software Best Practice' (EC, 1995). Software

Best Practice is a group of actions aimed at helping organizations in all industry sectors to increase their efficiency, provide better quality and provide better value for money, through improvements in their software development process. The specific goal of the Software Best Practice initiative is 'to promote improvements in the software development in industry, through the take-up of well founded and established – but insufficiently deployed – methods and technologies, so as to achieve greater efficiency, higher quality, and greater economy' (EC, 1995).

The strategy to achieve that goal has been to encourage European organizations to implement actions that will:

- raise awareness of the importance of the software development process to the competitiveness of all European industry;
- demonstrate what can be done to improve software development practices through experimentation;
- create communities of interest in Europe working to a common goal of improving software development practices; and
- raise the skill levels of software development professionals in Europe.

These goals have been achieved through the support and sponsorship of the following focused actions:

- Standalone assessments
- Process Improvement Experiments (PIEs)
- Dissemination actions
- Experience network
- User network
- Training actions.

Process Improvement Experiments (PIEs) form the bulk of the Software Best Practice initiative. Their aim is to demonstrate the benefits of software process improvement through user experimentation. A summary of the results of a selected number of PIEs has been published (EC, 1996) with the purpose 'to show quantifiable business benefits to be gained from adopting software best practice'.

Other European initiatives focusing on identifying the business benefits of software process improvement include the establishment of the European Software Institute (ESI). The ESI conducted a survey of software best practice in Europe, and published the results in a report (ESI, 1996). The report summarizes an analysis of the responses to a questionnaire enclosed with the project proposals submitted during the ESSI call for proposals in June 1995. There were 463 valid responses received from 17 different countries and covering 33 different sectors. The ESI actively promotes the adoption of software process improvement strategies and coordinates its effort with the SEI, the ESSI and the ISO/IEC 15504 project.

19.2.2 IBM'S EUROPEAN SOFTWARE DEVELOPMENT BENCHMARK

In late 1994 IBM initiated a project to benchmark software development organizations throughout Europe (IBM 1997, Goodhew 1997). IBM's internal software development organization in Europe wished to understand how their performance compared with non-IBM organizations. Also several customers in the UK approached IBM requiring a benchmark for their software development activities. In response to these requests a team was established to develop a benchmark approach. This benchmark has been deployed throughout Europe with great success.

IBM benchmark is based on the analysis of data gathered during a self-assessment questionnaire which covers both performance and practices used within software organizations in Europe. The practice questions ask about how software development is done, and the performance questions ask what levels of performance are achieved.

The self-assessment questionnaire comprised 66 questions covering performance and practices. The questions were grouped into the following seven categories:

Organization & Culture	(12 questions)
Process	(14 questions)
Quality	(12 questions)
Methods and Tools	(10 questions)
Technology and Innovation	(4 questions)
Planning and Innovation	(5 questions)
Measurements	(9 questions)

The respondents were asked to rate their organization's practice and performance by choosing a position on a scale of 1 to 5. Three score descriptions for each question characterize the scores 1, 3, and 5 (with any ratings valid between 1 and 5).

The response has been overwhelming with more than 400 organizations from 15 countries taking part. The largest representation was from finance and insurance industries with nearly 100 participants from each. Participants from the manufacturing, distribution, and IT services sectors have also been significant. Northern European countries provided most respondents, with Germany, the UK, Netherlands and Switzerland being particularly strong. Participant development organizations varied in size from less than 50 people to more than 500 people.

Tables 19.1 and 19.2 summarize some results of the performance profiles for the best organizations versus the worst organizations (Leaders and Laggers). Some interesting facts were revealed by the survey:

Table 19.1 Variations in the performance of the best performing (Leaders) and the worst performing (Laggers) software organizations in Europe. (Source: IBM 1997)

Area of comparision	Leaders (best performing)	Laggers (worst performing)	Relative performance Leaders versus Laggers
Development Productivity	Development productivity in excess of 25 function points per person per month	Development productivity below 5 function points per person per month	Productivity > 5 × Better
Defect Removal	Remove over 95% of defects before delivery	Remove less than 50% of defects before delivery	Quality > 30 × Better
Estimate consistency	Estimate consistency within 10% of the actual cost and duration of a project	Have projects which often exceed estimates by more than 40%	Delivery > 30 × Better
Defect correction after delivery	Spend less than 1% of the development effort on defect correction in the first 12 months after delivery	Spend more than 10% of the development effort on defect correction after delivery	Expenditure on Defect Correction after delivery > 10 × Better

Table 19.2 Strengths and weaknesses of large versus small organizations.

	Small organizations	Large organizations
Strength	Employee morale Innovations	Measurements Skills
Weakness	Testing approach (methods, tools, process) Quality assurance Insufficient critical mass	Reuse Design for Operations

- The IT sector has the highest performance levels.
- The adoption of best practices correlates strongly with the achievement of highest level of performance.
- Rarely do organizations with good practices perform badly. Organizations that have poor practices are unlikely to perform well over an extended period of time.
- At the individual level, performance and practices are frequently uneven. Organizations are often quite strong in some areas, but disappointingly weak in others.
- One of the significant results is that leaders are strong in all key areas impacting process – culture, methods, technology, measurements, organization and skills.

The practices that correlate most strongly with performance were found to be non-technical. They are human-centric rather than technological. They relate to the overall culture of the organization, and the management approach to human resources and skills. One key finding is that employee morale has a significant impact on the way an organization is performing. Organizations that encourage and reward innovation and entrepreneurial behaviour achieve significantly higher levels of employee morale. If management does not recognize these 'soft' factors, they will not be able to look critically at how they are managing the organization.

19.2.3 SELECTED CASE STUDIES FROM EUROPE

In the following sections we summarize the results of some European SPI case studies as a proof of how software process improvement results in business benefits. For every case study, the summary is provided under the following headings:

- *The organization:* A brief identification of the organization that undertook the process improvement effort.
- *Objectives and motivation:* A brief description of the business objectives and motivation for conducting software process improvement.
- *The approach:* A brief description of the approach that the organization has followed to improve its software process.
- *Business benefits:* A brief summary of the business benefits that resulted from software process improvement.

The case studies have been selected to form a representative sample and a cross-section. There are many more cases of process improvement programme in Europe than those summarized here. Readers interested in more details of any specific case study should contact the organization concerned, or the European Commission. While we quote here the successful SPI programmes, no one can deny that there are also many unsuccessful ones. We discussed in earlier chapters the critical factors that could make SPI effort successful and the challenges that may lead to failure.

Case study I: Improving the project estimation process

The organization
Engineering Ingegneria Informatica SPA is a large Italian software house with 420 staff and a turnover of 35 million ECU in 1994.

Objectives and motivation
The main motivation was the problems encountered with the accuracy of estimation. Average deviations in estimates were 25% (varying from minus 76% to plus 19%) over ten projects prior to the experiment. Too many projects

were running over the initial estimates made during the commercial negotiations, resulting in lost opportunities or lost profit.

The approach
To extend the development methodology to cover the formal specification of non-functional requirements (such as ease of use, reliability and portability) so that their impact could be traced throughout the development process. This then set up a self-reinforcing cycle, where better knowledge of these impacts leads to better estimation and project planning. Figure 19.1 illustrates the strategy adopted.

Business benefits
Deviation from the original estimates went down from 25% to 8% (ranging from minus 11% to plus 19%) in six projects in which the experiment had been applied. (The methodology was applied only to projects with a value of at least 250,000 ECU.)

The following quotation from an executive for the organization concerned highlights the business benefits of process improvement:

> 'By optimising our software development process and being able to produce better project estimates, we were much more able to convince clients of the soundness of our proposed approach.' (Nicola Morfuni, Engineering Ingegneria Informatica SPA)

Case study 2: Using formal specification methods to improve subcontracting management

The organization
ENEL SPA CRA is the second largest electricity supplier worldwide. They have an overall staff of 102,000 employees. Their IT investment was around 40 million ECU in 1994.

Objectives and motivation
The main motivation has been the company outsourcing the development of most of its applications. The company faced a major problem with the technical definition of the work to be undertaken, and the product acceptance phase. Well-defined software specifications are crucial where major lifecycle activities are outsourced to external suppliers. The objective is to improve the definition of work to be subcontracted to external suppliers, thus reducing the business and project risk.

The approach
The use of techniques and tools to support the improvement of the requirement specification guarantees a clear separation from the subsequent design and implementation phases and a higher degree of maintainability of the final

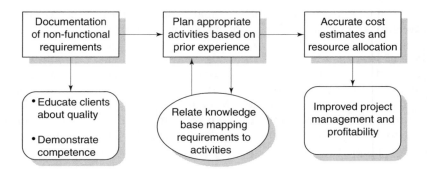

Figure 19.1 Strategy for project estimation improvement (Engineering Ingegneria Informatica SpA)

application. ENEL introduced a formal specification method for a project that aims at the development of a hydroelectric power plants control system.

Business benefits
Two projects with similar magnitude were tracked. One project used the formal specification method, and the other used the classic development approach. Two main results of using the new method have been achieved:

- A cost reduction of 18%
- Increased effort in the specification phase resulting in less effort at the acceptance phase.

The following quotation from an executive for the organization concerned highlights the business benefits of process improvement:

> 'By improving the definition of the software requirements, the risks of subcontracting work have been significantly reduced.' (Ermani Crivelli, ENEL SPA CRA)

Case study 3: Introduction of configuration management

The organization
Datamat Ingegneria dei Sistemi SpA (Datamat) is a large systems integration company based in Rome, undertaking turnkey software projects in a number of sectors including defence, aerospace, finance and public administration. The Datamat group employs over 1,000 people with a 1994 turnover exceeding 110 million ECU.

Objectives and motivation
The company delivers complex software systems to a number of its clients. Each client requires customized variants of the basic system, and requires their supplier to be able to amend their systems in response to market or legislation

changes. This could be achieved through formalized procedures for keeping track of the product components (such as source code modules, libraries and documentation). An initial assessment showed that many key procedures relating to configuration management were informal, unplanned and undocumented.

The approach
Introducing configuration management techniques and tools into Datamat's software development process for financial application products. The first step was to plan and document the procedures defining the lifecycle for objects to be managed by the configuration management system. This was followed by the selection and introduction of a suitable flexible configuration management tool.

Business benefits
Assessment after the implementation of configuration management showed an improvement in managing change, reproducibility of product releases, validation of product versions and passing of components between workers.

The following quotation from an executive for the organization concerned highlights the business benefits of process improvement:

'By being able to respond quickly and accurately to customer requests for change, we have greatly increased customer satisfaction levels, as well as reducing product development costs.' (Gianfranco del Duca, Datamat)

Case Study 4: Establishing a software process organizational and management infrastructure

The organization
Computer-Logic SA is a leading European software house, based in Greece, developing and marketing business-oriented software packages.

Objectives and motivation
In response to the market demands, senior management took a decision to develop a new product line based on object-oriented technology. This decision was strategic to the future success of the company. An R&D team was formed which successfully implemented a project to introduce and establish the new technology in the development lifecycle. The result was the OMEGA development platform for developing the new product line. It was soon evident that for the new technology to be most effective, there was a need to support it with a well-defined and effective organizational and management process infrastructure. With sponsorship from the European Commission, a software process improvement project was undertaken to achieve this objective. It started in 1996 and was successfully completed in 1997.

The approach
The development organization went through a complete process improvement cycle. The initial CMM-based assessment highlighted the strengths and weaknesses of the current processes and infrastructure, and resulted in a set of recommendations. The process maturity at that time was found to be CMM Level-1 with traces of Level-2. The recommendations were transformed into an improvement action plan, which was implemented over a 12 month period. A number of process improvement teams undertook the main improvement actions. These covered process design for key process areas of requirement management, project planning and tracking, configuration management, and quality assurance. An organizational schema was designed, which defines the roles and responsibilities necessary to support the software engineering process. Achievements included the establishment of a process and quality group, enhancing the project management role, defining and allocating the role of technical architect, definition of process training requirements and allocation of training responsibilities. After about 12 months of process improvement effort, a second CMM-based assessment was conducted. The process maturity level was found to be a strong CMM Level-2 with traces of Level-3. The process improvement teams and the process roles are now established as part of the overall culture of the software development organization.

Business benefits
The following quotations from the Technical Director and the R&D Director best illustrate the value of the software process improvement to the whole business:

'The SPI efforts, for developing a well defined process infrastructure for the OMEGA development process, have increased software development project's visibility and predictability. It has provided substantial competitive advantages to penetrate the market and to plan better and to meet our business objectives. Process thinking and support for continuous improvement provide confidence and hope for future business expansion.' *Dr. Pantelis Nikolopoulos, Technical Director, Computer Logic SA.*

'Our process infrastructure SPI efforts proved absolutely necessary to sustain and improve the quality and productivity gains provided by our OO-framework-based OMEGA development process. Passing from research to production development and applying considerable load, the process started to deteriorate. The CMM-based improvement plan has supported us to streamline the process, motivate and involve the key players and build an infrastructure to enable continuous improvement. *Dr. Charalampos Avratoglou, Software R&D Director, Computer Logic SA.*

19.3 EVIDENCE FROM THE USA

19.3.1 THE SOFTWARE ENGINEERING INSTITUTE

The Software Engineering Institute (SEI) leads the way in the USA and across the world to develop models and promote the practice of software process improvement. It also monitors, records, analyses and publishes the results of CMM-based software process improvement (Hayes and Zubrow, 1995; Herbsleb *et al.*, 1994; Kitson and Masters, 1992; Brodman and Johnson, 1995). This leading role of the SEI is well recognized and acknowledged by European organizations, as stated in a report on the business benefits of software best practice: 'In this domain . . . the USA have clearly taken the lead and significant achievements have resulted in increased competitiveness of the American industry' (EC, 1996).

Since the SEI developed a method for software process assessment in 1987, it has been collecting assessment results from organizations using the method, and implementing a CMM-based software process improvement. The first step is an assessment of the current software development capability of the organization. The SEI maintains a database of assessment results. While this database contains just a fraction of all assessments reported to the SEI, it serves as a reasonable indicator. It is used as basis for reporting on the practical experiences and results of software process improvement efforts in the USA. In the following section we summarize the main findings of a number of published reports that address the business benefits of software process improvement.

A report prepared by Will Hayes and Dave Zubrow and published by the SEI investigates the experiences of organizations following the CMM as a model for software process improvement (Hayes and Zubrow, 1995). The report analysed the data for 48 organizations that had conducted two or more assessments over the period from 1987 to 1994. It specifically addressed the following two questions:

- How long does it take for an organization to move up a maturity level?
- What are the process challenges that distinguish those who move from the initial level (level 1) to the repeatable level (level 2) and those who remain at the initial level?

The report provides good practical insights into the course of completing one or more software process improvement cycles (assessment, improvement, reassessment). One interesting finding is that 'The most prevalent "conventional wisdom" has been that it takes 18 to 30 months to improve a full maturity level but depending on the situation it could take much longer than this' (Hayes and Zubrow, 1995).

Another SEI report analysed data from 13 organizations to obtain information on the results of CMM-based software process improvement efforts (Herbsleb *et al.*, 1994). It reports the cost and business value of improvement efforts, as well as the yearly improvement in productivity, early defect detection, time to market, and post-release defect reports. Improvement efforts and results in five organizations are reported as case studies in more depth.

The most relevant aggregated findings of both reports are summarized in the lessons learned section below. The case studies summarized in the following section have been selected as a representative sample. More details and more case studies can be found in the reports.

The United States Air Force sponsored research to provide US industry with data on the positive, quantifiable benefits, or return-on-investment (ROI) for software process improvement programmes based on the SEI's Capability Maturity Model. A summary of the main findings of the report is published in a paper in the pilot issue of the *Software Process Improvement and Practice Journal* (Brodman and Johnson, 1995). The research investigated the published ROI claims for software process improvement. It sought evidence of the existence of new ROI data in organizations that had been engaged in software process improvement over the past several years. The paper reports that 'Evidence of new ROI data was found, though not typically in the form of a dollar returned for a dollar invested. Instead, ROI existed in the form of benefits, such as increased productivity, reduced schedule time, etc. – benefits defined in terms of meeting organizational and customer goals' (Brodman and Johnson, 1995).

19.3.4 SELECTED CASE STUDIES FROM THE USA

In the following sections we summarize a selection of the results of some case studies from the USA as a practical proof of how software process improvement results in business benefits. For every case study, the summary is provided under the following headings:

- *The organization:* A brief identification of the organization that undertook the process improvement experiment.
- *Objectives and motivation:* A brief description of the business objectives and motivation for conducting software process improvement.
- *The approach:* A brief description of the approach that the organization has followed to improve its software process.
- *Business benefits:* A brief summary of the business benefits that resulted from software process improvement.

The case studies have been selected to form a representative sample and a cross-section. There are many more cases of process improvement experiences in the USA than those summarized here. Readers interested in more details of any specific case study should contact the organization concerned, or the reference quoted. We have chosen to summarize three of the best known case studies on software process improvement – those at Hughes, Raytheon, and the Onboard Shuttle. This is because of their pioneering effort that enabled them to complete a number of software process improvement cycles. This leads to rich learning and insight in the different phases of implementing software process improvement. Other case studies covered in the literature include Bull HN Information Systems Inc., Schlumberger, Texas Instruments, and Oklahoma City Air Logistics Center: Tinker Air Force Base (Herbsleb *et al.*, 1994).

Case study I: Software Engineering Division (SED) at Hughes Aircraft

The organization
The SED is a division of Hughes Aircraft in California. It is the largest software organization in the Ground Systems Group that provides contract support to many other divisions. It primarily focuses on US Department of Defense contracts. The SED employs roughly 500 professionals.

Objectives and motivation
The SED primarily focuses on US Department of Defense (DoD) contracts. This explains the SED's interest in Watts Humphrey's early work on software process assessment in 1987. The motivation for the first assessment was the need to improve the consistency of their technical review process, and correct its training policy. There were a number of procedures in place for measuring and reporting project tracking data. These efforts were haphazardly implemented and lacked a central focus.

The approach
The SED has been one of the early adopters of software process improvement. Its story is becoming a classic case study for software process improvement efforts. The approach adopted since 1987 has been based on the SEI CMM-based assessment. Two assessments have been conducted: the first took place in 1987, and the second in 1990 (Humphrey *et al.*, 1991). A third self-assessment took place in May 1992. The first assessment in 1987 found the SED to be a level 2 organization. The second assessment in 1990 found the SED to be a strong level 3 organization. The third assessment in 1992 found it as level 4 maturity based on the early version of the CMM and of the SEI questionnaire. The assessors of the 1992 assessment noted, however, that SED would be at maturity level 3 using the newer version of the CMM v1.1. Table 19.1 summarizes the main findings of the three assessments.

Business benefits
The business benefits reported were both qualitative and quantitative. Qualitative benefits included:

• Improved project quality through predictability
• Increased team spirit, pride and morale

- Easier technology insertion
- Simpler language, design, and models
- Improved working conditions.

Quantitative benefits included:

- Improved productivity through increased detection and elimination of defects
- Reduction in the cost of rework
- Substantial improvement in the accuracy of overall predicted costs
- Improvement in meeting schedules.

Return on investment (ROI) of 4.5 to 1 has been reported, based on cost of about $400,000 and benefit of about $2 million. As benefits continue to accumulate and the up-front costs are spread over the years, the ROI ratio should continue to increase.

Case study 2: Raytheon: another pioneer of software process improvement

The organization
Raytheon is a diversified international technology-based company. It is one of the 100 largest corporations in the USA. The Equipment Division is one of eight divisions and 11 major operating subsidiaries within Raytheon, with annual sales in electronic systems that comprise about 13% of the corporation's $9.1 billion sales in 1993. Most of these electronic systems are software-driven and real-time, and most of the software is developed by the division's Software Systems Laboratory, which employs more than 400 engineers.

Objectives and motivation
A key requirement for the success of a new software development process is the accurate evaluation of how effective it is in reducing the bottom-line cost of getting the job done. Software process improvement has been the way to achieve this.

The approach
Raytheon adopted a three-phase paradigm for process improvement. The three phases of stabilization, control and change are based on the principles of Deming and Juran. The SSL conducted a self-assessment based on the SEI questionnaire, and rated itself at level 1. The results of the self-assessment prompted the Equipment Division to initiate, in mid 1988, a process improvement programme. Considering the results of the self-assessment, they created an organizational infrastructure to support process improvement. It comprised a number of roles and responsibilities: Steering Committee, Policy and Procedures working group, Training working group, Tools and Methods working group, and a Process Database working group (Dion, 1993).

Table 19.1 Summary of findings of the three Hughes Aircraft SED assessments

Main findings of the 1987 assessment:

- Formalize technology management
- Standardize and centralize the collection and reporting of defect data
- Fill gaps in the training programme, including project management, internal reviews, requirements writing, testing, and quality assurance
- Standardize the review process
- Define the software engineering process
- Strengthen software quality assurance

Main findings of the 1990 assessment:
- Integrate software into systems engineering
- Fill gaps in computer-aided software engineering (CASE) technology
- Expand scope of quantitative process management (QPM)
- Optimize QPM to business goals
- Increase participation in software requirements
- Ensure adequate software quality assurance (SQA) support

Main findings of the 1992 self-assessment:
- Predict and track errors
- Analyse error data for root causes
- Continuously improve the efficiency of reviews
- Institute a process of prototyping
- Develop a technology assessment mechanism

Business benefits
In 1993, Raytheon reported that software process improvements have yielded the following benefits:

- A $7.7 return on every dollar invested (a $4.48 million return on a $0.58 million investment)
- A two-fold increase in productivity
- An evolution from the CMM's process maturity Level 1 (1988) to Level 2 (1990), and then to Level 3 (1991).

Other quantitative benefits reported included winning additional business, $9,600,000 bonus on early delivery, and testing effort reduced by 2 to 1 (Curtis and Statz, 1996). Qualitative benefits reported include less overtime and lower staff turnover.

Case study 3: Space Shuttle Onboard Software (a model for a level 5 environment)

The organization
The Space Shuttle Onboard Software project is a subcontractor to NASA to develop the onboard flight software for the shuttle. The project was originally

performed by IBM Federal Systems Company in Houston, Texas. In the spring of 1994 this organization was sold to Loral Corporation and has merged into Loral's Space Division (Paulk *et al.*, 1994). The project employs approximately 270 people. Of those project staff, 26% are involved in flight software verification, but only 18% are involved in developing it.

Objectives and motivation
For over a decade the Onboard Shuttle project team has striven to ensure that there were no faults in the Space Shuttle flight software when new releases are delivered to NASA. To satisfy NASA's requirements for software that meets the highest safety and reliability standards, the Onboard Shuttle project evolved a software process that yields a highly predictable quality result. With NASA occasionally changing the requirements late in an operational increment because of functional priorities, the environment surrounding the Onboard Shuttle project is one of constantly changing requirements. To respond effectively in this environment without sacrificing product quality, the Onboard Shuttle project found that it had to have a formally defined process. This is to ensure that crucial steps were not missed while trying to satisfy the customer. The team found that most automated project management tools were not sufficient for such a dynamic environment and many management functions were not effectively performed manually.

The approach
The team believed that the best way to ensure that the next product will exhibit high quality is to execute the process faithfully to a process standard. This is especially valid given a defined process with a proven record to produce at a known level of quality. The project made continuous improvements to its software process, beginning in the 1970s.

The Onboard Shuttle project identified four primary hurdles that inhibit the production of high-quality software:

- Poor project management, especially the inability to manage within the constraints set by cost, schedule, functionality and quality
- Driving projects from schedule, not quality requirements
- Failure to control the contents of requirements and software product baselines
- Failure to track errors and to make process changes that eliminate their causes.

The continuing process improvement programme that the Onboard Shuttle project implemented over the past two decades has been designed to systematically overcome and eliminate these inhibitors. The project established the process infrastructure with roles and responsibilities to support all the key process areas including those of level 5 (Optimizing). These included Project Management Planning and Tracking, Intergroup Coordination, Configuration Control, Requirements Management, Peer Reviews and Inspections, Software

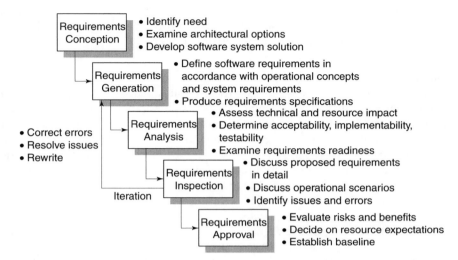

Figure 19.2 The Requirements Management process for the Onboard Shuttle Software project of Lockheed Martin (Paulk *et al.*, 1994)

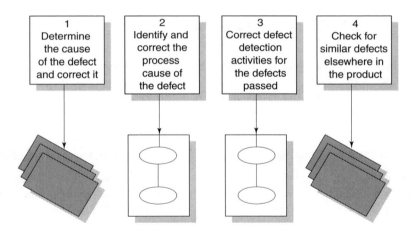

Figure 19.3 The Defect Prevention process for the Onboard Shuttle Software project of Lockheed Martin (Paulk *et al.*, 1994)

Product Engineering (Prototyping and Independent Verification), Software Quality Management, Defect Prevention, and Process Change Management.

Figure 19.2 illustrates the Requirements Management process for the Onboard Shuttle project, and Figure 19.3 illustrates the Defect Prevention process.

In some cases, process changes took up to two years to demonstrate results. However, the aggregate of the changes being made in different areas over time combine to demonstrate steady and continuous improvement in project results. The project reported a 300% improvement in productivity and two orders of magnitude reduction in defect rates.

Business benefits
After two decades of work, the shuttle's flight software is being developed using a process that exhibits some of the same characteristics exhibited by manufacturing processes under statistical control. As a result, the flight software produced by this process is predictably near zero-defects. A culture of excellence has been internalized by the staff. Executives in the Onboard Shuttle project have found that they need not be concerned with the drive for excellence by the individual staff members. The process has helped overcome variations in individual staff skills. It is extremely unlikely that the result of poor performance could escape detection and be delivered to the customer. The Onboard Shuttle project has developed the capability to consistently predict its cost within 10% of actual expenditures, and they have missed only one deadline in 15 years (Paulk *et al.*, 1994). Productivity went up three-fold (Curtis and Statz, 1996).

19.4 LESSONS LEARNED

Each of the case studies summarized above has its own set of lessons learned, but one can easily recognize common threads across them. The following paragraphs summarize the general lessons gained as a result of implementing software process improvement.

Alignment with business needs and customer satisfaction

Companies really benefit from software process improvement activities, when they are designed to meet the specific business needs of the company and to satisfy the needs of their customers. The technical dimension of software process improvement is important only when it is seen from the perspective of a means to support the business objectives.

Focused investment makes significant benefits possible

Investment in software process improvement has to be focused on those areas that can be expected to deliver the best possible results. Such areas of focus will depend on the business and company concerned. For example, a company producing Air Traffic Control systems may focus on improving the reliability of its software, with safety as the main driving factor. On the other hand, a commercial company may consider time-to-market as the key to its business, leading to a focus on faster delivery.

Demonstrate the benefits

The business benefits resulting from software process improvements and reported by organizations that completed the European process improvement experiments can be used as the basis for a convincing cost–benefit justification. This should help to make a business case for managers to decide to invest in software process improvement.

Benefits will materialize in the mid to long term

The results of software process improvement projects do not happen overnight. The key lesson is not to become disheartened because quantifiable results are not immediately available.

Take an incremental approach

An incremental approach works best and contributes to the avoidance of unnecessary risks. Choosing the right size of project for a pilot is of crucial importance. One way of achieving this is by adopting an overall architecture for the software process and its environment (such as the one described in this book), and devising an incremental implementation strategy for its realization. Also this approach will enable the organization to build up its own portfolio of 'lessons learned' of the software process improvement increments.

Sell the idea to the whole organization

The whole organization should be made aware of the importance of software process improvement and its anticipated business benefits. All the staff that may be affected by software process improvement should be involved and motivated to improve the process. Regular information flow should disseminate information about the progress of software process improvement (and its impact on the business). This is critical.

SUMMARY

Business benefits of software process improvement are a reality

Evidence is mounting of real-life SPI programmes which prove the business benefits of software process improvement. Figures of return on investment resulting from software process improvement range between 5:1 and 13:1.

Software process improvement should become a mainstream concern of management

Software is becoming a critical part of nearly all modern products. The quality of software is of critical importance to both consumers and business. Poor-quality software can lead to disasters, while high-quality software can lead to competitive advantage and business success.

Benefits of software process improvement are both qualitative and quantitative

While most managers will be seeking quantitative evidence of return on investment of software process improvement, there is a need to bring their attention to the qualitative benefits that could lead to long-term improvements in the business. Examples of qualitative benefits of software process improvement include improved staff morale, retention of software engineering skills, improved management visibility of the progress of software projects, fewer defects, improved focus on project and business goals, and so on.

The people factor

Software organizations should focus more on 'soft' factors such as culture, leadership and human resources. IBM benchmark programme in Europe has revealed that practises that correlate most strongly with performance are non-technical. They relate to the overall culture of the organizations and its approach to human resource management. The Software Engineering Institute has developed and promote the People CMM (P-CMM) to highlight the people factor in software development.

CHAPTER 20

Epilogue: future of software process improvement

20.1 PROCESS MATURITY:

IS IT ANOTHER BUZZWORD?

In a fast-moving industry like the computer industry and the software industry, many trends appear quickly and go as quickly as they appear. The question that could be in the minds of many people is whether software process improvement is yet another trend that will come and go like any others. The evidence and the common logic are contrary to this (I may be biased). The concept of 'Process' is a fundamental concept for many disciplines such that it is one of the foundations for many industries and systems. I will argue that process discipline builds civilizations, while chaotic behaviour destroys them. As we can all notice, order makes the universe full of beauty. In any disciplined team, you can notice patterns of behaviour. Without a process focus and process training, such patterns will not be as ordered and as effective as they are. The software industry will increase its success rates through mature processes. Thanks are due to the quality pioneers such as Shewhart, Deming and Juran, and to the software process pioneers such as Watts Humphrey.

20.2 ROLE OF INTERNATIONAL STANDARDS

The International Standards Organization (ISO) has published the ISO/IEC 15504 standard for software process assessment. A question that must come to mind is: What is the impact on current initiatives and will the new standard be a help or a hindrance to the software process movement? I believe that ISO/IEC 15504 is a very good step that will spread the awareness of the software process and will strengthen other models and initiatives such as the Capability Maturity Model. Now the standard is in place, everyone should strive towards conformance. After all, it is the software community that has developed the standard. There is coordination between all those working on the standard and on other initiatives. We in the software process movement are more fortunate than those who are involved in the methods war. In the process movement there are no conflicting trends and no sign (yet) of atrocious wars between camps. This is largely due to the clear direction and the strong leadership provided by the software process pioneers.

20.3 PROCESS DISCIPLINE IS A PREREQUISITE FOR SOFTWARE INDUSTRIALIZATION

Software process maturity is described as the second wave of the software industry. The third wave is software industrialization. Usually transitions between these waves are not abrupt. They rather transform gradually from one wave into the next. We believe that the disciplined software process is necessary before we think of software industrialization. The process discipline provides the best foundation for software industrialization. This is the route that manufacturing industry has followed, and how the industrial revolution transformed cottage industry to mass production. The question is: Is the software industry going along a similar route? Time will tell. In the meantime let us faithfully fulfil our role in paving the way for the future.

20.4 WHAT NEXT?

Process improvement should catch on at all levels of the organization. Business managers should be interested because of the potential business benefits. Software project managers should be interested because of the improved visibility into the software progress. End users should be interested because of improved management of requirements and better chances of achieving schedule, cost and quality targets. Software engineers should be interested because improving their personal software process has individual as well as professional advantages. To convert software process improvement into business benefits, let us remember the words of the master: 'Process improvement works and it pays off. Process improvement, however, is a long-term activity. Process improvement must start at the top. And finally until everyone is involved, however, it will not produce its potential benefits' (from a presentation by Watts Humphrey in 1995).

Glossary

This glossary defines the terms used in this book that are most relevant to software process improvement. Some of these terms are common with, and are adapted from, international standards and common software process improvement models such as ISO/IEC 15504 and the SEI CMM. Additional terms have been newly introduced in this book. Readers interested in the standard definition of terms are advised to refer to vocabulary sources for software engineering, software process and software quality terms. The main sources include the following:

ISO 2382-1:1984, Data Processing – Vocabulary – Part 01: Fundamental Terms

ISO 8402:1986, Quality – Vocabulary

ISO 9001:1987, Quality Systems – Model for quality assurance in design/ development, production, installation and servicing

ISO 10011-1:1990, Guidelines for auditing quality systems – Part 1: Auditing

ISO/IEC 15504 (initially known as SPICE), Part 9: Vocabulary

SEI Publication CMU/SEI-91-TR-24: Capability Maturity Model for Software

ANSI/IEEE Software Engineering Standard: Glossary of Software Engineering

A

ability to perform – see common features.

acceptance – The activities undertaken by a purchaser (acquirer) to judge whether or not the product developed by the supplier is acceptable according to previously agreed criteria.

acceptance criteria – The criteria that a system or component must satisfy in order to be accepted by a user, customer or other authorized entity.

acceptance testing – Formal testing conducted to determine whether or not a system satisfies its acceptance criteria and to enable the customer to determine whether or not to accept the system.

action item – (1) A unit in a list that has been assigned to an individual or group (e.g. software process improvement team) for disposition. (2) An action proposal that has been accepted.

action proposal – A documented suggestion for change to a process or process-related item that will prevent the future occurrence of defects identified as a result of defect prevention activities.

activities performed – see common features.

activity – Any step taken or function performed, both mental and physical, towards achieving some objective. Activities include all the work the managers and technical staff do to perform the tasks of the project and organization. In the software development context, activities are worksteps in the software development process.

alignment – This refers to alignment between the software process improvement strategy and the business strategy in order to ensure maximum business advantage from software process improvement effort. Such alignment should filter through all other levels leading to alignment between the process goals and the project goals.

allocated requirements – see system requirements allocated to software.

ami (acronym for 'application of metrics in industry') – A European method developed as a result of a European Community project which aimed 'to make the technology and techniques of metrics and measurement available in a simple, straightforward and understandable form that could be easily implemented'. The project resulted in a handbook describing the **ami** method.

application domain – A bounded set of related systems (i.e. systems that address a particular type of problem). Development and maintenance in an application domain usually requires special skills and/or resources. Examples include payroll and personnel systems, command and control systems, compilers and expert systems.

artefact – A tangible output, such as a work product, produced from the execution of an implemented process.

assessment – see software process assessment.

assessment constraints – Restrictions placed on the freedom of choice of the assessment team regarding the conduct of the assessment and the use of the assessment outputs. Such restrictions may be positive (e.g. requiring that a specific group or individual provides information), or negative (e.g. requiring that a specific group or individual be excluded from providing information). The coverage of the constraints could include:

- specific process instances to be included or excluded from the assessment
- the minimum, maximum or specific sample size or coverage that is required for the assessment
- ownership of the assessment outputs and restrictions on how they may be used
- controls on information resulting from a confidentiality agreement.

assessment indicator – A key word or phrase that guides an assessor in recognizing characteristics of practice adequacy.

assessment input – The collection of information required before a process assessment can commence. This includes:
- the assessment purpose
- the assessment scope including the definition of any extended processes
- the assessment constraints
- the assessment responsibilities
- the identification of any additional information required to be collected to support process improvement or process capability determination.

assessment instrument – A tool or set of tools that is used throughout an assessment to support the evaluation of the existence or adequacy of practices within the scope of the assessment. It may provide assistance in collecting, recording, formalizing, processing, using, storing or retrieving information gathered during an assessment.

assessment output – The formal output from an assessment consisting of the process profile and the assessment record.

assessment owner – The management role that takes ownership of the assessment and the assessment output, and has the authority to make the assessment happen.

assessment purpose – A statement, to be provided before an assessment is commenced, which defines the purpose of the assessment. The purpose may include:
- to promote an understanding of the software process
- to support process improvement
- to support process capability determination.

assessment record – Any information which is pertinent to the assessment. This includes at a minimum:
- the assessment input
- the assessment approach
- the assessment instrument used
- the base practice ratings for each process instance assessed
- the date of the assessment
- the names of the team who conducted the assessment
- any additional information required that was identified in the assessment input to support process improvement or process capability determination
- any assessment assumptions and limitations.

assessment scope – A statement, to be provided before an assessment is commenced, which defines:
- which organizational unit processes are to be investigated
- the mapping from the organizational unit processes to the processes of the adopted standard and extended processes that are to be assessed
- the identification of, and justification for, the process instance(s) selected
- the organizational unit that deploys these processes
- the process context.

assessment sponsor – The individual, internal or external to the organization being assessed, who requires the assessment to be performed, and provides financial or other resources to carry it out.

assessor – A member of the software process assessment team. An assessor can be:
- *provisional assessor:* An assessor who has not yet demonstrated competence or obtained validation of the skills, education and training appropriate to conducting assessments in accordance with the provisions of a selected standard.
- *qualified assessor:* An individual who has attained the qualifications for carrying out process assessments, as defined in a selected standard.

audit – An independent examination of a work product or set of work products to assess compliance with specifications, standards, contractual agreements or other criteria. An audit can be one of three types:
- *first party audit:* When an organization carries out an internal audit.
- *second party audit:* An audit of an organization's relevant products and processes by a customer.
- *third party audit:* An audit of an organization at its own request and expense by an external, impartial body (e.g. certification body) which is not a direct customer.

B

base practice – A software engineering or management activity that directly addresses the purpose of a particular process and contributes to the creation of its output. A base practice is an essential activity of a particular process. (See practice.)

base practice adequacy – A judgement, within the process context, of the extent to which the implemented base practice contributes to satisfying the process purpose. (See practice.)

base practice existence – A judgement, within the process context, of whether a base practice is implemented and produces some output.

baseline – A specification or product that has been formally reviewed and agreed upon, that thereafter serves as the basis for further development, and that can be changed only through formal change control procedures.

baseline configuration management – The establishment of baselines that are formally reviewed and agreed on and serve as the basis for further development. Some software work products, e.g. the software design and the code, should have baselines established at predetermined points, and a rigorous change control process should be applied to these items. These baselines provide control and stability when interacting with the customer. (See also baseline management.)

baseline management – In configuration management, the application of technical and administrative direction to designate the documents and changes to those documents that formally identify and establish baselines at specific times during the lifecycle of a configuration item.

benchmark – A standard against which measurements or comparisons can be made.

bidder – An individual, partnership, corporation or association that has submitted a proposal and is a candidate to be awarded a contract to design, develop and/or manufacture one or more products.

BOOTSTRAP – A European assessment method developed as a result of a European Community project. The mission of the original project was 'to speed up the application of software engineering technology in the European software industry'. The project resulted in a method for software process assessment and improvement.

BPR – acronym for business process re-engineering.

C

capability evaluation – The process of comparing the capability of an organization with a set of criteria in order to identify, analyse and quantify strengths, weaknesses and particularly risks. Capability evaluation has a major use in procurement in the selection of suppliers, but it also has a use internally within an organization.

capability level – A set of common features (i.e. generic practices) that works together to provide a major enhancement in the capability to perform a process. According to ISO/IEC 15504, it can be one of several types:
- *target capability:* That process capability which the process capability determination sponsor judges will represent an acceptable process risk to the successful implementation of the specified requirement.
- *assessed capability:* The output of one or more recent, relevant process assessments conducted in accordance with the provisions of this International Standard.
- *constructed capability:* A capability constructed from existing organizational elements plus sub-contractors, consultants, partners, etc.
- *enhanced capability:* A capability greater than current assessed capability, justified by a credible process improvement programme.
- *proposed capability:* The process capability that the organization proposes to bring to bear in meeting the specified requirement.

capability maturity model (for software) – A description of the stages through which software organizations evolve as they define, implement, measure, control and improve their software processes. This model provides a guide for selecting process improvement strategies by facilitating the determination of current process capabilities and the identification of the issues most critical to software quality and process improvement. Although the CMM was originally developed for software process maturity, the concept has been extended to cover other areas. There is now an expanding family of capability maturity models developed by the SEI which cover software, systems engineering, people, acquisition and integration.

causal analysis – The process of studying the symptoms of a problem and determining their cause(s).

causal analysis meeting – A meeting, conducted after completing a specific task, to analyse defects uncovered during the performance of that task.

certification – The act of having your quality system assessed by an independent, accredited third party for the purpose of confirming its conformance to a series of standards and attesting to it in writing.

chaotic forces – The forces of disorder in a disciplined process environment. They appear in the form of behaviours and actions inconsistent with the defined processes. They are likely to degrade the process performance and jeopardize business results.

CMM – acronym for Capability Maturity Model.

CMM-based assessment – An assessment which uses the CMM (or a tailored version of the CMM) as the process model and the SEI assessment questionnaire as the assessment instrument.

commitment – A pact that is freely assumed, visible, and expected to be kept by all parties.

commitment to perform – see common features.

common cause (of a defect) – A cause of a defect that is inherently part of a process or system. Common causes affect every outcome of the process and everyone working in the process.

common features (in CMM context) – The subdivision categories of the CMM key process areas. The common features are attributes that indicate whether the implementation and institutionalization of a key process area is effective, repeatable and lasting. The CMM common features are the following:
- *commitment to perform:* The actions the organization must take to ensure that the process is established and will endure. Commitment to perform typically involves establishing organizational policies and senior management sponsorship.
- *ability to perform:* The preconditions that must exist in the project or organization to implement the software process competently. Ability to perform typically involves resources, organizational structures and training.

- *activities performed:* A description of the roles and procedures necessary to implement a key process area. Activities performed typically involve establishing plans and procedures, performing the work, tracking it, and taking corrective actions as necessary.

- *measurement and analysis:* A description of the need to measure the process and analyse the measurements. Measurement and analysis typically includes examples of the measurements that could be taken to determine the status and effectiveness of the activities performed.

- *verifying implementation:* The steps to ensure that the activities are performed in compliance with the process that has been established. Verification typically encompasses reviews and audits by management and software quality assurance.

common features (in ISO/IEC 15504 context) – A set of generic practices that address an aspect of process implementation or management.

competence – The work performance that results from effectively applying skills, knowledge and personal attributes.

competency – The skills, knowledge and personal attributes that enable effective work performance.

component – One of the parts that make up a system; a component may be hardware or software and may be subdivided into other components.

concurrent engineering – The techniques of engineering and management activities that minimize the development time and schedule (cycle-time) of a product; this is achieved through an optimization of the concurrency in the performance of product development tasks (e.g. specifications, design, code) and minimization of inter-organizational/functional communication through multifunctional teams.

configuration – In configuration management, the functional and physical characteristics of hardware or software as set forth in technical documentation or achieved in a product.

configuration control – An element of configuration management, consisting of the evaluation, coordination, approval or disapproval, and implementation of changes to configuration items after formal establishment of their configuration identification.

configuration identification – An element of configuration management, consisting of selecting the configuration items for a system and recording their functional and physical characteristics in technical documentation.

configuration item – An aggregation of hardware, software or both, that is designated for configuration management and treated as a single entity in the configuration management process; an entity within a configuration that satisfies an end-use function and that can be uniquely identified at a given reference pont.

configuration management – A discipline applying technical and administrative direction and surveillance to identify and document the functional and physical characteristics of a configuration item, control changes to those characteristics, record and report change processing and implementation status, and verify compliance with specified requirements.

configuration management library system – The tools and procedures to store, update and access the contents of the software baseline library.

configuration unit – The lowest-level entity of a configuration item or component that can be placed into, and retrieved from, a configuration management library system.

consistency – The degree of uniformity, standardization, and freedom from contradiction among the documents or parts of a system or component.

contingency factor – An adjustment (increase) of a size, cost or schedule plan to account for likely underestimates of these parameters due to incomplete specification, inexperience in estimating the application domain, etc.

contract terms and conditions – The stated legal, financial and administrative aspects of a contract.

critical path – A series of dependent tasks for a project that must be completed as planned to keep the entire project on schedule.

CSCI – acronym for Computer Software Configuration Item.

CSF – acronym for critical success factor.

culture – a set of shared basic assumptions that a group has learned as it solved its problems, or that has helped the group repeatedly in achieving its objectives (see process culture).

customer – The individual or organization that is responsible for accepting the product and authorizing payment to the developing organization.

D

defect – A flaw in a system or system component that causes the system or component to fail to perform its required function. A defect, if encountered during execution, may cause a failure of the system.

defect density – The number of defects identified in a product divided by the size of the product component (expressed in standard measurement terms for that product).

defect prevention – The activities involved in identifying defects or potential defects and preventing them from being introduced into a product.

defect root cause – The underlying reason (e.g., process deficiency) that allowed a defect to be introduced.

defined software process – see project's defined software process.

dependency item – A product, action, piece of information, etc., that must be provided by one individual or group to a second individual or group so that the second individual or group can perform a planned task.

derived rating – A rating that has been determined by aggregating two or more actual ratings to derive an aggregate or average rating.

development – All activities to be carried out to create/enhance a product.

developmental configuration management – The application of technical and administrative direction to designate and control software and associated technical documentation that define the evolving configuration of a software work product during development. Developmental configuration management is under the direct control of the developer. Items under developmental configuration management are not baselines, although they may be baselined and placed under baseline configuration management at some point in their development.

development environment – The tools and methods directly involved in the development of a product, as well as the office and laboratory working environments.

deviation – A noticeable or marked departure from the appropriate norm, plan, standard, procedure or variable being reviewed.

documentation – Any written or pictorial information describing, defining, specifying, reporting or certifying activities, requirements, procedures or results.

E

effective process – A process that can be characterized as practised, documented, enforced, trained, measured and able to improve. (See also well-defined process.) An effective process achieves its goals.

end user – The individual or group who will use the system for its intended operational use when it is deployed in its environment.

end user representatives – A selected sample of end users who represent the total population of end users.

engineering group – A collection of individuals (both managers and technical staff) representing an engineering discipline. Examples of engineering disciplines include systems engineering, hardware engineering, system test, software engineering, software configuration management and software quality assurance.

EIT – acronym for Executive Improvement Team.

evaluation – see software capability evaluation.

event-driven review/activity – A review or activity that is performed based on the occurrence of an event within the project (e.g. a formal review or the completion of a lifecycle stage). (See periodic review/activity for contrast.)

Executive Improvement Team – A management group that monitors, supports and coordinates the process improvement activities within the organization.

extended process – A process which differs from any process contained in the selected process standard, either by having additional base practices defined for an existing process or by being an entirely new process. An extended process should conform to the requirements laid down in that standard.

F

findings – The conclusions of an assessment, evaluation, audit or review that identify the most important issues, problems or opportunities within the area of investigation.

first-line software manager – A manager who has direct management responsibility (including providing technical direction and administering the personnel and salary functions) for the staffing and activities of a single organizational unit (e.g. a department or project team) of software engineers and other related staff.

formal review – A formal meeting at which a product is presented to the end user, customer or other interested parties for comment and approval. It can also be a review of the management and technical activities and of the progress of the project.

function – A set of related actions, undertaken by individuals or tools that are specifically assigned or fitted for their roles, to accomplish a set purpose or end. Functions vary depending on their context, for example:
- In management, a major activity or group of activities that are continuous. For example, the principal functions of management are planning, organizing, staffing, directing and controlling.
- In project management: an activity or set of activities that span the entire duration of a software project. Examples of project functions include configuration management, quality assurance and project cost accounting.
- In programming: a specific, identifiable task performed by one or more software components.

G

goals – A summary of the key practices of a key process area that can be used to determine whether an organization or project has effectively implemented the key process area. The goals signify the scope, boundaries and intention of each key process area.

group – The collection of departments, managers and individuals who have responsibility for a set of tasks or activities. A group could vary from a single individual assigned part time to several part-time individuals assigned from different departments, to several individuals dedicated full time.

H

host computer – A computer used to develop software. (See target computer for contrast.)

I

IDEAL – This is a model developed by the SEI for initiating and implementing a software process improvement cycle. It encompasses five phases:
- *Initiating:* to start the improvement programme.
- *Diagnosing:* to assess the current state of the practice.
- *Establishing:* to set the implementation strategy and action plan for the improvement programme.
- *Acting:* to execute the action plan and recommended improvements.
- *Leveraging:* to analyse the lessons and the business results of the improvement effort, and revise the approach.

Infrastructure – see software process infrastructure.

initial level – see maturity level.

institutionalization – The building of infrastructure and corporate culture that support methods, practices and procedures so that they are the ongoing way of doing business, even after those who originally defined them are gone.

integrated software management – The unification and integration of the software engineering and management activities into a coherent defined software process based on the organization's standard software process and related process assets.

item - Any part, component, device, subsystem, functional unit, equipment or system that can be individually considered; an item may consist of hardware, software or both, and may also in particular cases include people.

K

key practices – The infrastructures and activities that contribute most to the effective implementation and institutionalization of a key process area.

key process area – A cluster of related activities that, when performed collectively, achieve a set of goals considered important for establishing process capability. The key process areas have been defined to reside at a single maturity level. They are the areas identified by the SEI to be the principal building blocks to help determine the software process capability of an organization and understand the improvements needed to advance to higher maturity levels.
- The Level 2 key process areas in the CMM are Requirements Management, Software Project Planning, Software Project Tracking and Oversight, Software Subcontract Management, Software Quality Assurance, and Software Configuration Management.
- The Level 3 key process areas in the CMM are Organization Process Focus, Organization Process Definition, Training Programme, Integrated Software Management, Software Product Engineering, Intergroup Coordination, and Peer Reviews.
- The Level 4 key process areas are Quantitative Process Management and Software Quality Management.

– The Level 5 key process areas are Defect Prevention, Technology Change Management, and Process Change Management.

L

lifecycle – see software lifecycle.

M

maintenance – The process of modifying a software system or component after delivery to correct faults, improve performance or other attributes, or adapt to a changed environment.

managed and controlled – The process of identifying and defining software work products that are not part of a baseline and, therefore, are not placed under configuration management but that must be controlled for the project to proceed in a disciplined manner. 'Managed and controlled' implies that the version of the work product in use at a given time (past or present) is known (i.e. version control), and changes are incorporated in a controlled manner (i.e. change control).

managed level – see maturity level.

manager – A role that encompasses providing technical and administrative direction and control to individuals performing tasks or activities within the manager's area of responsibility. The traditional functions of a manager include planning, resourcing, organizing, directing and controlling work within an area of responsibility.

maturity level – A well-defined evolutionary plateau towards achieving a mature software process. The five maturity levels in the SEI's Capability Maturity Model are:
– *initial:* The software process is characterized as *ad hoc*, and occasionally even chaotic. Few processes are defined, and success depends on individual effort.
– *repeatable:* Basic project management processes are established to track cost, schedule and functionality. The necessary process discipline is in place to repeat earlier successes on projects with similar applications.
– *defined:* The software process for both management and engineering activities is documented, standardized and integrated into a standard software process for the organization. All projects use an approved, tailored version of the organization's standard software process for developing and maintaining software.
– *managed:* Detailed measures of the software process and product quality are collected. Both the software process and products are quantitatively understood and controlled.
– *optimizing:* Continuous process improvement is enabled by quantitative feedback from the process and from piloting innovative ideas and technologies.

maturity questionnaire – A set of questions about the software process that sample the key practices in each key process area of the CMM. The maturity questionnaire is used as a springboard to appraise the capability of an organization or project to execute a software process reliably.

measure – A unit of measurement (such as source lines of code or document pages of design).

measurement – The dimension, capacity, quantity or amount of something (e.g. 300 source lines of code or 7 document pages of design).

method – A reasonably complete set of rules and criteria that establish a precise and repeatable way of performing a task and arriving at a desired result.

methodology – A collection of methods, procedures and standards that defines an integrated synthesis of engineering approaches to the development of a product.

milestone – A scheduled event for which some individual is accountable that is used to measure progress.

N

non-technical requirements – Agreements, conditions and/or contractual terms that affect and determine the management activities of a software project.

O

operational software – The software that is intended to be used and operated in a system when it is delivered to its customer and deployed in its intended environment.

organization – A company, corporation, firm, enterprise or institution, or part thereof, whether incorporated or not, public or private, that has its own functions and administration. In the software process improvement context, an assessment is generally applied to a complete organization, or part thereof, that is responsible for the development of a specific product.

organizational unit – A unit within a company or other entity (e.g. government agency or branch of service) within which many projects are managed as a whole. All projects within an organization share a common top-level manager and common policies.

organizational unit (target for assessment) – That part of an organization that is the subject of an assessment. An organizational unit deploys one or more processes that have a coherent process context and operates within a coherent set of business goals. An organizational unit is typically part of a larger organization, although in a small organization the organizational unit may be the whole organization. An organizational unit may be, for example:
– a specific project or set of (related) projects
– a unit within an organization focused on a specific lifecycle phase (or phases) such as acquisition, development, maintenance or support

– a part of an organization responsible for all aspects of a particular product or product set.

organization's measurement programme – The set of related elements for addressing an organization's measurement needs. It includes the definition of organization-wide measurements, methods and practices for collecting organizational measurement data, methods and practices for analysing organizational measurement data, and measurement goals for the organization.

organization's software process assets – A collection of entities, maintained by an organization, for use by projects in developing, tailoring, maintaining and implementing their software processes. These software process assets typically include:
– the organization's standard software process
– descriptions of the software lifecycles approved for use
– the guidelines and criteria for tailoring the organization's standard software process
– the organization's software process database
– a library of software process-related documentation.

Any entity that the organization considers useful in performing the activities of process definition and maintenance could be included as a process asset.

organization's software process database – A database established to collect and make available data on the software processes and resulting software work products, particularly as they relate to the organization's standard software process. The database contains or references both the actual measurement data and the related information needed to understand the measurement data and assess it for reasonableness and applicability. Examples of process and work product data include estimates of software size, effort and cost; actual data on software size, effort and cost; productivity data; peer review coverage and efficiency; and number and severity of defects found in the software code.

organization's standard software process – The operational definition of the basic process that guides the establishment of a common software process across the software projects in an organization. It describes the fundamental software process elements that each software project is expected to incorporate into its defined software process. It also describes the relationships (e.g. ordering and interfaces) between these software process elements.

orientation – An overview or introduction to a topic for those overseeing or interfacing with the individuals responsible for performing in the topic area. (See train for contrast.)

P

Pareto analysis – The analysis of defects by ranking causes from most significant to least significant. Pareto analysis is based on the principle, named after the 19th-century economist Vilfredo Pareto, that most effects come from relatively few causes, i.e., 80% of the effects come from 20% of the possible causes.

peer review – A review of a software work product, following defined procedures, by peers of the producers of the product for the purpose of identifying defects and improvements.

peer review leader – An individual specifically trained and qualified to plan, organize and lead a peer review.

periodic review/activity – A review or activity that occurs at specified regular time intervals.

phase – A defined segment of work, usually comprising a number of tasks and activities leading to a major milestone in the development cycle. A phase does not imply the use of any specific lifecycle model, nor does it imply a period of time in the development of a software product.

PIP – acronym for process improvement plan or process improvement programme.

PIT – acronym for process improvement team (see software process improvement team).

policy – A guiding principle, typically established by senior management, adopted by an organization or project to influence and determine decisions.

practice – A software engineering or management activity that contributes to the creation of the output (work products) of a process or enhances the capability of a process. In ISO/IEC 15504 a practice can be one of two types:
- *base practice:* A software engineering or management activity that directly addresses the purpose of a particular process and contributes to the creation of its output. A base practice is an essential activity of a particular process.
- *generic practice:* A process management activity that enhances the capability to perform a process. A generic practice supports the implementation or management of a process and may be applied to any process.

prime contractor – An individual, partnership, corporation or association that administers a subcontract to design, develop and/or manufacture one or more products.

procedure – A written description of a course of action to be taken to perform a given task.

process – A sequence of steps performed for a given purpose, for example the software development process. Also defined as a set of interrelated resources and activities which transform inputs into outputs; resources may include personnel, facilities, equipment, technology and methodology.

process assessment – The disciplined examination of the processes used by an organization to determine the capability of those processes to perform within quality, costs and schedule goals; the aim is to characterize current practices, identifying strengths and weaknesses and the ability of the process to control or avoid significant causes of poor quality, cost and schedule performance. Also defined as a disciplined evaluation of an organization's software processes against the process model or variant model described in a selected standard.

process assets – Process-related documentation previously developed by projects in the organization.

process capability – The range of expected results that can be achieved by following a process. (See process performance for contrast.)

process capability baseline – A documented characterization of the range of expected results that would normally be achieved by following a specific process under typical circumstances. A process capability baseline is typically established at an organizational level.

process capability determination – A systematic assessment and analysis of selected software processes within an organization against a target capability, carried out with the aim of identifying the strengths, weaknesses and risks associated with deploying the processes to meet a particular specified requirement.

process capability level rating – A representation of the extent to which a process achieves the set of capabilities represented by that capability level. A process capability level rating consists of an aggregation of generic practice adequacy ratings of the generic practices within a particular capability level.

process category – A set of processes addressing the same general area of activity. The process categories address five general areas of activity: customer–supplier, engineering, project, support, and organization.

process context – Those factors that influence the judgement, comprehension and comparability of process ratings. These factors include at a minimum:
- the application domain of the products or services
- the size, criticality and complexity of the products or services
- the quality characteristics of the products or services (see, for example, ISO)
- the size of the organizational unit
- the demographics of the organizational unit.

process culture – Shared basic assumption across the organization of the value of process discipline and its positive impact on the business results. A process culture should be driven by vision and strategic direction coming from the top of the organization.

process database – see organization's software process database.

process description – The operational definition of the major components of a process. This usually takes the form of documentation that specifies, in a complete, precise, verifiable manner, the requirements, design, behaviour or other characteristics of a process. It may also include the procedures for determining whether these provisions have been satisfied. Process descriptions may be found at the task, project or organizational level.

process development – The act of defining and describing a process. It may include planning, architecture, design, implementation and validation.

process improvement – Action taken to change an organization's processes so that they meet the organization's business needs and achieve its business goals more effectively.

process improvement action – An action planned and executed to improve all or part of the software process. A process improvement action can contribute to the achievement of more than one process goal.

process improvement programme – All the strategies, policies, goals, responsibilities and activities concerned with the achievement of specified improvement goals. A process improvement programme can span more than one complete cycle of process improvement.

process improvement project – Any subset of the process improvement programme that forms a coherent set of actions to achieve a specific improvement.

process instance – A single instantiation of a process, where its purpose is fulfilled in terms of taking the process inputs, performing the set of base practices and producing a set of process outputs.

process measurement – The set of definitions, methods and activities used to take measurements of a process and its resulting products for the purpose of characterizing and understanding the process.

process performance – A calculated measure of the efficiency and effectiveness achieved by following a process. (See process capability for contrast.)

process performance baseline – A documented characterization of the actual results achieved by following a process, which is used as a benchmark for comparing actual process performance against expected process. A process performance baseline is typically established at the project level, although the initial process performance baseline will usually be derived from the process capability baseline. (See process capability baseline for contrast.)

process profile – The actual and derived generic practice adequacy ratings, and the process capability level ratings for each process identified in the assessment scope.

process purpose – A summary description of the intention or functional objectives of a process and its base practices.

process repository – A library of documented processes.

process tailoring – The activity of creating a process description by elaborating, adapting and/or completing the details of process elements or other incomplete specifications of a process. Specific business needs for a project will usually be addressed during process tailoring.

product – The result of activities or processes. A product may include service, hardware, processed materials, software or a combination thereof.

profile – A comparison, usually in graphical form, of plans or projections versus actuals, typically over time.

project – An undertaking requiring concerted effort, which is focused on developing and/or maintaining a specific product. The product may include hardware, software and other components. Typically a project has its own funding, cost accounting and delivery schedule.

project's defined software process – The operational definition of the software process used by a project for achieving a specific purpose. The project's defined software process is a well-characterized and understood software process, described in terms of software standards, procedures, tools and methods. Also defined as the operational definition of a set of activities. It is developed by tailoring the organization's standard software process to fit the specific characteristics of the project. (See organization's standard software process.)

project manager – The role with total business responsibility for an entire project; the individual who directs, controls, administers and regulates a project building a software or hardware/software system. The project manager is the individual ultimately responsible to the customer.

project software manager – The role with total responsibility for all the software activities for a project. The project software manager is the individual the project manager deals with in terms of software commitments and who controls all the software resources for a project.

Q

quality – (1) The degree to which a system, component or process meets specified requirements. (2) The degree to which a system, component or process meets customer or user needs or expectations.

quality assurance – see software quality assurance.

quality management – All activities of the overall management function that determine the quality policy, objectives and responsibilities and implement them by means such as quality planning, quality control, quality assurance and quality improvement, within the quality system. Quality management is the responsibility of all levels of management but must be driven by top management and its implementation involves all members of the organization. This can be applied to software (see software quality management).

quantitative control – Any quantitative or statistically based technique appropriate to analyse a software process, identify special causes of variations in the performance of the software process, and bring the performance of the software process within well-defined limits.

R

ratings – According to ISO/IEC 15504 there are different types of process ratings:
- *actual rating:* A rating determined by assessing a specific process instance.
- *derived rating:* A rating determined by aggregating two or more actual ratings to derive an aggregate or average rating.

– process capability level rating: A representation of the extent to which a process achieves the set of capabilities represented by that capability level. A process capability level rating consists of an aggregation of generic practice adequacy ratings of the generic practices within a particular capability level.

required training – Training designated by an organization to be required to perform a specific role.

requirements – An essential set of conditions that a system has to satisfy.

risk – Possibility of suffering loss.

risk management – An approach to problem analysis which weighs risk in a situation by using risk probabilities to give a more accurate understanding of the risks involved. Risk management includes risk identification, analysis, prioritization and control.

risk management plan – The collection of plans that describe the risk management activities to be performed on a project.

role – A unit of defined responsibilities that may be assumed by one or more individuals.

S

SCE – acronym for software capability evaluation.

SCM – acronym for software configuration management.

senior manager – A management role at a high enough level in an organization that the primary focus is the long-term vitality of the organization, rather than short-term project and contractual concerns and pressures. In general, a senior manager for engineering would have responsibility for multiple projects.

software – A set of programs, associated data, procedures, rules, documentation and materials concerned with the development, use, operation and maintenance of a computer system. In some contexts (e.g. Trillium) this includes firmware regardless of its final manufactured form (e.g. PROM, Gate Array).

software baseline audit – An examination of the structure, contents and facilities of the software baseline library to verify that baselines conform to the documentation that describes the baselines.

software baseline library – The contents of a repository for storing configuration items and the associated records.

software build – An operational version of a software system or component that incorporates a specified subset of the capabilities the final software system or component will provide.

software capability evaluation – An appraisal by a trained team of professionals to identify contractors who are qualified to perform the software work or to monitor the state of the software process used on an existing software effort.

software configuration control board – A group responsible for evaluating and approving or disapproving proposed changes to configuration items, and for ensuring implementation of approved changes.

software development plan – The collection of plans that describe the activities to be performed for the software project. It governs the management of the activities performed by the software engineering group for a software project. It is not limited to the scope of any particular planning standard which may use similar terminology.

software engineering group – The collection of individuals (both managers and technical staff) who have responsibility for software development and maintenance activities (i.e. requirements analysis, design, code and test) for a project. Groups performing software-related work, such as the software quality assurance group, the software configuration management group and the software engineering process group are not included in the software engineering group.

software engineering process group (SEPG) – A group of specialists who facilitate the definition, maintenance and improvement of the software process used by the organization. In the key practices, this group is generically referred to as 'the group responsible for the organization's software process activities'.

software integration – A process of putting together selected software components to provide the set or specified subset of the capabilities the final software system will provide.

software lifecycle – The period of time that begins when a software product is conceived and ends when the software is no longer available for use. The phases of the software lifecycle typically comprise concept, requirements, design, implementation, test, installation and checkout, operation and maintenance and, sometimes, retirement.

software manager – Any manager, at a project or organizational level, who has direct responsibility for software development and/or maintenance.

software plans – The collection of plans, both formal and informal, used to express how software development and/or maintenance activities will be performed. Such plans could cover, for example, software development, software quality assurance, software configuration management, software test, risk management, and process improvement.

software process – A set of activities, methods, practices and transformations that people use to develop and maintain software and the associated products (e.g. project plans, design documents, code, test cases and user manuals). Also defined as the process or set of processes used by an organization or project to plan, manage, execute, monitor, control and improve its software related activities.

software process assessment – An appraisal by a trained team of software professionals to determine the state of an organization's current software process, to determine the high-priority software process-related issues facing an organization, and to obtain the organizational support for software process improvement.

software process assets – see organization's software process assets.

software process description – The operational definition of a major software process component identified in the project's defined software process or the organization's standard software process. It documents, in a complete, precise, verifiable manner, the requirements, design, behaviour or other characteristics of a software process. (See also process description.)

software process element – A constituent element of a software process description. Each process element covers a well-defined, bounded, closely related set of tasks (e.g. software estimating element, software design element, coding element, and peer review element). The descriptions of the process elements may be templates to be filled in, fragments to be completed, abstractions to be refined, or complete descriptions to be modified or used unmodified.

software process improvement plan – A plan, derived from the recommendations of a software process assessment, that identifies the specific actions that will be taken to improve the software process and outlines the plans for implementing those actions. Sometimes referred to as an action plan.

software process improvement proposal – A documented suggestion for change to a process or process-related item that will improve software process capability and performance.

software process improvement teams (software PITs) – Focus groups of software engineering staff and management responsible for the improvement of specific software processes (e.g. a group for improving the requirements management process, a group for improving the project planning process, etc.). Usually they act as a team (see definition of a team) and their involvement in software process improvement activities is alongside their normal engineering or management activities.

software process infrastructure – the software process infrastructure is the underlying framework and structural foundations that support the software process. It covers both the organizational and management roles and responsibilities as well as the technical tools and platforms necessary to support defining the process, performing the process activities, capturing and analysing feedback on process performance, and ongoing process improvement activities.

software process maturity – The extent to which a specific process is explicitly defined, managed, measured, controlled and effective. Maturity implies a potential for growth in capability and indicates both the richness of an organization's software process and the consistency with which it is applied in projects throughout the organization.

software process performance – see process performance.

software process-related documentation – Example documents and document fragments, which are expected to be of use to future projects when they are tailoring the organization's standard software process. The examples may cover subjects such as a project's defined software process, standards, procedures, software development plans, measurement plans and process training materials.

software product – The complete set, or any of the individual items of the set, of computer programs, procedures and associated documentation and data designated for delivery to a customer or end user. (See software work product for contrast.)

software project – An undertaking requiring concerted effort, which is focused on analysing, specifying, designing, developing, testing and/or maintaining the software components and associated documentation of a system. A software project may be part of a project building a hardware/software system.

software quality assurance – (1) A planned and systematic pattern of all actions necessary to provide adequate confidence that a software work product conforms to established technical requirements. (2) A set of activities designed to evaluate the process by which software work products are developed and/or maintained.

software quality goal – Quantitative quality objectives defined for a software work product.

software quality management – The process of defining quality goals for a software product, establishing plans to achieve these goals, and monitoring and adjusting the software plans, software work products, activities and quality goals to satisfy the needs and desires of the customer and end users. (See quality management.)

software-related group – A collection of individuals (both managers and technical staff) representing a software engineering discipline that supports, but is not directly responsible for, software development and/or maintenance. Examples of software engineering disciplines include software quality assurance and software configuration management.

software requirement – A condition or capability that must be met by software needed by a user to solve a problem or achieve an objective.

software work product – Any artefact created as part of defining, maintaining or using a software process, including process descriptions, plans, procedures, computer programs and associated documentation, which may or may not be intended for delivery to a customer or end user.

SPA – acronym for software process assessment.

specification – A document that specifies, in a complete, precise, verifiable manner, the requirements, design, behaviour or other characteristics of a service, product, system or component, and often the procedures for determining whether these provisions have been satisfied.

SPI – acronym for software process improvement.

SPM – acronym for software process maturity.

SPU – acronym for software producing unit.

SPICE – acronym for Software Process Improvement and dEtermination.

sponsor (for software process improvement) – A senior manager who authorizes the budget for software process improvement activities and signs off the job description for those involved in software process improvement activities.

SQA – acronym for software quality assurance.

staff – The individuals, including task leaders, who are responsible for accomplishing an assigned function, such as software development or software configuration management, but who are not managers. In the context of software they are the software technical people (e.g. analysts, programmers and engineers), including software task leaders, who perform the software development and maintenance activities for the project, but who are not managers.

stage – A partition of the software effort that is of a manageable size and that represents a meaningful and measurable set of related tasks which are performed by the project. A stage is usually considered a subdivision of a software lifecycle and is often ended with a formal review prior to the onset of the following stage.

standard – Mandatory requirements employed and enforced to prescribe a disciplined uniform approach to software development.

standard software process – see organization's standard software process.

statement of work – A description of all the work required to complete a project, which is provided by the customer.

subcontract manager – A manager in the prime contractor's organization who has direct responsibility for administering and managing one or more subcontracts.

subcontractor – An individual, partnership, corporation or association that contracts with an organization (i.e. the prime contractor) to design, develop and/or manufacture one or more products.

system – A collection of components organized to accomplish a specific function or set of functions.

system engineering group – The collection of individuals (both managers and technical staff) who have responsibility for specifying the system requirements; allocating the system requirements to the hardware, software, and other components; specifying the interfaces between the hardware, software, and other components; and monitoring the design and development of these components to ensure conformance with their specifications.

system requirement – A condition or capability that must be met or possessed by a system or system component to satisfy a condition or capability needed by a user to solve a problem.

system requirements allocated to software – The subset of the system requirements that are to be implemented in the software components of the system. The allocated requirements are a primary input to the software development plan. Software requirements analysis elaborates and refines the allocated requirements and results in software requirements which are documented.

system testing – Testing software under conditions that simulate typical installation environments.

systems engineering – The application of the mathematical and physical sciences to develop systems that utilize economically the materials and forces of nature for the benefit of mankind.

T

tailor – To modify a process, standard or procedure to better match process or product requirements.

target computer – The computer on which delivered software is intended to operate. (See host computer for contrast.)

task – (1) A sequence of instructions treated as a basic unit of work. (2) A well-defined unit of work in the software process that provides management with a visible checkpoint into the status of the project. Tasks have readiness criteria (preconditions) and completion criteria (postconditions).

team – A collection of people, often drawn from diverse but related groups, assigned to perform a well-defined function for an organization or a project. Team members may be part-time participants of the team and have other primary responsibilities.

technical requirements – Those requirements that describe what the software must do and its operational constraints. Examples of technical requirements include functional, performance, interface and quality requirements.

technology – The application of science and/or engineering in accomplishing some particular result.

testability – (1) The degree to which a system or component facilitates the establishment of test criteria and the performance of tests to determine whether those criteria have been met. (2) The degree to which a requirement is stated in terms that permit establishment of test criteria and performance of tests to determine whether those criteria have been met.

traceability – The degree to which a relationship can be established between two or more products of the development process, especially products having a predecessor–successor or master–subordinate relationship to one another. Also defined as the ability to trace the history, application or location of an entity (e.g. product, activity, process, organization, person) by means of recorded identifications.

train – To make proficient with specialized instruction and practice.

training group – The collection of individuals (both managers and staff) who are responsible for coordinating and arranging the training activities for an organization. This group typically prepares and conducts most of the training courses and coordinates use of other training vehicles.

training programme – The set of related elements that focus on addressing an organization's training needs. It includes an organization's training plan, training materials, development of training, conduct of training, training facilities, evaluation of training and maintenance of training records.

training waiver – A written approval exempting an individual from training that has been designated as required for a specific role. The exemption is granted because it has been objectively determined that the individual already possesses the needed skills to perform the role.

U

unit – (1) A separately testable element specified in the design of a computer software component. (2) A logically separable part of a computer program. (3) A software component that is not subdivided into other components.

user (end user) – The individual or group who will use the system for its intended operational use when it is deployed in its environment.

V

validation – The process of evaluating software during or at the end of the development process to determine whether it satisfies specified requirements.

verification – The process of evaluating software to determine whether the products of a given development phase satisfy the conditions imposed at the start of that phase.

verifying implementation – see common features.

W

well-defined process – A process that includes readiness criteria, inputs, standards and procedures for performing the work, verification mechanisms (such as peer reviews), outputs, and completion criteria that are documented, consistent, and complete. (See also effective process.)

work product – An artefact associated with the execution of a practice (e.g. a test case, a requirement specification, code, or a work breakdown structure). The existence of the work product indicates that the practice is performed.

work product characteristic – An attribute of a type of work product that indicates the adequacy of an implementation of a practice.

References

(To avoid repetition, the Software Engineering Institute, Carnegie Mellon University, Pittsburgh, PA is abbreviated to SEI.)

Basili V. and Selby R. (1991). Paradigms for experimentation and empirical studies in software engineering. *Reliability Engineering and System Safety*, 32, 171–91.

Baumert J. (1995). SEPG highlights maturing software industry, *IEEE Software*, September, 103–104.

Baumert J. (1996). Experiences developing and deploying a corporate-wide process asset library. In *Proc. 1996 SEPG Conf.*, Atlantic City, NJ, 20–23 May.

Baumert J. and McWhinney M. (1992). Software Measurements and the Capability Maturity Model. *Technical Report CMU/SEI-92-TR-25*, SEI.

Bennis W. (1989). *On Becoming a Leader*. Hutchinson.

Bicego A. and Kuvaja P. (1996). Software process maturity and certification. *Journal of Systems Architecture* (Elsevier), 44.

Boehm B. W. (1981). *Software Engineering Economics*. Prentice Hall.

Brodman J. G. and Johnson D. L. (1995). Return on investment (ROI) from software process improvement as measured by US industry. *Software Process Improvement and Practice Journal* (Wiley), pilot issue, 37–47.

Brooks F. (1995). *The Mythical Man-Month*, Anniversary Edition. Addison-Wesley.

BSI (1992). *TickIT Guide to Software Quality Management System Construction and Certification Using ISO9001/EN29001*. British Standards Institution.

BSI (1995). *The TickIT Guide: A Guide to Software Quality Management System Construction and Certification to ISO9001*. British Standards Institution.

Bush M. and La Manna M. (1996). The value of combining software process improvement models. In *Proc. 1996 SEPG Conf.*, Atlantic City, NJ, 20–23 May.

Crosby P. (1980). *Quality is Free: The Art of Making Quality Certain*. McGraw-Hill.

Crosby P. (1984). *Quality without Fear*. McGraw-Hill.

Curtis B. and Statz J. (1996). Building the cost–benefit case for software process improvement. In *Proc. 1996 SEPG Conf.*, Atlantic City, NJ, 20–23 May.

Davenport T. (1993). *Process Innovation: Reengineering Work through Information Technology*. Harvard Business School Press.

De Marco T. (1982). *Controlling Software Projects*. Prentice Hall.

Deming W. E. (1982). *Out of the Crisis*. Cambridge University Press.

Dion R. (1993). Process improvement and the corporate balance sheet. *IEEE Software*, July, 28–35.

DoD (1994). *Military Standard for Software Development and Documentation MIL-STD-498*. AMSC No. N7069, US Department of Defense, 5 December.

Dorling A. (1997) Private communication, April 1997.

Dorsey T. and McDonald D. (1996). Structured for success: a Software Engineering Process Group (SEPG) model. In *Proc. 1996 SEPG Conf.*, Atlantic City, NJ, 20–23 May.

EC (1995). *Building the Information Society, RTD in Information Technologies, Software Best Practice (ESSI) Information Package*. IT Programme/ESPRIT Information Desk, DGIII/F, European Commission, BU29-7/10, 200 rue de la Loi, B-1049 Brussels, Belgium.

EC (1996). *The Business Benefits of Software Best Practice: Case Studies*. ESSI office, DGIII, European Commission, N105-3/43, 200 rue de la Loi, B-1049 Brussels, Belgium.

EFQM (1995). *Self-Assessment Guidelines*. European Foundation for Quality Management.

El Emam K., Drouin J.-N. and Melo W. (1997). *SPICE: The Theory and Practice of Software Process Improvement and Capability Determination*. IEEE.

ESA (1991). *ESA Software Engineering Standards ESA PSS-05-0*, Issue 2. ESA Board of Software Standardisation and Control, European Space Agency, Paris, February.

ESI (1996). 1995 Software Best Practice Questionnaire, Analysis of Results. *Technical Report ESI-PIA-960464v5*, European Software Institute, April.

Fenton N. (1993). How effective are software engineering methods? *Journal of Systems and Software*, 22, 141–6.

Florac W. (1992). Software Quality Measurement: A Framework for Counting Problems and Defects. *Technical Report CMU/SEI-92-TR-22*, SEI.

Fowler P. and Rifkin S. (1990). Software Engineering Process Group Guide. *Technical Report CMU/SEI-90-TR-24*, SEI, September.

Furnham A. (1994). Seven strategies to change your company. *Financial Times*, 16 March.

GAO (1992). *Embedded Computer Systems: Significant Software Problems on C-17 Must Be Addressed*. GAO/IMTEC-92-48, US Government Accounting Office, May.

Gilb T. (1988). *Principles of Software Engineering Management*. Addison-Wesley.

Ginsberg M. P. and Quinn L. H. (1995). Process Tailoring of the Software Capability Maturity Model. *Technical Report CMU/SET 94-TR-025*, SEI.

Goldenson D. and Herbsleb J. (1995a). After the Appraisal: A Systematic Survey of Process Improvement, Its Benefits, and Factors that Influence Success. *Technical Report CMU/SEI-95-TR-009*, SEI.

Goldenson D. and Herbsleb J. (1995b). What happens after the appraisal: a survey of process improvement effort. In *Proc. 1995 SEPG Conf.*, May.

Goodhew P. (1996). European Best Practise in Software Development – the true state of Software Engineering in Europe. In *ESEPG Conf.*, June.

Hammer M. and Champy J. (1993). *Reengineering the Corporation*. Nicholas Brealey Publishing.

Hargraves T. (1995). Project Risk Assessment and Management (PRAM). Internal training material, Bull Information Systems Ltd, UK.

Harrington H. J. (1991). *Business Process Improvement*. McGraw-Hill.

Hayes W. and Zubrow D. (1995). Moving On Up: Data and Experience Doing CMM-based Improvement. *Technical Report CMU/SEI-95-TR-008*, SEI.

Herbsleb J., Carleton A. *et al.* (1994). Benefits of CMM-based Software Process Improvement: Initial Results. *Technical Report CMU/SEI-94-TR-13*, SEI, August.

Holmes B. (1995). *European Systems and Software Initiative (ESSI)*. European Commission, Brussels.

Humphrey W. (1987). Characterizing the Software Process: A Maturity Framework. *Technical Report CMU/SEI-87-TR-11*, SEI, June.

Humphrey W. (1988). Characterizing the software process: a maturity framework. *IEEE Software*, 5(2), March, 73–9.

Humphrey W. S. (1989). *Managing the Software Process*. Addison-Wesley.

Humphrey W. (1995). *A Discipline for Software Engineering*. Addison-Wesley.

Humphrey W. (1996). *Managing Technical People: Innovation, Teamwork, and the Software Process*. Addison-Wesley.

Humphrey W. (1997). *Introduction to the Personal Software Process*. Addison-Wesley.

Humphrey W. S. and Sweet W. L. (1987). A Method for Assessing the Software Engineering Capability of Contractors. *Technical Report CMU/SEI-87-TR-23*, SEI, September.

Humphrey W., Snyder T. and Willis R. (1991). Software process improvement at Hughes Aircraft. *IEEE Software*, July, 11–23.

IABG (1992). *The V-Model – General Directive 250, Software Development Standard for the German Federal Armed Forces*, August. Available from Industrieanlagen-Betriebsgesellschaft mbH-IABG, Einsteinstr. 20, D-85521 Ottobrum, Germany.

IBM (1996). IBM's Software Development Benchmark: A Powerful Competitive Edge. In *AD Effectiveness Programme*, IBM Europe.

IEEE (1988). *Software Engineering Standards*. ANSI/IEEE Stds, Institute of Electrical and Electronic Engineers.

IEEE (1991). *IEEE Standard Glossary of Software Engineering Terminology*. ANSI/IEEE Std 610.12-1990, Institute of Electrical and Electronic Engineers, February.

ISO (1987). *Quality Systems: Model for Quality Assurance in Design/Development, Production, Installation and Servicing*. ISO 9001, International Standards Organization.

ISO (1991, 1994). *Quality Management and Quality Assurance Standards, Part 3: Guidelines for the ISO 9001 to the Development, Supply and Maintenance of Software*. ISO 9000-3, International Standards Organization.

ISO (1995). *Information Technology – Software Life Cycle Processes*. ISO/IEC 12207, International Standards Organization.

ISO (1997). ISO/IEC 15504 Draft Standard for Software Process Assessment (Parts 1–9). ISO/IEC 15504 Draft Technical Report (DTR), International Standards Organization.

ISPI (1995). *Guidance for Action Planning. Instructors' Guide*. Institute for Software Process Improvement, 15 North Collinwood Drive, Pittsburgh, PA 15215, USA. ISPI Europe, Klein Heiken 101, 2950 Kapellen, Belgium.

Johnson D. and Brodman J. (1997). Tailoring the CMM for small businesses, small organizations, and small projects. *Software Process Newsletter* (IEEE Computer Society), 8, Winter.

Jonassen, A. M. (1996). *See Your Software Development Therapist*. DELTA, Denmark.

Jones, C. (1991). *Applied Software Measurement: Assuring Productivity*. McGraw-Hill.

Jones L., Kusanic M. and Ginn M. (1996). Implementing the IDEAL model in a less than ideal world. In *Proc. 1996 SEPG Conf.*, Atlantic City, NJ, 20–23 May.

Juran J. M. (1981). Product quality – a prescription for the West. *Management Review*, June.

Juran J. M. (1988). *Juran on Planning for Quality*. Free-Press Macmillan.

Kanter R. M. (1989). *When Giants Learn to Dance*. Simon & Schuster.

Kennedy C. (1996). *Managing with the Gurus*. Century Business Books.

Kitson D. H. and Masters S. (1992). An Analysis of SEI Software Process Assessment Results: 1987–1991. *Technical Report CMU/SEI-92-TR-24*, SEI.

Konrad M., Chrissis M. B., Ferguson J., Garcia S., Heffley B., Kitson D. and Paulk M. (1996). Capability Maturity Modelling at the SEI, *Software Process Improvement and Practice Journal*, 2, 21–34.

Kuvaja P. and Bicego A. (1994). BOOTSTRAP – a European assessment methodology. *Software Quality Journal*, 3, 117–27.

Kuvaja P., Simila J., Krzanik L., Bicego A., Soukkonen S. and Koch G. (1994). *Software Process Assessment and Improvement: The BOOTSTRAP Approach*. Blackwell.

Lai R. (1993). The move to mature process. *IEEE Software*, July.

Mackie K. and Rigby P. (1993). Practical experience in assessing the health of the software process. *Software Quality Journal*, 2(4), December.

Masters S. and Bothwell C. (1995). CMM Appraisal Framework Version 1.0. *Technical Report CMU/SEI-95-TR-001*, SEI.

Messnarz R. (1997). A comparison of BOOTSTRAP and SPICE. *Software Process Newsletter* (IEEE Computer Society), 8, Winter.

Myers C. (1996). Ingredients of a successful improvement effort. In *Proc. 1996 SEPG Conf.*, Atlantic City, NJ, 20–23 May.

Olson T., Humphrey W. and Kitson D. (1989). Conducting SEI-assisted Software Process Assessments. *Technical Report CMU/SEI-90-TR-7*, SEI, February.

Paulk M. (1995a). How ISO 9001 compares with the CMM. *IEEE Software*, January, 74–83.

Paulk M. (1995b). Trends in software process and quality. Presentation notes.

Paulk M., Curtis B., Chrissis M. B. *et al.* (1991). Capability Maturity Model for Software. *Technical Report CMU/SEI-91-TR-24*, SEI, August.

Paulk M., Curtis B., Chrissis M. B. and Weber C. V. (1993a). Capability Maturity Model for Software, Version 1.1. *Technical Report CMU/SEI-93-TR-24*, SEI. Also *IEEE Software*, July.

Paulk M., Weber C., Garcia S., Chrissis M. B. and Bush M. (1993b). Key Practices of the Capability Maturity Model for Software, Version 1.1. *Technical Report CMU/SEI-93-TR-25*, SEI.

Paulk M., Weber C., Curtis B. and Chrissis M. B. (1994). *The Capability Maturity Model – Guidelines for Improving the Software Process*. Addison-Wesley.

Paulk M., Garcia S. and Chrissis M. B. (1996). An architecture for CMM version 2. In *Proc. 1996 SEPG Conf.*, Atlantic City, NJ, 20–23 May.

Peters T. (1988). *Thriving on Chaos*. Macmillan.

Peterson B. (1995). Transitioning the CMM into practice. In *Proc. SPI '95 Conf.*, Barcelona, Spain, 30 November–1 December. Published by Meetings Management Ltd, UK.

Popel B. and Wise C. (1996). Trillium and the CMM: differences between the two models and assessment methods. In *Proc. 1996 SEPG Conf.*, Atlantic City, NJ, 20–23 May.

Pressman R. S. (1988). *Making Software Engineering Happen: A Guide for Instituting the Technology*. Prentice Hall.

Pressman R. S. (1994). *Software Engineering: A Practitioner's Approach*. McGraw-Hill.

Process Professional (1996). *The Process Professional Portfolio*. Available from Qualigy AS, PO Box 23, Smostad, N-0309 Oslo, Norway.

Pulford K., Kuntzmann-Combelles A. and Shirlaw S. (1996). *A Quantitative Approach to Software Management: The* ami *Handbook*. Addison-Wesley.

Putnam L. H. and Myers W. (1992). *Measures for Excellence: Reliable Software on Time, within Budget*. Yourdon Press, Prentice Hall.

Radice R., Harding J. T., Munnis P. E. and Phillips R. W. (1985). A programming process study. *IBM Systems Journal*, 24(2).

Reed R. (1996). Planning software improvement after assessment. In *Proc. 1996 SEPG Conf.*, Atlantic City, NJ, 20–23 May.

Royce W. W. (1970). Managing the development of large software systems. In *Proc. Wescon*, IEEE Press, New York, 1–9.

Rozum J. (1993). Concepts on Measuring the Benefits of Software Process Improvements. *Technical Report CMU/SEI-93-TR-09*, SEI.

Shewhart W. (1931). *Economic Control of Quality of Manufactured Product*. Van Nostrand. Reprinted 1980 by the American Society for Quality Control.

Shewhart W. (1939). *Statistical Method from the Viewpoint of Quality Control*. The Graduate School, Washington DC.

Singh R. (1996). International Standard ISO/IEC 12207 Software Life Cycle Processes. *Software Process Improvement and Practice Journal*, 2(1), March, 35–50.

Steinen H., Engelman F., Lebsanft E. (1997), BOOTSTRAP: Five Years of Assessment Experience, Proc. Software Technology and Practice, STEP '97, July.

Trillium (1994). *Trillium: Model for Telecom Product Development and Support Process Capability, Release 3.0*. Bell Canada Acquisitions, Canada.

Waterman R. Jr (1987). *The Renewal Factor*. Bantam.

Weber C. V., Paulk M. C., Wise C. J. and Withy J. V. (1991). Key Practices of the Capability Maturity Model. *Technical Report CMU/SEI-91-TR-25*, SEI, August.

Zahran S. (1994). The software process: what it is, and how to improve it. In *Proc. Int. Conf. on Software Quality Management, SQM '94*, UK.

Zahran S. (1995a). A model for process improvement environment. In *British Computer Society Software Process Improvement Network (SPIN) Group Meeting*, Birmingham, UK, May.

Zahran S. (1995b). A software process improvement framework: theory and practice. In *Proc. European Software Process Improvement Conf., SPI '95*, Barcelona, Spain.

Zahran S. (1996). Establishing a systems integration process. In *Proc. Int. Conf. on Software Quality Management, SQM '96*, Cambridge, UK. Also *SQM Journal*, December.

Zubrow D., Hayes W., Siegel J. and Goldenson D. (1994). Maturity Questionnaire. *Special Report CMU/SEI-94-SR-7*, SEI, June.

Index

This index covers Chapters 1 to 20. Index entries are to page numbers. Alphabetical arrangement is word-by-word, where a group of letters followed by a space is filed before the same group of letters followed by a letter, for example 'Organization Process Focus' will appear before 'organizational change'.

Main entries to the title of the book 'Software Process Improvement' have been kept to a minimum, and references should be sought elsewhere.